The Obama Presidency in the Constitutional Order

The Obama Presidency in the Constitutional Order

A First Look

Edited by
Carol McNamara and Melanie M. Marlowe

ROWMAN & LITTLEFIELD PUBLISHERS, INC.
Lanham • Boulder • New York • Toronto • Plymouth, UK

Published by Rowman & Littlefield Publishers, Inc.
A wholly owned subsidary of The Rowman & Littlefield Publishing Group, Inc.
4501 Forbes Boulevard, Suite 200, Lanham, Maryland 20706
http://www.rowmanlittlefield.com

Estover Road, Plymouth PL6 7PY, United Kingdom

Copyright © 2011 by Rowman & Littlefield Publishers, Inc.
First paperback edition 2012

British Library Cataloguing in Publication Information Available

Library of Congress Cataloging-in-Publication Data

The hardback edition of this book was previously cataloged by the Library of Congress
as follows:

The Obama presidency in the constitutional order : a first look / edited by Carol
McNamara and Melanie M. Marlowe.
     p. cm.
  Includes index.
  1. United States—Politics and government—2009– 2. Obama, Barack. 3.
Constitutional history—United States. I. McNamara, Carol, 1961– II. Marlowe,
Melanie M.
  JK275.O33 2011
  973.932092—dc22   2010052913

ISBN: 978-1-4422-0530-7 (cloth : alk. paper)
ISBN: 978-1-4422-0531-4 (pbk. : alk. paper)
ISBN: 978-1-4422-0532-1 (electronic)

Printed in the United States of America

~

Contents

~

Preface

The objective of this book is to step back from the partisan divide and examine the early days of the Obama presidency in light of the Constitution's theory, structure, and powers. As we consider President Obama's words and actions, we seek to answer a broad set of questions. First, what is President Obama's understanding of executive power under the Constitution? Second, how does he exercise his executive power within the parameters of the Constitution, especially in relation to the other branches of government? And, finally, how does this relate to the nonconstitutional, or informal, powers of the presidency—in particular, the rhetorical and educative responsibilities of the modern presidency? The organizing idea of this collection is to set a constitutional standard for examining the actions and policies of the Obama presidency.

The essays collected in this volume began as a lecture series titled "The Obama Presidency in the Constitutional Order," held at Utah State University in April 2010 under the auspices of the Project on Liberty and American Constitutionalism and the Political Science Department. Funding for the lecture series and resulting book was generously provided by the Earhart Foundation and the Merrill Endowment in the USU Political Science Department. We would like to thank Utah Public Radio for hosting the speakers from this lecture series on its morning news and events program, *Access Utah*. We are grateful for all the support we received at Utah State from Anthony Peacock and Peter McNamara, the directors of the Project on Liberty and American Constitutionalism, and from Brandee Halverson, who provided indispensable administrative assistance for the lecture series. We would also like to thank Abigail Joy Ledman for compiling the bibliography and index for this volume, and Stephanie Cook for other research assistance. We are appreciative of the eight authors who were willing to contribute their original observations on the early days of the Obama presidency. Finally, we would like to thank our families and friends. Melanie thanks Tyson Marlowe for putting up with late nights. She is grateful to Tom Karako, Ryan Barilleaux, and Christopher Kelley for opportunities to refine, in discussion and writing, thoughts on presidential power. Carol would like to express her appreciation for the patience with which her friends, in particular Phebe Jensen, and especially her family, Peter, Isabella, and Adelaide, have supported her in this project.

Carol McNamara
Melanie Marlowe

~

Introduction

Joseph M. Bessette

It is a truism to say that the American presidency is a constitutional office. It exists because it was created by the fifty-five men who wrote the Constitution in Philadelphia during the summer of 1787. Yet we modern Americans sometimes forget that the presidency exists in the form it does because of the many specific decisions the framers made about mode of election, structure and term of office, and powers. Change a provision here or there and a very different institution would have resulted. Give the occupant a single one-year term; have Congress elect the president; deny the president a veto power; make the executive a committee of three or require an executive council to approve the president's actions; allow Congress to appoint the commander-in-chief of the armed forces; require Senate approval before the president can remove a department head; have the Senate appoint ambassadors and make treaties—make any of these changes and the American presidency, as well as American political history, might have been—likely would have been—dramatically different.

The framers well understood the importance of their decisions. All but five had served in executive positions at the national, state, or local level. Most had held positions of considerable executive responsibility such as governor (nine), governor's council (nine), a state's committee of safety during the early revolutionary period (ten), and officer in the Continental Army (fourteen). These leaders had seen enough of weak state governors (and

the resulting legislative tyranny) and of the executive incapacities of the
Confederation Congress. Bringing to bear the lessons of the "critical period,"
they created an institution whose unity, mode of election, four-year term,
re-eligibility, and substantial independent powers would give it energy and a
will of its own. Such an office would be capable of effectively administering
the nation's laws, of securing its safety and interests in a dangerous world,
and, by recommending measures to Congress and occasionally vetoing statutes, of guiding the lawmaking process.[1]

How, then, would this new office, and its occupant, relate to the people
and public opinion? Although the Constitution derives its legitimacy from
its popular ratification, the president receives his powers and duties not
directly from the people but from and through their charter of government.
His highest obligations, specified in his formal oath, confirm this: "I will
faithfully execute the Office of President of the United States, and will to
the best of my Ability, preserve, protect and defend the Constitution of the
United States." The first obligation focuses the president on the nature and
purposes on his particular constitutional office; the second, on the constitutional order as a whole.[2]

The president takes no oath to make good on his campaign promises, to
advance the views of the majority responsible for his election, or even to
follow the broad contours of public opinion. Rather, as Publius writes in *The
Federalist*, presidents (and other elected officials) were expected to draw on
their "wisdom," "patriotism," and "love of justice" to "refine and enlarge the
public views."[3] In some cases, this might require actively resisting public pressure for some policy or action adverse to the people's true interests. Dangerous politicians—"parasites and sycophants," "the ambitious, the avaricious,
the desperate"—are sometime successful at stimulating and corrupting public
opinion. When this happens, presidents (and others) must "withstand the
temporary delusion in order to give [the people] time and opportunity for
more cool and sedate reflection."[4] In this way, "the cool and deliberate sense
of the community" will prevail. The "republican principle" demands no less.[5]

Note that all this would be true even if the framers had established direct
popular election of the president. The constitutional demands of the office
were one thing; the method of selection was quite another. In their long and
hard deliberations in Philadelphia about how to select the president, the
framers sought three main goals: the selection of fit characters, executive
independence, and the creation of incentives for presidents to do a good
job. Congressional election might achieve the first, but if the president
were re-eligible he would have too strong an incentive to curry favor with
Congress, thus undermining independence. Although denying re-eligibility

might solve the dependence problem, it would undermine incentives to do a good job. Direct popular election, though supported by several leading framers, promised to achieve the second and third goals but at the cost of the first. The country was too big and communication too primitive to expect most Americans to make informed judgments about the merits of leaders from other states or regions. Choice by electors, the framers came to believe, would achieve all three goals. It would also ensure that "the sense of the people [would] operate in the choice of the person to whom so important a trust was to be confided."[6] Because the electors would be chosen either by the very democratic state legislatures or by the people themselves, the choice of president would likely reflect broad public preferences.

Although the contribution of public opinion to the selection of the president would boost public confidence in the national government, it was not intended to channel public sentiments into the operation of the executive branch. As Harvey Mansfield has written, the framers sought to give public officials "constitutional space" in which to govern, insulating them to some degree from public pressures.[7] No such space had existed in the ancient republics where, as Madison cautioned, "the whole body of the people assembled in person, [and] a single orator, or an artful statesman, was generally seen to rule with as complete a sway as if a scepter had been placed in his single hand." When there are no mediating institutions between leaders and people, ambitious men of "eloquence and address," skilled in "sophistry and declamation," can play upon the ignorance and passions of the people to achieve their own self-interested and often dangerous ends.[8] Constitutional government undermines the politician's ability to gain power and direct events through direct popular appeal, while it simultaneously diminishes the people's hold over the actions of their leaders. In an almost paradoxical sense, it makes leaders both weaker—no absolute rule through "eloquence and address"—and stronger—no need to follow every popular whim while governing in the space created by the Constitution. There is, then, a necessary tension between the constitutional character of the presidential office and the occupant's connection to public opinion. No recent presidency better illustrates this tension than that of Barack Obama, the subject of this timely collection of essays.

Although the rise of the party system in the 1790s converted the electoral college into an arm of partisan politics, the parties themselves came to moderate the linkage between the people and their presidents by choosing the candidates and thereby filtering out demagogic appeals.[9] Yet, beginning in the 1970s, a candidate-centered selection process replaced the party-dominated system. Direct popular appeal became the key to success as candidates competed for votes in primaries over which the parties as such had little influence. As Anthony Corrado shows in "The Obama Campaign Revolution," the spectacular success of the Obama campaign "intensifie[d] the plebiscitarian character of the electoral process." Using the Internet to speak directly to an army of enthusiastic supporters, the campaign perfected new techniques of mass communications and mass persuasion. In the process, it raised a staggering $746 million, most of it from online donations. In the primary campaign alone, Obama raised $409 million—almost $190 million more than his main rival, Hillary Clinton. In the general election, Obama, flush with funds, "did not integrate his operations with those of the party," freeing him from any dependence on the national party apparatus.

Yet, if Obama showed that plebiscitary politics could take one from the Illinois state senate to the presidency in four short years, once in office he was much less successful in actually governing through public opinion. Corrado gives two basic reasons: first, it is difficult to sustain popular activism over time and, second, Congress has its own independent authority and power. The debate over health care illustrates the point well; for despite Obama's best efforts he was unable to generate widespread public support for his plan. In the end, his success turned not on his rhetorical skills but on "institutional and internal party pressures that encouraged compromise and political bargaining." This theme—how governing through the framers' institutions constrains and directs behavior—echoes throughout these essays.

Successful candidates enter the presidency not only with the lessons of their own electoral success but also with some understanding, more or less comprehensive and sophisticated, of the nature and role of the nation's highest office. The essays by David Nichols and Joshua Dunn detail Obama's constitutional understanding. Despite Obama's thin political resume, we can expect from him a more fully developed constitutional view than from other new presidents if only because he taught constitutional law at the University of Chicago, one of the nation's top law schools, for seven years before entering the U. S. Senate. Indeed, while serving in the Senate, Obama was not reluctant to tout his own qualifications when challenging President George W. Bush's theory of a "unitary executive." In "Professor Obama and the Constitution," for example, Nichols recounts what Obama told one audience in 2007: "I joined a civil rights law practice, and I started teaching constitutional law—because unlike some occupants of the White House, I actually believe in the Constitution."

Drawing upon his course syllabi, some final exam questions, memos to students, and a few student anecdotes, Nichols explores the constitutional understanding of "Professor Obama." (Analysis is restricted to these materials because Obama produced no scholarly writings on law.) Nichols discovers that Obama's courses on constitutional law covered equal protection, substantive due process, voting rights, and race. He never taught courses on the structure of government, separation of powers, or executive power. "In other words," Nichols asserts, "Obama's teaching had nothing to do with the issues on which he was claiming professional expertise." Nonetheless, a close analysis of the courses he did teach reveals "a progressive conception of law, in which history moves the law in an ever more positive direction." When Nichols turns to Obama's actual governance, he finds that on many issues—such as the "state secrets" doctrine, the habeas corpus rights of detainees at Bagram Air Force Base in Afghanistan, preventive detention, rendition, military tribunals, recess appointments, and signing statements—the new administration advanced constitutional positions closer to those of its predecessor than to Obama's earlier critique. "The constitutional office," Nichols concludes, "inevitably shapes the behavior and even the beliefs of its occupant."

In "The Spirit Is Partially Willing: The Legal Realism and Halfhearted Minimalism of President Obama," Joshua Dunn shifts the focus from Obama's understanding of executive power to his broader constitutionalism and his views on the role and power the Supreme Court. Drawing particularly from *The Audacity of Hope*, Obama's first State of the Union Address (2010) during which he publicly criticized the Court's decision in *Citizens United v. Federal Election Commission*, and Obama's various remarks about the need for "empathy" in federal judges, Dunn finds that Obama is both a "legal realist" and a "judicial minimalist." The first view "argues that there is no escaping justices imposing their own political and policy preferences through decisions." What matters here is not legal reasoning but the actual consequences of judicial behavior. Obama's "judicial minimalism," on the other hand, tempers his realism by holding that "social change is best pursued through political mobilization rather than litigation."

The thrust of Obama's constitutionalism is to reject the notion that many parts of the Constitution have a fixed meaning. Rather, the Constitution creates a "framework" for organizing "the way we argue about the future." This "celebration of deliberation" empowers the political branches to chart a progressive course for the country. Indeed, in a 2001 interview, Obama admitted his skepticism that courts could bring about "major redistributive change." Thus, Dunn argues, "it would not be entirely surprising if President Obama rejects judicial supremacy." By the end of his analysis, however, Dunn acknowledges that Obama "is willing to abandon minimalism when political obstacles frustrate his very ambitious political goals." At best, his judicial minimalism is "halfhearted." Despite some mixed signals from the administration, Dunn concludes that Obama views both the Court and the Constitution as "politically" lacking a "fixed meaning to which we can appeal."

Obama's constitutionalism, then, is linked to his broader progressive political thought. David Alvis explores this connection in "The End of Small Politics? Barack Obama and the Progressive Movement." Although Obama occasionally voices pragmatic themes, as in his Inaugural Address—"The question we ask today is not whether our government is too big or too small, but whether it works"—at a deeper level his pragmatism gives way to his progressive outlook. "So much of his thinking," Alvis writes, "resonates with the reformers of the early twentieth century. . . . Obama is a Progressive and the polar strands of his governing philosophy reflect precisely the character of that period." These strands include the need for greater government regulation of the economy, the recognition that our democratic institutions have failed to keep pace with social change, the embrace of the "living constitution" thesis, and the value of seeing the Constitution less as a document for securing basic liberties than as a framework for forcing a national conversation about our goals and purposes.

In one of his most revealing insights, Alvis documents Obama's embrace of the progressive theme of "promise," a word he used thirty-one times in his speech accepting the Democratic Party nomination in 2008. According to Obama, "America's promise . . . pushes us forward even when the path is uncertain; . . . binds us together in spite of our differences; . . . makes us fix our eye not on what is seen, but what is unseen, that better place around the bend." In Alvis's interpretation, Obama sees promise as "the antidote to the individualism of the past." Promise "restructures political life by cultivating a common bond and sense of purpose." Obama asks Americans to embrace "Change We Can Believe In," but we are left to ponder "from what; to what?"

In January of 2009, Barack Obama brought his constitutional and political philosophy and his considerable rhetorical skills to the task of governing. Three essays in this volume explore in some detail how the job of president molded his thought and behavior. In "President Obama and Executive Independence," Melanie Marlowe contrasts Obama's prepresidential critique of the "unitary executive" theory of presidential power with his decisions and acts as president. Insisting that "the President is not above the law," candidate Obama had criticized the Bush–Cheney administration for "extreme arguments" in terrorism cases and "abuse of prerogative" in signing statements. Some of Obama's supporters, perhaps not surprisingly, had expected the new administration to be much less assertive about executive power and more deferential to Congress.

Marlowe looks closely at the actions of the new administration in four key areas: access to information, signing statements, control of administration, and national security. In each case she finds the president and his subordinates aggressively defending the prerogatives of the office. As the White House Counsel told *CBS News*, the president did not want "to do anything that would undermine or weaken the institution of the presidency." In one case, Obama issued a statement in signing a bill to provide loan guarantees to the International Monetary Fund that insisted that his administration would not be bound by language in the bill that directed the president to take certain positions in foreign negotiations and to consult with Congress in advance. Marlowe notes that "Congress, as a whole, was furious" and Barney Frank (D-MA), who had negotiated the language in the bill, "was especially irate: 'It's outrageous. It's exactly what the Bush people did.'" And even though the administration has not publicly embraced the full Bush–Cheney defense of presidential power, "President Obama has thus far been a champion of the unitary executive."

In "President Obama, the Intelligence Community, and the War on Terror: 'Change We Can Believe In'?" Stephen Knott focuses on national security issues and the war on terror. He notes favorably the shift in Obama's position from his days as a candidate, when he seemed to embrace the predominant opinion in the American legal community that courts should define "the appropriate parameters of presidential emergency measures," to his service as president. Early on, he refused to endorse calls for a "truth commission" to investigate Bush-era abuses. Later, he acted aggressively in the war on terror by authorizing the military targeting of an American citizen, Anwar al-Awlaki, increasing American forces in Afghanistan, escalating the Predator War in Pakistan, endorsing the renewal of the Patriot Act, and appointing "solid mainstream realists" to top positions. Although Knott gives Obama high marks for these actions, he takes the administration to task for "legalizing" the war on terror. He particularly faults Attorney General Eric Holder for seeing terrorism "as a law enforcement and judicial problem," as evidenced by Holder's proposal to try Khalid Sheikh Mohammed in a civilian court and by treating both Umar Farouk Abdulmutallab, the Christmas Day "Undie Bomber," and Faisal Shahzad, who attempted to explode a car bomb in Times Square, as suspected criminals, meriting Miranda rights, rather than as terrorists. There are, in fact, "deep divisions within Obama's administration over the best approach to conduct the war on terror."

In Knott's view, these divisions are exacerbated by judicial and congressional efforts to encroach on executive power. In several key war-on-terror cases the Supreme Court ruled against the executive branch, essentially killing off the "political questions doctrine." Congress, for its part, insists on micromanaging the intelligence operation and is moving aggressively to increase oversight of covert operations. All of this, according to Knott, goes against a long tradition of deferring to the judgment of the executive branch on vital national security matters. Indeed, "expansive notions of presidential power . . . are as old as the American Constitution."

Andrew Busch's essay "President Obama and Congress: Deference, Disinterest, or Collusion?" shifts the focus to domestic matters, where Congress is on firmer constitutional ground. Here Busch distinguishes Obama's formal constitutional relations with Congress from his informal relations. As with other authors in this volume, he finds a marked difference between candidate Obama and President Obama. Most strikingly, at one campaign appearance Obama promised that he would never use signing statements to identify parts of laws he would refuse to enforce for constitutional reasons. This violation of separation of powers, he told the audience, was "part of the whole theory of George Bush that he can make law as he goes along." Yet, President Obama resumed the practice, giving essentially the same constitutional defense as had Bush, though he issued fewer statements and vowed to use the device only when the constitutional interpretation at issue was "well-founded." By also examining vetoes and appointments, Busch shows that in the realm of the constitutional relations between the branches, the Obama administration was not much different from its predecessor.

In the informal realm it is more difficult to reach confident conclusions. Entering the office on a wave of popular approval for his promise of fundamental change, Obama, it appeared to many, would embrace the role of legislative leader and impose his will on the lawmaking process. Instead, on many major policies he seemed largely to defer to Congress, apparently eschewing the leadership role embraced by the likes of Woodrow Wilson, Franklin Roosevelt, and Lyndon Johnson. By examining four key pieces of legislation, Busch assesses three possible explanations. The first is "deference": that Obama believes the president should on constitutional grounds defer to Congress on legislative details. The second is "disinterestedness": that Obama simply lacks interest in the details of governing. The third is "collusion": that Obama only *appears* disengaged, but is "actually closely involved behind the scenes." In the end, Busch concludes that "collusion" best fits the data. The president controls the agenda, establishes the broad principles of legislation, allows Congress to work out the details, attempts to generate public support, and "actively intervenes only when necessary to iron out disagreements or push for final passage." This model combines Wilson's "aggressive leadership of public agenda-setting" and Jefferson's "apparent deference on legislative detail" but "active involvement beneath the surface." Such a model, however, requires a Congress friendly to the president's policy agenda. It provides little guidance for how to navigate the shoals of divided government.

Pursuing the comparison to former presidents, Marc Landy addresses the comparison of Obama to FDR in "Presidential Masks: Barack Obama and FDR." The similarities are many: coming to power during a time of economic collapse; hailing from "patrician bastions" (coincidentally with the same name: Hyde Park); possessing a calm, unflappable temperament; not fitting the stereotype of insider or outsider; enduring difficult nomination battles but easy general election victories; and sharing a similar progressive ideology. The differences, however, are more decisive and are captured by the military historian John Keegan's phrase, "the mask of command," which "is composed of words and deeds that convey a sense of confidence, steadfastness, strength, patience, wisdom and courage." Obama's public gaffes, haste, and impatience in pushing major legislation, and ambivalence as war leader—all in sharp contrast to FDR—undermine the qualities that the mask of command should project. Landy concludes that Obama's "combination of impatience regarding domestic policy and ambivalence regarding foreign policy" resembles not FDR but Lyndon Johnson, whose "half hearted mobilization [of the Vietnam war] and . . . ostentatious eagerness for peace" undermined the national will.

Carol McNamara explores another kind of presidential ambivalence in "Barack Obama's Postracial Presidency: A New Joshua for a New Civil Rights Era." The history of the American presidency, she maintains, is one of "ambivalent leadership in racial politics." Although our presidents have "often fallen short with regard to moral and political leadership on matters of race," part of the reason stems from the limits that federalism and separation of powers place on presidential power. In the modern era, it was not until Lyndon Johnson that a president "seize[d] the leadership of the civil rights movement." Although Obama, the first black president, saw his election as "a new stage or step in the civil rights movement," he faced from the beginning an ambivalence, if not a contradiction, in his relationship to the agenda of civil rights groups. On the one hand, his victory and his broad appeal seemed to promise a postracial politics and society for the country. "In no other country on earth," he said in his major campaign speech on race, would his story even be possible. On the other hand, racial disparities persist in the United States, and many of Obama's supporters believed that he had a special responsibility to address them.

McNamara shows that Obama seeks to resolve the ambivalence by melding his civil rights agenda into his broader progressive policy agenda. Embracing FDR's redefinition of rights, Obama interprets social and material goods such as health care, education, and a higher minimum wage as economic rights in which all have an interest. As he wrote in *The Audacity of Hope*, "What would help minority workers are the same things that would help white workers." That this "universalization of economic rights" has not yet freed Obama from the pressures of identity politics is evidenced by his charge, before he knew all the facts, that a white Cambridge, Massachusetts, police officer had "acted stupidly" in arresting prominent African American professor, Henry Louis Gates, Jr. It remains to be seen whether President Obama will "be able to satisfy both his narrow and broader constituencies, the African American and minority communities, and the American public at large, without falling back on the identity politics he has publicly rejected."

In "The Changing Face of Barack Obama's Leadership," James Ceaser concludes this volume by returning us to the theme of rhetoric and governance, charging that Obama is damaging the office by introducing populism and demagoguery "into the 'normal' conduct of the presidency." This dramatically reverses the founders' design: "The Constitution was crafted to prevent a populist presidency; Obama today is in the midst of creating one." In targeting opposition symbols—such as "speculators" and "fat cat bankers"—assailing political opponents by name, disparaging Republicans in general, and repeating "the old populist mantra of rallying the people—'I won't stop fighting for you,'" Obama practices what Alexander Hamilton called "the little arts of popularity." Hamilton and his colleagues, fearful of the effects of the "popular arts" on sound democratic governance, devised selection methods for the Senate and presidency that would reward the kind of stature that came from a reputation for distinguished public service and sound political judgment.

Related to popular appeal and populism is charisma and charismatic politics. Charisma, Ceaser argues, "sits uneasily with a republic form of government" for at least two reasons. First, it can render the press obsequious, abandoning "even the pretense to objectivity." Second, it tempts its bearer "to try to guard it at all cost." For Obama, this means sustaining his international image even if this entails disparaging his predecessor or questioning America's motives in the world: "The nation's foreign policy has arguably become hostage to the president's charisma." To counteract the dangers of populism and charismatic politics, Ceaser urges a recovery of the framers' aim to promote presidential statesmanship and statesmanlike rhetoric. There is no better guide here than President George Washington who, in effect, "invented presidentialism" and established the norms for appropriate presidential behavior. One of these norms "is for the president to appear as president of all the people, even when others may not choose to accept him as such." To violate this norm by waging a populist campaign to achieve policy success necessarily damages the dignity of the office. Obama's "political counselors," Ceaser concludes, "do not have the slightest clue of the damage they have done to him, because they have no conception of what the office of the presidency is all about."

The framers were keenly aware how governing institutions mold political behavior. When Madison famously wrote that "ambition must be made to counteract ambition," he meant that institutions like the House of Representative, the Senate, and the presidency had to be designed so that the occupants would feel a personal interest in carrying out their constitutional duties. As the Obama presidency and the reflections compiled in this volume make clear, the constitutional design continues to mold behavior, attaching presidents to their duties. But this is not the full story. Powerful countervailing forces also exist and pose new and sobering challenges to American constitutionalism.

Notes

1. For the lessons learned during the "critical period," see especially Charles C. Thach, Jr., *The Creation of the Presidency, 1775–1789: A Study in Constitutional History* (Indianapolis, IN: Liberty Fund, 2007; originally published by The Johns Hopkins University Press, 1923). On the importance of executive energy and an independent will, see especially Alexander Hamilton, James Madison, and John Jay, *The Federalist Papers*, ed. Clinton Rossiter, with a new Introduction and Notes by Charles R. Kesler (New York: New American Library, Mentor Books, 2003), No. 70, pp. 421–29; No. 71, p. 431.

2. For more on the powers and duties vested by Article II of the Constitution, see Joseph M. Bessette and Gary J. Schmitt, "The Powers and Duties of the President: Recovering the Logic and Meaning of Article II," in *The Constitutional Presidency*, ed. Joseph M. Bessette and Jeffrey K. Tulis (Baltimore, MD: Johns Hopkins University Press, 2009), 28–53.

3. Hamilton, Madison, and Jay, *The Federalist Papers* No. 10, p. 76.

4. Ibid., No. 71, p. 431.

5. Ibid., No. 63, p. 382; Ibid., No. 71, p. 430.

6. Ibid., No, 68, p. 410.

7. Harvey C. Mansfield, *America's Constitutional Soul* (Baltimore, MD: Johns Hopkins University Press, 1991), 16.

8. Hamilton, Madison, and Jay, *Federalist* No. 58, p. 358. On the founders' concerns about political rhetoric, see James W. Ceaser, Glen Thurow, Jeffrey Tulis, and Joseph M. Bessette, "The Rise of the Rhetorical Presidency" in *Presidential Studies Quarterly* 11, no. 2 (Spring 1981): 158–71, and Jeffrey Tulis, *The Rhetorical Presidency* (Princeton, NJ: Princeton University Press, 1987).

9. See especially James W. Ceaser, *Presidential Selection: Theory and Development* (Princeton, NJ: Princeton University Press, 1979).

CHAPTER ONE

~

The Obama Campaign Revolution

Presidential Electioneering in the Digital Age

Anthony Corrado

Barack Obama has been described as "the first Internet president,"[1] a characterization that reflects the emphasis he placed on online political activity and the importance of its role in his campaign. Although Obama made extensive use of broadcast media and other commonly practiced campaign strategies, what distinguished his campaign from those of his opponents was his use of new digital technologies and web-enabled services as tools for building an organization and mobilizing voter support.

From the beginning of his quest for the Oval Office, Obama made online communications a core component of his campaign, seeking to capitalize on the organizational potential of the Internet and the new communications environment that had emerged since the 2004 election. In doing so, he was able to incorporate an interactive, grassroots approach to electioneering that engaged citizens in innovative ways. This approach centered on the creation of online networked communities in which information and actions were initiated by individual supporters or groups, as well as by the central campaign organization. The Obama campaign thus advanced a model of plebiscitary politics grounded in citizen activism that demonstrated the possibilities for broad-based citizen participation inherent in the new communications environment. His success marks a watershed in the course of electoral politics, highlighting the effects of technology on the conduct of presidential campaigns in a new era of citizen interaction.

Popular Consent

Our constitutional system of government is based on the fundamental principle of the consent of the governed. Government receives its legitimacy through its dependence on the will of the people, who are responsible for establishing its structure and functions, selecting those who exercise government authority, and monitoring the actions of elected leaders to ensure their accountability in office. Elections are the primary means by which citizens express their support for elected officials and hold these representatives accountable for their actions. Elections require candidates to persuade members of the electorate of their suitability for office, thereby linking candidates to citizens' interests and preferences, and fostering citizens' sense of political efficacy.

While the framers of the Constitution designed a system that would be responsive to the public will, they were aware of the risks inherent in unfettered popular passions and the possibility of ambitious politicians seeking favor by supporting popular causes that might conflict with the public good.[2] To minimize these risks, they established a republican form of government that would serve to filter public opinion and thus restrain the influence of public views in government deliberations. With respect to the office of president, the Constitution set forth an indirect selection process, establishing an electoral college consisting of electors chosen in a manner established by each state legislature, who were free to use their own judgment as to the individual most capable of serving in the nation's highest office. Some statesmen at the time of the Founding advocated direct popular election of the president, but the framers of the Constitution chose not to adopt this method. Their decision was largely premised on their desire to insulate the president from a dependence on popular appeals as a means of gaining office, as well as their recognition of the need to establish an electoral base distinctive from that of the Congress in order to promote the "independence" of the executive in a system of separated powers. This constitutional framework also in part reflected the difficulties of conducting a direct popular election, given suffrage requirements that varied from state to state.[3]

Since the adoption of the Constitution, the presidential selection process has undergone a series of transformations. The process has evolved in response to the rise of party-nominating processes and the emergence of a tradition of casting electoral college ballots on the basis of a state's popular vote outcome, as well as deepening conceptions of the value of citizen participation in the electoral process and the role of the president as a representative of the people as a whole.[4] These developments have converted what was once a "mixed system," in which party leaders and organizations played an essential role in the selection of presidential candidates, into a system of candidate-centered campaigns in which popular balloting is the principal factor in determining nomination and election. Consequently, the modern election process is perhaps best described as a "plebiscitary system"[5] in which presidential aspirants seek election by building a personal mass constituency through their own policies and personal appeals, and by mobilizing their supporters to vote through personal campaign organizations.

Recent presidential campaigns have underscored the notion of popular consent by connecting candidates and citizens in a more direct manner than that envisioned by the founders. Today, aspirants campaign by making direct appeals to the public through the techniques of mass persuasion, rather than by simply recruiting the support of party elites. Presidential campaigns have become endeavors in mass communications and electioneering, an outcome that has been facilitated not only by the structural changes that have been made in the selection process—for example, the establishment of formal party-nominating processes where selection is based on the votes cast in primary contests—but also by the changes that have taken place in communications technology.

Just as first radio and then television dramatically altered presidential electioneering, the growth of the Internet and other digital technologies are revolutionizing the ways in which candidates communicate with citizens and citizens connect with campaigns. The digital revolution is transforming the political world, altering the means by which individuals receive and use political information, and spurring new prospects for citizen participation.

Most notably, communications between candidates and individuals are becoming more personalized, decentralized, and interactive through the use of email, text messaging, and social networking applications, such as MeetUp, MySpace, or Facebook. Candidates can now contact their supporters on a regular basis at minimal cost, distributing information widely through an email, text message, or web posting, even orienting the messages to the particular interests or preferences of the individual recipient. These online tools also facilitate more collaborative and participatory information sharing between individuals and a presidential campaign, as well as among citizens themselves, thus adding a viral component to political outreach. The many can now communicate with the many without the intervention of the few; that is, without the intermediation of political elites, party organizations, or news media.[6] Digital communications thus offer presidential aspirants the capacity to build personal electoral constituencies with a level of efficiency and on a scale considered impracticable only a decade ago.

Online communications have not replaced broadcast media as a principal means of communicating with voters and they are unlikely to do so in the near future. Candidates still need to appeal to a mass audience, including those who do not seek out political information and only come upon political information inadvertently through print media or television. But there is little doubt that web-based capabilities are fundamentally changing the character of the communications that occur in the context of a presidential campaign.

The Rise of Web 2.0

Obama was not the first candidate to recognize the potential benefits of the Internet in a presidential campaign. Presidential candidates have made use of the Internet since 1992, when the Clinton campaign employed it for the limited purposes of communicating within the campaign by email and listserv distribution of information.[7] By 2004, candidates were mounting extensive Internet operations to distribute and gather information via websites, email, blogs, and other applications, and the benefits of online activity were clear to see, most demonstrably in the insurgent campaign of former Vermont governor Howard Dean in his bid for the Democratic presidential nomination. Dean made web-based outreach a centerpiece of his campaign, relying on the Internet to garner the support of liberal activists and others responsive to his antiwar message and severe criticisms of President George Bush. The Dean campaign, which can be described as the first Internet campaign, displayed the power of the Internet as a tool for organizing and recruiting support.[8] Dean relied on the Internet to maintain regular contact with supporters and solicit their ideas for campaign events and volunteer activities. He used an independent social networking website, MeetUp.com, to arrange campaign events and meetings with local activists interested in his candidacy. In all, the Dean campaign ended up with 190,000 enrollees on MeetUp.com and 170,000 supporters on GetLocal, which was his campaign's version of a grassroots-organizing program.[9] Moreover, he highlighted the value of the Internet as a fundraising vehicle, raising $27 million in online contributions, which represented more than half of his total $51 million in campaign receipts.[10]

Dean was the candidate most associated with online campaigning in 2004, but he was not the only candidate to benefit from its capacities. Both of the major party nominees, then-President George Bush and his Democratic challenger John Kerry, made extensive use of the Internet in carrying out campaign functions. After he secured the Democratic nomination in early

March, Kerry raised tens of millions of dollars from online contributions during the months leading up to the Democratic nominating convention, and ended the campaign with an email list of three million addresses.[11] Bush tended to focus on more traditional fundraising methods, such as major fundraising events and direct mail. His campaign focused its online campaigning on the distribution of information, including videos, and as a portal for organizing volunteers. And it did so with great success. By the end of the campaign, Bush had recruited 1.2 million online volunteers and constructed an email list of six million addresses.[12]

The 2004 presidential campaign was a harbinger of things to come. To a certain extent, the Obama campaign followed the path established by the 2004 contenders and hoped to build on their experiences. But technological innovation continued at a rapid pace, producing a more powerful communications infrastructure and capabilities that were not available in 2004. Specifically, the 2008 election would be the first contest held in the world of Web 2.0—the collective term used to describe the wide range of online activities and applications that provide network-enabled interactive services.[13] This technological advance greatly enhanced the possibilities for online electioneering by creating even more interactive means of connecting supporters and involving them in a campaign.

Web 2.0 applications are designed to move away from static web pages to more dynamic websites that enable online "communities" or "social networks." These sites provide virtually seamless interaction and communications among users. Many of the online applications that have come into common use, such as Facebook, MySpace, or YouTube, are based on Web 2.0 capabilities, and most did not achieve great scale until after the 2004 election. For example, MySpace was launched in January 2004 and grew to five million users by November of that year.[14] By the beginning of 2008, it was the web's largest social networking site. Facebook was launched in 2004 with access limited to students at certain colleges and was not opened to anyone with a valid email address until 2006. In 2007, its user base nearly doubled from fourteen million users to twenty-six million.[15] YouTube was opened to the public in November 2005. By July 2006, more than sixty-five thousand videos were being uploaded on the site each day, with one hundred million daily views.[16]

The rapid growth of these new Internet applications was spurred by the expansion of broadband availability, which has gained public penetration more quickly than either the computer or the cell phone, its nearest kin.[17] Broadband or other high-speed Internet connections are essential for Web 2.0 applications, and 2008 was the first election year in which more than half of all Americans had broadband access at home.[18] Broadband helped to create a more distributed computing environment, allowing individuals to access the Internet from computers, cell phones, or other mobile communication devices.

By the beginning of 2008, these technological advances had created a more personal, mobile, and interactive communications environment. Surveys conducted by the Pew Internet and American Life Project estimated that 75 percent of adults and 90 percent of teenagers were online by the beginning of the 2008, and at least 80 percent of all adults had cell phones.[19] By March of 2008, 62 percent of all Americans had some experience with mobile access to digital data or services, which meant that they were becoming more familiar with the use of web-enabled services no matter where they were physically located.[20] A substantial share of the public was increasingly online, accessing news and other information, watching video content, and participating in social networks. Technological and behavioral changes thus presented a new context for communications in 2008. Web-based networking had become part of the social fabric. The Obama campaign recognized this early on, and better than all others.

The Obama Campaign

Given his experience as a community organizer, Obama recognized the political potential of the Internet. As he noted during the campaign, "One of my fundamental beliefs from my days as a community organizer is that real change comes from the bottom up. And there's no more powerful tool for grassroots organizing than the Internet."[21] This emphasis on technology and grassroots politicking was also shaped by the strategic challenge he faced in opposing Hillary Clinton, whom Obama's campaign manager, David Plouffe, described as "the strongest establishment frontrunner in our party's history."[22] The Obama campaign would frame its campaign as a grassroots, volunteer-driven organization in order to draw a contrast with Clinton and her campaign, which was based on a more traditional strategy. This meant relying on the Internet to recruit support on a broad scale.[23]

From the very start, Obama made online communications an integral component of his campaign operation. Before he launched his candidacy in February 2007, he retained the services of Blue State Digital, a market research firm specializing in new media founded by four former members of Howard Dean's 2004 presidential campaign. He hired one of the partners, Joe Rospars, to serve as his campaign's director of new media.[24] He also hired Julius Genachowski, a former chief counsel at the Federal Communications

Commission who co-founded LaunchBox Digital and served as a senior partner at the Fortune 500 company IAC/InteractiveCorp, to serve as chief technology advisor. In addition, Chris Hughes, one of the cofounders of Facebook, took a sabbatical from the company to join the campaign's staff.

Led by these Internet-savvy entrepreneurs, the Obama campaign constructed a state-of-the-art website, the central feature of which was a social networking hub, My.BarackObama.com, which became known as MyBO. The goal was to make this hub the central coordinating point of all Internet-related activity that took place during the campaign and use it to build an "online relationship" with supporters that would encourage them to identify with the candidate, contribute to the campaign, undertake volunteer activities, and mobilize others to vote.[25] The basic idea was to provide a place online where the campaign could connect and directly interact with supporters, maintain regular contact with them, share ideas, and assign campaign tasks in order to build a personal constituency for Obama by building a community of supporters. The approach is best captured by the underlying concepts of his grassroots outreach: "respect, empower, and include."[26] In this way, the campaign endeavored to give their supporters a sense of personal involvement in the campaign and a stake in the election, in hopes of encouraging them to participate in campaign activities both online and—more importantly—offline in their local precincts and at the polls.

Social Networking and Outreach

Obama's website was modeled on existing social networking sites such as Facebook. This structure, while considered innovative for a presidential campaign, was familiar to those who were already participants in similar networks. For example, even before Obama had formally announced his decision to run, individuals were registering support for his candidacy. One Facebook group, "Barack Obama for President in 2008," had more than fifty thousand members prior to the time Obama threw his hat into ring, while another, "Students for Obama," had sixty thousand members. A group called "One Million Strong for Barack" was established on January 16, 2007, the day Obama released a video stating that he would explore a run for the presidency, and within a week had two hundred thousand members.[27]

Visitors to Obama's website were invited to enter an email address to receive regular updates from the campaign and were provided access to a wealth of campaign-related content, ranging from speeches and policy papers to videos of campaign appearances and messages from staff members to volunteer training videos and tasks. Supporters were also given the opportunity to build their own personal profiles on the site, which provided the campaign with the data needed to tailor messages to a recipient's political interests, demographic characteristics, or level of involvement in the campaign. Two million supporters created personal profiles on MyBO, which gave the campaign a wealth of data that could be used to better personalize and target messages.[28]

Once MyBO was established, the campaign linked this hub to other social networking sites in order to encourage those who had expressed support for Obama to connect directly with the campaign. Obama established a profile in more than fifteen online communities, including Facebook, MySpace, BlackPlanet (a social network for African Americans), and Eons (a site established for baby boomers).[29] The campaign also invited supporters to share links to MyBO with their own networks of associates, which led individuals to spread information person to person through social connections.[30] By October 2008, Obama had attracted five million connections on social networks, including 2.4 million Facebook "supporters" and more than eight hundred and thirty thousand MySpace "friends."[31]

While MyBO was established as the principal locus for coordinating online activity, the campaign's predominant method of contacting individuals was through email. A wide variety of tactics was employed to gather as many email addresses as possible. In addition to capturing addresses through the website, the campaign collected addresses at events, through online advertisements, and by offering some incentive such as a free bumper sticker in exchange for contact information. In all, the campaign amassed thirteen million addresses and distributed approximately seven thousand separate email messages, many of which were targeted based on a recipient's prior contact with the campaign and most of which directed recipients to visit MyBO for more information or subsequent action. In all, more than one billion emails were sent out by the campaign.[32]

Email messages were sent out on a regular basis throughout the course of the campaign. These messages typically highlighted campaign developments, encouraged participation, suggested actions to be taken by grassroots supporters, and solicited contributions. This outreach effort continued right through to Election Day, when emails were distributed that not only included a get-out-the-vote message, but also the names of five people in an individual's neighborhood who were targeted as likely to vote for Obama.[33]

The Obama campaign also employed text messaging more than any of the other candidates. This was a strategy designed to reach younger voters, with custom-made wallpapers, ring tones, and a personalized text message number of 62262, which spelled "Obama" on a cell phone.[34] This program allowed the campaign to reach individuals wherever they were located, as long as they were carrying a cell phone or other mobile communications device. A million people signed up for the campaign's text-messaging program, and participants received on average five to twenty text messages per month, depending on the kind of messages they had opted to receive and where they lived, as the program targeted supporters by state, regions, zip codes, and colleges.[35] On Election Day, every voter in battleground states who had signed up for alerts received at least three text messages with a reminder to vote.[36]

Building from the Ground Up

Obama's Internet version of grassroots politicking did more than allow him to recruit supporters and involve them in his efforts. It also let him build off of the initiatives of his supporters. Chris Hughes urged supporters to "get busy on your own" and "take the campaign into your own hands."[37] To encourage this sense of "ownership," MyBO made tools and content material available so that supporters could share ideas on how to best promote Obama's candidacy, create their own organized groups based on location or interest, establish personal blogs, upload videos, organize and advertise local events, and solicit contributions. In other words, individuals were encouraged to act as campaign agents and advocate on behalf of Obama among their own social circles or in the online networks to which they belonged. This capacity served to exponentially increase the breadth of the campaign's outreach, adding a viral effect to his grassroots program that far surpassed the kind of individual interaction made possible by such techniques as direct mail or telephone calls.

Obama's Internet strategy facilitated the development of an extensive grassroots political operation that was in large part constructed from the bottom up, rather than the top down. Supporters were able to initiate actions on their own or with the direction of the central campaign organization, which resulted in an unparalleled scope of volunteer activity. Through MyBO, thirty-five thousand volunteer groups were created, including more than a thousand that were initiated on the day that Obama announced his candidacy; two hundred thousand campaign events were planned and advertised; four hundred thousand blog postings were written; and more than four hundred thousand videos were posted to YouTube.[38]

Yet while promoting individual and localized grassroots electioneering, the Obama campaign was not about to cede control to local volunteer organizations. The campaign coordinated and directed these efforts to ensure that they conformed to its strategic plans and objectives. To this end, the campaign established elaborate, top-down organizational structures—in some cases extending down to specific neighborhoods within precincts—to incorporate volunteers and supporters as they were identified into their centralized operations. This organizational hierarchy was set up to serve and reinforce the activities of local volunteers. It also ensured that the information garnered from such activities would be reported back for inclusion in the Obama database, and offered a means of monitoring and guiding volunteer efforts. Control was also exerted by centrally coordinating the messages distributed to volunteers. Even the graphic designs used in campaign materials, including everything from pamphlets to yard signs and bumper stickers, were made available through MyBO to ensure consistency throughout the country. As David Plouffe, Obama's campaign manager, noted after the election: "We wanted to control all aspects of our campaign. . . . We wanted control of our advertising and, most important, we wanted control of our field operation."[39] Thus, individuals were encouraged to stake a claim to ownership, but the campaign management still set the terms of the deal.

Obama's voter identification and mobilization telephone call program offers but one example of the way Obama used the Internet to facilitate localized volunteer participation, but on a centralized basis. The campaign established a virtual telephone bank through its website. No matter where they were located physically or geographically, volunteers could download lists of targeted voters to be called in states where primaries were being held or, in the general election, states targeted as electoral battlegrounds. These volunteer callers would then canvass the individuals on their list, identify their candidate preference, likelihood of voting, and any other requested information, and then relay the results to the campaign, which integrated the information into its voter database to provide an almost seamless, real-time update of their voter records. The updated voter files could then be accessed online by local campaign staff or volunteers. A supporter in California or New York, where the general election outcome was not in question, could therefore help the campaign simply by taking time during a lunch hour to download and make ten calls to prospective Obama supporters in a key general election state such as Florida or Ohio. All that was required on the part of the volunteer was online access, a willingness to use one's cell phone minutes, and a recording of the result of a call.

Similarly, an application was created for the Apple iPhone that organized the telephone numbers in a user's personal contact list by state in the order of electoral college priority. The iPhone user could then call friends and acquaintances to discern their voting preference and upload results to the campaign's database. This application also made calling statistics available to users to indicate how their caller statistics compared to those of other iPhone users.[40] This feature constituted a subtle means of trying to induce users to make more calls.

Virtual telephone banks allowed the Obama campaign to involve supporters from throughout the nation in their voter identification and mobilization efforts, and apply their labor to those states where it was needed most. They recruited an army of phone canvassers as capable of making calls to selected voters in other states as they were of making personal calls to their friends, with all of these contacts integrated into the operations of the campaign. Consequently, Obama was able to mount a volunteer calling program on a grand scale. In the final four days of the election, volunteers working through MyBO's virtual phone-banking platform made three million telephone calls urging voters to turn out for Obama.[41]

Fundraising

The aspect of Obama's campaign that best demonstrated the benefits of his online organizational model was his fundraising success. MyBO set a new standard for using the Internet to recruit and engage a vast network of financial supporters.[42] Obama became the first presidential candidate since the establishment of the public funding program in 1976 to forgo public funds—and its accompanying spending restrictions—in both the primary and the general election. In all, he raised a total of $746 million during the 2008 election cycle, a record sum that far surpassed the amount taken in by any other presidential contender. Obama raised more than twice the amount garnered by his general election opponent, John McCain, who received more than $300 million, including $220 million in primary campaign contributions and $84 million in general election public funds.[43] During the primary campaign alone, Obama collected $409 million, which was more than the rest of the Democratic field combined, and almost $190 million more than his principal rival, Hillary Clinton.[44] Even more notable, a significant share of Obama's total—$500 million according to one estimate—was raised through donations made online.[45] Obama received 6.5 million donations via the Internet, with six million of these contributions made in the amount of one hundred dollars or less.[46]

Obama employed a variety of means to promote online giving that went beyond such standard tools as a "donate" click button to facilitate online credit-card contributions. Individuals were steadily solicited by email and text messages. The campaign spent significant sums on Internet advertising to expand their presence on specific websites and search engines to drive traffic to MyBO, and used paraphernalia sales, limited edition memorabilia offers, prize offers (such as debate tickets or an opportunity to meet the candidate), and other inducements to generate initial donations of five dollars or ten dollars or more to increase the pool of donors who could then be solicited for additional contributions.[47] Those who gave were sometimes asked to make another contribution that would be matched by another donor. Contributors could also sign up for a "recurring gift" program in which a donation of as little as twenty-five dollars could be charged on a regular basis to a credit card.

Supporters could also assist Obama by establishing their own fundraising page on MyBO. This application helped them solicit their friends or contacts, establish a personal fundraising goal of their choice, and set up a "fundraising thermometer" that they could watch rise as individuals gave in response to their requests. To promote such volunteer fundraising, the campaign established a grassroots fundraising committee that helped train individuals online in how to collect donations from friends, relatives, and coworkers. This tactic proved so successful that it eventually led to a corps of seventy thousand individuals who were willing to solicit their own contacts for campaign dollars. These volunteer fundraisers generated $30 million for the campaign.[48] No political campaign had ever had such a broad scope of participation in its fundraising efforts.

By Election Day, Obama had received contributions from almost four million donors, including close to two million individuals who joined his ranks during the general election contest.[49] Obama successfully raised large sums of money from donors across the spectrum, but the defining characteristic of his campaign fundraising was the scope of small-donor participation. According to Federal Election Commission reports, Obama raised $246 million in contributions of two hundred dollars or less; $166 million in contributions of more than two hundred dollars but less than one thousand dollars; and $229 million in contributions of one thousand dollars or more, including $136 million from contributions of at least two thousand dollars.[50] But many of those who supported Obama gave more than one contribution. Indeed, this was one of the major advantages of his online approach: it made it easy to solicit donors for additional contributions. An analysis by the nonpartisan Campaign Finance Institute identified more than two hundred thousand individuals who began by making small contributions of less than two hundred dollars, but eventually gave two hundred dollars or more, including thirteen thousand individuals who ended up giving a total of one thousand dollars or more.[51]

Another way to assess the role of small donors is on the basis of the aggregate amount given by individual donors, instead of on the basis of the separate donations made by individuals. Such an analysis, again conducted by the Campaign Finance Institute, provides a clearer depiction of the role of small donors, defined as those who gave less than two hundred dollars. In all, Obama raised $235 million of his $746 million total, or about 32 percent of his total funding from small donors. In the primaries alone, he received $121 million from these donors, or about three times as much as Clinton ($42.5 million) or McCain ($42.2 million).[52] In the shorter general election period, he received $114 million from small contributors.

To put Obama's fundraising in another perspective, the Democratic and Republican National Committees raised a combined total of $688 million in the two-year 2008 election cycle, or almost $60 million less than the sum Obama amassed for his own campaign.[53] In terms of small contributors, the Democratic National Committee raised a total of $70 million from individuals who gave a total of two hundred dollars or less during the 2008 cycle, while the Republican National Committee received $117 million from such donors.[54] Obama therefore received almost $50 million more than the national party committees ($235 million as compared to a combined $187 million) from small donors. When it came to fundraising, Obama was, in effect, a party unto himself.

Plebiscitary Politics: Prospects and Problems

The Obama campaign highlighted a revolution that is taking place in American politics—a revolution in the ways people communicate. Technological innovation has lowered the costs of participating in presidential elections—it has made it easier for citizens to become personally involved in electioneering and for candidates to organize personal constituencies. But it has not changed the logic of participation. Citizens still must perceive some benefit from political engagement; they must have a sense that their participation matters and that a candidate shares their views. Candidates are therefore encouraged to make personal appeals and link themselves more closely to public views in the wake of changing technology. Such behavior serves to enhance the influence of public opinion on the conduct of presidential campaigns and intensifies the plebiscitarian character of the electoral process.

In adopting a grassroots strategy, Obama was not breaking new ground. Grassroots organizational development has been a common feature of presidential electioneering, especially in the case of insurgent candidates challenging established party frontrunners, dating back at least to Goldwater's bid for the Republican nomination in 1964. In recent elections, it has come to be regarded as an essential component of a presidential campaign, as demonstrated by the Republican voter turnout efforts that contributed to George Bush's victories in 2000 and 2004. In fact, the architects of the Obama strategy carefully studied Bush's 2004 campaign to gain insights into localized, person-to-person voter turnout, and culled other lessons from the experience of candidates in 2004.[55] They even sought advice from Marshall Ganz, a former organizer under Cesar Chavez for the United Farm Workers turned Harvard professor, who conducted training sessions for Obama organizers on grassroots mobilization techniques.[56]

Obama's extraordinary success in building a grassroots movement was fueled by the distinctive aspects of his candidacy and the political dynamics that formed the context of the presidential race. He was a charismatic candidate with accomplished rhetorical skills who had the ability to communicate with a mass audience. He already had the attributes of celebrity, particularly within the ranks of his own party, as a result of his highly regarded address to the 2004 Democratic National Convention and the popularity of his best-selling books.[57] More important, his campaign's thematic message resonated with the prevalent attitudes of voters. He ran as a candidate advocating "change" in an election defined by an electorate greatly dissatisfied with the direction of the country under the incumbent administration. At a time when many Americans were expressing frustration with the divisive partisan politicking exhibited on Capitol Hill, he called for a "new kind of politics," based on "post-partisan" approaches that would allow "Democrats and Republicans [to] actively give birth to ideas together."[58] These themes helped him attract enthusiastic support from young voters and liberal activists already well versed in online activity. Finally, Obama's candidacy constituted an historic moment, since he sought to be the first African American to win a major party's presidential nomination, and, once he achieved that, the first to win the presidency. These aspects of his candidacy created a level of public excitement in his campaign that spurred millions of Americans to become involved.

By relying on technology, Obama was able to mount a campaign focused on the mobilization of a personal constituency that was largely independent of his party. While many scholars have noted that the modern selection process diminishes the link between candidates and parties,[59] it is fair to say that Obama sought office with less reliance on the party organization than any other recent candidate. For example, in 2004, John Kerry, who, like Bush, was competing in the general election under the spending restrictions accompanying the acceptance of public funding, received substantial assistance from the party during the final months of the campaign. The Democratic National Committee (DNC) spent at least $160 million during the general election to assist Kerry, not including millions of dollars that were spent on voter identification and mobilization efforts designed to mobilize voters in the presidential contest.[60] Similarly, the Republican National Committee (RNC) spent at least $80 million on advertising in support of President Bush, as well as millions of dollars more on get-out-the-vote operations, which were primarily conducted by the party rather than the Bush campaign.[61]

Unlike the Kerry and Bush campaigns in 2004, Obama did not integrate his operations with those of the party. In fact, Obama was unwilling to rely on party support. This was one of the reasons he decided to refuse public funding; he did not want to be in the same position as Kerry and have to depend on the party for advertising and field support. As David Plouffe noted after the election, "We did not want to outsource these millions of people, and these hundreds of thousands of full-time volunteers to the DNC . . . or another entity."[62] Consequently, the DNC spent only $7.5 million during the entire 2008 election year on advertising and direct mail in connection with the presidential race, most of which was devoted to messages opposing McCain, rather than advocating Obama.[63]

To the extent that Obama did work with his party, it was primarily to assist the party with fundraising. For instance, Obama participated in joint fundraising activities with the party. These events, which were jointly sponsored by the Obama campaign and national and state party committees, were designed to solicit contributions from individuals capable of giving the maximum permissible contribution to his campaign ($2,400) and to the DNC ($28,500). McCain and the RNC also engaged in this tactic. In this way, Obama helped raise $203 million, including $87 million that was deposited in his own campaign account.[64]

The Obama campaign also transferred some of its campaign money to party committees in October to help the party contest targeted congressional seats and turn out the vote. After first rejecting a request by Senate majority leader Harry Reid in early September to share $10 million for use in Senate races, the campaign eventually transferred $4.5 million from its campaign fund to the Senate campaign committee and $4 million to the House campaign committee.[65] The campaign also transferred $33 million to state parties, mostly in battleground electoral college states, to assist with party voter mobilization efforts.[66]

Aside from these financial transactions, Obama for the most part conducted his campaign independently of his party. The distinction between his personal constituency and the party structure was laid bare after the election, when a decision had to be made concerning the future of his organization. Obama officials debated whether to maintain his organization as a separate entity that would advocate independently in support of the president-elect's agenda, or associate it with the national party structure. A few days before the inauguration, Obama announced a decision in a YouTube video: the organization would be maintained as a "special project" of the DNC under a new name, Organizing for America (OFA).[67] A press release described the new group as "the next phase for the organization that was built during the campaign, offering volunteers the continued opportunity to work for change in their communities by organizing in support of reform in Washington."[68]

As Jeffrey Tulis has noted, the role of the president in our system of government is influenced by two "constitutions."[69] The first is the framework erected by the founders in 1789, which establishes an executive as a constitutional officer whose authority and power derives ultimately from the Constitution itself. The president operates within a system of separated powers wherein his actions are shaped by his interaction with the other branches of government and constrained by their independent sources of power. In this conception, the president is intended to be representative of the people, but not solely responsive to a popular will.

The second "constitution" is the conception of the executive as a leader of public opinion, whose role is to persuade and galvanize public support. This understanding, which emphasizes popular rhetoric as a principal tool of presidential governance, is also deeply rooted in American political thinking, extending back to the presidencies of Theodore Roosevelt and Woodrow Wilson. In describing how this conception of the president's role has gained prominence in modern politics, Tulis observes, "It is taken for granted that presidents have a *duty* constantly to defend themselves publicly, to promote policy initiatives nationwide, and to inspirit the population."[70]

This second conception of the president's role has been greatly advanced by the rise of mass media and development of a more plebiscitary election process. It is made manifest by Obama's approach to campaigning and the effects of emerging technologies. Obama demonstrated the electoral advantages that can be achieved through popular appeals and a capacity to mobilize public support in a digital age. He showed how candidates who have the skills or qualities needed to excite public enthusiasm—such as rhetorical abilities, popular celebrity, or the personal qualities that engender public favorability—or who are clearly responsive to public views can convert the amorphous support they generate within the electorate into direct personal contact and meaningful campaign resources. He thus highlighted the value of citizen-based strategies in today's robust communications environment.

Obama's strategy also reinforced the notion of the utility of public opinion as a means of presidential governance. Indeed, in the immediate aftermath of the election, many pundits speculated that Obama's organization would give him great influence with the Democratic Congress. Howard Dean's 2004 campaign manager Joe Trippi, among others, predicted that Obama would be a particularly powerful chief executive because "never before has a president been connected to that many Americans."[71] The president was cast not only as chief executive in command of the bully pulpit, but also as chief lobbyist, in command of a powerful, permanent, grassroots apparatus—Organizing for America—that could be used to leverage public opinion to place pressure on Congress and thus build support for his policy initiatives.

Popular activism, however, is difficult to sustain over time. The fervor and intensity of citizen involvement generated by an election campaign are hard to replicate in the ordinary course of events. Conversely, the principles of the constitutional framework endure. A president must still construct a governing coalition with members of Congress, who are elected by constituencies of their own and given independent authority and power under the Constitution to perform their constitutional responsibilities, in order to achieve his legislative goals. In this regard, the complex relationships that shape institutional practice in our constitutional system function to constrain popular leadership as a means of accomplishing programmatic objectives.[72]

The limits of Obama's campaign model were evident in the debate over health care reform. Health care reform was one of the major issues emphasized by Obama throughout the campaign and a principal policy concern of many of his supporters. OFA therefore employed its resources to build support for national health care reform. According to a tabulation of emails sent by OFA that was posted on its website, the organization sent out more emails on this subject in 2009 than on any other. In all, 44 percent of OFA's emails focused on health care, as compared to 17 percent that addressed economic and budget issues, the next highest category.[73] OFA hired paid organizers to direct campaign-style outreach efforts and events to encourage Obama activists to participate in grassroots events, sign statements of support for health care reform, call their members of Congress, visit congressional district offices, and organize their local neighborhoods to promote congressional action. By January 2010, OFA claimed that its efforts had led 2.5 million to take some action to influence the congressional debate, including more than one million calls to Congress in support of reform.[74]

Yet this lobbying had little apparent effect in furthering the adoption of health care legislation. Although the Democrats held a majority in Congress, this majority was a result of the election outcomes in 2006 and 2008, and included moderate and conservative Democrats, many of whom were first elected in 2006 and 2008 from districts formerly held by Republicans. For example, thirty of the Democratic House freshmen elected to Congress in 2006 were from districts formerly held by Republicans.[75] The House Democrats first elected in 2008 included fourteen members who beat Republican incumbents and twelve who captured Republican open seats.[76] These members were the most likely targets for persuasion to generate support for legislation supported by Obama's constituents, such as a public health care option. And OFA initially sought to pressure these members to align themselves with the president by undertaking such tactics as running advertisements in their districts backing health care reform. But moderate and conservative members objected to such lobbying, creating a backlash that elevated the tensions between party leaders and OFA, which in turn threatened to undermine the President's prospects for bargaining with legislative leaders and cobbling together the votes needed to pass a major reform package.[77]

Furthermore, the lessons of the Obama campaign with respect to the role of web-based activism were not lost on his opponents. They, too, relied on the ability to mobilize others through web-enabled social networks to generate attendance at town hall meetings and organize protests that spurred, at times, vitriolic public opposition to reform.[78] They thus used the Internet to help mobilize opinion against a greater government role in health care services, which served as a counterforce to OFA's lobbying and gave recalcitrant members of Congress further reason to maintain some distance from the president in their deliberations on legislative options.

Consequently, OFA had to restrain its advocacy of particular policies and settle for backing the President and whatever alternative he could achieve. In the end, the passage of a health care plan was an outcome shaped more by institutional and internal-party pressures that encouraged compromise and political bargaining than by the influence of the President's personal constituency.

Future presidential aspirants will certainly take account of Obama's electoral strategy and seek to emulate his success in using digital technology as a tool for political campaigning. Given the rapid pace of technological innovation, it seems unlikely that Obama's organizational tactics will not become widely accepted practice. In future elections, candidates are likely to have even more powerful means at their disposal to connect with citizens and incorporate citizen-based electioneering into their campaigns. Obama's strategy thus signals a new era in campaigning, one defined by a diminishing distance between candidates and the public at large. This change offers the prospect of enhanced citizen participation in elections and greatly improved capacity of citizens to express their views. It will also make a candidate's popular leadership skills a more important factor in electoral success. But it may diminish a candidate's capacity to build the type of partisan or institutional coalitions required to govern in our constitutional order.

Notes

1. Samuel Greengard, "The First Internet President," *Communications of the ACM* 52, no. 2 (February 2009): 16–18.

2. James W. Ceaser, *Presidential Selection: Theory and Development* (Princeton, NJ: Princeton University Press, 1979), 52–75.

3. Alexander Hamilton, James Madison, and John Jay, *The Federalist Papers*, ed. Clinton Rossiter (New York: Mentor, 1999), 68, 379–83, and Charles C. Thach, Jr., *The Creation of the Presidency 1775–1789* (Baltimore, MD: The Johns Hopkins University Press, 1969), 97–104, 133–34.

4. For an insightful discussion of the transformations that have taken place in the presidential selection process, see Ceaser, *Presidential Selection.*

5. The description of the presidential election process as a "plebiscitary system" is found in Ceaser, *Presidential Selection*, 5.

6. Anthony J. Corrado, Michael J. Malbin, Thomas E. Mann, and Norman J. Ornstein, *Reform in an Age of Networked Campaigns* (Washington, DC: Campaign Finance Institute, 2010), 11.

7. John Allen Hendricks and Robert E. Denton, Jr., "Political Campaigns and Communicating with the Electorate in the Twenty-First Century," in *Communicator-in-Chief*, ed. John Allen Hendricks and Robert E. Denton, Jr. (Lanham, MD: Rowman & Littlefield, 2010), 3.

8. Michael Cornfield, Pew Internet and American Life Project, *The Internet and Campaign 2004: A Look Back at the Campaigners*, Commentary, www.pewinternet.org/~/media/Files/Reports/2005/Cornfield_commentary.pdf.pdf (accessed May 28, 2010), and Joe Trippi, *The Revolution Will Not Be Televised* (New York: Regan Books, 2004).

9. Trippi, *The Revolution Will Not Be Televised*, 88.

10. David Talbot, "The Geeks Behind Obama's Web Strategy," *Boston Globe*, January 8, 2009, www.boston.com/news/politics/2008/articles/2009/01/08/the_geeks_behind_obamas_web_strategy/ (accessed May 28, 2010), and John C. Green, "Financing the 2004 Presidential Nomination Campaigns," in *Financing the 2004 Election*, ed. David B. Magleby, Anthony Corrado, and Kelly D. Patterson (Washington, DC: Brookings Institution Press, 2006), 100.

11. Melissa Smith, "Political Campaigns in the Twenty-First Century: Implications of New Media Technology," in *Communicator-in-Chief*, 142.

12. John F. Harris and Jonathan Martin, "The George W. Bush and Bill Clinton Legacies in the 2008 Elections," in *The American Elections of 2008*, ed. Janet M. Box-Steffensmeier and Steven E. Schier (Lanham, MD: Rowman & Littlefield, 2009), 7–8.

13. Jenn Burleson Mackay, "Gadgets, Gismos, and the Web 2.0 Election," in *Communicator-in-Chief*, 23–24.

14. "MySpace," www.crunchbase.com/company/myspace (accessed June 2, 2010).

15. Jody C. Baumgartner and Jonathan S. Morris, "Who Wants to Be My Friend? Obama, Youth, and Social Networks in the 2008 Campaign," in *Communicator-in-Chief*, 54.

16. Larry Powell, "Obama and Obama Girl: YouTube, Viral Videos, and the 2008 Presidential Campaign," in *Communicator-in-Chief*, 84.

17. John Horrigan, *Why We Don't Know Enough About Broadband in the U.S.*, Pew Internet and American Life Project, November 14, 2007, www.pewinternet. org/Reports/2007/Why-We-Don't-Know-Enough-About-Broadband-in-the-US.aspx (accessed September 19, 2009).

18. John Horrigan, *Home Broadband 2008*, Pew Internet and American Life Project, July 2, 2008, www.pewinternet.org/Reports/2008/Home-Broadband-2008.aspx (accessed September 19, 2009).

19. Susannah Fox, *Privacy Implications of Fast, Mobile Internet Access*, Pew Internet and American Life Project, February 13, 2008, www.pewinternet.org/Reports/2008/ Privacy-Implications-of-Fast-Mobile-Internet-Access.aspx (accessed September 19, 2009).

20. John Horrigan, *Mobile Access to Data and Information*, Pew Internet and American Life Project, March 5, 2008, www.pewinternet.org/Press-Releases/2008/ Mobile-Access-to-Data-and-Information.aspx (accessed September 19, 2009).

21. Quoted in Brian Stelter, "The Facebooker Who Friended Obama," *New York Times*, July 7, 2008, www.nytimes.com/2008/07/07/technology/07hughes.html (accessed May 30, 2010).

22. David Plouffe, *The Audacity to Win* (New York: Viking, 2009), 21.

23. Ibid.

24. Tom Lowry, "Obama's Secret Digital Weapon," *Business Week*, June 24, 2008, www.businessweek.com/magazine/content/08_27/b4091000977488.htm (accessed May 30, 2010).

25. Matthew Mosk, "Obama Rewriting Rules for Raising Campaign Money Online," *Washington Post*, March 28, 2008, www.washingtonpost.com/wp-dyn/content/ article/2008/03/27/AR2008032702968.html (accessed May 30, 2010).

26. Brandon C. Waite, "E-mail and Electoral Fortunes: Obama's Campaign Internet Insurgency," in *Communicator-in-Chief*, 110.

27. Baumgartner and Morris, "Who Wants to Be My Friend?" 57.

28. Ibid., 58.

29. Jose Antonio Vargas, "Obama Raised Half a Billion Online," *washingtonpost. com*, November 20, 2008, http://voices.washingtonpost.com/the-trail/2008/11/20/ obama_raised_half_a_billion_on.html (accessed March 9, 2009).

30. "What Does "Viral" Mean?" *epolitics.com*, January 14, 2009, www.epolitics. com/2009/01/14/what-does-viral-mean/ (accessed June 2, 2010).

31. Ibid., and Baumgartner and Morris, "Who Wants to Be My Friend?" 51.

32. Vargas, "Obama Raised Half a Billion Online," and Colin Delany, "Learning from Obama's Online Outreach: How to Find and Build Support on the Internet," *epolitics*, March 2, 2009, www.epolitics.com/2009/03/02/learning-from-obamas-online-outreach-how-to-find-and-build-support-on-the-internet/ (accessed June 2, 2010).

33. Waite, "E-mail and Electoral Fortunes," 110.

34. Hendricks and Denton, "Political Campaigns," 10.

35. Vargas, "Obama Raised Half a Billion Online."

36. Ibid.

37. Quoted in Plouffe, *The Audacity to Win*, 92.

38. Baumgartner and Morris, "Who Wants to Be My Friend?" 58.

39. Quoted in *Electing the President, 2008: The Insiders' View*, ed. Kathleen Hall Jamieson (Philadelphia: University of Pennsylvania Press, 2009), 37.

40. Mackay, "Gadgets, Gismos, and the Web 2.0 Election," 20.

41. Vargas, "Obama Raised Half a Billion Online" and Baumgartner and Morris, "Who Wants to Be My Friend?" 58.

42. This section draws on the more detailed discussion in Anthony Corrado, "Fund-Raising Strategies in the 2008 Presidential Campaign," in *Campaigns and Elections American Style*, 3rd ed., ed. James A. Thurber and Candice J. Nelson (Boulder, CO: Westview Press, 2010), 114–17, and Corrado et al., *Reform in an Age of Networked Campaigns*, 12–13.

43. Federal Election Commission, "2008 Presidential Campaign Financial Activity Summarized: Receipts Nearly Double 2004 Total," press release, June 8, 2009, www.fec.gov/press/press2009/20090608PresStat.shtml (accessed May 30, 2010).

44. Federal Election Commission, "2008."

45. Vargas, "Obama Raised Half a Billion Online."

46. Ibid.

47. Mosk, "Obama Rewriting Rules."

48. Vargas, "Obama Raised Half a Billion Online."

49. David Plouffe quoted in The Institute of Politics, John F. Kennedy School of Government, Harvard University, *Campaign for President: The Managers Look at 2008* (Lanham, MD: Rowman & Littlefield, 2009), 181. In August, it was reported that the Obama campaign had reached the two million donor mark, hence the estimate that he recruited close to two million additional donors during the general election contest. See Foon Rhee, "Obama Reaches 2 Million Donors," *Boston Globe*, August 14, 2008, www.boston.com/news/politics/politicalintelligence/2008/08/obama_reaches_2.html (accessed June 2, 2010).

50. See the Federal Election Commission's summary of Obama's campaign receipts, which is available at www.fec.gov/DisclosureSearch/mapApp.do (accessed June 3, 2010).

51. Campaign Finance Institute, "Reality Check: Obama Received About the Same Percentage from Small Donors in 2008 as Bush in 2004," press release, November 24,

2008, www.cfinst.org/Press/Releases_tags/08-11-24/Realty_Check_-_Obama_Small_
Donors.aspx (accessed June 3, 2010). For the purposes of disclosure, it should be
noted that the author serves as chair of the Campaign Finance Institute's Board of
Trustees.

52. Campaign Finance Institute data as reported in Corrado et al., *Reform in an Age
of Networked Campaigns*, Table 1: Sources of Funds for Presidential Candidates, 16.

53. Federal Election Commission, "Party Financial Activity Summarized for the
2008 Election Cycle," press release, May 28, 2009, www.fec.gov/press/press2009/052
82009Party/20090528Party.shtml (accessed June 3, 2010).

54. Michael J. Malbin, Aaron Dusso, Gregory Fortelny, and Brendan Glavin, "The
Need for an Integrated Vision of Parties and Candidates: National Party Finances,
1999–2008," in *The State of the Parties*, ed. John C. Green (Lanham, MD: Rowman &
Littlefield, forthcoming). A summary of the findings of this research is available on
the Campaign Finance Institute website. See "Small and Large Donors to National
Political Parties and Candidates," press release, March 25, 2010, Table 1, www.cfinst.
org/Press/PReleases/10-03-25/Small_and_Large_Donors_to_National_Political_Par
ties_and_Candidates.aspx (accessed June 3, 2010).

55. Plouffe in *Electing the President, 2008*, 37–38, 40.

56. Zack Exley, "Obama Field Organizers Plot a Miracle," *Huffington Post*, August
27, 2007, www.huffingtonpost.com/zack-exley/obama-field-organizers-pl_b_61918.
html (accessed June 3, 2010).

57. Barack Obama, *Dreams from My Father* (New York: Times Books, 1995; later
print edition, New York: Three Rivers Press, 2004), and *The Audacity of Hope* (New
York: Crown Publishers, 2006).

58. James W. Ceaser, Andrew E. Busch, and John J. Pitney, Jr., *Epic Journey: The
2008 Elections and American Politics* (Lanham, MD: Rowman & Littlefield, 2009), 16.

59. See, among others, Ceaser, *Presidential Selection* and *Reforming the Reforms*
(Cambridge, MA: Ballinger Publishing, 1982), and Nelson W. Polsby, *Consequences
of Party Reform* (New York: Oxford University Press, 1983).

60. Anthony Corrado, "Financing the 2004 Presidential General Election," in
Financing the 2004 Election, 142–43.

61. Ibid.

62. Plouffe, *Electing the President, 2008*, 37–38.

63. Anthony Corrado, "Financing the 2008 Presidential General Election," in
Financing the 2008 Election, ed. by David B. Magleby and Anthony Corrado (Washington, DC: Brookings Institution Press, forthcoming).

64. Ibid.

65. John Bresnahan, "Cash-poor Obama Says No to Reid," *Politico.com*, September 16, 2008, www.politico.com/news/stories/0908/13485.html (accessed June 5,
2010), and Federal Election Commission, "2008 Presidential Campaign Financial
Activity Summarized."

66. Federal Election Commission, "2008 Presidential Campaign Financial Activity Summarized."

67. Chris Cillizza, "Obama Announces 'Organizing for America,'" *The Fix* Weblog, entry posted January 17, 2009, http://voices.washingtonpost.com/thefix/white-house/obama-announces-organizing-for.html (accessed June 4, 2010), and Lydia DePillis, "Disorganized," *The New Republic*, October 29, 2009, www.tnr.com/article/politics/disorganized?page=0,2 (accessed June 4, 2010).

68. "President-Elect Obama Announces Organizing for America," January 17, 2009, available at www.gwu.edu/~action/2008/chrntran08/orgforam011709pr.html (accessed June 6, 2010).

69. Jeffrey K. Tulis, *The Rhetorical Presidency* (Princeton, NJ: Princeton University Press, 1987), 17.

70. Ibid., 4.

71. Jonathan D. Salant, "Obama's Army of E-Mail Backers Give Him Clout to Sway Congress," *Bloomberg.com*, December 1, 2008, www.bloomberg.com/apps/news?pid=20601087&sid=aEVXKOC3s8.k (accessed June 6, 2010).

72. Tulis, *The Rhetorical Presidency*, 145–72.

73. Micah Sifry, "Section I: Year One of Organizing for America: The Permanent Field Campaign in a Digital Age," www.techpresident.com/ofayear1/I (accessed June 6, 2010).

74. Jeremy Bird, "Organizing for America: Looking Back, Marching Ahead," *Huffington Post*, January 6, 2010, www.huffingtonpost.com/jeremy-bird/organizing-for-america-lo_b_413000.html (accessed June 6, 2010).

75. Ceasar, Busch, and Pitney, *Epic Journey*, 168.

76. Ibid., 179.

77. Ben Smith and Alex Isenstadt, "Obama Political Arm Under Fire," *Politico.com*, January 13, 2010, www.politico.com/news/stories/0110/31428.html (accessed June 7, 2010).

78. Philip Rucker and Dan Eggen, "Protests at Democrats' Health-Care Events Spark Political Tug of War," *Washington Post*, August 6, 2009, www.washingtonpost.com/wp-dyn/content/article/2009/08/05/AR2009080502780.html?sid=ST2009080504000 (accessed June 7, 2010), and Mark Z. Barabak, "Thousands Gather in D.C. to Protest Healthcare Overhaul Plan," *Los Angeles Times*, September 13, 2009, http://articles.latimes.com/2009/sep/13/nation/na-capitol-rally13 (accessed June 7, 2010).

CHAPTER TWO

~

Professor Obama
and the Constitution

David K. Nichols

Barack Obama is our first professor president since Woodrow Wilson. On the campaign trail in 2008 he frequently mentioned his experience as a professor at the University of Chicago, claiming that unlike various Republicans, he understood the Constitution and would obey it, particularly in the use of his war powers. Obama declared: "I was a constitutional law professor, which means unlike the current president I actually respect the Constitution."[1] It seems only appropriate, therefore, that we look seriously at President Obama's understanding of the Constitution beginning with what he actually taught about the Constitution at the University of Chicago. We will then turn to Obama's comments on constitutional matters during the campaign, and compare them with his performance as President to see if the office has "taught" President Obama anything about the Constitution. Finally, we will speculate about what else he may learn from the Court about the Constitution during the remainder of his term.

Professor Obama

In 1990 Obama was recommended to the head of the appointments committee at the University of Chicago Law School by conservative professor (and later Circuit Court Judge) Michael McConnell. As editor of the *Harvard Law Review*, Obama had made helpful comments on an article McConnell

25

published there. Although Obama responded that he was not interested in a teaching position, he was interested in becoming a Law and Government Fellow, a position that would provide him with an office, a small stipend, and the opportunity to complete a book on voting rights. Obama never completed the book on voting rights, but instead wrote his memoir, *Dreams From My Father*. In 1992 he was hired as a lecturer at Chicago, and served in that capacity until 1996 when he became a senior lecturer, a position he held until 2004 when he left to run for the U.S. Senate. For much of this period he was a member of the law firm of Davis, Miner, Barnhill & Galland, and he also served on the board of several foundations. He was a member of the State Senate of Illinois from 1997 to 2004.

During the 2008 campaign there was much debate over the question of whether Obama was actually a professor at the University of Chicago, critics complaining that he served in a part-time, nontenured, and nontenure-track position. The University, however, defended Obama's claims to the title of professor,[2] and for our purposes it is sufficient to note that as a senior lecturer he regularly taught three courses a year for the law school. He had a record teaching some of the brightest law students in the country on matters related to constitutional law. While we have only a few anecdotal accounts from Obama's students, we do have copies of his course syllabi, some of his final exam questions, as well as two of his memos to students summarizing what he considered to be good answers to his questions.[3] From these materials we can begin to develop a picture of Obama's views of the Constitution.

Several prominent professors of constitutional law have already reviewed these materials and concluded they were the product of a serious scholar. Pamela Karlan, Stanford law professor and former clerk to Justice Harry Blackmun, sees evidence of "a first-rate mind for legal doctrine," and Yale's Akhil Amar says that: "I came away impressed—dazzled, really—by the analytic intelligence and sophistication of these questions and answers." Even more conservative scholars saw much to praise. Randy Barnett, a well-known libertarian law professor at Georgetown University, found that: "The exam question and answer keys manifest a keen comprehension of then-prevailing Supreme Court Due Process and Equal Protection Clause doctrine," and he was particularly struck by the balanced viewpoints in his course on "Racism and the Law." John C. Eastman, a former law clerk to Justice Clarence Thomas, was equally impressed with the reading list for the "Racism" course, ranging as it did from Derrick Bell and Malcolm X on one end of the political spectrum to Chuck Cooper and Lino Graglia on the other. Amar went so far as to conclude that based on these materials alone, the University of Chicago would have been warranted to offer Obama tenure.[4]

Not everyone would agree with that conclusion, and numerous commentators have pointed out that it would be very rare for a major law school to offer tenure to anyone who had never published any scholarly work. The more common complaint about Obama's time at Chicago, however, is that Obama was very reticent to share his opinions with his students or to engage in scholarly debate with his colleagues. Barnett concludes:

> He either was skillful at concealing his own take on these issues both in these materials and in the classroom (as reported by his former students) or he held no deep commitments on what one would think were matters of central concern to him. While this latter possibility would make him a flexible politician, it is bound to disappoint his most vehement supporters and detractors alike. In the end, while they confirm that the former president of the *Harvard Law Review* is a smart guy, and an exceptionally fair-minded teacher, they tell us little about his core beliefs on the very sensitive issues covered by these courses. Nor perhaps should we have expected them to.[5]

It is possible, however, that Barnett and others did not push very far in the search for Obama's views in his course materials.

First, we might get some sense of Obama's constitutional thought from his choice of courses, and perhaps even more from what he did not teach. It turns out that Obama's professing about the Constitution was focused on a relatively few areas of constitutional law. Chicago's curriculum offers several courses in constitutional law. Constitutional Law I focuses on the structure of government, issues such as the separation of powers, federalism, commerce powers, and the contract clause. Professor Obama never taught that course. Constitutional Law II examines free speech, whereas Constitutional Law IV examines both freedom of speech and freedom of religion. Constitutional Law V looks only at freedom of religion. Professor Obama never taught any of those courses. He did teach Con Law III, a course that examines equal protection and substantive due process. He also taught a course on voting rights and the above mentioned course on "Racism and the Law." As even Karlan admits, Obama's courses "did not examine many of the issues that have come to the forefront of constitutional debate . . . such as the president's inherent powers under Article II of the Constitution to disregard limitations placed on his authority by Congress or other aspects of what's referred to as 'separation of powers' (the checks and balances among the three branches of government)."[6] In other words, Obama's teaching had nothing to do with the issues on which he was claiming professional expertise during the campaign.

If, however, Obama had indeed demonstrated a balanced scholarly approach toward the Constitution in the courses he did teach, one might assume that this professional perspective would carry over to the exploration of other constitutional issues. Let us then look at the three courses that Obama did teach. "Racism and the Law" was the course that was singled out for its display of balance and fairness.[7] This was a seminar class that met nine times. Professor Obama structured the seminar so that he would assign readings and direct the discussion for the first four sessions, the next four classes would be led by students, based on readings they would choose, and the final session would be devoted to a summary and a reading quiz. Given that half of the first class, according to the syllabus, was to be devoted to getting organized, Obama's "balanced" reading list that was so impressive to Barnett and Eastman covered only three-and-a-half classes.

What constituted balance in this reading list? Three selections are often cited. Two are articles from a 1991 issue of the *Harvard Journal of Law and Public Policy*—a ten-page article by Lino Graglia titled "Title VII of the Civil Rights Act of 1964: From Prohibiting to Requiring Racial, Discrimination in Employment" and a nine-page article by Charles Cooper on the *Wards Cove* decision. The third is a three-page article in the *New Republic* from 1964 by Robert Bork entitled "Civil Rights—A Challenge." The Bork essay, hardly his most recent or most substantial scholarly work, was used extensively to discredit Bork during his confirmation hearings. The Graglia and Cooper articles are more serious efforts. Nonetheless, it suggests a certain lack of imagination on Obama's part if these are the three best articles to carry the weight for the conservative position on civil rights in a balanced discussion of the topic.

Randy Barnett also praises the courage of Obama in "including several readings by Frederick Douglass, who many modern race theorists have come to disparage as insufficiently radical."[8] Given that Douglass was the leading black abolitionist in the United States, this comment may tell us more about the modern race theorists than it does about Obama's courage. It should also be noted that the "several" articles consisted of two required readings, an editorial supporting the killing of officials enforcing the Fugitive Slave Laws, and a speech entitled "The Right to Criticize American Institutions" (although the title is shortened to "The Right to Criticize" on Obama's syllabus) in which Douglass proclaims:

> I have no love for America, as such; I have no patriotism. I have no country. What country have I? The institutions of this country do not know me, do not recognize me as a man. I am not thought of, spoken of, in any direction, out of the anti-slavery ranks, as a man. I am not thought of, or spoken of, except as a piece of property belonging to some *Christian* slaveholder, and all the

religious and political institutions of this country, alike pronounce me a slave and a chattel.[9]

It is difficult to imagine what even modern race theorists would find objectionable in these works. Nor would it be difficult to find other Douglass speeches, for example his "Oration in Memory of Abraham Lincoln," that would provide a more complex and balanced view of Douglass's thought.[10]

A large part of the reading list consists of Supreme Court opinions, but Obama kindly suggests that it is not necessary to read the opinions if the students are familiar with them from other courses, or he tells the students that they can rely on the summaries of the cases provided by Derrick Bell, one of the founders of critical race theory. To substitute Bell's description of the cases for the primary source material may be justified to make the students' lives easier, but it can hardly be justified if the goal is a full and balanced presentation of the issues.

Much of the course, however, is devoted to student presentations. Professor Obama is also praised for his considerate treatment of these topics by Randy Barnett. "What particularly impressed me was how even handed were his presentations of the competing sides the students might take. These summaries were remarkably free of the sort of cant and polemics that all too often afflicts academic discussions of race. Were this not a seminar on 'racism and the law' I doubt one could tell which side of each issue the teacher was on."[11] However, not only the title of the course, but also the suggested topics, might provide a clue as to the professor's leanings. They included: all black all male schools, reparations, media bias, racial gerrymandering, sentencing discrimination, school funding, hate crimes, welfare policy, immigration, and reproductive rights. Each begins with the assumption of an ongoing problem of racism that must be addressed.

Professor Obama does try to give a balanced description of each topic, and in many cases he succeeds. For example, he asks a series of questions regarding reproductive rights: "Should we change welfare policy so that welfare grants no longer increase with each child? Should judges of welfare agencies have the authority to restrict the reproductive choices of mothers who are found to have neglected their children or take drugs during pregnancy? Are commentators who say such policies smack of 'racial genocide' misguided?"[12] Liberals and conservatives might each see reasons to support or be horrified by such policies, although the move at the end to the question of "racial genocide" may tilt the discussion in a certain direction.

The syllabus for his second course on "Voting Rights & the Democratic Process" appears less concerned with competing opinions.[13] He assigns a standard textbook by three well-known law professors, and lists no other readings on the syllabus. He begins the course with a discussion of the reapportionment cases and spends the next several weeks on vote dilution and racial gerrymandering, and concludes the course with sections on direct democracy and alternative voting systems. There is nothing about the long history of the debate over theories of representation prior to the 1960s, or of the founding perspective on questions of representation. The description of the course concludes with the question of whether "voting even matter[s] in a complex, modern society where campaigns are dominated by money and issues are framed by lobbyists."[14] As in so many other cases, he frames a question in such a way as to encourage a general direction for the discussion. This is almost unavoidable, and is not a reason for condemning him as a professor, but it does raise questions as to why so many thoughtful scholars from across the political spectrum would suggest that it is impossible to determine anything about his politics from his course materials.

We have much more information regarding his third course, "Constitutional Law III: Equal Protection and Substantive Due Process," and the available information certainly supports the claims of Obama's legal sophistication.[15] This course is the broadest of the three, and reveals the most about Obama's approach to the Constitution. For this class we have both Obama's exam questions and in some cases, his proposed answers. Again it is interesting to look at the topics Obama chooses for his hypothetical exam questions. They include cases involving in vitro fertilization for lesbian couples and whether the state is obligated to pay for it, forbidding sale of alcohol or cigarettes to pregnant women, the states' authority to prevent Abraham and Sarah from entering into a contractual arrangement with a surrogate mother, the necessity of court-ordered affirmative action to remedy a case of racial profiling by customs agents, affirmative action for gays and lesbians on law review, and, perhaps most striking, a case involving the right of Mary and Joseph to clone their daughter Dolly, who is in a persistent vegetative state.

These hypothetical cases are packed with interesting legal questions that force students to develop a complex legal argument, and Obama's sample answers clearly demonstrate that he has worked his way through the relevant legal arguments and precedents. The cloning case is a good example. He begins by arguing that we should start with two questions: (1) Is there a fundamental right that would have protected Dolly's right to clone herself, and (2) What standard of review should be used in determining the constitutionality of any law restricting Dolly's, Mary's, or Joseph's right to clone? Obama admits there may be disagreement about whether there is a fundamental right to clone and he explores the possible objections to it. He begins with the standard for fundamental rights established by Justice Scalia in a paternity case, *Michael H. v. Gerald D.*[16] Scalia's argument is that "Constitutionally protected substantive rights under the due process clause must be defined at their most specific, traditionally defined level." Obama says that if the Court followed Scalia's argument it would leave little room for Dolly to claim a substantive due process violation if she were prevented by law from cloning herself, but Obama goes on to say that "whether a majority of the current Court would in fact embrace such a cramped reading of the Constitution is not entirely clear."[17] The decision would turn on whether or not the Court was willing to accept tradition as the basis for defining due process rights, but Obama points out that one could argue, as Justice Souter does, that tradition is fluid, and therefore might evolve to include such rights. Souter's approach would clearly be less "cramped" than Scalia's.

Obama next argues that even if there is no fundamental right to clone oneself, a government restriction on cloning might violate the "liberty interests" of Dolly under the doctrine of substantive due process, in the same way restrictions on abortion were said to violate the liberty interests of Jane Roe in *Roe v. Wade*. Obama explains, however, that liberty does not mean that one can do anything one wants with one's body. He carefully lays out the arguments for restricting liberty interests, but presents them largely as difficulties to be overcome by Dolly and her parents. He concludes that the choice between the constitutionally protected liberty interests and the state's right to restrict them would ultimately turn on the question of what standard of review would be adopted by the Court, and this in turn would be based on whether the state has any legitimate reason to regulate cloning.

Obama proposes three possible justifications for the state to regulate cloning: (1) Protecting the cloned child from future psychological damage, (2) preventing objectification of a human being and the possible commercial uses of cloning, and (3) protecting the sanctity of life and familial bonds. He argues the first justification is clearly the weakest of the three. "The hypothetical offers no evidence that cloned children would suffer a disproportionate amount of psychological damage or social ostracism." Even if it could be shown, it would not provide a sufficient rationale for the state to prevent the coming into being of such children, "any more than [the state] can use bigotry to justify discriminatory child custody policies. . . . If the state wants to prevent discrimination against the cloned, it can pass anti-discrimination laws."[18]

Obama finds the second justification only slightly more persuasive, arguing that it "rest[s] on the assumption that cloned children will be treated differently from children produced in traditional fashion, an assumption that is not supported by the evidence."[19] According to Obama, there is no reason to believe that cloned children are more likely to be used to harvest organs or as objects of child abuse than other children. He goes on to suggest that any problems related to objectification could be addressed through bans on organ harvesting or child abuse laws.

This leaves the state with the third and presumably strongest argument for restricting cloning: the sanctity of life and familial bonds. Although the state has a legitimate interest in protecting actual human life,[20] Obama argues, that "this does not necessarily mean that the state also has a compelling interest in preventing what it considers to be a 'devaluation' of human life that might result from cloning." Furthermore, "It is hard to see how a compelling interest in protecting human life translates into a compelling interest in preventing human life."[21] Obama is also suspicious of the claims of the state to protect family bonds. He contends that "the Court has indicated that the individual has constitutionally protected rights to determine his or her familial relations."[22] It is not clear how laws related to incest or polygamy would fare under this standard. Obama might claim that incest could be regulated as a form of abuse and polygamy as a denial of equal protection, but what is clear is that the standard suggested by Obama leaves little room for regulation by the state to protect familial bonds.

Just when it looks as though Obama will reject any legitimate basis for the state to regulate cloning, he adds a slight variation on the third justification for state regulation—whether the state's "moral judgment regarding the potential harms that cloning will have on our current conceptions of life and family serve as a sufficient basis for instituting an outright ban." Given his arguments so far, one might think that Obama would dismiss this claim. Indeed it is difficult to distinguish it from those made above. Surprisingly, however, Obama hypothesizes that the Court might sustain such moral regulation if it chose to adopt a rational basis test, although it would be a close call if the Court used some heightened basis of scrutiny. Still Obama resists reaching a firm conclusion. Just as he shifted the ground from the question of a liberty interest to a question of the level of scrutiny at the end of his discussion of the due process rights of Dolly and her parents, he now shifts the ground back to the question of Dolly's liberty interest rather than decide which level of scrutiny would be most appropriate. He concludes that the Court might wish to avoid establishing the "troubling precedent that the state's moral judgments, standing alone, can override the individual's fundamental rights or liberty interests."[23]

What are Obama's conclusions? They may be difficult to discern, at least if one looks where one would expect to find them, at the end of his arguments. Obama leaves the outcome of the case in question, thereby supporting the claims of his scholarly impartiality. But if one looks at the argument itself, one gets the impression that Obama is slightly more interested in finding a way to justify cloning than in defending the state's right to restrict it. Although he has one section exploring the strengths and weaknesses of the pro-cloning position and one looking at the strengths and weaknesses of the state's position, his perspective is that of one who is trying to find a way to defend the rights of Dolly and her parents. When examining the state's justifications, Obama carefully undermines each argument. He concludes that the Court might adopt a rational basis test, which he assumes would uphold virtually any justification the state would like to offer, but Obama leaves the impression that such a decision would rest on the Justices' arbitrary preferences rather than a reasoned constitutional argument. On the other hand, each time he comes up with an objection to Dolly's, or Mary's, or Joseph's claims to a fundamental right or liberty interest, he finds a way that they might be able to overcome those objections.

Moreover, his creation of this particular hypothetical and others tell us something about his perspective. In each of his hypothetical cases Obama is clearly trying to push the envelope. He has no interest in revisiting what he obviously considers to be settled questions regarding abortion or equal protection. The possibility of returning to an earlier understanding of the Constitution does not seem to occur to Obama. Most of his hypothetical cases are based on situations in which individuals are trying to expand the definition of rights in a more liberal direction—support for cloning, state-funded in vitro fertilization for lesbian couples, contractual rights for surrogate parents, requiring affirmative action for gays and lesbians to participate on a law review, or affirmative action as a mandatory remedy for findings of racial profiling. Obama provides a detailed legal analysis of each of these cases, and considers competing points of view, but these cases all point to a Progressive conception of law, in which history moves the law in an ever more positive direction. There may be obstacles, there may even be legitimate objections, but there is no real question about the direction in which the law should move. The name of the state in the hypothetical cloning case is Futura. Cloning might cause problems for "our current conceptions of life and family," but Obama points to the possibility that this too may change.

Although Obama's classes do not appear to have been exercises in heavy-handed indoctrination, they may have betrayed more ideological bias than has been frequently claimed. A cynic might say that he merely used his classes as a testing ground for the best rhetoric to use to move his agenda forward. Clearly his Progressive assumptions are in evidence in his choice of topics and his presentation of arguments, but what is also in evidence is his desire to at least appear to be balanced. Perhaps this is all we can ask from an academic or a politician. By confronting the range of objections he might encounter in pursuing his Progressive goals in the areas of privacy or equal protection, Obama may have learned the need to temper at least his rhetoric in these areas. It is interesting to note that at this point in his administration, his major problems have not come either in the area of civil rights or abortion. His speech on race in response to the Reverend Wright controversy during the campaign is considered one of his best, and although he is not likely to be embraced by pro-life voters, when the abortion issue threatened to sink his health care bill he was able to help to craft language that offered an acceptable compromise, at least to congressional Democrats. When he announced his executive order to reverse Bush's policy and allow federally funded stem cell research, he was careful to point to needed restriction, declaring: "We will ensure that our government never opens the door to the use of cloning for human reproduction. It is dangerous, profoundly wrong, and has no place in our society, or any society."[24] Mary, Joseph, and Dolly would have little hope under this policy. Obama's teaching and study of the law may have given him at least some appreciation for the complexity of these issues. This appreciation may be more tactical than principled, but in either case it has probably helped to moderate his policy choices.

Campaign Promise, Presidential Performance, and the Constitution

In 2007 Obama disparaged the Bush administration, telling audiences: "I joined a civil rights law practice, and I started teaching constitutional law—because unlike some occupants of the White House, I actually believe in the Constitution."[25] Candidate Obama argued that Bush's theory of a "unitary executive" led him to disregard the constitutional rights of individuals, and the constitutional role of Congress and the Courts. He elaborated these complaints in August 2007. "When I am President, America will reject torture without exception. . . . I will close Guantanamo, reject the Military Commissions Act, and adhere to the Geneva Conventions. . . . No more ignoring the law when it is inconvenient."[26] Obama was also clear in his promise to end the policy of extraordinary renditions, where detainees were transferred to countries that had fewer restrictions on detentions and interrogations. As he said in a 2007 article in *Foreign Affairs*:

> To build a better, freer world, we must first behave in ways that reflect the decency and aspirations of the American people. This means ending the prac-

tices of shipping away prisoners in the dead of night to be tortured in far-off countries, of detaining thousands without charge or trial, of maintaining a network of secret prisons to jail people beyond the reach of the law.[27]

In December of 2007, in response to a questionnaire from the *Boston Globe*, Obama offered several additional concerns, stating categorically: "I reject the Bush administration's claim that the President has plenary authority under the Constitution to detain U.S. citizens without charges as unlawful enemy combatants," and "I believe the Administration's use of executive authority to over-classify information is a bad idea."[28]

Obama's criticisms were not limited to Bush's conduct of national security policy. He complained that Bush was interfering with the constitutional rights of Congress through his use of signing statements. According to Obama: "What George Bush has been trying to do, as part of his effort to accumulate more power in the presidency, is he's been saying, 'Well, I can basically change what Congress passed by attaching a letter saying, I don't agree with this part or I don't agree with that part. I'm going to choose to interpret it this way or that way.'" In the Obama administration: "We're not going to use signing statements as a way of doing an end-run around Congress."[29]

Furthermore, Obama objected that the Bush administration had frequently refused to provide Congress the information it needed to carry out its constitutional functions. Explaining his vote against the confirmation of John Roberts to be Chief Justice of the United States, Obama remarked: "I remain distressed that the White House during this confirmation process . . . failed to provide critical documents . . . that could have provided us with a better basis to make our judgment with respect to the nomination. This White House continues to stymie efforts on the part of the Senate to do its job."[30]

Senator Obama also vigorously criticized Senate Republicans when they threatened to end the practice of allowing a filibuster on presidential nominees, arguing:

> The American people sent us here to be their voice. They understand that those voices can at times become loud and argumentative, but they also hope that we can disagree without being disagreeable. . . .
>
> What they don't expect is for one party—be it Republican or Democrat—to change the rules in the middle of the game so that they can make all the decisions while the other party is told to sit down and keep quiet. The American people want less partisanship in this town, but everyone in this chamber knows that if the majority chooses to end the filibuster—if they choose to change the rules and put an end to democratic debate—then the fighting and the bitterness and the gridlock will only get worse.[31]

Obama's campaign message was clear. He wanted to "turn the page on the imperial presidency."[32]

When he came into office, President Obama seemed poised to follow through on his promises. On January 21, 2009 he issued two executive memoranda, one ordered the creation by the Office of Management and Budget of an "Open Government Directive" that would apply to all independent agencies,[33] and a second proclaimed that in dealing with requests under the Freedom of Information Act agencies should adopt a "presumption in favor of disclosure."[34] The days of unnecessary secrecy were over. The following day he issued three executive orders regarding the treatment of detainees. The first, Executive Order 13491, revoked Executive Order 13440 (issued by the Bush administration), which had interpreted the "Geneva Conventions" to allow harsh interrogation techniques with regards to enemy combatants, and declared instead that interrogations be conducted under the requirements of the Army Field Manual.[35] He also issued Executive Order 13492, which stated: "The detention facilities at Guantánamo for individuals covered by this order shall be closed as soon as practicable, and no later than 1 year from the date of this order."[36] Finally, the President issued Executive Order 13493, which called for the creation of a task force "to develop policies for the detention, trial, transfer, release, or other disposition of individuals captured or apprehended in connection with armed conflicts and counterterrorism."[37]

It became apparent, however, that the shift on national security policy might be less pronounced than many of Obama's supporters had hoped. In February 2009 the Obama Justice Department adopted the argument of the Bush administration defending state secrets in the case of *Mohamed v. Jeppesen Dataplan*.[38] The case involved Binyam Mohamed, an Ethiopian national, and four other detainees who had brought suit against Boeing for arranging flights for Bush's extraordinary rendition program. Mohamed alleged that he had been tortured both in U.S. custody and after being transported to Morocco. The Obama administration argued that the case should be dismissed, because even a discussion of the details involved would breach national security. Anthony Romero, Executive Director of the American Civil Liberties Union, was outraged by the administration's position:

> "This is not change," he said in a statement. "This is definitely more of the same. Candidate Obama ran on a platform that would reform the abuse of state secrets, but President Obama's Justice Department has disappointingly reneged on that important civil liberties issue. If this is a harbinger of things to come, it will be a long and arduous road to give us back an America we can be proud of again."[39]

Later the same month the Obama Justice Department supported the Bush administration's argument that the writ of habeas corpus did not extend to detainees at Bagram Airforce Base in Afghanistan.[40] President Obama has made no mention of any desire to close the Bagram detention facility, nor has the closure of Guantanamo proceeded according to schedule. January 2010 came and went, and as of June 2010, 181 detainees remain at the facility.

Critics have also pointed out that major loopholes remain in the Obama administration's new torture policy. Although Executive Order 13491 states that the Army Field Manual will be followed for military interrogations, it also established a special task force to "study and evaluate whether the interrogation practices and techniques in Army Field Manual, when employed by departments or agencies outside the military, provide an appropriate means of acquiring the intelligence necessary to protect the Nation, and, if warranted, to recommend any additional or different guidance for other departments or agencies."[41] The door was left wide open as to what was allowed in nonmilitary interrogations. Moreover, even the under the Army Field Manual there was a great deal of leeway. As Matthew Alexander, a former Air Force interrogator, argued: "If I were to return to one of the war zones today . . . I would still be allowed to abuse prisoners. . . . When it comes to the specifics the manual contradicts itself, allowing actions that no right-thinking person could consider humane."[42] Finally, any restrictions would be subject to change if the president were to issue a new executive order, a fact of which the Obama administration is well aware.

Jack Goldsmith, a former Bush administration member and later critic, argues in the *New Republic*: "The new administration has copied most of the Bush program, has expanded some of it, and has narrowed it only a bit. Almost all of the Obama changes have been at the level of packaging, argumentation, symbol, and rhetoric."[43] Goldsmith goes on to outline twelve areas, including preventive detention, state secrets, rendition, surveillance, the use of military tribunals, and habeas corpus, where Obama has largely accepted Bush's policy prescriptions. As Senator Sue Collins of Maine explained: "The administration came in determined to undo a lot of the policies of the prior administration . . . but in fact is finding that many of those policies were better-thought-out than they realized—or that doing away with them is a far more complex task."[44] Goldsmith concludes that this is not surprising: "The presidency invariably gives its occupants a sober outlook on problems of national security. The intense personal responsibility of the president for national security, combined with the continuing reality of a frightening and difficult-to-detect threat, has unsurprisingly led President Obama, like President Bush, to want to use the full arsenal of presidential tools."[45] The constitutional office inevitably shapes the behavior and even the beliefs of its occupant.

This is true not only in the area of foreign affairs, but also in the area of domestic policy. In March 2010 President Obama announced fifteen recess appointments (the same number Bush had made at this point in his administration), complaining that "in the interest of scoring political points" Republican Senators have refused to allow a final vote on his nominees.[46] There was a similar shift on the use of signing statements. As reported in the *New York Times*: "President Obama has issued signing statements claiming the authority to bypass dozens of provisions of bills enacted into law since he took office, provoking mounting criticism by lawmakers from both parties."[47] Although Obama contends that he has used signing statements only to defend "interpretations of the Constitution that are well founded," the same would also have been claimed by President Bush.[48] President Obama was also quick to defend Karl Rove's claims of executive privilege regarding the dismissal of U.S. attorneys. A statement from White House Counsel Gregory Craig explained that President Obama did not want "to do anything that would undermine the institution of the presidency."[49] When Social Secretary Desiree Rogers was invited to testify before a Congressional Committee following a breach of security at a state dinner, press secretary Robert Gibbs explained: "I think you know that based on separation of powers, staff here don't go to testify in front of Congress."[50] Finally, Obama's commitment to the filibuster as a mechanism for protecting minority rights in the Senate confirmation process, was less in evidence during the passage of health care reform.

Many would argue that Obama has failed to live up to his principles as president, but the problem may be with his principles rather than his pragmatism. Professor Obama, like many constitutional law scholars, has not spent much time studying the constitutional structure of government. He began with a very simplistic, although perhaps all-too-common, understanding of the role of the executive in the constitutional separation of powers. Although he frequently claimed during the campaign that we do not have to choose between our constitutional principles and the exigencies of government, he often framed the debate in a way that left us with precisely that choice. President Obama soon learned that the presidency could not function according to the principles he laid out during the campaign, and this led him to reconsider those principles. Whether he carried out that reconsideration from a motive of expediency or from the perspective of one who was open to learning may not matter. The genius of the constitutional separation of powers is that we need not always have to be able to distinguish between the two motives. Nonetheless, it would be better for Obama and the country if principle and practice were in harmony. Otherwise we are left with a conception of constitutional constraints that will undermine effective government, or we rely on claims of necessity that are bound to lead to cynicism about the possibility of constitutional government.

Learning from the Court

When President Obama directly confronted the Supreme Court over its recent campaign finance decision *Citizens United v. Federal Election Commission* (558 U.S. ___ [2010]) during his State of the Union address, commentators were quick to point to the parallel with Franklin Delano Roosevelt's epic battle with the Supreme Court over his New Deal legislation.[51] Of course, FDR's "court packing" plan proved a failure, but conventional wisdom has long accepted that FDR was successful in convincing the Court to change its tune over the long run. Perhaps President Obama, following once again in the tradition of FDR, was taking a preliminary shot across the bow, one directed not only at the campaign finance decision, but at possible future decisions regarding business regulation and most importantly health care.

If so, President Obama may have been too quick to accept conventional wisdom regarding FDR and the Court. Works such as G. Edward White's *The Constitution and the New Deal* have argued that it was not political pressure from Roosevelt, but a gradual evolution of doctrine within the Court that was responsible for change.[52] As Barry Cushman explains, the Court in the early 1930s had been anything but doctrinaire in its rejections of government regulation. Prior to 1937 the Court upheld such far-reaching programs such as collective bargaining for railway workers, nullification of the gold clause in private contracts, a moratorium on mortgage payments, state regulation of the price of milk, and the creation of the Tennessee Valley Authority.[53] It was less that the Court changed in 1937, than that Congress and Roosevelt, after the *Schechter* decision, learned to craft legislation that took into account constitutional and legal precedents.[54] There was no sudden "switch in time that saved nine." Even a president with as little regard for the Court as Roosevelt was forced by his own pragmatism to take seriously constitutional concerns.

If President Obama is wise, he may learn that lesson more quickly than FDR did. There are signs that such constitutional learning is already taking place. The legislation Obama is supporting in response to the *Citizens United* decision would, in his words,

> require that when corporations and other special interests take to the airwaves, whoever is running and funding the ad would have to appear in the

advertisement and claim responsibility for it. . . . Under the bill Congress will consider, we'll make sure that foreign corporations and foreign nationals are restricted from spending money to influence American elections, just as they were in the past—even through U.S. subsidiaries. And we'd keep large contractors that receive taxpayer funds from interfering in our elections as well, to avoid the appearance of corruption and the possible misuse of tax dollars.[55]

Republicans may well oppose these reforms for no other reason than partisan politics, but whatever their response, one could argue that Obama and Congressional Democrats have actually listened to what the Court had to say about finance reform and the First Amendment. Far from overturning the *Citizens United* ruling, the proposed legislation shows evidence of a major shift in the Democrats' approach to campaign finance reform. More disclosure rather than more regulation has long been a refrain of Republicans, and it has the virtue of avoiding many of the conflicts with the First Amendment with which the Court has been concerned.

It will be interesting to see if the Court will play a similar role in the contemporary debates over health care reform and economic regulation. When Cushman quotes Senate Judiciary Committee Chairman Henry Ashurst's comments on the early New Deal, he might just as well have been speaking of health care reform.

We ground out laws so fast that we had no time to offer even a respectful gesture to grammar, syntax and philology. We counted deuces as aces, reasoned from nonexistent premises and, at times, seemed to accept chimeras, fantasies, and exploded social and economic theories as our authentic guides.[56]

There was little debate on questions of constitutionality. The same has been true of the process leading up to passage of the health care reform bill. Since President Obama signed the bill into law, however, we have seen twenty-one states file suits claiming that the legislation is unconstitutional. As usual there is always a presumption that laws passed by Congress are constitutional. The Obama administration obviously believes that Congress has the power to mandate insurance coverage for individuals under both the commerce clause and the taxing power, but the Court has an opportunity to at least weigh in on questions regarding the limits of the power to regulate interstate commerce, the use of the taxing power as an enforcement tool, as well as questions of the contract clause, the ninth and tenth amendments, and the liberty interests of individuals under the Constitution. Whether the Court accepts or rejects the arguments regarding the constitutionality of this particular bill, its opinion will have important implications for the character of any additional reform proposals. If the Court offers guidance on the constitutional limits on reform, President Obama would do well to listen.

Learning to Be a Liberal

More than any recent political figure, President Obama refers to himself as a Progressive rather than a liberal. Part of the reason for this linguistic distinction is surely the fact that Democrats have come to believe that the value of the liberal label has diminished in recent years. The move from liberalism to progressivism could be seen as little more than a marketing ploy—Colonel Sanders' Kentucky Fried Chicken becomes KFC. It is likely, however, that Obama appreciates a far more important distinction between liberalism and progressivism. Whereas progressivism looks forward to the evolution of a more comprehensive national community and government, as well as the growing professionalism of the bureaucratic state, liberalism rests on a language of rights, a language that can be expanded to provide much room for government action, but one that maintains its commitment to a government whose primary purpose is the preservation and protection of rights from those who would abuse them.

Curiously, FDR, to whom Obama is often compared, also began his administration drawing on the rhetoric of the Progressives. In his First Inaugural, Roosevelt echoed Progressive principles, claiming: "We now realize as we have never realized before an interdependence on each other; that we cannot merely take but we must give as well; that if we are to go forward, we must move as a trained and loyal army willing to sacrifice for the good of a common discipline."[57] By 1936, however, FDR had already begun to shift his rhetoric away from community and towards rights. FDR came to see that he did not have to reject the doctrine of rights; he could instead offer to expand it. "If the average citizen is guaranteed equal opportunity in the polling place, he must have equal opportunity in the market place."[58]

This rhetorical move reflected a deeper move on the level of policy. The National Industrial Recovery Act that was struck down by the Supreme Court in 1936 was a model Progressive program. Representatives of business and labor would, together with government experts, establish regulations for wages, prices, and the other business practices. Decisions would be made in the name of society as a whole. In contrast, the National Labor Relations Act that was upheld by the Supreme Court in 1937 defended the rights of workers to organize so that they could defend their rights in negotiations with corporations. The NLRA did not require the government to guarantee a particular outcome to those negotiations. It merely provided a framework in which they could occur, a framework that would protect the rights of all involved. The New Deal liberalism of the NLRA reflected an appreciation of the constitutional limits on the ends and means of government action.

Without the assistance of the Supreme Court, Roosevelt might never have seen that such a shift was politically or constitutionally desirable. Indeed many would argue that Roosevelt was at best a C student of that lesson, but if he had not made at least some movement in the direction of the constitutional language of rights, in all likelihood the New Deal would not be as fondly remembered as it is today. Whether Professor Obama learns the same lesson from history or the Court will in all likelihood determine how he is remembered by future generations.

Notes

1. See FactCheck.Org, March 28, 2008, www.factcheck.org/askfactcheck/was_barack_obama_really_a_constitutional_law.html (accessed July 3, 2010).

2. "Statement Regarding Barack Obama," University of Chicago School of Law, www.law.uchicago.edu/media (accessed June 29, 2010).

3. Jodi Kantor, "Teaching Law, Testing Ideas, Obama Stood Slightly Apart," *New York Times*, July 30, 2008, www.nytimes.com/2008/07/30/us/politics/30law.html (accessed July 3, 2010).

4. Jodi Kantor, "Inside Professor Obama's Classroom," *New York Times* Caucus blog, July 30, 2008, http://thecaucus.blogs.nytimes.com/2008/07/30/inside-professor-obamas-classroom/ (accessed July 3, 2010).

5. Kantor, "Inside Professor Obama's Classroom."

6. Ibid.

7. Course reading packet for "Current Issues in Racism and the Law," Spring 1994, www.nytimes.com/packages/pdf/politics/2008OBAMA_LAW/Obama_CoursePk.pdf (accessed July 3, 2010).

8. Kantor, "Inside Professor Obama's Classroom."

9. Frederick Douglass, "The Right to Criticize American Institutions," May 11, 1847, http://teachingamericanhistory.org/library/index.asp?document=1101 (accessed June 29, 2010).

10. Frederick Douglass, "Oration in Honor of Abraham Lincoln," April 14, 1876, http://teachingamericanhistory.org/library/index.asp?document=39 (accessed June 29, 2010).

11. Kantor, "Inside Professor Obama's Classroom."

12. "Current Issues in Racism and Law."

13. Barack Obama, "Syllabus for Voting Rights Law, Winter 2002," http://electionlawblog.org/archives/obama-votingrightssyllabus.pdf (accessed June 29, 2010).

14. *University of Chicago Law School Announcements* (Fall 2002): 81, http://catalogs.uchicago.edu/law-folder/Law%2002-03.pdf (accessed July 3, 2010).

15. Kantor, "Inside Professor Obama's Classroom."

16. *Michael H. v. Gerard D.* (491 U.S. 110) (1989).

17. Barack Obama, "Answer Memo" (Fall 1997): 2, http://graphics.nytimes.com/packages/pdf/politics/2008OBAMA_LAW/conlaw3.obama.1997.fall.memo.pdf (accessed June 29, 2010).

18. Obama, "Answer Memo," 5.

19. Ibid.

20. See, for example, *Cruzan v. Director, Missouri Department of Health* (497 U.S. 261) (1990) and *Washington v. Glucksberg*, (521 U.S. 702) (1997).

21. Obama, "Answer Memo," 5.

22. Ibid., 6.

23. Ibid., 7.

24. "Remarks of President Barack Obama—As Prepared for Delivery, Signing of Stem Cell Executive Order and Scientific Integrity Presidential Memorandum," March 9, 2009, www.whitehouse.gov/the-press-office/remarks-president-prepared-delivery-signing-stem-cell-executive-order-and-scientifi (accessed June 29, 2010).

25. "Remarks of Senator Barack Obama: Take Back America 2007," Washington, DC, June 19, 2007, www.barackobama.com/2007/06/19/remarks_of_senator_barack_obam_16.php (accessed June 29, 2010).

26. "Remarks of Senator Obama: The War We Need to Win," Washington, DC, August 1, 2007, www.barackobama.com/2007/08/01/the_war_we_need_to_win.php (accessed June 29, 2010).

27. Barack Obama, "Renewing American Leadership: Campaign 2008," *Foreign Affairs*, (July/August 2007): 14.

28. Charlie Savage, "Barack Obama's Q & A," December 20, 2007, *Boston Globe*, www.boston.com/news/politics/2008/specials/CandidateQA/ObamaQA/ (accessed July 3, 2010).

29. "Remarks at Obama Town Hall Meeting," Billings, MT, May 20, 2008, http://blogs.cqpolitics.com/beyond/2008/05/obamas-pledge-on-signing-state.html (accessed June 29, 2010).

30. "Remarks of Senator Barack Obama on the Confirmation of Judge John Roberts," September 22, 2005, www.barackobama.com/2005/09/22/remarks_of_senator_barack_obam_10.php (accessed June 29, 2010).

31. "Statement of Senator Barack Obama on the Nuclear Option," April 13, 2005, www.barackobama.com/2005/04/13/statement_of_senator_barack_ob.php (accessed June 29, 2010).

32. "Remarks of Senator Barack Obama: A New Beginning," Chicago, October 2, 2007, www.barackobama.com/2007/10/02/remarks_of_senator_barack_obam_27.php (accessed July 3, 2010).

33. "Memorandum for the Heads of Executive Departments and Agencies: Transparency and Open Government," January 21, 2009, www.whitehouse.gov/the_press_office/Transparency_and_Open_Government/ (accessed July 3, 2010).

34. "Executive Order 13492: Review and Disposition of Individuals Detained at the Guantanamo Bay Naval Base and Closure of Detention Facilities," January 22, 2009, www.whitehouse.gov/the_press_office/Closure_Of_Guantanamo_Detention_Facilities/ (accessed July 3, 2010).

35. "Executive Order 13491: Ensuring Lawful Interrogations," January 22, 2009, www.whitehouse.gov/the_press_office/EnsuringLawfulInterrogations/ (accessed June 29, 2010).

36. "Executive Order 13492."

37. "Executive Order 13493: Review of Detention Policy Options," January 22, 2009, http://edocket.access.gpo.gov/2009/pdf/E9-1895.pdf (accessed July 3, 2010).

38. Mohamed v. Jeppesen Datapla, 579 F.3d 943.

39. John Schwartz, "Obama Backs Off Reversal on Secrets," *New York Times*, February 9, 2009, www.nytimes.com/2009/02/10/us/10torture.html?_r=2 (accessed July 3, 2010).

40. Charlie Savage, "Obama Upholds Detainee Policy in Afghanistan," *New York Times*, February 21, 2009, www.nytimes.com/2009/02/22/washington/22bagram.html?_r=1&scp=2&sq=bagram&st=cse (accessed July 3, 2010).

41. "Executive Order 13491."

42. Matthew Alexander, "Torture's Loopholes," *New York Times*, January 20, 2010, www.nytimes.com/2010/01/21/opinion/21alexander.html (accessed June 29, 2010).

43. Jack Goldsmith, "The Cheney Fallacy: Why Barrack Obama is Waging a More Effective War on Terror Than George Bush," *The New Republic*, May 18, 2009, www.tnr.com/article/politics/the-cheney-fallacy?id=1e733cac-c273-48e5-9140-80443ed1f5e2&p=1 (accessed June 29, 2010).

44. Peter Baker, "Obama's War Over Terror," *New York Times Magazine*, January 4, 2010, www.nytimes.com/2010/01/17/magazine/17Terror-t.html?pagewanted=all (accessed June 29, 2010).

45. Ibid.

46. "President Obama Announces Recess Appointments to Key Administrative Positions," March 27, 2010, www.whitehouse.gov/the-press-office/president-obama-announces-recess-appointments-key-administration-positions (accessed July 3, 2010).

47. Charlie Savage, "Obama Embrace of Bush Tactic Riles Congress," *New York Times*, August 8, 2009, www.nytimes.com/2009/08/09/us/politics/09signing.html (accessed June 29, 2010).

48. Savage, "Obama Embrace of Bush Tactic."

49. Mark Knoller, "White House Not Challenging Rove's Privilege," *CBS News* Political Hotsheet, February 14, 2009, www.cbsnews.com/8301-503544_162-4803349-503544.html (accessed June 29, 2010).

50. Michael Scherer, "No Testifying for Obama's Social Secretary?" *Time*, December 3, 2009, www.time.com/time/politics/article/0,8599,1945192,00.html (accessed June 29, 2010).

51. *Citizens United v. Federal Election Commission*, 558 U.S. ___ (2010).

52. G. Edward White, *The Constitution and the New Deal* (Cambridge, MA: Harvard University Press, 2000).

53. *Texas & N.O.R. Co. v. Brotherhood of Railway Clerks 281 U.S.* (538, 1930); *Home Building & Loan* Association *v. Blaisdell*, 290 U.S. 398 (1934); *Nebbia v. New York*, 291 U.S. 502 (1934); and *Ashwander v. Tennessee Valley Authority*, 297 U.S. 288 (1936).

54. Barry Cushman, *Rethinking the New Deal Court: The Structure of a Constitutional Revolution* (New York: Oxford University Press, 1998), 33–43.

55. Jake Tapper, "Obama Calls for Support of Campaign Finance Reform Bill, Post-Citizens United Ruling," *ABC News* Political Punch Blog, May 1, 2010, http://blogs.abcnews.com/politicalpunch/2010/05/obama-calls-for-support-of-campaign-finance-reform-bill-post-citizens-united-ruling.html (accessed June 29, 2010).

56. Cushman, *Rethinking the New Deal Court*, 37.

57. Franklin D. Roosevelt, *The Public Papers and Addresses of Franklin D. Roosevelt*, ed. Samuel Rosenman (New York: Random House, 1938), 2:14.

58. Franklin D. Roosevelt, "Acceptance of Nomination for Second Term," June 27, 1936, http://teachingamericanhistory.org/library/index.asp?document=611.

CHAPTER THREE

~

President Obama and Executive Independence

Melanie M. Marlowe

During the presidency of George W. Bush, much was made of the "unitary executive" theory of presidential power. Public understanding, led by the American and international press, seemed to be that the theory was created in the Bush White House to give the president (and vice president) limitless power and permit him to subvert the rule of law.[1] What many considered the excesses of the Bush–Cheney years gave those looking to criticize executive power no shortage of targets.

The theory of the unitary executive, however, is concerned with who exercises the executive power, and therefore who controls the executive branch of government. Those who advocate the correct form of this theory do not claim the president should be free of all constitutional restraints, but argue that the separation of powers requires the president to be responsible for and able to effectively defend those powers that the Constitution gives him. Cass Sunstein, President Obama's Administrator of the Office of Information and Regulatory Affairs, explained that while one may find disagreement among supporters of the unitary executive theory (and it is important to recognize this fact),

> the most important point is that the claim for the unitary executive is not a general claim about the president's power to act on his own or to contradict the will of Congress. You can believe in a strongly unitary executive branch

while also believing that the president cannot make war, or torture people, or engage in foreign surveillance without congressional authorization. You can also believe that the president can do a lot on his own, or a lot in violation of Congress' will, while also accepting the view that Congress can create independent agencies and independent prosecutors. In short, the debate over the unitary executive is an important but narrow one, and it is a small, distinct subpart of the general debate over presidential power.[2]

Candidate Barack Obama made what many believed were President Bush's—and, just as often, Vice President Dick Cheney's—exercises of executive power a focal point of his campaign. In a candidate "Q & A," Barack Obama clearly referenced the Bush administration when he stated, "The President is not above the law," said that there had been "extreme arguments" made in terrorism cases, and asserted there had been an "abuse of prerogative" regarding signing statements.[3] It appeared his vision of executive power was a very deferential one.

Immediately after winning the 2008 election, President Obama moved to establish his administration. It was soon clear that his view of executive power was not as meek as some had hoped it would be. In fact, by looking at his actions in areas such as access to information, signing statements, control of administration, and national security, it is becoming clear that whether he calls it so or not, and whether it is a conscious "theory" he subscribes to or not, President Obama has thus far been a champion of the unitary executive.

The Unitary Executive

Article II, section 1, clause 1 of the Constitution vests "the executive Power" in "a President of the United States." The framers opposed a plural executive or an executive with a privy council, and instead created a unitary executive who would be able to employ "decision, activity, secrecy, and dispatch" as he exercised his powers and fulfilled his duties. Serious concerns about the great powers given to the president would be tempered by the fact that the unitary nature of the office would force him to be politically accountable to the public.[4]

The energetic president established by Article II was a response to the ineffective national government and tyrannical state legislatures that developed under the Articles of Confederation. The framers viewed this as a necessary constitutional feature if the executive branch were to protect itself against encroachments on its power by the other branches.[5] The president possesses "the executive Power" subject to specific constitutional restrictions, not simply some or part of the executive power. This distinction is seen clearly when compared to Article I, which vests Congress only with "All legislative Powers herein granted," not with a general legislative power. (Article III grants federal courts "The judicial Power," but clearly limits what it "shall extend to.") The president, it is argued, has independent constitutional authority to control the executive branch in terms of policy and personnel.

The president is the nation's chief law enforcement officer. The Constitution obligates him to "take Care that the laws be faithfully executed," and here presidents have claimed and been given a fair amount of discretion.[6] The president must enforce the laws Congress makes, and he may provide for the implementation of laws as he sees fit through executive instructions. In the absence of a congressional requirement, he may determine what laws may apply in a specific circumstance, and how the laws will be enforced.[7] He may have to rely on his own interpretation of what the Constitution and laws mean as he assesses how the laws will be enforced.[8] Congress cannot, by the use of the Necessary and Proper clause or other Article I powers, divest the president of his constitutional authority to execute the laws.[9] But Congress will try, and the president must be able to effectively and publicly defend himself.

To fulfill the requirements of the "take care" clause, the president must appoint and direct trusted subordinates whose actions he will coordinate and oversee.[10] This promotes the accountability that the framers understood was necessary in the only truly national office. The Constitution's "opinion clause" makes it evident that the president may rely on those under his supervision for information and recommendations, yet he may over rule their discretion and make a final determination.[11] Hamilton thought inclusion of this clause in the Constitution to be "a mere redundancy in the plan, as the right for which it provides would result of itself from the office."[12] To maintain the separation of powers and his own political stature, the president may invoke executive privilege to prevent certain executive branch officials from giving information he deems confidential from falling into the hands of the other branches.

Article II, section 1 of the Constitution specifies the presidential oath of office. The president must take the oath as it is written in the Constitution (it is the only oath in quotation marks and the only officer oath entirely written in the text of the Constitution[13]). The president swears to "preserve, protect, and defend the Constitution of the United States." This means he has to bring his independent judgment to bear on measures that come before him. Article I, section 7 explains the way that bills get to the president's desk. Once there, if he sees a constitutional violation, he may ignore the violation, veto the bill and send it back with recommendations for Congress's next attempt, or he may refuse to enforce the legislation as signed. The important thing, again, is that what he does is done publicly, with accountability.

Article II, section 2 of the Constitution requires the president to act as commander in chief. He has wide discretion over military tactics and the movement of troops, as well as over the prosecution of individuals who violate national security legislation. But his power may be circumscribed by Congress's constitutional prerogatives, especially that of appropriating funding for military operations. The president, as the head of state, may receive ambassadors, recognize foreign governments, and negotiate treaties (which must be ratified by the Senate).[14] Obviously, his constitutional place in foreign affairs provides the foundation for substantive actions, which he may undertake alone or with the consent of Congress. In military and foreign affairs, it is particularly critical to the president that he is able to efficiently direct the actions of his subordinates.

While the Constitution provides a permanent basis for the president's authority, political context matters here as well. The ambiguity of certain constitutional clauses and practice or tradition provides presidents with a fair amount of discretion, but it also restrains him. In all sorts of situations, government officials, including presidents, "are forced to accommodate their behavior to generally accepted constitutional requirements."[15] Besides giving the president a great deal of power, the Constitution limits his actions, as he must "find some constitutional grounds for questionable political acts."[16]

All three branches have recognized that the president must be able to fulfill the constitutional and statutorily delegated responsibilities of office. Presidents must gather and protect information, address problems, fix crises, and manage staff. Presidents have a wide array of instruments available to fulfill the requirements of office and implement policy in areas such as foreign affairs, defense, administration, economy, personnel management, and civil rights. These unilateral tools include executive orders, executive agreements, bill drafting, executive reorganization plans, veto statements, presidential signing statements, and proclamations, as well as various national security tools.[17] The president usually cites his authority for issuing the directive in the text of the document.[18] Executive orders and proclamations are the most frequently used tools for announcing and implementing public presidential policy.

Access to Information

On January 21, 2009, citing simply "the authority vested in me by the Constitution and laws of the United States of America," President Obama signed his first executive order.[19] According to the order, only the incumbent president may designate presidential records as confidential, and such records must go through a review process that is headed by the Attorney General and the White House Counsel. This revoked a controversial Bush order that provided for unlimited delay in document release beyond the earlier twelve-year mandatory disclosure period. The new order was heralded by public interest groups and the press as these organizations looked forward to a new era of openness where the public would have access to information about the decision makers and decision-making processes in government.[20] The administration's commitment to openness, however, would soon be questioned.

Less than a month after Obama took office, the White House notified the press that it would not challenge a claim of executive privilege that President Bush was invoking on behalf of Karl Rove.[21] Rove had been subpoenaed by the House Judiciary Committee to publicly explain what he knew about the firings of several U.S. Attorneys in the second Bush term. In a statement, White House Counsel Gregory Craig told *CBS News* that the president was "very sympathetic to those who want to find out what happened," but he also did not want "to do anything that would undermine or weaken the institution of the presidency." The president continued to support the investigation into the firing of the attorneys.

Mark Rozell and Mitchel Sollenberger explained the predicament in which the president found himself:

> The new president assumed the constitutional powers of the executive at noon on Jan. 20. And here we have a former presidential aide, at the determination of private citizen George W. Bush asserting executive privilege, something normally thought to be a constitutionally-based power of the incumbent president. The new president . . . now has to decide whether and how he involves himself in this latest Bush-era dust-up, and his decision could have important consequences for his own future exercise of a presidential power that every president since George Washington has relied upon at some point.
>
> Indeed, Obama's decision will have a significant impact not only on his administration, but will create a precedent for future presidents as well. How much protection will Obama claim under what is an implied Article II power? Bush thought Article II grants to former White House staffers an absolute immunity from congressional testimony. Does Obama believe this as well?[22]

The issue was later resolved in an agreement negotiated between Rove and the Committee, with the assistance of Obama administration aides. Mr. Rove would testify in a closed hearing, but under penalty of perjury.[23] The agreement stalled a lawsuit on the matter, an outcome that was supported by both the President and Congress.[24] It is clear that the president wanted to avoid an adverse ruling that would be a constitutional bar to his assertions of privilege in the future.

The president's decision not to involve himself in the fight between Congress and former Bush administration aides was roundly criticized by many on the left who not only wanted to see Rove squirm under questioning by a majority-Democratic committee, but also those who thought the new administration would make a more clear commitment to administrative openness. This invocation of the separation of powers and Greg's statement demonstrate the president was concerned with defending himself and the prerogatives of his office. The most important thing was to avoid a legal ruling that would hinder the president's ability to freely communicate with his subordinates in the future.

In an event perhaps most known for its apparent triviality, the Obama administration invoked the separation of powers to prevent White House Social Secretary Desiree Rogers from testifying before the House Homeland Security Committee. This matter involved a couple that crashed a White House dinner, hoping the incident would give them the publicity they needed to land a reality television show. In the days following the event, as the press and Congress found out what happened and a photo surfaced of the couple shaking the president's hand, questions about White House security were raised and hearings were scheduled.

Mark Rozell said in an interview with *Time*, "I would completely fall out of my chair if they invoked executive privilege with regards to a social secretary arranging a party."[25] One hopes he has soft carpet: in his daily briefing, White House Press Secretary Robert Gibbs took that view, telling the press, "I think you know that, based on separation of powers, staff here don't go to testify in front of Congress."[26] The president's constitutional position is now clear.

Attempting to deal with a very unpleasant holdover issue from the Bush administration, President Obama announced in April 2009 that he would release to the ACLU forty-four photos of abused detainees in Iraq and Afghanistan.[27] The photos were at the heart of a 2003 Freedom of Information Act request denied by the Bush administration for privacy reasons and being fought over in federal court. This policy position shift was applauded by human rights advocates.

However, in mid-May, the president "chose secrecy over disclosure" and informed the press that he would challenge the photos' release on national security grounds. President Obama noted his and others' concerns that release of the photos would not "add any additional benefit to our understanding" of what happened to inmates under American supervision, and it would place American troops in danger.[28] In this case, he was not only defending the concept of separation of powers, but asserting his responsibility as commander in chief, further discussed below. Rahm Emanuel, President Obama's chief of staff, said of the president's commander in chief responsibility, "When you have a window that you were told had been shut that is still open, an argument that's never been made and a secretary of defense who is telling you that your commanders on the ground are concerned, you make this decision."[29]

These examples demonstrate that the Obama administration is interested in maintaining an executive branch zone of confidentiality within which it can formulate policy and make decisions without interference from Congress and even the public. The president has made transparency and openness a theme of his administration, but his support of the executive privilege claim in the Rove case shows that the president puts the protection of the office (and perhaps his own longer-term political safety) above that. He also publicly recognizes a military responsibility. This may serve him and the office of the presidency well. However, by making claims on more trivial matters, such as the dinner security lapse, he runs the risk of making the invocation of executive privilege illegitimate in the eyes of the public and provoking petty contests with Congress.

Signing Statements

Signing statements are documents issued by the president at the time a bill is signed that include his interpretation of a law or comments on what he understands the law to be. Rhetorical signing statements are mainly designed for public and press consumption. They explain to particular constituencies or important interest groups what the legislation being signed will mean to them. These are usually written in way that will publicize the president's action as he would like.[30] Constitutional signing statements focus on "constitutional defects," as viewed by the president, in laws Congress has passed but the president will sign in spite of his constitutional concerns. They generally contain an objection to an intrusion on executive power, and sometimes clarify what the president views as an ambiguous legislative provision.[31] We are concerned with the constitutional signing statement here, as the use of it reflects recognition on the part of the president that he has a responsibility to defend the Constitution as he understands it.

Although they have been used since the presidency of James Monroe, signing statements became particularly controversial during George W. Bush's administration when they were used to advance broad claims of executive power and to reject attempts by Congress to interfere with that power. Christopher Kelley has determined that in his two terms, President Bush used signing statements to object to almost 1,200 sections of bills. This is twice as many as all provisions challenged by presidents from Washington to Clinton combined.[32]

While accusations of President Bush's abuse of signing statements became a part of candidate Obama's campaign, and Obama strongly criticized those statements, he did not promise to avoid using them altogether.[33] (His Republican opponent, John McCain, said he would "never" use them.[34]) In 2007, he said that if he were elected, he would "not use signing statements to nullify or undermine congressional instructions as enacted into law. . . . No one doubts that it is appropriate to use signing statements to protect a president's constitutional prerogatives; unfortunately, the Bush Administration has gone much further than that."[35]

Shortly after taking office, the president issued a memorandum recognizing the historical importance of these statements and explaining how they would be utilized in his administration.[36] He explained that statements can assist the president in his responsibility to "take care that the laws be faithfully executed," and he indicated four principles he would follow in the issuance process:

1. The executive branch will communicate with the Congress to address constitutional concerns regarding pending legislation.
2. The president will presume enrolled bills are constitutional. President Obama noted his obligation to make an independent constitutional judgment in this respect, but said his standard would be "interpretations of the Constitution that are well-founded."[37]
3. Constitutional signing statements will explain in clear terms what, specifically, the constitutional objections are.
4. He will do his best avoid constitutional objections to legislation, but if he sees a constitutional problem, he will not ignore it.

He also ordered executive officials to consult with the Attorney General when relying on statements issued in previous administrations for their actions.

Two days after the memorandum was delivered, President Obama issued his first constitutional signing statement.[38] In it, he listed several constitutional reservations under five different headings: foreign affairs, United Nations peacekeeping missions, executive authority to control executive branch communications with Congress, legislative aggrandizements, and

Recommendations Clause concerns. The president specifically noted his unease with provisions in the bill that might limit his choice of appointees, restrict his constitutional authority to negotiate with foreign governments, impermissibly intrude on communications, take budgetary control away from the executive, and force the president to submit legislation in a way that Congress, not the president, thought important.

In his signing statement on the creation of the Ronald Reagan Centennial Commission, President Obama stated that, based on the separation of powers and the Ineligibility Clause of the Constitution, members of Congress appointed to the Commission would be able to serve only in a ceremonial role. What is most interesting here is that as precedential authority he invoked a signing statement issued by President Reagan in 1983.[39] The unilateral exercise of power in one instance became the justification for it later.[40]

An example of a more controversial signing statement came in June 2009. To win congressional support for legislation,[41] which included $108 billion in International Monetary Fund loan guarantees, the Obama administration brokered deals with important members of Congress, including Barney Frank and John Kerry. Some of these agreements required the president to insist that the IMF and World Bank provide increased transparency, strengthen labor laws, and permit poor countries to maintain educational and social programs even when receiving emergency loans.[42]

But when he signed the bill, the president also issued a signing statement, noting in the last paragraph that he would not be bound by these provisions, claiming that they would interfere with his constitutional responsibility to conduct foreign relations. The president, he said, cannot be required to "take certain positions in negotiations or discussions with international organizations and foreign governments," and cannot be required to consult "with the Congress prior to such negotiations or discussions."[43]

Congress, as a whole, was furious. On July 9, 2009, the House of Representatives voted 429-2—hardly a mixed message—on an amendment sponsored by Republican Kay Granger of Texas to reinstate the restrictions the bill originally required.[44] Responding to the signing statement, Barney Frank (D-MA) was especially irate: "It's outrageous. It's exactly what the Bush people did." Congressmen Frank and Obey (D-WI) and Congresswoman Lowey (D-NY) sent a letter to the president, asking him "to accept the terms and conditions under which the legislation was passed," or else suffer Congress's refusal to allocate funds for the IMF and World Bank.[45]

What does this mean for President Obama? While making justifiable, public assertions about his constitutional concerns, he still has to live with the Bush legacy of signing statements. The number and scope of the Bush statements eventually garnered publicity—almost none of it good. Now the public is aware of them and President Obama has to deal with the ramifications. Not only must he measure general public sentiment, but he must assess the kind of conflict a statement will set up with Congress. Congress will not object every time, but it can be counted on to defend itself when it senses it is being undercut as an institution or when individual members have the prominence and will necessary to fight back.

Administration: Control over Policy and Personnel

Perhaps the most important and yet least understood area of centralization of political control in the Obama administration has been in the area of executive oversight of agency rulemaking activity. This follows a long line of presidents who found that control over the bureaucracy leads to much greater accomplishments in terms of policy success. As presidents are able to direct policy matters within the executive branch itself, they can avoid the compromises and setbacks involved in the normal legislative process. Presidents can focus valuable resources on initiatives that are important to them and their favored constituencies. A bit of historical understanding may be useful here.

In an attempt to command the reins of regulatory authority at a time when environmental and consumer protection regulations were rapidly growing in number and scope, President Nixon reorganized the Bureau of the Budget into the Office of Management and Budget.[46] "Quality of Life" reviews were implemented in several executive branch agencies to provide OMB with significant procedural control over rulemaking in those agencies.[47] President Ford issued an executive order that authorized the Council on Wage and Price Stability to consider the economic impact proposed regulations might have as compared with the benefits they might furnish.[48] In 1978, President Carter issued an executive order that provided for a more public rulemaking process and an even more stringent economic review process that mandated regulatory impact analysis and alternative regulation consideration for each proposed rule.[49] He established the Regulatory Analysis Review Group and the Regulatory Council to, among other things, coordinate regulatory review programs among different agencies and monitor publication of proposed rules.[50] Perhaps most importantly, President Carter signed the Paperwork Reduction Act in 1980, establishing the Office of Information and Regulatory Affairs (OIRA) in the Office of Management and Budget (OMB).[51] While the office initially supervised agency compliance with reporting requirements, it was soon on its way to becoming one of the most important offices in the federal government.

While each of these presidential actions had an effect on the regulatory review process, none had the impact of President Reagan's program. In the first month of his presidency, he signed Executive Order 12,291,[52] which required that every proposed rule undergo a thorough cost-benefit analysis in OIRA.[53] If a regulatory impact analysis showed that a regulation's benefits did not outweigh its costs, the regulation was eliminated.[54] OMB imposed the standards agencies would use in the analysis process[55] and signed off on publication of proposed rules.[56] In January 1985, just prior to the commencement of his second term, President Reagan signed Executive Order 12,498,[57] which permitted OMB to review agencies' "draft regulatory programs" for the coming calendar year[58] and make recommendations for agency action.[59] OMB entrance at the beginning of the review process gave it great influence at the point when it is easiest to manipulate the substance of regulations.

These orders were highly controversial as they were the most aggressive oversight actions taken on regulatory review to that time. Despite the disagreement about their propriety, succeeding presidents used them as they moved to establish their regulatory review programs. Immediately following Reagan, President George H. W. Bush kept the orders in place and established the business-friendly Council on Competitiveness, headed by Vice President Dan Quayle, to continue the centralization of executive authority over agency rulemaking.[60]

Eight months into his first administration, President Clinton revoked the Reagan orders with Executive Order 12,866.[61] The terms of the new order, however, further solidified agency oversight in the executive branch, and a close reading shows that the Reagan orders were really absorbed into the new one. Important rules had to undergo cost-benefit analysis, Vice President Gore was given authority to determine which existing regulations would be subject to review,[62] and, for the first time, independent agencies would have to submit to participation in the plan.[63] If there was disagreement between agency heads and OMB, there remained the possibility that the vice president or even the president himself might step in to settle the matter.[64] This order was a firm foundation for a president with a pro-regulatory agenda.

President George W. Bush used the Clinton order as the basis of his regulatory review program until he lost the Republican congressional majorities in the 2006 midterm elections. On January 18, 2007, Bush issued Executive Order 13,422,[65] which revised Executive Order 12,866. The new order imposed a mandate on covered agencies to "identify in writing the specific market failure . . . or other specific problem" that a new rule might address.[66] The order also called for each agency to name a presidential appointee as a Regulatory Policy Officer[67] who would authorize the initiation of rulemaking procedures.[68] It was the order of a president who no longer had congressional majorities and needed to assert political control where he could. Critics argued that the Bush order was inherently antiregulatory and that it so tightened the political connection between the agency and the president that the agencies would be essentially unable to fulfill their legal responsibilities.[69]

However, the order had a short life: On February 20, 2009, newly inaugurated President Obama revoked the Bush order and went back to Clinton's 12,866.[70] The reversion back to such a strong order instead of a weaker one signaled that the administration would, at a minimum, retain the expansive oversight goals of previous administrations. The president issued a memo requiring OMB to consult with representatives of the regulatory agencies and produce a set of recommendations for a new executive order on regulatory review. Public participation was also encouraged.[71] Government watchdog groups looked forward to a revision of cost-benefit standards and more transparent regulatory reviews in which the public would "see the differences between draft regulations that come into the office and versions that go out."[72]

It was anticipated that a new regulatory order would be in place by the end of 2009, but the delay in confirming Cass Sunstein as OIRA head no doubt slowed the formulation process.[73] He was finally confirmed by the Senate on September 10, 2009. However, in July 2010 the *New York Times* reported that academics and open-government advocates do not believe a new executive order on regulatory review is forthcoming.[74] Although the president spoke against politicization of the rulemaking process, it is likely that the he sees the advantages of shaping policy at the front end of the process, and Executive Order 12,866 ably facilitates this. "Once any administration gets in power, it's difficult to expect them to abdicate any responsibilities or powers they have."[75] And issuing a new executive order that has essentially the same effect as 12,866 may mean a public disagreement with senators (including those of the president's party who are opposed to cost-benefit analysis), and a loss of political capital.

The choice of Cass Sunstein to head OIRA is significant. The president appointed one of the most frequently cited legal scholars in the nation,[76] someone with a top-tier reputation who held positions at some of the most prestigious universities in the country. When he was appointed to the Harvard Law School faculty to head the Program on Risk Regulation, then-Dean (and former Solicitor General and current Supreme Court Justice) Elena Kagan called him "the preeminent legal scholar of our time—the most wide-ranging, the most prolific, the most cited, and the most influential."[77]

In his confirmation hearings, when asked if it was appropriate for OIRA to push regulation in certain directions, Sunstein responded, "I believe that OIRA has a role to play in promoting compliance with the law and with the President's commitments and priorities—and that it can do so in a manner fully consistent with its mission."[78] It is hard to believe that the president would place someone with his credentials and views as Administrator of OIRA if the president's objective is to limit his influence in regulatory review.

President Obama is also employing several "czars" in order to consolidate policy making in the executive branch. There are czars who coordinate policy efforts in areas such as pay, green jobs, faith-based initiatives, and international climate. While some of these policy specialists must be confirmed by the Senate (for example, the drug czar and information czar), many do not, and therefore are accountable solely to the president and do not have to report to Congress as many other appointees do.[79]

President Obama is not the first president to have appointed czars—they have been around as such at least since the Nixon administration. But perhaps the number of czars President Obama has named and the secrecy the administration has maintained about their activities has set up a confrontation with Congress. The late Senator Robert Byrd (D-WV) expressed his discomfort with the number of czars and the possibility that they will threaten congressional power (especially, one may understand, Congress's ability to oversee the executive branch as it would like). In a letter to President Obama, Senator Byrd noted that "the rapid and easy accumulation of power by White House staff can threaten the Constitutional system of checks and balances. At the worst, White House staff have taken direction and control of programmatic areas that are the statutory responsibility of Senate-confirmed officials."[80] He asked the president to restrict claims of executive privilege on behalf of the czars and to keep the lines between czars and Senate-confirmed cabinet officials clear.

In October 2009, the Senate Judiciary Subcommittee on the Constitution held hearings on the constitutionality of czars. Although no White House representative appeared at the event, Gregory Craig sent a three-page letter outlining the administration's position on czars and asserted that they do not "raise valid concerns about accountability, transparency or congressional oversight."[81]

Consistent with presidents before him, President Obama will continue an energetic program of executive oversight of regulatory activity. Going back to the Nixon administration, it is clear that presidents of both parties and differing views of the benefits of regulation have found that control over administrative clearance and policy formulation helps the White House to coordinate and promote the president's priorities and agenda. President Obama will be no different. Take, for example, the passage of the health care and financial reform bills—legislation that he strongly supported. These bills run into the thousands of pages and confer extensive discretionary authority on executive branch officials. It is only reasonable to believe that he will want to maintain as much control as possible over the writing, revision, and implementation of regulations.

National Security

Obama administration legal policy in national security matters has also been fairly consistent with that of the Bush administration. Consider first the indefinite detention of terrorism suspects at Guantanamo Bay, Cuba. In September 2009, the administration declined to seek legislation from Congress that would specifically authorize the president to keep these individuals in American custody without charges, noting in a statement that "the Administration is currently not seeking additional authorization."[82] Instead, President Obama would rely on the Authorization for the Use of Military Force (AUMF) passed by Congress and signed by President Bush after the 9/11 terrorist attacks to indefinitely hold about fifty suspects.[83]

This view was reaffirmed when it was announced on January 22, 2010, that a task force[84] headed by the Department of Justice concluded that almost a quarter of the 196 detainees still at Guantanamo were too dangerous to be released but "unprosecutable" because of intelligence issues and the possibility that some detainees might claim the use of harsh interrogation techniques resulted in coerced testimony.[85] The Obama administration has also argued in federal court that detainees being held at the Bagram Air Force base in Afghanistan have no legal right to contest their confinement,[86] continuing a policy created during the Bush administration.

In other national security matters, the Obama administration is continuing the Bush rendition program, sending alleged terrorists to particular countries for detention and interrogation, but with an assurance that suspects will not be tortured.[87] The Patriot Act was extended without any changes.[88] The Obama administration has accepted and even furthered Bush administration claims about "state secrets" to eliminate a lawsuit brought by five men who claim the CIA seized them and interrogated them under the "extraordinary rendition" program of that administration.[89] The president has claimed for the government "sovereign immunity," based on the Patriot Act, to protect government agencies and officials from lawsuits springing out of that administration's "warrantless wiretapping" program.[90] He accepted the resignation of General Stanley McChrystal, the top United States military commander in Afghanistan, on whose loyalty and good judgment he could no longer rely.[91]

One area of national security policy where President Obama has taken an aggressive and unique approach is currently unfolding. On April 6, 2010, it was publicly announced that President Obama had issued a targeted killing order for Anwar al-Awlaki, an American citizen who is thought to be hiding in Yemen. Mr. al-Awlaki, who was born in New Mexico, is a radical Muslim cleric whose followers have included Nidal Malik Hasan (the accused Fort Hood shooter) and Umar Farouk Abdulmutallab (the man who allegedly attempted to take down an airline flight on Christmas Day, 2009).[92] While this development has drawn less attention than one might have expected, there are those who question the authority of the president to make such a move.[93] However, it seems that this would be covered, from the president's perspective, in the AUMF and in international law.[94]

President Obama has displayed a willingness to follow in the steps of his predecessor as he negotiates the difficult terrain of war and national security policy. The commander-in-chief power is one of the core functions of the presidency, one in which unilateral action can be an effective tool. In high-profile circumstances, President Obama has shown a reluctance to submit it to congressional and judicial supervision.

Conclusion

Today, there is disappointment on the part of some supporters who thought there would be a significant departure from the policies and legal justifications for them that were made during the Bush years. "Change" was promised on the campaign trail, so supporters of candidate Obama expected things would be much different—perhaps a "tamer" president would occupy the White House. As president, Obama seems reluctant to make strong claims of executive power in the areas discussed above, even as his lawyers, press assistants, executive branch officials, and official documents make a case for it.[95]

But whether one embraces the president's constitutional and political positions, there should be little surprise about what has transpired. The president is acting like the Chief Executive, not like a U.S. senator or state legislator, as he defends the constitutional prerogatives of his office and tries to move his agenda. He has new constitutional responsibilities and national concerns (and a national election) to consider. He is behaving as Madison might have generally predicted he would: "Ambition would be made to counteract ambition. The interest of the man must be connected with the constitutional rights of the place."[96]

Upon assuming the presidency, President Obama's attitude became that of a line of presidents who have sought to use the Constitution and practical tools available to them to defend the office from the other branches (especially Congress) and to secure its independence. His actions are clearly unitary. He has protected access to information in instances where he thought it might harm the deliberations or legitimacy of the executive branch. He has issued signing statements to protect his constitutional authority, or at least to "get it on record" that he did not acquiesce in what he perceived as a threat to that authority. President Obama, like several executives before him, sees the rise of the administrative state and the exponential increase in agency authority and activity, and seeks to centralize his control over the government bureaucracies. Czars have been appointed to give the president control over a fragmented policy-making process where agency heads are held accountable to Congress as well as to the president. President Obama has chosen a regulatory administrator who is supportive of presidential influence in the regulatory process.

It is true that President Obama has been very clear in his orders and memos to executive branch officials that there will be new procedures in place to guard against "unwarranted" or "excessive" invocations of executive power. But the president may revoke any order—including his own—with a subsequent order or other directive. The Department of Justice may be more involved in reviewing policy actions, signing statements, and other presidential devices, but the fact remains that in the end, it is the president's administration, not the attorney general's or any other executive official's, and it is his policy that will prevail in the executive branch if he so chooses.[97] As one commentator noted, "If you were hoping that the Obama team would come into the White House and aggressively undercut its own power it's time to change dreams."[98]

Notes

1. John Finn, "Enumerating Absolute Power? Who Needs the Rest of the Constitution?" *Hartford Courant*, April 6, 2008, http://articles.courant.com/2008-04-06/news/commentaryfinn0406.art_1_combatants-presidential-power-constitutional (accessed April 7, 2010). Peter Baker, "When 535 Take on Number 1," *New York Times*, October 5, 2008, http://query.nytimes.com/gst/fullpage.html?res=9901E3DB1339F936A35753C1A96E9C8B63 (accessed March 14, 2010). "The 'unitary executive' theory he embraced held that because the Constitution provides for only one executive branch, Congress cannot intrude upon the president's duties to manage the government. . . . With the acquiescence of a Republican Congress and a public

eager to fight terrorism, Mr. Bush and Mr. Cheney advanced their cause for years—the secret deliberations of an energy task force; the Patriot Act; 'signing statements' that express reservations about enforcing a bill; warrantless surveillance; unrestricted detention of terrorism suspects; the reinterpretation of the Geneva Conventions."

2. Cass Sunstein, "What the 'Unitary Executive' Debate Is and Is Not About," The Faculty Blog, August 6, 2007, http://uchicagolaw.typepad.com/faculty/2007/08/what-the-unitar.html (accessed January 19, 2010).

3. Charlie Savage, "Barack Obama's Q & A," *Boston Globe*, December 20, 2007, www.boston.com/news/politics/2008/specials/CandidateQA/ObamaQA/ (accessed March 17, 2010).

4. Alexander Hamilton, "Federalist no. 70," *The Federalist Papers*, ed. Charles Kesler (New York: Penguin, 2003), 422.

5. The president was given extensive independent constitutional powers in order to protect the executive branch from the other branches, particularly the legislature, which the framers were concerned would encroach upon the president's powers. James Madison, in "Federalist no. 48": "The legislative department is everywhere extending the sphere of its activity and drawing all power into its impetuous vortex." In "Federalist no. 51," he writes: "In republican government, the legislative authority predominates." He then goes on to explain how Congress will be structured so as to "remedy this inconveniency" and "guard against dangerous encroachments." He notes that to counter the powerful and ambitious legislature, "the weakness of the executive may require . . . that it should be fortified." All of this is not to say that the office of the president is superior to the other branches, but that it is not constitutionally inferior to either, thus leaving room for political conflict.

6. The president's constitutional responsibility to "take care that the laws be faithfully executed" includes not just "enforcement of acts of Congress or of treaties according to their express forms," but also "the rights, duties, and obligations growing out of the Constitution itself . . . and all the protection implied by the nature of the government under this Constitution." J. Miller, *In Re Neagle*, 135 U.S. 1 (1899), 64.

7. A recent example is the determination of the Obama administration to advise federal prosecutors not to criminally prosecute those who abide by state law while using or supplying medical marijuana. Attorney General Eric Holder stated, "It will not be a priority to use federal resources to prosecute patients with serious illnesses or their caregivers who are complying with state laws on medical marijuana. But we will not tolerate drug traffickers who hide behind claims of compliance with state law to mask activities that are clearly illegal." Justin Blum, "Medical Marijuana Policy Eased by Justice Department," *Bloomberg.com*, October 19, 2009, www.bloomberg.com/apps/news?pid=newsarchive&sid=aZyHHGxOpwz0 (accessed January 19, 2010).

8. "By the Constitution of the United States the President is invested with certain important political powers, in the exercise of which he is to use his own discretion, and is accountable only to his country in his political character, and to his own conscience." John Marshall, C.J., opinion in *Marbury v. Madison* 1 Cranch 137, 166 (U.S. 1803).

9. Steven Calabresi and Saikrishna Prakash, "The President's Power to Execute the Laws," *Yale Law Journal* 104 (1994): 586.

10. Hamilton, in "Federalist no. 72," 434: "The persons, therefore, to whose immediate management these different matters [the administration of government] are committed ought to be considered as the assistant or deputies of the chief Magistrate, and on this account they ought to derive their officers from his appointment, at least from his nomination, and ought to be subject to his superintendence."

11. "The President . . . may require the Opinion in writing, of the principal Officer in each of the executive Departments, upon any subject relating to the duties of their respective Offices." Article II, section 2.

12. Hamilton, "Federalist no. 74," 446.

13. Recall that when Chief Justice John Roberts incorrectly gave the oath to President-elect Obama, they had a "do-over" the following day just to be on the "safe side." Most constitutional scholars did not believe this was necessary, but it does make a statement about the seriousness with which the oath is taken.

14. Article II, section 3.

15. Joseph M. Bessette and Jeffrey Tulis, "The Constitution, Politics, and the Presidency," in *The Presidency in the Constitutional Order*, ed. Joseph M. Bessette and Jeffrey Tulis (Baton Rouge: Louisiana State University Press, 1981), 10.

16. Ibid.

17. Harold C. Relyea, "Presidential Directives: Background and Overview," *CRS Report for Congress*, April 23, 2007, www.fas.org/irp/crs/98-611.pdf (accessed March 10, 2010). Some of these instruments are rarely used. Louis Fisher, *The President and Congress: Power and Policy* (New York: Free Press, 1972), 44–54. See also generally Phillip Cooper, *By Order of the President: The Use and Abuse of Executive Direct Action* (Lawrence: University Press of Kansas, 2002).

18. House Committee on Governmental Operations, *Executive Orders and Proclamations: A Study of the Use of Presidential Power*, 85th Congress, 1st sess., 1957, Committee Print, vii. But the stated authority may be vague, such as a general reference to the Constitution or "the laws of the United States."

19. Executive Order 13,489, "Presidential Records," 74 *Federal Register* 4669, January 26, 2009. A procedure was established for former presidents to request executive privilege.

20. Clint Hendler, "Day One: New FOIA Rules," *Columbia Journalism Review*, January 21, 2009, www.cjr.org/campaign_desk/day_one_new_foia_rules.php (accessed March 31, 2010).

21. Mark Knoller, "White House Not Challenging Rove's Privilege," CBS News Political Hotsheet, February 14, 2009, www.cbsnews.com/8301-503544_162-4803349-503544.html (accessed March 31, 2010).

22. Mark Rozell and Mitchel Sollenberger, "Taking Executive Privilege to Absurd Levels?" *Roll Call*, February 6, 2009, www.rollcall.com/news/32134-1.html (accessed March 19, 2010).

23. Nedra Pickler, "Rove, Miers, Will Testify about Prosecutor Firings," *Houston Chronicle*, March 4, 2009, www.chron.com/disp/story.mpl/front/6294041.html (accessed March 17, 2010). Former White House Counsel Harriett Miers was also involved in the executive privilege conflict and eventually testified in June 2009.

24. John Bresnahan and Josh Gerstein, "Rove Deposed in U.S. Attorney Probe," *Politico*, July 7, 2009, http://dyn.politico.com/printstory.cfm?uuid=578CDD0A-18FE-70B2-A87147E37EC2C3DB (accessed March 17, 2010).

25. Michael Scherer, "No Testifying for Obama's Social Secretary?" *Time*, December 3, 2009, www.time.com/time/politics/article/0,8599,1945192,00.html (accessed March 22, 2010).

26. Sheryl Gay Stolberg and Janie Lorber, "White House Blocks Testimony on Party Crashers," *New York Times* Caucus blog, December 2, 2009, http://thecaucus.blogs.nytimes.com/2009/12/02/white-house-revises-rules-for-major-events/ (accessed March 22, 2010). Rogers was not subpoenaed by the Committee, but rather was invited to testify by Rep. Peter King (R-NY), so no legal action was taken against her. Scherer, "No Testifying for Obama's Social Secretary?"

27. Jake Tapper, "Obama Administration to Release Detainee Abuse Photos," ABC.com Political Punch blog, April 24, 2009, http://blogs.abcnews.com/political punch/2009/04/obama-adminis-3.html (accessed March 27, 2010).

28. Scott Wilson, "Obama Shifts on Abuse Photos," *Washington Post*, May 14, 2009, www.washingtonpost.com/wp-dyn/content/article/2009/05/13/AR2009051301751.html (accessed March 27, 2010).

29. Wilson, "Obama Shifts on Abuse Photos."

30. Christopher S. Kelley, "The Unitary Executive and the Presidential Signing Statement," (PhD diss., Miami University, 2003): 50, available at http://etd.ohio link.edu/send-pdf.cgi/Kelley%20Christopher%20S.pdf?miami1057716977.

31. Kelley, "The Unitary Executive," 46.

32. Charlie Savage, "Obama Looks to Limit Impact of Tactic Bush Used to Sidestep New Laws," *New York Times*, March 9, 2009, www.nytimes.com/2009/03/10/us/politics/10signing.html (accessed March 17, 2010).

33. At a town hall meeting in Billings, Montana, candidate Obama said, "Congress's job is to pass legislation. The president can veto it or he can sign it. But what George Bush has been trying to do, as part of his effort to accumulate more power in the presidency, is he's been saying, 'Well, I can basically change what Congress passed by attaching a letter saying, I don't agree with this part or I don't agree with that part. I'm going to choose to interpret it this way or that way.' That's not part of his power, but this is part of the whole theory of George Bush that he can make laws as he's going along. I disagree with that. I taught the Constitution for ten years. I believe in the Constitution, and I will obey the Constitution of the United States. We're not going to use signing statements as a way of doing an end-run around Congress, all right?" David Nather, "Obama's Pledge on Signing Statements," CQ Beyond the Dome blog, May 20, 2008, http://blogs.cqpolitics.com/beyond/2008/05/obamas-pledge-on-signing-state.html (accessed March 17, 2010). Video available

at http://opiniojuris.org/2009/07/01/did-anyone-oppose-signing-statements-just-koh-the-aba-and-some-guy-named-barack/ (accessed April 4, 2010).

34. Debra Cassens Weiss, "McCain Says He Won't Use Signing Statement," ABA Journal, February 25, 2008, www.abajournal.com/news/article/mccain_says_he_wont_use_signing_statements/ (accessed July 14, 2010).

35. Savage, "Barack Obama's Q & A."

36. Memorandum of March 9, 2009, "Presidential Signing Statements: Memorandum for the Heads of Executive Departments and Agencies," 74 Federal Register 10669 (March 11, 2009).

37. This is obviously a swipe at the Bush administration.

38. "Statement on Signing the Omnibus Appropriations Act, 2009," Daily Comp. Pres. Doc. No. DCPD 200900145 (March 11, 2009), www.gpoaccess.gov/presdocs/2009/DCPD200900145.pdf (accessed March 21, 2010).

39. Statement on the Signing of the Ronald Reagan Centennial Commission Act, www.presidency.ucsb.edu/ws/index.php?pid=86243 (accessed April 10, 2010).

40. For an excellent discussion of this kind of activity, see Ryan J. Barilleaux, "Venture Constitutionalism and the Enlargement of the Presidency," in Executing the Constitution, ed. Christopher S. Kelley (Albany: SUNY Press, 2006), 37–52.

41. Supplemental Appropriations Act of 2009, Pub.L. 111-32, H.R. 2346.

42. Jonathan Weisman, "Obama's Fiats Anger Lawmakers," Wall Street Journal, June 2, 2009, http://online.wsj.com/article/SB124761651200542351.html (accessed March 21, 2010).

43. Signing Statement on the Supplemental Appropriations Act of 2009, www.whitehouse.gov/the_press_office/Statement-from-the-President-upon-signing-HR-2346/ (accessed March 21, 2010).

44. David Nather, "Congress Suddenly Remembers It Can Cut Off Funds," CQ Balance of Power blog, July 10, 2009, http://blogs.cqpolitics.com/balance_of_power/2009/07/congress-suddenly-remembers-it.html (accessed March 21, 2010).

45. Letter from Members of Congress Barney Frank, David Obey, and Nita Lowey, to President Obama, www.house.gov/frank/pressreleases/2009/07-21-09-signing-statements-letter-obama.html (accessed March 23, 2010).

46. Executive Order 11,541, Code of Federal Regulations, title 3, p. 939 (1966–1970). Unless otherwise specified, all of the executive orders in this section were done under the authority vested by the Constitution in the president and a general reference to the statutes of the United States.

47. House Committee on Energy and Commerce, Presidential Control of Agency Rulemaking: An Analysis of Constitutional Issues That May Be Raised by Executive Order 12291, 97th Cong., 1st sess., June 15, 1981, 10.

48. Executive Order 11,821, 39 Federal Register 41501 (November 29, 1974). This order was amended by Executive Order 11,949 on December 31, 1976, and expired on December 31, 1977.

49. Executive Order 12044, Code of Federal Regulations, title 3, p. 152 (1979).

50. Paul R. Verkuil, "Jawboning Administrative Agencies: Ex Parte Contacts by the White House," *Columbia Law Review* 80 (1980): 948–49.

51. Public Law 96-511, *U.S. Statutes at Large* 94 (1980): 2812.

52. Executive Order 12,291, Code of Federal Regulations, title 3, p. 127 (1981). Ronald Reagan, "Program for Economic Recovery: Address before Joint Session of Congress," 17 *Weekly Comp. Pres. Doc.* 130 (February 18, 1981). James F. Blumenstein, "Regulatory Review by the Executive Office of the President: An Overview and Policy Analysis of Current Issues," *Duke Law Journal* 51, no. 3 (December 2001): 859–60.

53. Executive Order 12,291, 6(a)(2), at 131. Existing rules could also be subject to scrutiny. 6(a)(5)-(8), at 131.

54. Executive Order 12,291, 2(b), at 128. The order recognized that not all costs can be "quantified in monetary terms." Ibid., 3(d)(1)-(4), at 129.

55. Executive Order 12,291, 6(a)(2), at 131.

56. Executive Order 12,291, 3(e)(1), at 129.

57. Executive Order 12,498, "Regulatory Planning Process," *Code of Federal Regulations*, title 3, p. 323 (1985).

58. Executive Order 12,498, 2(a), at 324.

59. Executive Order 12,498, 3(a)(i) and (ii), at 324.

60. Robert B. Percival, "Checks Without Balance: Executive Office Oversight of the Environmental Protection Agency," *Law and Contemporary Problems* 54, no. 4 (1991): 155. See also Barry D. Friedman, *Regulation in the Reagan–Bush Era, The Eruption of Presidential Influence* (Pittsburgh: University of Pittsburgh Press, 1995), 165.

61. Executive Order 12,866, "Regulatory Planning and Review," *Code of Federal Regulations*, title 3, p. 638 (1993).

62. Executive Order 12,866, 5(c), at 644.

63. Executive Order 12,866, 4(c), at 642.

64. Elena Kagan, Deputy Director of the Domestic Policy Council in the Clinton administration and current Supreme Court Justice, noted that this provision reveals "something significant about the relationship between the agencies and the President—to say that they were *his* and so too were their decisions." "Presidential Administration," *Harvard Law Review* 114, no. 8 (2001): 2290.

65. Executive Order 13,422, "Further Amendment to Executive Order 12,866 on Regulatory Planning and Review," 72 *Federal Register* 2763 (January 18, 2007).

66. "Market failure" is explained as "externalities, market power," and "lack of information." Executive Order 13,422, 1(a)(1), p. 2763.

67. Executive Order 13,422, 5(b), at 2764.

68. Executive Order 13,422, 4(b), at 2764.

69. Testimony of Sally Katzen, House Committee on Science and Technology, Subcommittee on Investigation & Oversight, on February 13, 2007, http://judiciary .house.gov/hearings/printers/110th/33312.PDF (accessed July 10, 2010). Some might argue that this was the case in March of 2008 when President Bush himself

personally intervened minutes before EPA Administrator Steve Johnson was to give a press conference to announce new ambient air quality standards. When the press conference was held five hours later, Mr. Johnson announced the standards as requested by the president. See Juliet Eilperin, "Ozone Rules Weakened at Bush's Behest," *Washington Post*, March 14, 2008, www.washingtonpost.com/wp-dyn/content/article/2008/03/13/AR2008031304175.html (accessed March 22, 2010).

70. Executive Order 13,497, "Revocation of Certain Executive Orders Concerning Regulatory Planning and Review," 74 *Federal Register* 6113 (February 4, 2009), www.reginfo.gov/public/jsp/Utilities/EO_13497.pdf (accessed April 7, 2010).

71. "Memorandum for the Heads of Executive Departments and Agencies: Regulatory Review," 74 *Federal Register* 5977 (February 3, 2009), www.reginfo.gov/public/jsp/EO/fedRegReview/POTUS_Memo_on_Regulatory_Review.pdf (accessed March 21, 2010).

72. Gabriel Nelson, "Obama Overhaul of Regulatory Reviews Now Seen as Unlikely," *New York Times* Greenwire, July 14, 2010, www.nytimes.com/gwire/2010/07/14/14greenwire-obama-overhaul-of-regulatory-reviews-now-seen-45978.html (accessed July 16, 2010).

73. Sunstein stated that the lengthy comments submitted to OIRA regarding the possible order contributed to the delay in its issuance. Rena Steinzor, "Eye on OIRA: Sunstein Says Ambitious Efforts to Revamp Regulatory Review Tabled for the Time Being," Center for Progressive Reform blog, March 12, 2010, www.progressivereform.org/CPRBlog.cfm?idBlog=52D5FC2E-F9E4-2834-4EEF1A5EB76DA41B (accessed April 7, 2010).

74. Nelson, "Obama Overhaul of Regulatory Reviews Now Seen as Unlikely."

75. Matt Media, regulatory policy analyst at OMB Watch, in Nelson, "Obama Overhaul of Regulatory Reviews Now Seen as Unlikely." In the same article, OIRA associate administrator Michael Fitzpatrick "defended cost-benefit analysis and said that subjecting the regulatory review process to public scrutiny would have a 'whole host of complications.'" It "'could create an inability to have full and frank conversations about what's going on. . . . To open up the whole process transparently could actually take the value of it.'"

76. He is the most frequently cited law professor in the area of constitutional/public law, according to Leiter's Law School Rankings, www.leiterrankings.com/faculty/2007faculty_impact_areas.shtml (accessed April 2, 2010).

77. Announcement regarding Sunstein joining the Harvard Law School Faculty, www.law.harvard.edu/news/2008/02/19_sunstein.php (accessed April 2, 2010). The author appreciates Ryan Barilleaux for bringing this to her attention.

78. "OIRA Nominee Promises Law and Pragmatism Will Guide Decisions," OMBWatch, www.ombwatch.org/node/10010 (accessed April 2, 2010).

79. "President Obama's 'Czars,'" *Politico.com*, September 4, 2009, http://dyn.politico.com/printstory.cfm?uuid=870D765C-18FE-70B2-A86B4FAE48EF7FBB (accessed April 9, 2010).

80. Letter dated February 23, 2009, www.eenews.net/public/25/9865/features/docu ments/2009/02/25/document_gw_02.pdf (accessed April 2, 2010).

81. Kate Phillips, "Senators Take on Czar Wars," *New York Times* Caucus blog, October 7, 2009, thecaucus.blogs.nytimes.com/2009/10/07/senators-take-on-the-czar-wars/ (accessed March 17, 2010).

82. Peter Baker, "Obama to Use Current Law to Support Detentions," *New York Times*, September 24, 2009, www.nytimes.com/2009/09/24/us/politics/24detain.html (accessed January 22, 2010). Baker notes that in asserting this claim, "the Obama administration is adopting one of the arguments advanced by the Bush administration in years of debates about detention policies."

83. Authorization for the Use of Military Force, Public Law 107-40 [S. J. RES. 23], September 18, 2001.

84. This task force was created by Executive Order 13,492.

85. Peter Finn, "Justice Task Force Recommends about 50 Guantanamo Detainees Be Held Indefinitely," January 22, 2010, *Washington Post*, www.washingtonpost.com/wp-dyn/content/article/2010/01/21/AR2010012104936.html (accessed January 22, 2010).

86. Charlie Savage, "Obama Upholds Detainee Policy in Afghanistan," *New York Times*, February 22, 2009, www.nytimes.com/2009/02/22/washington/22bagram.html (accessed January 20, 2010).

87. David Johnston, "US Says Rendition to Continue, but with More Oversight," *New York Times*, August 25, 2009, www.nytimes.com/2009/08/25/us/politics/25rendition.html (accessed September 19, 2009).

88. Michael B. Farrell, "Obama Signs Patriot Act Extension without Reforms," *Christian Science Monitor*, March 1, 2010, www.csmonitor.com/USA/Politics/2010/0301/Obama-signs-Patriot-Act-extension-without-reforms (accessed March 2, 2010).

89. Glenn Greenwald, "The 180-degree Reversal of Obama's State Secrets Position," *Salon*, February 10, 2009, www.salon.com/news/opinion/glenn_greenwald/2009/02/10/obama (accessed March 21, 2010).

90. Glenn Greenwald, "New and Worse Secrecy Claims from the Obama Department of Justice," *Salon*, April 6, 2009, www.salon.com/news/opinion/glenn_greenwald/2009/04/06/obama (accessed March 21, 2010).

91. Tony Pierce, "Gen. Stanley McChrystal Resigns, Obama Nominates Gen. David Petraeus to Lead the War in Afghanistan," *Los Angeles Times* Comments blog, June 23, 2010, http://latimesblogs.latimes.com/comments_blog/2010/06/gen-stanley-mcchrystal-general-david-h-petraeus.html (accessed July 23, 2010).

92. Scott Shane, "US Approves Targeted Killing of Muslim Cleric," *New York Times*, April 6, 2010, www.nytimes.com/2010/04/07/world/middleeast/07yemen.html (accessed April 7, 2010).

93. Glenn Greenwald, "Confirmed: Obama Authorizes Assassination of U.S. Citizen," *Salon*, April 7, 2010, www.salon.com/news/opinion/glenn_greenwald/2010/04/07/assassinations (accessed April 9, 2010).

94. Shane, "US Approves Targeted Killing of Muslim Cleric."

95. Charlie Savage, "Obama's Embrace of a Bush Tactic Riles Congress, *New York Times*, August 9, 2009, www.nytimes.com/2009/08/09/us/politics/09signing.html (accessed April 10, 2010). "But unlike Mr. Bush, Mr. Obama has not mentioned the Unitary Executive Theory." There is no reason to think that President Obama would actually claim to have adopted the unitary executive theory. However, one does not have to publicly state a belief in a particular theory in order to behave in a way that squares with it.

96. Hamilton, "Federalist no. 51," 319.

97. In the wake of the highly politicized Department of Justice headed by Alberto Gonzales, much was made during Eric Holder's confirmation hearings of his being selected for his independence from the president. In those hearings, Holder noted, "I understand that the attorney general is different from every other cabinet officer. Though I am a part of the president's team, I am not a part of the president's team in the way that any other cabinet officer is. I have a special and unique responsibility. There has to be a distance between me and the president. The president-elect said when he nominated me that he recognized that, that the attorney general was different from other cabinet officers." But the news that the Obama administration is seeking to try terrorists in military trials as part of a compromise with members of Congress, as opposed to the trials in New York City as Holder had announced and defended, demonstrates where the final authority is. Hearing testimony available at www.nytimes.com/2009/01/16/us/politics/16text-holder.html?pagewanted=all (accessed April 3, 2010). For background on the possible change of decision, see Evan Perez, "Decision on 9/11 Trial Could Undercut Holder," *Wall Street Journal*, March 10, 2010, http://online.wsj.com/article/SB100014240527487041459045751120723 80877534.html?mod=WSJ_hpp_MIDDLTopStories (accessed April 3, 2010).

98. Andrew Cohen, "Maneuvering Room on Signing Statements," *CBS News*, March 3, 2009, www.cbsnews.com/8301-503544_162-4854750-503544.html (accessed March 17, 2010).

~

CHAPTER FOUR

President Obama and Congress

Deference, Disinterest, or Collusion?

Andrew E. Busch

This chapter will examine Barack Obama's understanding of the constitutional and institutional relationship of the president and executive branch with Congress. This relationship has both a formal component having to do with separation of powers (exemplified by issues such as vetoes, recess appointments, and presidential signing statements) and an informal component having to do with the institutional role of the president relative to Congress in a broader sense (most notably the role of the president in developing and promoting a legislative program). Obama's campaign and early presidency have been characterized by tensions between competing strands of his thinking. As a candidate, Obama strongly criticized signing statements under George W. Bush, though he subsequently used them as president; while he has exhibited a Progressive concept of the presidency as an institution pushing for a new policy direction, he has also been cited by some analysts as possessing a whiggish streak that has left the "heavy lifting" of legislation such as health care or the stimulus package to Congress. As Obama moved through the first sixteen months of his presidency, observers were sometimes struck by the apparent distance he maintained from affairs in Congress, even on some of his signature initiatives such as the stimulus package and the health care reform bill. As these observers noted, the president often seemed to leave important legislative details to the Democratic leadership in Congress.

This chapter will explore and assess these tensions, analyzing as well continuities or discontinuities between Obama as candidate and as president. Three general interpretations are plausible.

One possibility is that Obama, on principle, took a more limited view of the proper role of the president in the American constitutional order. Perhaps he believes that the president ought to propose broad initiatives or help set priorities but defer to the Congress to fill in details. This can be called "deference."

A second possibility is that Obama was indeed detached from much policy making, but not out of principled deference to Congress. Rather, this detachment was the result of a less noble preference for grand rhetoric over the hard work of shaping legislation. In this view, the president was not exhibiting respect for the Constitution, but lack of interest in the details of governing. Call this "disinterestedness."

The third possibility is that Obama appeared disengaged but was actually closely involved behind the scenes. When he appeared to let Congress have its way, it was because Congress was doing more or less what he wanted anyway. In this view, forlorn criticisms that the president was allowing Democrats in Congress to pursue polarizing policies missed the point: he was allowing them to do so because those policies were, roughly speaking, his policies, too. This can be called "collusion."

Which interpretation is correct—and it should not be taken for granted at the outset that only one is in play—is important, for a number of reasons. It can provide insight into the constitutional relationship between the branches, cast light on policy making in the Obama era, and provide a clue about how Obama may approach Congress in the future.

Presidential Traditions

As president, Obama could draw on a number of traditions of presidential relations with Congress. George Washington, anxious to convince Americans that the presidency was a "safe" institution, generally acted with deference to Congress. However, he also wanted more open cooperation between the two branches than Congress was willing to provide, and he took a stronger executive hand on matters of foreign affairs and national security. His Secretary of Treasury, Alexander Hamilton, fancied himself the president's "prime minister," and advocated a more active legislative role for the president. Although decrying parties in the abstract, Thomas Jefferson filled the role of party leader, often writing legislation and actively promoting outcomes behind the scenes in coordination with his party's majority in Congress. By the mid-nineteenth century, the party division between Whigs and Democrats revolved to a large degree around different visions of presidential power, with Democrats (such as Andrew Jackson and James Polk) supporting a more active president and Whigs fearing it as potentially monarchical and preferring a more deferential executive. Compared with the twentieth century, though, presidents of both parties in the nineteenth century were usually passive, subject to a general norm that presidents were not to exert too much "popular leadership" and were not to interfere very much with the legislative process, especially in domestic matters. This norm went hand-in-hand with a norm of presidential candidates not openly appealing for votes in public campaigns. Not until William Jennings Bryan's 1896 transcontinental train excursion did a presidential candidate make a modern-style canvass for votes—and he lost to William McKinley, who gave speeches from his front porch in Canton, Ohio.

These norms were upended by the Progressives in the early twentieth century. Woodrow Wilson, notably, argued that presidential candidates should appeal directly to voters on the basis of a detailed policy platform. The winner, Wilson posited, should bring that platform to Congress and insist upon its adoption as part of his electoral "mandate." It was Franklin Roosevelt, though, who permanently changed expectations about the president and relations between the president and Congress. Roosevelt famously won enactment of a flood of major legislation in the "Hundred Days Session" at the beginning of his presidency. From then on, he brought to Congress a detailed legislative agenda and compiled a "must pass" list. FDR also vetoed more bills than any president in U.S. history.

Presidents since Roosevelt have varied in their degree of legislative activity. Lyndon Johnson duplicated the attention FDR paid to developing and promoting a vast legislative agenda; Ronald Reagan came to office with a handful of top legislative priorities, which he pursued with considerable success; others had fewer ambitions or less success. Nevertheless, none reverted to the nineteenth-century model, with the possible exception of George H. W. Bush, whose chief of staff remarked about halfway through his term that Bush would be perfectly satisfied if Congress did not come back into session. Whether this comment should be seen as the manifestation of a humble presidency with few domestic ambitions or of an arrogant one that had no use for its coordinate branch was not clear. Bush notwithstanding, almost all presidents who followed Roosevelt understood that they were being judged at least partially in his light.[1]

Obama's immediate predecessor, George W. Bush, held to an especially vigorous view of executive power. Particularly in the area of national security, but extending into other areas as well, Bush and Vice President Richard

Cheney advanced the notion of the president as largely independent from constraints imposed by other branches. This position raised the ire of many liberals, as well as some conservatives and libertarians appealing to an older conservative tradition that emphasized limited executive power.[2]

Congress and Candidate Obama

It is worth noting at the outset that Obama is the first president elected directly from the U.S. Senate since John F. Kennedy in 1960. Most recent presidents have had a majority of their political experience as state governors (Carter, Reagan, Clinton, George W. Bush) or in the federal executive branch (George H.W. Bush, though he also served two terms as a congressman). However, by most accounts, Obama had few significant legislative accomplishments to his name during his short career in the Illinois legislature and even shorter span in the U.S. Senate. As a lecturer in constitutional law at the University of Chicago, he had probably given more thought to the Constitution than any Democratic Presidential candidate since Woodrow Wilson (or any Republican since Reagan).

As a candidate, Obama positioned himself to benefit from the backlash against his predecessor's use of executive power, expressing concerns about the erosion of separation of powers resulting from an overassertive presidency. In *The Audacity of Hope*, Obama's campaign autobiography, he complains that, under George W. Bush, "the White House stood fast against any suggestion that it was answerable to Congress or the Courts. . . . It was as if those in power had decided that habeas corpus and separation of powers were niceties that only got in the way, that they complicated what was obvious (the need to stop terrorists) or impeded what was right (the sanctity of life) and could therefore be disregarded, or at least bent to strong wills."[3] On the campaign trail, Obama again criticized Bush for excessive executive secrecy and promised to accommodate better executive–legislative coordination.[4] He also pledged to cease Bush's practice of using presidential signing statements to stipulate areas of legislation that the executive branch will not enforce due to constitutional concerns. When asked at a campaign appearance if he would promise never to use signing statements, he answered, "Yes." Elaborating, he told the audience that he saw such statements as a violation of separation of powers and "part of the whole theory of George Bush that he can make law as he goes along."[5] However, later in the campaign, Obama said signing statements were "a legitimate way to protect a president's constitutional prerogatives" if used with more restraint than Bush showed. This meant not issuing signing statements that "undermine the legislative intent" or "nullify or undermine congressional instructions as enacted into law."[6]

The 2008 Democratic national platform declared that "We reject sweeping claims of 'inherent' Presidential power," and promised appointment of judges who "respect our system of checks and balances and the separation of power among the Executive Branch, Congress, and the Judiciary."[7] It should be noted that most of the concerns raised by Obama and his fellow Democrats related to foreign and security affairs.

At the same time, Obama seemed to embrace Progressive theories of the presidency. Indeed, *The Audacity of Hope* is filled with praises of Woodrow Wilson and, even more, of Franklin Roosevelt for exerting presidential leadership to attain enactment of reforms such as creation of the Federal Reserve and the New Deal safety net. His own campaign fit the Progressive model of pledging himself to an extensive legislative program if elected. Once he was elected, Obama broke with precedent to fill a number of important positions on his White House staff with individuals possessing hands-on experience in Congress. Chief of Staff Rahm Emanuel actually served as a member of Congress from 2003–2009; upon taking office, Obama named to his Legislative Affairs team fourteen former Capitol Hill staffers including Legislative Affairs director Phil Schiliro, who had served as chief of staff for powerful California congressman Robert Waxman.[8] Obama, it seemed, was preparing for an all-out legislative drive, in coordination with Congress.

Formal Constitutional Relations between Obama and Congress

The formal constitutional relationship between President and Congress—what one might call the relationship having to do with the large "C" Constitution—can be measured by the president's use of devices such as the veto, the recess appointment, and the signing statement. In view of these devices, as president, Barack Obama's constitutional relations with Congress have not been radically different than those of his immediate predecessors.

The veto presents an obvious opportunity for the President to confront Congress and pressure it to respect his priorities. Obama has continued a recent trend of Presidents rarely exercising their veto power against Congress. In the first sixteen months of his presidency—months in which his own party held large majorities in Congress—Obama never utilized his veto. Similarly, in Bill Clinton's first two years and the first four years of George Bush's presidency, when Clinton enjoyed friendly partisan control of Congress and Bush enjoyed it for two-and-a-half years, neither used their veto pens a single time.

Another device that can test a president's deference to Congress is the recess appointment. The power to make recess appointments—appointments made during congressional recesses for limited terms without requiring Senate confirmation—is explicitly granted to the president in the Constitution. Although the provision was initially thought necessary in order to allow for the machinery of government to continue operating even during the very long congressional recesses of the eighteenth and nineteenth centuries, recent presidents, including George W. Bush and Bill Clinton, have sometimes used recess appointments to give an executive position to someone who already seemed unlikely to win Senate confirmation through the regular route. In fact, in many such cases, the recess appointees had been appointed through the regular channels first but had been stalled in the Senate, so the president turned to recess appointment to trump Senate rules.

During Congress's 2010 Easter recess, Obama used the power of recess appointment to install fifteen controversial appointees who had heretofore been blocked in the Senate. These nominations included union lawyer Craig Becker, opposed by all forty-one Republican Senators, to a spot on the National Labor Relations Board. In the wake of Obama's recess appointments, veteran columnist Dan Thomasson noted that the fifteen recess appointments were exactly the same number that George W. Bush had used to that point in his presidency, and wrote that the president's action "was almost an in your face rebuke of the two-party system with a decided touch of kingly arrogance thrown in for good measure."[9] Obama's use of presidential power to bypass the Senate with recess appointments was not, in the early part of his presidency, noticeably different from that of his immediate predecessor.

When it comes to signing statements, Obama has been more deferential to Congress than Bush was, but not as much as many of his strongest supporters had hoped. In March 2009, Obama issued a memorandum suspending Bush's signing statements (along with those of his predecessors) and requiring executive agencies to consult with the Justice Department before acting on them further. However, Obama's memorandum gave him considerable latitude, limiting his use of the device only to "interpretations of the Constitution that are well-founded" in his administration's own view. Two days later, Obama resumed the practice himself, and between March 2009 and May 2010 issued five signing statements declaring the executive branch exempted from some portion of the law he was signing. Some of the five cited multiple provisions in the law, and a total of nineteen provisions were called into question. From January 2009 through May 2010, the president issued an additional two signing statements that were purely ceremonial, extolling the merits of the legislation.

The first of the constitutionally oriented signing statements came on March 11, 2009, related to the Omnibus Appropriations Act of 2009. In it, Obama argued that "it is a legitimate constitutional function, and one that promotes the value of transparency, to indicate when a bill that is presented for Presidential signature includes provisions that are subject to well-founded constitutional objections." Specific constitutional concerns cited in the signing statement included provisions that would "unduly interfere with my constitutional authority in the area of foreign affairs by effectively directing the Executive on how to proceed or not proceed in negotiations or discussions with international organizations and foreign governments;" constrain presidential appointment powers; detract from the president's ability to prevent executive branch employees from revealing information "that is properly privileged or otherwise confidential;" attempt to give congressional committees authority in the allocation of appropriated funds; and attempt to dictate to the executive branch particular forms that budget requests from the executive branch must take. In each case, Obama indicated that he would not consider himself or his administration bound by the provisions in question.[10]

Other Obama signing statements have targeted "impermissible restriction on the appointment power,"[11] provisions requiring executive branch agencies to furnish information to the Financial Crisis Inquiry Commission,[12] and the role of members of Congress appointed to commissions. The latter cited a Reagan signing statement directing that members of Congress "will be able to participate only in ceremonial or advisory functions of [such a] Commission, and not in matters involving the administration of the act" in light of separation of powers and the Appointments and Ineligibility Clauses of the Constitution.[13] One signing statement, targeting the Supplemental Appropriations Act of 2009, repudiated provisions that would "interfere with my constitutional authority in the area of foreign affairs by effectively directing the Executive on how to proceed or not proceed in negotiations or discussions with international organizations and foreign governments, or by requiring consultation with the Congress prior to such negotiations or discussions." The president's answer to Congress was that "I will not treat these provisions as limiting my ability to engage in foreign diplomacy or negotiations."[14]

On one hand, in his first sixteen months Obama issued fewer signing statements registering constitutional concerns and pledging a sort of noncompliance than George W. Bush did in his first sixteen months, five by Obama versus seventeen by Bush. Bush also issued fifteen such signing statements, not including purely ceremonial statements, in the first sixteen months of his second term, when he had a partisan majority. (As in Obama's case, several of Bush's signing statements targeted multiple congressional provisions.) He only enjoyed such a majority for five of the first sixteen months of his first term. Obama has clearly been less eager to use this tool of presidential power against Congress.

On the other hand, he has clearly renounced in action the constitutional doctrine that he espoused early on the campaign trail that had led him to an absolute promise that he would not use such statements. From a standpoint of constitutional theory, once one moves from rejecting to accepting the argument that signing statements are sometimes a "legitimate constitutional function," one has crossed the threshold into a new view of the proper constitutional relationship between president and Congress, whether one issues five such statements or fifteen. As one Duke University law professor put it, referring to Obama's March 2009 memorandum, "President Bush could have issued this, because it has all those caveats in it."[15] Indeed, several key House Democrats, including David Obey and Barney Frank, felt compelled to write a letter to Obama complaining that "during the previous administration, all of us were critical of the President's assertion that he could pick and choose which aspects of Congressional statutes he was required to enforce. We were therefore chagrined to see you appear to express a similar attitude."[16]

Moreover, although there is some disagreement among analysts as to whether the content of Obama's signing statements has been fundamentally different from Bush's, a glance at Bush's signing statements indicates that the answer is mostly no—Bush's, like Obama's, placed a heavy emphasis on safeguarding the president's authority to conduct foreign affairs, his right to make appointments, and the constitutional illegitimacy of the "legislative veto." While Obama cited the relevant *INS v. Chadha* decision only implicitly, Bush frequently did so explicitly.

Informal Constitutional Relations: Obama as Legislative Leader

If vetoes, recess appointments, and signing statements form part of the picture of Obama's relation to Congress—the formal constitutional part—there is another, arguably equally important, part. That part is his informal relationship with Congress—his small "c" constitutional relationship—in what Clinton Rossiter called the president's role as "Chief Legislator." As Rossiter noted in his classic *The American Presidency*, the president is "intimately associated, by Constitution and custom, with the legislative process." The complexity of problems faced by the modern nation has made "external leadership" necessary for congressional action, and "the President alone is in a political, constitutional, and practical position to provide such leadership."[17]

Although grounded in the provision of the Constitution giving the president the right to recommend to Congress "such Measures as he shall judge necessary and expedient,"[18] the role of legislative leader has grown to be a much bigger part of his job.

Here, one might distinguish between president as legislative agenda setter and president as legislative mechanic. As agenda setter, the president presents Congress with a legislative program and aggressively pushes it to devote its limited time and energy to that task. The Progressive view of the presidency, exemplified by Woodrow Wilson, touts the president as active agenda setter. As legislative mechanic, the president involves himself deeply in the details of legislation, actively brokering compromises and taking ownership of the legislative process and product.

A view of Obama as legislative leader can be gleaned by examining four key pieces of legislation promoted by the president in his first sixteen months in office: the American Recovery and Reinvestment Act (otherwise known as the economic stimulus bill); the health care reform bill, passed and signed in March 2010; the cap-and-trade bill aimed at reducing carbon emissions; and the financial regulation reform bill.

Stimulus Bill

Obama made enactment of the ARRA his most immediate priority upon assuming office in January 2009. In his inaugural address, Obama declared that "the state of the economy calls for action, bold and swift, and we will act not only to create new jobs but to lay a new foundation for growth."[19] Three weeks later, in Obama's first news conference, the president called on Congress "to act without delay in the coming week to resolve their differences and pass this plan." He expressed confidence that the nation could escape its economic troubles, but "step number one," he said, was that "we have to pass an economic recovery and reinvestment plan."[20]

Despite the president's central role in promoting the legislation as the nation's number-one legislative priority, there was debate over how active he was as legislative mechanic. A widespread view among observers was that Obama, having set the agenda, stood back and allowed congressional Democratic leaders to fashion the details. Michael Gerson, former speechwriter for George W. Bush, exemplified this view when he wrote that "it will seem strange to history, and probably, eventually, to Obama himself, that the President's main expenditure of political capital and largest legislative achievement was a $787 billion stimulus package he did not design. . . . President Obama staked the initial reputation of his administration on the wisdom, restraint and economic innovation of House Speaker Nancy Pelosi and the rest of the Democratic congressional leadership. It was a mistake."[21] Indeed, this view has nearly hardened into conventional wisdom.

It is not the only view of the president's role in the stimulus package, however. At the Brookings Institution, congressional expert Thomas E. Mann countered that "Obama's hands were all over this bill from start to finish." Mann argued that

> the basic shape of the stimulus—rough allocations between tax cuts, fiscal relief to the states, direct assistance to individuals suffering directly from the recession, and spending for infrastructure, strategic investments in health IT, renewable energy and education, and other priorities—were set by the President-elect. The nitty-gritty legislative work identifying where and how these decisions could be implemented—it was no easy task moving these huge amounts of funds into the pipeline—was done in Congress with the direct participation of key Obama administration staff.

Moreover, Mann concluded, the final product was "remarkably close to what Obama sought." Obama won a key victory "working with Congress, not in deference to it."[22]

Health Care

Health care reform was also a high legislative priority for Obama from the beginning. Rhetorically, he listed health care as one of a handful of top priorities in his nomination acceptance speech, his inaugural address (in which he promised to "wield technology's wonders to raise health care's quality and lower its cost"), and his first address to a joint session of Congress. In that address, on February 24, 2009, Obama declared that "we must address the crushing cost of health care. . . . We can no longer afford to put health care reform on hold." To put an exclamation point on this declaration, Obama emphasized, "I know that nearly a century after Teddy Roosevelt first called for reform, the cost of our health care has weighed down our economy and our conscience long enough. So let there be no doubt: Health care reform cannot wait, it must not wait, and it will not wait another year."[23] Moreover, this priority was not only Obama's, but was a long-term commitment of the Democratic Party since Franklin Roosevelt's call for an "Economic Bill of Rights" in his 1944 State of the Union message.

Until passage of the Patient Protection and Affordable Care Act in March 2010, Obama gave a total of fifty-eight speeches on the subject, including one to another joint session of Congress in September 2009. He became closely enough associated with the drive for health care reform that it became widely known as "Obamacare." There is no question that he put the issue front and center, and pressed Congress to keep moving forward (or backward, depending on your view of the bill), going so far as to establish a number of sliding deadlines for congressional passage of a bill. Both in his campaign and as president, Obama clearly served as an activist agenda-setter on health care.

Yet, at several points in the process, Obama appeared to many observers to be disconnected from the process of designing the legislation and shepherding it through Congress. Indeed, in point of fact, the administration made a calculated decision not to lead with its own health care blueprint. It reportedly made this decision on the basis of its reading of the failure of the Clinton health care reform effort. By leading with his own proposal, according to this view, Clinton had made himself vulnerable to immediate attack. Better, the reasoning went, to let Congress work up proposals in a more decentralized fashion that was harder to pin down and attack.

When the initial House bill began drawing a negative public reaction in the summer of 2009, some criticized Obama for taking a hands-off approach that allowed liberal House Democratic leaders to construct a left-leaning bill with questionable appeal to moderates. Gerson, who similarly criticized Obama on the stimulus bill, contended that "once again, Obama deferred to Democratic congressional leaders instead of producing a detailed plan of his own. Once again, their failures have become his own."[24] This interpretation was not limited to conservative critics. When Congress reconvened after a difficult August recess, during which many members faced hostile questioning at town hall meetings, complaints were heard from Democratic members of Congress that the president had not been active enough in making clear what he wanted and what he was willing to give up. For example, was the "public option"—the provision creating a government-run insurance plan to compete with private insurance—nonnegotiable, or could it be traded away?

In early September 2009, Obama made his much-awaited appeal to a joint session of Congress. He laid down a few markers (the program should not cost more than $900 billion dollars over ten years, for example) but did little to satisfy critics. Given an opportunity to seize the moment and finally produce a plan of his own—perhaps a moderate compromise plan including substantial concessions to Republicans—he demurred. As late as February 3, 2010, when Democrats were still struggling to regain their footing after Scott Brown's surprise win in the vacancy election for U.S. Senate in Massachusetts, some congressional Democrats were angry over what they perceived to be Obama's lack of involvement in the process. At a private meeting with presidential advisor David Axelrod, Senator Al Franken (D-Minn.) declared,

"I'm just livid. . . . You're talking platitudes, and we have to go home and defend ourselves. We're getting the crap kicked out of us!" Senator Bill Nelson of Florida added, "There's a great deal of frustration that the President isn't getting the feelings that a lot of us are feeling. The President needs to be more hands-on with the health care bill." After Axelrod assured participants that the White House had a plan, Senator Carl M. Levin (D-Mich.) demanded, "What is it? What exactly is the plan?"[25] Throughout the months of deliberation on the bill, the president on several occasions demonstrated an incomplete grasp of the content of the legislation. Some suggested that the president simply was not interested in the nitty gritty of legislative work, that he was what congressional scholars would once have called a "show horse" instead of a "work horse."

It was never clear that Obama was as disengaged as his critics imagined. Early in his term, he had kicked off the health care drive by reaching a private agreement with insurance and pharmaceutical industry representatives that they would back his push as long as it included an individual insurance mandate (thus forcibly increasingly their customer base) and significant subsidies. Though the deal came under attack by many Democrats, including powerful House Commerce Committee chairman Henry Waxman, it essentially held. As the process unfolded, it also became increasingly implausible to believe that congressional liberals had hijacked the process and fashioned a bill while Obama was looking the other way. And, just before Brown's victory in Massachusetts upset the apple cart, intense negotiations between the House and the Senate were taking place, not in conference committee as is customary, but in the White House, with Obama as an active participant.

In any event, in the end, Obama took a much more openly active role as legislative mechanic than he had at any previous point. First, he made the decision to move ahead with a large reform bill rather than take a "small bill" fallback position after the Massachusetts election. Then, he pressed House Speaker Nancy Pelosi to adopt the strategy of passing the Senate bill in the House, despite its unpopularity there. Literally days before the House vote, he delivered to Congress the changes that he wanted to incorporate as part of the final package.

Not least, by all accounts he threw himself deeply into the task of winning over skeptical House Democrats. Obama travelled to Ohio for rallies and meetings that convinced members such as Dennis Kucinich and Ken Boccieri to flip to yes votes. He met privately with many others, insisting in the end on a hard sell that argued that defeat on health care would mean the effective end of his presidency. Crucially, he also offered to sign an executive order on abortion funding that kept Congressman Bart Stupak and about half a dozen other pro-life Democrats on the "yes" side, putting Pelosi's vote-counters over the top. In the midst of all of this, Obama offered an important though controversial constitutional argument: that the job of the President was to do "the right thing" in terms of policy, regardless of public opinion—and that the job of members of Congress was to follow him rather than their constituents. An endless debate could result from the question of whether Obama was exercising Burkean leadership by urging that Congress not subject policy to the whims of public opinion, or anti-Burkean leadership by foregoing humility and normal political prudence; regardless, his position here had profound constitutional implications for representation and consent.

Cap-and-Trade

As with the stimulus bill and health care reform, Obama made cap-and-trade a high priority in his campaign and his early presidential speeches, though perhaps in a second tier of issues. Obama also drew attention back to the issue through his high-profile participation in the Copenhagen international summit on climate change. The White House also tried to limit damage by studiously declining to engage with the possible implications of the East Anglia climate scandal that broke in late 2009, which seemed to indicate that the scientific models predicting global warming were not as solid as the administration and cap-and-trade advocates had contended. Not least, the administration tried to prod Congress into action by asserting that the Environmental Protection Agency had the right to regulate carbon emissions even without passage of congressional legislation.

The mechanics of cap-and-trade were strikingly similar to the health care bill, insofar as Obama left to Democrats in Congress the task of writing the legislation. In the summer of 2009, the House version narrowly passed after an intense lobbying effort by the White House, though some provisions (such as increased trade tariffs) were not to Obama's liking. The Senate, then, struggled. The original Senate bill left open a number of key details, and was ultimately shelved as Democratic leaders realized that nothing like the House bill could command the sixty votes necessary to overcome a filibuster. A new push for a bipartisan solution commenced, until key Republican supporter Lindsey Graham of South Carolina concluded that no agreeable compromise was likely. In May 2010, it was clear that a final bill, if one ever reached the floor, would be fashioned by Harry Reid.[26] At that point, the White House had not yet intervened heavily to try to force a resolution.

Financial Reform

As a contributing factor to the economic meltdown of late 2008, the mistakes and malfeasance of the financial sector drew Obama's attention and reached the high second tier of issues during his early presidency. In his February 24, 2009 address to a joint session of Congress, Obama declared, "To ensure that a crisis of this magnitude never happens again, I ask Congress to move quickly on legislation that will finally reform our outdated regulatory system. It is time to put in place tough, new, commonsense rules of the road so that our financial market rewards drive and innovation, and punishes shortcuts and abuse."[27]

In June 2009 the Treasury Department issued a white paper establishing key principles. Unlike the other examples, the White House followed up its exposition of broad principles by actually sending detailed legislative language to Congress two months later. As legislation wound through Congress, the Senate version diverged considerably from the House version that closely tracked the White House proposal and that passed in December 2009.[28] In May 2010, the Senate passed a financial reform bill and congressional negotiators prepared to reconcile the two versions.

Observers noted several important differences between the way the Obama administration approached financial reform and the way it had approached health care. The White House not only made a legislative proposal, it then engaged heavily in detailed negotiations from the beginning. Senate Republicans also claimed that the administration actively intervened to scuttle bipartisan talks later in the process, and at a critical point Obama personally shifted the direction of the Senate bill by insisting that a provision for a $50 billion bailout fund be scrapped. Altogether, largely because of stronger and earlier direction from the White House, the bill passed the Senate with little of the unseemly bargaining that marked the frenzied endgame on health care.[29]

Assessments

It is not easy to draw from these facts a clear answer to the question of how to assess Barack Obama's constitutional relation to Congress, formal or informal. Shortly after the bipartisan summit on health care convened by Obama, political analyst Fred Barnes declared that Obama was "No FDR." The President, Barnes contended, "has weakened the presidency and strengthened the power of Congress. . . . In Obama's Washington, Speaker Nancy Pelosi and Majority Leader Harry Reid are powerhouses. The job of actually writing bills—the economic stimulus, health care, cap and trade, the omnibus appropriation—was turned over to them and their colleagues. To put it more bluntly, Obama has abdicated where FDR ruled like a king." Roosevelt, Barnes concluded, had "a far more expansive idea of the presidency than Obama has. . . . Obama seems to see Presidential power as purely rhetorical."[30] Days after passage of the health care bill, columnist Maureen Down, calling Obama "the Conquering Professor," suggested that Obama (and Pelosi) had "steered [Democrats] off Jimmy Carter Highway and onto F.D.R. Drive." In Dowd's view, "When push came to shove, he shoved (and let Nancy push). He treated politics not as an intellectual exercise, but a political one. He realized that sometimes you can't rise above it. You have to sink down into it. You have to stop being cerebral and get your hands dirty."[31]

Nevertheless, it is possible to try to assess each of the interpretations offered of Obama's relation with Congress—deference, collusion, and disinterest.

In two important ways—one formal and the other informal—it is possible to see Obama as more deferential to Congress than some of his predecessors. His use of signing statements has been less frequent than George W. Bush's, and he has refrained from submitting to Congress his own detailed legislative blueprint on some key priorities. Of the four high-priority bills discussed here, the White House led with detailed legislative language only once; members of Congress and the public were kept guessing about its detailed health care preferences for some time.

However, this deference is limited, and may be conditional. Obama has continued to utilize signing statements, has formally asserted his constitutional right to do so, and has, in practice, used them for reasons not radically unlike the reasons underlying most of Bush's signing statements. Moreover, he has not vetoed less often, nor used recess appointments more often, than his predecessor. As legislative leader, Obama has not hesitated to aggressively act as an agenda-setter, has usually offered a guideline of key principles to drive the congressional discussion, and (especially in the case of health care) has involved himself deeply in legislative mechanics at crucial junctures; the White House was deeply involved in legislative details of the financial reform bill from the beginning. It is impossible to see a president as being rigidly deferential to Congress when he convinces reluctant members to vote for unpopular health care legislation on the grounds that failure will ruin his presidency.

To the degree that there seems to be deference to Congress, it is hard to know whether it represents a deep deference—that is, a principled decision to forego presidential activism out of genuine concern for constitutional principle—or only a tactical deference, based on public relations concerns and highly conditioned by the fact that Democrats controlled the Congress to which he was deferring. Certainly in regard to health care, evidence is strong that the White House chose to allow Congress to lead for the tactical reason that Bill Clinton's 1993–1994 effort, when Congress received a detailed presidential proposal, had failed.

For similar reasons, disinterest as an interpretation is only plausible in a limited sense. The president does indeed seem to be relatively uninterested in the narrow details of legislation, in comparison to presidents such as Bill Clinton or Jimmy Carter. However, Obama's model is not unprecedented. Although the caricature of Ronald Reagan as uninterested in policy detail was overdrawn, it was based on a kernel of truth. Reagan was most interested in broad principles and in getting results, not unlike Obama (though the principles they espoused were quite different). Likewise, there was considerable similarity between Obama's health care drive and George W. Bush's drive for Social Security reform, when Bush offered a set of broad principles and then left it to Congress to work out the details; of course, in Bush's case, Congress did not come through, due to internal Republican divisions and lack of a filibuster-proof Senate. In the end, ironically, Obama won passage of health care not with his lofty rhetoric, which consistently failed to move the needle of public opinion after the summer of 2009, but with his inside game, alternately cajoling and muscling skeptical members of Congress and helping to broker deals, including the last-minute executive order on abortion funding that won over wavering pro-life Democrats. Again, partisan considerations must come into play: at the outset of his presidency, Obama could afford some disinterest about legislative details because it was Nancy Pelosi and not John Boehner who was shaping them.

Collusion remains as the model that best fits the disparate facts of the case. Collusion is not dictation, so actions (or inactions) that are consistent with it can also appear to be deference or disinterestedness. In this model, Obama controlled the agenda, established broad principles for legislation, allowed a friendly Congress to work out the details, gave public backing and cover to the enterprise while it was ongoing, and actively intervened only when necessary to iron out disagreements or push for final passage. The president could retain authority and some political capital by remaining above the fray, but in the end a liberal Congress gave a liberal president more or less what he wanted. In this sense, Obama was part Wilson, exercising an aggressive leadership of public agenda-setting, and part Jefferson, whose apparent deference on legislative detail often masked active involvement beneath the surface.

Of course, this approach is only workable when the president is dealing with a solidly liberal Congress. A Congress that is less solidly liberal or under partial or complete control by Republicans (as after the 2010 elections) will require Obama to significantly revise his approach. Under the former conditions, elements of deference and disinterestedness can coexist comfortably within a strategy of collusion. Under the latter conditions, that coexistence will be imperiled and choices will have to be made.

In a related vein, it is also a combination that works best on offense, when proposing change. When Obama is thrown on defense—for example, having to fight off attempts to repeal or significantly scale back health care reform—any constitutional scruples that he has favoring deference will be put sorely to the test. When all possible legislative outcomes (other than defeat) are acceptable, just unequally so, a president can afford a level of disinterest in detail that is not possible when some legislative outcomes might be positively bad from the president's point of view. And if Democratic members of Congress become less willing to take a leap of faith with the president against the inclinations of their constituents, Obama will likewise be forced to adjust his approach.

Notes

1. For an insightful examination of early American presidents see Thomas E. Cronin, ed., *Inventing the American Presidency* (Lawrence: University Press of Kansas, 1989), chapters 10–14. For an excellent overview of presidential history, see Sidney A. Milkis and Michael Nelson, *The American Presidency: Origins and Development, 1776–2007*, 5th ed. (Washington, DC: Congressional Quarterly Press, 2007).

2. For a favorable assessment of Bush's strong presidency, see John Yoo, *Crisis and Command: A History of Executive Power from George Washington to George W. Bush* (New York: Kaplan, 2010). Other accounts ranging from mixed to strongly hostile include Mickey Edwards, *Reclaiming Conservatism: How a Great American Movement Got lost—And How It Can Find Its Way Back* (New York: Oxford University Press, 2008); Gene Healy and Timothy Lynch, *Power Surge: The Constitutional Record of George W. Bush* (Washington, DC: Cato Institute, 2006); James P. Pfiffner, *Power Play: The Bush Presidency and the Constitution* (Washington, D.C.: Brookings Institution, 2008); Charlie Savage, *Takeover: The Return of the Imperial Presidency and the Subversion of American Democracy* (Boston: Back Bay Books, 2008); and selected chapters from Mark J. Rozell and Gleaves Whitney, ed., *Testing the Limits: George W. Bush and the Imperial Presidency* (Lanham, MD: Rowman & Littlefield, 2009), and George C. Edwards III and Desmond S. King, *The Polarized Presidency of George W. Bush* (New York: Oxford University Press, 2007).

3. Barack Obama, *The Audacity of Hope: Thoughts on Reclaiming the American Dream* (New York: Vintage Books, 2006), 92–93.

4. For a discussion of Obama's treatment of constitutional issues in the 2008 campaign, see Andrew E. Busch, "Constitutional Discourse and American Govern-

ment," The Heritage Foundation, August 22, 2008, www.heritage.org/Research/
Reports/2008/08/Constitutional-Discourse-and-American-Government (accessed
June 29, 2010).

5. For a video of the appearance, see Politics Daily, www.politicsdaily.
com/2009/03/13/obama-breaks-own-signing-statements-standard/ (accessed March
24, 2010).

6. Charlie Savage, "Obama's Embrace of a Bush Tactic Riles Congress," *New
York Times*, August 8, 2009, www.nytimes.com/2009/08/09/us/politics/09signing.
html (accessed June 29, 2010).

7. *Renewing America's Promise*, Democratic National Platform, www.presidency.
ucsb.edu/papers_pdf/78283.pdf (accessed March 23, 2010).

8. Anna Palmer, "Legislative Affairs Team Gets to Work," *Roll Call*, January
21, 2009, www.rollcall.com/issues/54_75/lobbying/31589-1.html (accessed May 20,
2010).

9. Dan Thomasson, "Recess Appointments Another Slap at GOP," *Boston
Herald*, April 2, 2010, www.bostonherald.com/news/opinion/op_ed/view.
bg?articleid=1244079 (accessed April 4, 2010).

10. "Statement on Signing the Omnibus Appropriations Act, 2009," March
11, 2009, *Administration of Barack H. Obama, 2009*. See also Jonathan Weisman,
"Signing Statements Reappear in Obama White House," *Wall Street Journal*, March
12, 2009, http://online.wsj.com/article/SB123688875576610955.html (accessed
June 29, 2010).

11. "Statement on Signing the Omnibus Public Land Management Act of 2009,"
March 30, 2009, *Administration of Barack H. Obama, 2009*.

12. "Statement on Signing the Fraud Enforcement and Recovery Act of 2009,"
May 20, 2009, *Administration of Barack H. Obama, 2009*.

13. "Statement on Signing the Ronald Reagan Centennial Commission Act,"
June 2, 2009, *Administration of Barack H. Obama, 2009*.

14. "Statement on Signing the Supplemental Appropriations Act, 2009," June 24,
2009, *Administration of Barack H. Obama, 2009*.

15. Josh Gerstein, "Obama: Ignore Signing Statements," *Politico*, March 9, 2009,
www.politico.com/news/stories/0309/19795.html (accessed March 24, 2010).

16. Savage, "Obama's Embrace of a Bush Tactic Riles Congress."

17. Clinton Rossiter, *The American Presidency* (New York: Harcourt Brace,
1960), 26.

18. This provision is found in Article II, section 3.

19. Barack Obama, "Inaugural Address, January 20, 2009," www.presidency.ucsb.
edu/ws/index.php?pid=44 (accessed March 24, 2009).

20. "The President's News Conference, February 9, 2009," www.presidency.ucsb.
edu/ws/index.php?pid=85728 (accessed March 24, 2010).

21. Michael Gerson, "Political Honeymoon Over for President," *State Journal-
Register*, August 8, 2009, www.sj-r.com/opinions_columnists/x1558731508/Michael-
Gerson-Political-honeymoon-over-for-President (accessed June 29, 2010).

22. Thomas E. Mann, "Whose Stimulus: President Obama's or the Democratic Congress'?" The Brookings Institution, August 18, 2009, www.brookings/opinions/2009/0807_obama_mann.aspx?p=1 (accessed August 18, 2009).

23. "Address Before a Joint Session of Congress," February 24, 2009, www.presidency.ucsb.edu/ws/print.php?pid=85753 (accessed August 14, 2009).

24. Gerson, "Political Honeymoon Over for President."

25. Ceci Connolly, "How Obama Revived His Health-Care Bill," *Washington Post*, March 23, 2010.

26. See Coral Davenport and Avery Palmer, "A Landmark Climate Bill Passes," *Congressional Quarterly Weekly Report*, June 29, 2009, p. 1516; Carol Davenport, "2009 Legislative Summary: Climate Change Mitigation," *Congressional Quarterly Weekly Report*, January 4, 2010, p. 42.

27. "Address Before a Joint Session of Congress," February 24, 2009.

28. See *Financial Regulatory Reform: A New Foundation—Rebuilding Financial Supervision and Regulation*, Washington, DC: Treasury Department, June 17, 2009; "Administration's Regulatory Reform Agenda Reaches New Milestone: Final Piece of Legislative Language Delivered to Capitol Hill," U.S. Department of the Treasury, August 11, 2009.

29. Jonathan Weisman and Damian Paletta, "Financial-Bill Playbook: Don't Mess Around," *Wall Street Journal*, May 22–23, 2010.

30. Fred Barnes, "He's No FDR," *Weekly Standard*, March 8, 2010, www.weeklystandard.com/articles/hes-no-fdr (accessed March 23, 2010).

31. Maureen Dowd, "Hail the Conquering Professor," *New York Times*, March 23, 2010, www.nytimes.com/2010/03/24/opinion/24dowd.html (accessed March 24, 2010).

~

CHAPTER FIVE

The Spirit Is Partially Willing

The Legal Realism and Half-Hearted Minimalism of President Obama

Joshua Dunn

For a graduate of Harvard Law School, editor of its law review, and visiting professor at the University of Chicago Law School, Barack Obama has said remarkably little about his views of the Constitution and the role of the Supreme Court in American politics.[1] Indeed his only sustained reflection on the Court and the Constitution, the subject of this chapter, is found in his campaign biography *The Audacity of Hope*.[2] Despite the scarcity of material it is still possible to construct a clear picture of the president's views.[3] His previous statements and interviews, along with *The Audacity of Hope* and his actions and declarations as president, point to a comprehensible view of constitutional interpretation and the Court's role in our constitutional order. Furthermore, his silence on the subject tells us something about his position, namely that he considers the Court and legal action of much less importance to him than elected institutions and political mobilization.

Examination of his record reveals that while Obama unsurprisingly accepts central tenets of progressivism and legal realism, such as the notions of a living Constitution and the indeterminacy of legal texts, he also tends toward the judicial minimalism of his friend, former colleague, and now member of his administration, Cass Sunstein. The import of Obama's view is that judges must treat the Constitution as having no fixed meaning but that most of the remaining political goals of liberals and Progressives are unlikely to be accomplished through the judiciary. In this view, instead of dramatically expanding the frontiers of liberal progressivism, the Court should consolidate and perhaps gradually expand the "gains" of the Warren Court era. Appearing to accept academic critiques of judicial policy making, he acknowledges the limitations of the Court and instead views elected institutions as the most promising venues for pursuing social change. As another of his former colleagues at the University of Chicago Law School, David Strauss, has maintained, Obama is not a "court-focused" president.[4] That does not mean that he is unwilling to use the judiciary to push his political agenda. Obama's version of judicial minimalism seems to be one that accepts that courts are ineffective at changing society but that the courts should be used anyway. Already his administration has found it difficult to resist the siren song of judicial action to accomplish objectives obstructed by the political process.

The State of the Union

President Obama's first State of the Union address offers the most compelling place to begin this analysis. While his address does not provide a complete picture of his views of the Court and Constitution, it does at least provide a glimpse of his legal realism and judicial minimalism. Somewhat infamously, President Obama attacked the Supreme Court for its recent decision in *Citizens United v. Federal Election Commission*.[5] His attack was just a short paragraph:

> With all due deference to separation of powers, last week the Supreme Court reversed a century of law to open the floodgates for special interests—including foreign companies—to spend without limit in our elections. Well I don't think American elections should be bankrolled by America's most powerful interests, and worse, by foreign entities. They should be decided by the American people. And I'd urge Democrats and Republicans to pass a bill that helps to correct some of these problems.

Although brief, this shot across the Court's bow was remarkable. It marked the first time in modern history that a president has directly attacked the Supreme Court during the State of the Union Address. The criticism was also factually incorrect. The Court's decision left in place existing prohibitions on foreign citizens and corporations and it did not reverse a century of law. The precedent the Court overruled was a mere nineteen years old. Furthermore, six of nine justices were in attendance and according to protocol must sit expressionless during the speech (although Justice Alito found it impossible and was caught silently mouthing "not true" after the president's attack). Most importantly, Justice Anthony

Kennedy, the author of the Court's opinion and also the most influential member of the Court, was in attendance. Kennedy is the swing vote on the Court and controls the outcome of almost all controversial political decisions where the justices divide on ideological lines. The four conservatives along with Kennedy appear healthy and unlikely to retire anytime soon. Potentially alienating the swing member of the Court for temporary political gain seems like a blunder of the first order, particularly for someone with Obama's legal background.

Nonetheless Obama's attack indicates two components to his view of the Court and the Constitution. First, legal reasoning is of secondary importance to him compared to political considerations. While one could not reasonably expect a sustained legal exegesis, Obama did not offer anything even approaching a constitutional argument against the Court's decision. Instead, he focused on the consequences of the decision and, of course, was trying to use the decision for political gain. By implication the Court made the wrong decision because of the alleged baleful effects of the ruling. Undoubtedly he disagrees with the Court's legal reasoning but it is telling that he did not even attempt to counter it.

Second, the attack also indicates that he has a diminished view of the role the Court plays in our political system. In fact, his statement raises the interesting question of whether he believes in judicial supremacy, the idea that the Court is the final authoritative interpreter of the Constitution. Since 1958 the Court has maintained its interpretive supremacy and the public seems to have accepted for even longer the idea that the Court's interpretations supersede the president's and Congress's.[6] Obama, however, called on Congress to correct a constitutional decision of the Court. Perhaps the president envisions legislation that does not directly countermand the Court's ruling but instead places onerous regulatory burdens on corporations and unions that wish to spend on elections. Of course, statutory requirements that discourage the exercise of constitutional rights risk being struck down by the Court.

It would not be entirely surprising if President Obama rejects judicial supremacy. Constitutional scholars, and particularly scholars on the political left, have become increasingly critical of the idea. Larry Kramer, Dean of the Stanford Law School, has argued for "popular constitutionalism" where the people are the ultimate interpreter's of the Constitution. The people who waged the Revolutionary War and then wrote and ratified the Constitution, he argues, would have been astonished at the notion that unelected, life-tenured judges would be the final repository of constitutional meaning.[7] Mark Tushnet has also called for rejecting judicial supremacy and sharply limiting the power of judicial review.[8] The Court, despite conservative critics of judicial activism, has more often in Tushnet's view been a hidebound and reactionary obstacle to Progressive social action than the vanguard of liberalism.[9]

At the very least, Obama seems to have crept as close to attacking judicial supremacy as any modern president. Even Franklin Roosevelt, when objecting to Court decisions striking down the core of his New Deal programs, did not imply that Congress could directly contradict or "correct" the Court's constitutional decisions. Instead, he tried to change the Court's jurisprudence by increasing its size, but even then he had to—unsuccessfully—disguise his court-packing plan as a relief program for elderly judges.

Obama's attack does indicate that he views the Court through the lenses of both legal realism and judicial minimalism. The former argues that there is no escaping justices imposing their own political and policy preferences through decisions and thus the focus of judicial decision making should be on the consequences of court rulings. The latter argues that the left has placed too much emphasis on the Court and that social change is best pursued through political mobilization rather than litigation. The president seems to have lost faith, as many liberals have, in judicial policy making and instead would prefer for the Court's role in our system to be cabined. Thus, Obama's legal realism, which would seem to lift most restraints on the Court, is tempered by his judicial minimalism.

Obama's Legal Realism

During his campaign for president, Obama repeatedly asserted that he would nominate judges with empathy. This empathy litmus test did not receive much attention until Justice Souter announced his retirement and Obama reiterated his preference and explained what he meant by it:

> I will seek someone who understands that justice isn't about some abstract legal theory or footnote in a case book. It is also about how our laws affect the daily realities of people's lives—whether they can make a living and care for their families; whether they feel safe in their homes and welcome in their own nation.
>
> I view that quality of empathy, of understanding and identifying with people's hopes and struggles as an essential ingredient for arriving as [sic] just decisions and outcomes. I will seek somebody who is dedicated to the rule of law, who honors our constitutional traditions, who respects the integrity of the judicial process and the appropriate limits of the judicial role. I will seek somebody who shares my respect for constitutional values on which this nation was founded, and who brings a thoughtful understanding of how to apply them in our time.[10]

During the campaign Obama used the example of the Supreme Court's 2007 decision in *Ledbettter v. Goodyear Tire & Rubber Co.* to illustrate the importance of empathy.[11] Lily Ledbetter had brought a discrimination claim against Goodyear but under the law she had to bring claims within 180 days of filing a claim of discrimination, which she had failed to do. In a 5-4 decision, the Court ruled that based on prior case law and the plain meaning of the Civil Rights Act, Ledbetter could not bring claims after 180 days. Congress and President Obama effectively overturned the Court's decision with the Lily Ledbetter Fair Pay Act, which Obama signed into law shortly after his inauguration.

But Obama's empathy test, which seemed popular or at least received little attention during the campaign, became controversial when Obama reasserted it in 2009. Obama's critics seized on the apparent contradiction between empathy and the rule of law, since it implies that judges should not apply the law equally and that someone with sufficiently sad personal circumstances should get more favorable treatment from the Court than someone without a hard-luck story to tell. Enough of the public seemed to recoil at the idea that judges might not be impartial and apply the law equally that Sotomayor had to disavow it after receiving her nomination to the Court, telling the Judiciary Committee that "judges can't rely on what's in their heart."[12] And Obama himself pointedly refused to refer to empathy after Justice John Paul Stevens' retirement even though he reiterated that judges should insure that ordinary citizens should not be overrun by powerful interests in court. While generating political controversy, Obama's understanding of empathy should just be viewed as a shorthand version of legal realism. The public was simply not used to hearing such a straightforward presentation of what is commonly accepted in law schools.

At its core, legal realism advocates both an institutional and interpretive nihilism. According to legal realism, traditional constitutional doctrines such as separation of powers and federalism should not concern judges. Instead, judges should feel free to disregard them if they get in the way of good public policy. Furthermore, legal realism maintains that judges inevitably base their decisions on their personal political preferences so one should abandon the attempt to interpret the constitutional text properly.

Legal realism rose to prominence in the 1920s and 1930s. Among its most prominent advocates were Karl Llewellyn, Thurman Arnold, Max Radin, and Jerome Frank, but it had as its intellectual forbears Justice Oliver Wendell Holmes, Jr., and Roscoe Pound.[13] In The Common Law, Holmes had famously argued:

> The life of the law has not been logic; it has been experience. The felt necessities of the time, the prevalent moral and political theories, intuitions of

public policy, avowed or unconscious, even the prejudices which judges share
with their fellow men, have had a good deal more to do than the syllogism in
determining the rules by which men should be governed.[14]

This position was echoed in legal realism's central empirical claim: judges
do not make decisions based on legal materials or legal reasoning. Instead,
they make decisions based on how the facts of a case strike them. That is,
judges make up their minds about the proper outcome of a case and then
create the legal reasoning as a diversionary adornment. According to this
theory, political ideology plays a far greater role than constitutions or statutes
in determining the outcome of cases.

The upshot of legal realism is that the law as we normally think of it does
not exist at all. If judges make decisions in this way, they are really just deciding what they think is the best policy. The law becomes nothing but public
policy. In the parlance of legal realism, the law is "indeterminate," which
means that it is insufficient for determining the outcome of cases. Thus,
judges just do what they think is best. Or, more bluntly, the law is whatever
judges say it is.[15]

The clearest statement of the Obama's legal realism can be found in *The
Audacity of Hope* where he tells us that judges should reject originalism and
instead take context, history, and practical outcomes into account when deciding cases. Originalism maintains that the only legitimate method of interpreting the Constitution, and the only way to reconcile judicial review with
constitutional government, is to construe the document according to what its
words meant at the time it was adopted or amended. Originalism was much
ridiculed and mocked when it achieved national attention in the 1980s during
the nomination of Robert Bork. Today, though, it is a growth industry in the
legal academy. Even liberal constitutional scholars like Akhil Amar and Jack
Balkin of Yale declare themselves originalists.[16] Others have noted that the
reason for this turn is the fact that many decisions favored by liberals remain
vulnerable to being overturned and rejected unless the left convinces the
public that these controversial decisions are grounded in the Constitution.[17]

Barack Obama, however, rejects the idea that many parts of the Constitution contain any discernable meaning or that original understandings of the
document should constrain judges. While things like two- and six-year terms
for Representatives and Senators are not open to interpretation, the broad
guarantees of the Bill of Rights and Fourteenth Amendment have no definite
meaning. Instead, the Constitution creates the basis for a postmodern dialogue
that allows us to impose our own meaning on these words. Strangely, Obama
asserts that the same Americans who gave their assent to the Declaration and

its defense of self-evident truths rejected the idea of absolute truth. "Implicit in its [the Constitution's] structure," Obama says, "in the very idea of ordered liberty, was a rejection of absolute truth." The Constitution under this view is just "a framework" for organizing "the way we argue about our future." The Constitution, he says, "won't tell us whether abortion is good or bad, a decision for a woman to make or a decision for a legislature. Nor will it tell us whether school prayer is better than no prayer at all."[18] The document just invites us to discuss these questions but does not give any indication of the answers or even what institution should answer them. Of course, originalists like Scalia,[19] and for that matter nonoriginalists like John Hart Ely,[20] have also maintained that the Constitution does not tell us whether abortion is good or bad. But they point out that when the Constitution does not address an issue as in the case of abortion, the issue is left to state legislatures.

Obama's celebration of deliberation glides over another problem. The questions he raises have been answered, but there has been very little deliberation, at least under the Constitution, about them. Instead, what deliberation has occurred, or at least the deliberation that has mattered, has occurred among the nine members of the Supreme Court. This sleight of hand tries to avoid the core criticism of originalists like Scalia, which is that the Court is not constitutionally entrusted to make these decisions. If the Court is to be the ultimate repository of constitutional meaning, then, the notion of constitutional deliberation becomes circumscribed and cramped.

Instead of originalism, Obama declares his preference for Justice Stephen Breyer's mode of interpretation outlined in *Active Liberty: Interpreting Our Democratic Constitution.*[21] While allegedly offering a theory of interpretation, Justice Breyer really defends consequentialist judicial decision making: "Why should courts try to answer difficult federalism questions on the basis of logical deduction from text or precedent alone? Why not ask about the consequences of decision-making on the active liberty that federalism seeks to further?" Even those sympathetic to Justice Breyer lamented the fact that, his declarations to the contrary, he did not really offer a theory of interpretation. Instead, "active liberty" really functioned as a catch-all for his preferred outcomes. The problem with Justice Breyer's method of interpretation, James Ryan has noted, is that it is "incurably indeterminate" and "quite abstract and at times only loosely connected with the text of the Constitution." Instead, Justice Breyer's focus on consequences really, as legal realism emphasizes, means avoiding "bad public policy."[22]

President Obama also indicated his affinity for legal realism along with the Progressive notion of a living constitution during the debate over Proposition 8 in California. Proposition 8 was placed on the ballot in response to a state supreme court decision finding that marriage was a fundamental right and striking down a ban on same-sex marriage. During an interview with MTV, Obama expressed his opposition to the ballot measure saying, "Usually, our constitutions expand liberties, they don't contract them."[23] One doesn't want to place too much weight on remarks made on MTV, but this statement is illustrative of the chasm between originalists and Obama. A common assumption among liberal legal scholars and expressed by Obama is the notion of a living Constitution, which means that the document has no fixed meaning but instead evolves according to changing social circumstances. Just as importantly, when married with legal realism, the idea means that judges should expand liberties over time and, as indicated by Obama, once they have been expanded by a court, they should not be repealed or retrenched. As noted by Judge Richard Posner, the idea that a "living constitution" must move only in one direction is simply an undefended assumption of living constitutionalists.[24] If they were consistent, Posner argues, they would acknowledge that circumstances and society can change in different ways and that, therefore, the problems facing the nation today might necessitate interpreting constitutional rights more narrowly. To assume that that they must always expand simply means that you want judges to make decisions that agree with your policy preferences. Thus, the slogan of a living constitution is just a cover for the consequentialist judicial decision making preferred by legal realism.

Judicial Minimalism

While Obama's support for notions like a living constitution and legal realism would seem to incline him toward judicial activism, there appears to be evidence that Obama views himself as a judicial minimalist. Judicial minimalism was first articulated by Obama's colleague and friend at the University of Chicago, Cass Sunstein. Sunstein maintains that liberals, instead of seeking a fresh round of judicial activism, should instead seek to consolidate gains made during the Warren Court era and leave the pursuit of dramatic change to elected institutions. In his most recent explication of minimalism, Sunstein articulated several key tenets. Minimalists: do not have a "heroic view" of the federal judiciary; want to avoid broad, ambitious rulings; do not believe the Court should seek to be at the forefront of social movements; do not want judges to seize on ambiguous constitutional provisions to issue broad rulings that limit democratic prerogatives; and think Warren Court decisions were sometimes "radical," but don't want to overturn significant precedents.[25] Undergirding this minimalism seems to be a suspicion of judicial capacity to create social change. Sunstein gave these in his contribution to *The Constitution in 2020*, which was intended to provide a Progressive vision of constitutional law. A common theme running throughout many of the volume's essays is that the hopes of Progressives for the Constitution should not be excessively focused on the judiciary.

Viewed politically, the implication of minimalism for the left is that the Court has done what it could to advance the Progressive agenda and should now largely stay out of the way. Or as Pam Karlan, a professor at Stanford Law School and contributor to *The Constitution in 2020*, recently explained, the current goals of the left lie in the area of "affirmative rights," such as health care and housing that are "things courts aren't that good at."[26]

While Obama has never, to my knowledge, explicitly called himself a judicial minimalist, there are several pieces of evidence indicating that the label fits him and that he concurs to some degree with Sunstein. In fact, he quite clearly believes that the left has emphasized judicial action too much and that the courts are ineffective at accomplishing the goals of the Progressive movement.

Obama reveals his minimalism most clearly in a 2001 interview that achieved some notoriety during the 2008 presidential campaign. Conducted with two other scholars for a public radio program in Chicago, the interview became controversial in 2008 when Matt Drudge posted excerpts on his website. In the quoted excerpts, Obama says that the Warren Court was not as radical as its critics had contended: "But, the Supreme Court never ventured into the issues of redistribution of wealth, and of more basic issues such as political and economic justice in society. To that extent, as radical as I think people try to characterize the Warren Court, it wasn't that radical. It didn't break free from the essential constraints that were placed by the founding fathers in the Constitution, at least as it's been interpreted and the Warren Court interpreted in the same way, that generally the Constitution is a charter of negative liberties."[27]

Taken out of context it would appear that Obama would support the Court interpreting the Constitution as a guarantee of positive liberty and therefore of Court-mandated economic redistribution. But just following that excerpt, he criticized the civil rights movement for being too "court-focused" and losing "track of the political and community organizing and activities on the ground that are able to put together the actual coalition of powers through which you bring about redistributive change. In some ways we still suffer from that." Even later in the interview he said:

Maybe I'm showing my bias here as a legislator as well as a law professor, but I'm not optimistic about bringing about major redistributive change through the courts. The institution just isn't structured that way. You just look at very rare examples during the desegregation era the court was willing to for example order changes that cost money to a local school district. The court was very uncomfortable with it. It was very hard to manage, it was hard to figure out. You start getting into all sorts of separation of powers issues in terms of the court monitoring or engaging in a process that essentially is administrative and takes a lot of time. The court's just not very good at it and politically it's very hard to legitimize opinions from the court in that regard. So, I think that although you can craft theoretical justifications for it legally. . . . I think that as a practical matter our institutions are poorly equipped to do it.[28]

Here, Obama seems to be echoing the work of his colleague Gerald Rosenberg. In the early 1990s, Rosenberg argued in his book *The Hollow Hope* that courts lack the necessary resources to create social change. Exhibit A in his case was desegregation.[29] Rosenberg contended that the Court had almost no influence on desegregation despite the exalted reputation of *Brown v. Board of Education* and that it was not until the Civil Rights Act of 1964 that significant progress was made on desegregation. Obama drew on the very evidence Rosenberg used to prove his point, saying that "*Brown v. Board of Education* happens in 1954. By 1964, if you look essentially at what's happened on the ground, nothing has happened or very little has happened." But after 1964, the Department of Health, Education, and Welfare (HEW) is empowered to withhold federal funding from segregated school districts.

This interview also indicates a practical understanding, if not appreciation, of the difficulties that the Constitution places on social reformers. Progressives, such as Woodrow Wilson, lamented the restraints the Constitution placed on their ability to implement their agenda. Thus was born the notion of a living Constitution, which was intended to erode institutional impediments, such as separation of powers, to Progressive social change. But constitutional principles proved more durable than the Progressives hoped. Hence, courts still must wrestle to some extent with whether their actions intrude too far into another institution's proper sphere of authority.

President Obama has also, so far, paid little attention to reshaping the federal judiciary, an indication that it is not his highest priority. His rate of nominations for circuit and district court vacancies is far below that of past presidents. In his first year, Obama nominated thirty-three federal judges compared to forty-five in Clinton's first term and sixty-five in George W. Bush's. This shortage of nominations even led the American Constitution Society, the Left's answer to the Federalist Society, to hold a panel investigating this ostensibly perplexing subject. While many theories were proffered, the simplest and most plausible came from the panel's token conservative, Orin Kerr, who said, "I think the main reason is that the Obama Administration just has not made the judiciary a major priority and it's—it's as simple as that."[30] Presidents always have many demands on their time, but as Obama said during the 2008 campaign when McCain, in an act of desperation, tried to suspend the campaign, the president must "deal with more than one thing at once."[31]

This lack of concern from the Obama administration has led to much hand-wringing among liberal law school professors who want Obama to reclaim the judiciary from an alleged conservative takeover. Leading the chorus of lamentations has been Geoffrey Stone, Obama's former colleague at Chicago. In February 2010, he, along with other prominent legal academics, including Bruce Ackerman of Yale and Kathleen Sullivan of Stanford, sent a letter to Obama. The signatories wrote:

> We write out of a growing concern that your Administration must act with far more energy and dispatch in the vitally important task of nominating and confirming federal judges. We recognize that partisan obstructionism in the Senate has made this task increasingly difficult, but the successful management of the confirmation process is critical to the nation and, ultimately, is the White House's responsibility.[32]

While it could be that Obama will allay the fears of Stone and others in the next few years, it seems far more likely Obama will continue to view the judiciary as of secondary importance. His nomination of Sonia Sotomayor, and more recently Elena Kagan, illustrate that he is unwilling to spend political capital to satisfy his left flank.

While some commentators have speculated that Sotomayor is a judicial minimalist, which in turn led Obama to select her, there are more obvious and less speculative reasons that she points to Obama's minimalism. No one expects Sotomayor to be an intellectual leader on the Court, capable of challenging Scalia and other conservatives. Jeffrey Rosen famously questioned her intelligence. One former clerk for a colleague of Sotomayor's on the Second Circuit told Rosen that Sotomayor was "not that smart and kind of a bully on the bench." Rosen reported that "her opinions, although competent, are viewed by former prosecutors as not especially clean or tight, and sometimes miss the forest for the trees." She also apparently aggravates her colleagues: "several former clerks complained, she rankled her colleagues by sending long memos that didn't distinguish between substantive and trivial points, with petty editing suggestions—fixing typos and the like—rather than focusing on the core analytical issues."[33] If Obama was looking for an intellectual standard bearer to lead the liberal wing of the Court into a new era of Progressive constitutional change, presumably he would have nominated someone with greater acknowledged intellectual heft and perhaps more personal charm, who could help sway Justice Kennedy (even though the ability of any justice to influence other justices is always exaggerated). Instead, he picked someone with a compelling personal story and decent credentials and of a race previously unrepresented on the Court, in short, a nominee guaranteed to be confirmed by the Senate and perhaps win some political credit for Obama with an increasingly important ethnic group.

Perhaps it would not have been worth waging a more difficult political fight to get a more aggressive liberal on the Court, since Sotomayor was replacing Justice Souter and she would not dramatically affect the ideological balance on the Court. But if there was ever an opportune time to do so, it would have been early in Obama's first year in office, with his high approval ratings and a filibuster proof majority in the Senate. As everyone who has taken "Introduction to American Politics" knows, presidential popularity fades over time, and the president's party tends to lose seats in the Senate, particularly during midterm elections.

More recently, the nomination and confirmation of Elena Kagan provides additional evidence of Obama's minimalism. Kagan's nomination led to concerns from Obama's left that she was a reverse Souter who would move to the right once on the Court.[34] This alarmism was largely based on her tenure as dean at Harvard Law School, where she did something astonishing: hire well-qualified conservatives. As with Sotomayor, Obama appears to be far smarter than his critics on the Left. There is no indication that Kagan will do anything but uphold the shibboleths of *Roe v. Wade*[35] and *Planned Parenthood v. Casey*[36] and will reliably join the Court's other liberals on politically controversial cases. In addition, her willingness to treat conservatives with decency as Harvard dean meant that many prominent conservative legal scholars and attorneys lined up to support her nomination, giving her nomination broader support in the legal community.

Halfhearted Minimalism

While the preponderance of the evidence points to Obama's minimalism, his administration has made decisions indicating that he is willing to abandon minimalism when political obstacles frustrate his very ambitious political goals and to nominate judges who are much more willing to insert their preferences into the Constitution. Hence, one could say that Obama gives intellectual assent to minimalism but as a pragmatic politician is willing to sacrifice minimalism for political gain. Since, as Cass Sunstein has said, minimalism is not so much a doctrine but an attitude, this should not be surprising.

The most significant departure from minimalism came from Obama's Secretary of Education, Arne Duncan, who announced in March of 2010 that the Department of Education's Office of Civil Rights (OCR) would launch a new effort of civil rights enforcement in America's schools. The OCR, he said, will monitor racial disparities in three areas: enrollment in college prep classes, school discipline, and teacher assignment. The first is the one most likely to draw courts into a fresh round of expansive judicial action and into the very type of policy making that President Obama said that courts are not good at. Russlyn Alli, the director of the OCR, explained just how ambitious the effort would be, telling the Fordham Institute that the OCR would use "all the tools at the Disposal of the Office of Civil Rights" and that would include looking at "feeder patterns [for schools], and early interventions."[37] While the OCR said that it would either seek funding cutoffs or court injunctions for districts it deemed in noncompliance, ultimately court injunctions will be the enforcement mechanism of choice. Funding cutoffs end up harming the very students OCR claims to be helping, so, historically the OCR has used them as a threat and not actually followed through. Thus, Duncan's civil rights initiative will require litigation for enforcement and judges will be determining the effectiveness and appropriateness of these education remedies. In brief, the judiciary will be responsible for establishing and monitoring feeder patterns and early interventions.

The OCR's effort appears worrisomely similar to previous litigation. Anyone familiar with HEW's enforcement of the Title VI of the Civil Rights Act in the 1970s knows that we've been down this road before and it is a very bumpy ride. In the notorious *Adams v. Richardson* litigation, HEW became compelled in the same fashion Duncan has outlined, to take on enrollment disparities in school districts across the country. Stephen Halpern documented the "perverse and insidiously negative" consequences of pursuing these goals through the courts.[38] And Jeremy Rabkin showed how the interests of the students quickly got lost in a "fog of legalisms," to be replaced by the interests of advocacy groups allegedly acting on their behalf.[39] Both authors emphasized the unintended consequences caused by judicial enforcement. In the case of Duncan's announcement, the goal displacement rituals, where educational concerns are trumped by the need to satisfy the DOE, are practically limitless. At the very least, one can easily envision school districts putting unprepared students in AP classes simply to satisfy the Department of Education.[40]

Because of the fanfare surrounding Duncan's announcement (he announced it on the forty-fifth anniversary of "Bloody Sunday" at the Edmund

Pettus Bridge in Selma, Alabama), President Obama was surely aware of the
nature of the OCR's new initiative. Hence, it's reasonable to ask why his
administration is pursuing this policy in this manner. While an obvious reason is that it is something favored by his political base, that does not explain
why he would not use other means. The answer is quite likely that Congress
could easily frustrate the administration if they sought remedies through the
legislative process. Because these investigations and interventions impose
significant burdens on important constituencies of Representatives and
Senators who can block legislative action, pursuing this agenda through the
courts offers the path of least resistance. Hence, one can intellectually understand that courts are ineffective at this kind of policy making, as Obama
does, but feel politically compelled to pursue one's policy goals through them
nonetheless.

The limits of Obama's minimalism are also apparent in his nomination
of Goodwin Liu to the Ninth Circuit. Liu, a professor at the University of
California Berkeley's Boalt Hall School of Law, is far from a judicial minimalist. Rather than circumscribing the judiciary's role, he calls for courts to
recognize "constitutional welfare rights" such as welfare, shelter, subsistence,
and health care, the very kinds of positive or "affirmative rights" that Obama
said that courts were not structured to provide.

Liu claims that the judiciary's role should be limited and "interstitial" but
his own language belies his alleged judicial modesty: "I argue that judicial
recognition of welfare rights is best conceived as an act of interpreting the
shared understandings of particular welfare goods as they are manifested in
our institutions, laws, and evolving social practices."[41] Liu says that these
welfare rights should first develop via "democratic instantiation" through
a "legislative program" rather than the courts.[42] But in calling for courts to
divine our shared understandings, courts essentially become free to decide
what those understandings are, a task one normally thinks is best performed
by elected institutions. Liu anticipates this objection but his response is
not reassuring. Instead of being "didactic and interventionist," he desires
"dialogic and provisional" rulings.[43] Thus, courts, instead of commanding,
should engage in a conversation with elected institutions. Liu's conversation,
though, turns out to be very one-sided. Courts, in being dialogic and provisional, need to "leverage the legislature's own publicly stated commitment to
welfare provision and then inquire whether or not apparent qualifications on
that commitment comprise part of the social understanding of the commitment itself."[44] Translated, this terribly opaque prose means that courts should
tell legislatures that their welfare programs are insufficient and they must do
more, which it will fall to the courts to determine. Courts already have a

lengthy history of this kind of activism through statutory interpretation; calling it dialogic and provisional does nothing to change the problems with it.[45]

While one nomination does not make a trend, it does show that President Obama is not in principle averse to the kind of judicial decision making advocated by Liu. Once again, even its most ardent proponent seems to consider minimalism a disposition rather than a principled creed. Hence, departures from minimalism are not likely to cause significant pangs of conscience for violating its doctrines and such departures are to be expected if minimalism and politics are at odds. In fact, one is not likely to see a significant difference in voting behavior between a liberal minimalist compared to other liberal justices. The Supreme Court's decision in *Horne v. Flores* illustrates this. As usual for a controversial case, the Court split 5–4 with Justice Kennedy joining the conservatives to rule that money should not be the sole factor in determining whether a state was meeting its educational obligations under the Equal Educational Opportunity Act. Goodwin Liu would certainly agree with justices like Ginsburg and Breyer, who Cass Sunstein considers minimalists, but he would prefer the Court do more. In fact, he would like courts to place more emphasis on educational spending and to strike down state school-financing formulas in order to equalize spending. Minimalists on the Left might want to take a more leisurely pace but they are heading in the same direction.

Conclusion

What, then, can we say for certain about President Obama's view of the Court and the Constitution in our constitutional order? I think we can say with confidence that he views both politically. He does not fall for the false dogma that the Court somehow has special access to a world of constitutional meaning that is inaccessible to mere political mortals. The Court behaves politically and thus its interpretations are political. But this also affects his view of the Constitution, which is that it also must be construed politically except when brute reality, such as the meaning of two and six, imposes an interpretation. He, then, has general and flexible attitudes to both the Court and Constitution. Hence, we should expect him to behave like a legal realist and judicial minimalist, but we should not necessarily expect him to be consistent.

The best example of his constitutional flexibility in action can be seen *in The Audacity of Hope*. Early in his chapter on the Constitution, he criticizes President Bush and congressional Republicans for all manner of sins against the Constitution, including their treatment of enemy combatants and interventions to save Terri Schiavo. Their actions, he says, made it seem that "the rules of governing no longer applied, and that there were no fixed meanings or standards to which we could appeal. It was as if those in power had decided that habeas corpus and separation of powers were niceties that only got in the way."[46] A mere few pages later, he asserts that much of the Constitution has no fixed meaning to which we can appeal. Instead, it simply creates the framework for deliberation. Obama's opponents would say that the legal status of enemy combatants under the Constitution or the constitutional contours of executive power are even more open to debate than abortion. Questions about the extent of executive power go back to the drafting of the Constitution; significant debates over its limits erupted during George Washington's administration, while no one imagines that the Constitution had anything to say about abortion until the latter half of the twentieth century. Implying that the nature of presidential power is clear under the Constitution while abortion is not constitutes political special pleading. But for someone such as President Obama who views disputes over constitutional meaning as political all the way down, these charges of inconsistency will not have much force. In fact, for him they miss the point.

Notes

1. President Obama did author a note while on the *Harvard Law Review*, "Tort Law—Prenatal Injuries—Supreme Court of Illinois Refuses to Recognize Cause of Action Brought by Fetus Against Its Mother for Unintentional Affliction of Prenatal Injuries," *Harvard Law Review* 103 (1988): 823. It analyzed an Illinois Supreme Court decision denying a person the right to sue his or her mother for damages sustained as a fetus. The article offered a clear summary of the case and why he believed the "court rightly concluded that, at least in cases arising out of maternal negligence, women's interests in autonomy and privacy outweigh the dubious policy benefits of fetal-maternal tort suits." Instead of fetal tort rights, he argued, that "expanded access to prenatal education and health care facilities will far more likely serve the very real state interest in preventing increasing numbers of children from being born into lives of pain and despair" (828). The article is unexceptional, telling us nothing remarkable about its author, and offers a completely unsurprising defense of the decision.

2. Barack Obama, *The Audacity of Hope: Thoughts on Reclaiming the American Dream* (New York: Crown, 2006).

3. While in law school Obama also provided research assistance for an article written by Laurence Tribe allegedly showing the relevance of both quantum physics and the theory of relativity for constitutional interpretation; see Laurence Tribe, "The Curvature of Constitutional Space: What Lawyers Can Learn from Modern Physics," *Harvard Law Review* 103 (1989): 1. In 2010, Obama's political advisor, David Axelrod, while being interviewed for a sympathetic profile of Obama's deci-

sion making said that Obama had worked with Tribe on the article; see Ann E. Kornblut and Michael A. Fletcher, "In Obama's Decision-Making, A Wide Range of Influences," *Washington Post*, January 25, 2010. This led some to assume that he had done more than provide research assistance. Tribe's article has not aged well, so it is perhaps best that Obama's role was limited.

4. Quoted in Peter Slevin, "Obama Makes Empathy a Requirement for Court," *Washington Post*, May 13, 2009.

5. 558 U.S. ___ (2010).

6. The Court claimed supremacy in *Cooper v. Aaron* 358 U.S. 1 (1958).

7. Larry Kramer, *The People Themselves: Popular Constitutionalism and Judicial Review* (New York: Oxford University Press, 2004).

8. Mark Tushnet, *Taking the Constitution Away from the Courts* (Princeton, NJ: Princeton University Press, 2000).

9. For another spirited attack on the Court from the Left, see James McGregor Burns, *Packing the Court* (New York: Penguin, 2009).

10. "The President's Remarks on Justice Souter," *The White House Blog* www.whitehouse.gov/blog/09/05/01/The-Presidents-Remarks-on-Justice-Souter/ (accessed July 20, 2010). In those remarks, Obama also said that justices from both the left and right like Ginsburg and Scalia will agree in 95 percent of cases but that empathy becomes important in both. This claim of agreement turns out to be untrue but fits a pattern that seems to attempt to find unity where it does not exist.

11. 550 U.S. 618 (2007).

12. Quoted in Peter Baker, "In Court Nominees, Is Obama Looking for Empathy by Another Name?" *New York Times*, April 25, 2010.

13. Roscoe Pound and Karl Llewellyn famously disputed the claims of legal realism, leading many to overestimate the disagreement between realism and Pound's "sociological" jurisprudence. One is tempted to credit their dispute to the narcissism of minor differences.

14. Oliver Wendell Holmes, *The Common Law* (Boston: Brown Little, 1881), 1.

15. Peter Edelman, the former aide to Robert Kennedy, gave a shockingly candid example of legal realism in action. He recalled that when he was clerking for Justice Arthur Goldberg, Goldberg's "first question in approaching a case always was, 'What is the just result?' Then he would work backward from the answer to that question to see how it would comport with relevant theory or precedent." Translated this means that Justice Goldberg did not try to determine the outcome of the case based on the law. He tried to make his desired outcome determine what the law should be. See Tim Wells, "A Conversation with Peter B. Edelman," *Washington Lawyer Magazine* (April 2008), available at www.dcbar.org/for_lawyers/resources/publications/washington_lawyer/april_2008/legends.cfm (accessed May 16, 2010).

16. See Akhil Amar, *America's Constitution: A Biography* (New York: Random House, 2005), and Jack Balkin, "Original Meaning and Constitutional Redemption," *Constitutional Commentary* 24 (2007): 427.

17. See James E. Ryan, "Does It Take A Theory? Originalism, Active Liberty, and Minimalism," *Stanford Law Review* 58 (2006): 1623.

18. Obama, *Audacity*, 108.

19. See Scalia's dissent in *Planned Parenthood v. Casey*, 505 U.S. 833 (1992).

20. See Ely's critique of *Roe v. Wade* in "The Wages of Crying Wolf: A Comment on *Roe v. Wade*," *Yale Law Journal* 82 (1973): 920. Ely, while declaring that he would gladly support legislative legalization of abortion, says, Roe "is, nevertheless, a very bad decision. Not because it will perceptibly weaken the Court—it won't; and not because it conflicts with either my idea of progress or what the evidence suggests is society's—it doesn't. It is bad because it is bad constitutional law, or rather because it is not constitutional law and gives almost no sense of an obligation to try to be" (947).

21. Stephen Breyer, *Active Liberty: Interpreting Our Democratic Constitution* (New York: Vintage, 2006), 63.

22. Ryan, "Does It Take A Theory?" 1645, 1655.

23. "Barack Obama Answers Your Questions about Gay Marriage, Paying For College, More," *MTV*, www.mtv.com/news/articles/1598407/20081101/story.jhtml (accessed July 20, 2010).

24. Richard Posner, *Not a Suicide Pact: The Constitution in a Time of National Emergency* (New York: Oxford University Press, 2006).

25. Cass Sunstein, "The Minimalist Constitution," in *The Constitution in 2020*, ed. Jack M. Balkin and Reva B. Siegel (New York: Oxford University Press, 2009).

26. Quoted in Jess Bravin, "Liberals Sketch Out Dreams and Limits for Supreme Court," *Wall Street Journal*, May 26, 2009, A14.

27. Audio available at WBEZ radio http://audio.wbez.org/Odyssey/Courtand CivilRights.mp3 (accessed July 20, 2010).

28. Ibid.

29. Gerald Rosenberg, *The Hollow Hope: Can Courts Bring About Social Change?*, 2nd ed. (Chicago: University of Chicago Press, 2008).

30. Transcript and audio available at "The Lingering State of Obama's Judicial Nominations," *American Constitution Society*, www.acslaw.org/node/15393 (accessed July 20, 2010).

31. Quoted in "McCain, Obama headed to Washington for Bailout Talks," *CNN*, www.cnn.com/2008/POLITICS/09/24/campaign.wrap/index.html (accessed July 20, 2010).

32. Geoffrey R. Stone, "Obama's Judges," *Huffington Post*, March 2, 2010, www.huffingtonpost.com/geoffrey-r-stone/obamas-judges_b_483042.html (accessed July 20, 2010).

33. Jeffrey Rosen, "The Case Against Sotomayor: Indictments of Obama's Frontrunner to Replace Souter," May 4, 2009, *New Republic online*, www.tnr.com/article/politics/the-case-against-sotomayor (accessed July 20, 2010).

34. See for instance, Glenn Greenwald, "The Case Against Elena Kagan," *Salon*, April 13, 2010, www.salon.com/news/opinion/glenn_greenwald/2010/04/13/kagan/index.html (accessed July 20, 2010).

35. 410 U.S. 113 (1973).

36. 505 U.S. 833 (1992).

37. Mike Petrilli, "Russlyn Alli's "Remedy" Redux," *Flypaper*, March 9, 2010, www.edexcellence.net/flypaper/index.php/2010/03/russlynn-alis-remedy-redux/ (accessed July 20, 2010).

38. Stephen Halpern, *On the Limits of the Law: The Ironic Legacy of Title VI of the 1964 Civil Rights Act* (Baltimore: Johns Hopkins University Press, 1995), x.

39. Jeremy Rabkin, *Judicial Compulsions: How Public Law Distorts Public Policy* (New York: Basic Books, 2009), 148.

40. One indication of the peculiar nature of Duncan's initiative is that the Los Angeles Unified School District was the first target of OCR. The OCR announced that it would investigate the district's services to English language learners. While the Los Angeles school district is notorious for its educational problems, being insufficiently concerned about racial minorities would not be one of them. See Howard Blume, "Department of Education Targets L.A. Unified for Investigation," *Los Angeles Times*, March 9, 2010.

41. Goodwin Liu, "Rethinking Constitutional Welfare Rights," *Stanford Law Review* 61, no. 2 (2008): 203–4.

42. Ibid.

43. Ibid., 255.

44. Ibid., 264.

45. See Shep Melnick, *Between the Lines: Interpreting Welfare Rights* (Washington, DC: Brookings Institution Press, 1994), for an extensive critique of judicial policy making through statutory interpretation.

46. Obama, *Audacity*, 93.

CHAPTER SIX

~

President Obama, the Intelligence Community, and the War on Terror

"Change We Can Believe In"?

Stephen F. Knott

Barack Obama pledged in his presidential campaign to restore transparency and accountability to the executive branch, and frequently criticized the Bush administration for stretching, if not breaking, the constitutional safeguards on presidential power. Candidate Obama believed that President Bush, assisted by Vice President Cheney, betrayed the spirit of the founding fathers by conducting the war on terror in a manner at odds with American principles and practices. The new president noted in his inaugural address that "we reject as false the choice between our safety and our ideals. Our founding fathers, faced with perils that we can scarcely imagine, drafted a charter to assure the rule of law and the rights of man, a charter expanded by the blood of generations. Those ideals still light the world, and we will not give them up for expedience's sake."[1] Two days after his inauguration, the president signed an executive order directing the Central Intelligence Agency (CIA) to close its worldwide network of secret prisons and ordering that the terrorist detention facility at Guantanamo be closed no later than January, 2010.[2]

Additionally, the practice of waterboarding and other forms of torture led some members of Obama's coalition to call for criminal prosecutions against former Bush administration officials. The President continues to be dogged by questions surrounding the release of torture photographs and whether the Bush administration may have misled the intelligence committees in Congress.

These controversies led to the drafting of legislation designed to strengthen congressional oversight of the intelligence community. President Obama has expressed his displeasure with elements of this legislation, and has disappointed many of his core supporters by continuing various Bush administration security practices. This chapter will examine these issues and will do so by placing the Obama presidency in a broader historical and constitutional context.

As mentioned, candidate Obama was critical of the Bush administration's use of torture as part of its "enhanced interrogation" techniques, and appeared to promise an end to the more controversial aspects of the war on terror. In light of this, his selection of Leon Panetta as Director of the CIA (DCI), while somewhat surprising, signaled that change was coming to the agency. Panetta had written an essay in the *Washington Monthly* in 2008 arguing that "those who support torture may believe that we can abuse captives in certain select circumstances and still be true to our values, but that is a false compromise." He added, "We cannot and we must not use torture under any circumstances. We are better than that."[3] Nonetheless, Panetta was hardly a card-carrying member of MoveOn.org, and as a former White House Chief of Staff and Director of the Office of Management and Budget, he had developed a good working familiarity with the nation's intelligence community. Panetta was not President Obama's first choice for DCI; that honor belonged to John Brennan, who now serves as Assistant to the President and Deputy National Security Adviser for Homeland Security and Counterterrorism. Brennan withdrew his name from consideration after reports surfaced during the transition period that he was associated with some of the more controversial aspects of President Bush's war on terror, including rendition and waterboarding.[4] Complicating Leon Panetta's standing was the post-9/11 reform that created the new Office of Director of National Intelligence (DNI), a position initially held by former Navy Admiral Dennis Blair. Congress, in a move ultimately endorsed by President Bush, adopted the recommendations of the 9/11 Commission and decided to add another layer of intelligence bureaucracy on top of an already sclerotic and antiquated system. The Director of National Intelligence, it was hoped by its proponents, would end the problem of "stove piping" that had contributed to the 9/11 disaster. Unfortunately, while this reform has somewhat affected the status of the CIA, the legislation exempted the largest member of the American intelligence community, the Department of Defense, contributing to continuing problems in the coordination of American intelligence.

It was only a matter of months before Leon Panetta and Dennis Blair were at odds, and, according to some, deeply at odds, over who was ultimately in charge of the nation's intelligence community. The 9/11 commission proposed such a role for the DNI, but ultimately Panetta's Washington savvy carried the day, as the CIA was allowed to have a "direct line to the White House on covert operations" and its station chiefs continued to be the dominant intelligence officials in American outposts abroad.[5] The DNI, however, retained his veto power over the content of the President's Daily Brief, which is written primarily by CIA analysts, and the actual briefing responsibilities are now shared between CIA and other intelligence agencies under the DNI.[6] In the end, Blair lost his bureaucratic battle with Panetta, and he announced his resignation on May 20, 2010. Blair was the fourth DNI in six years; his short tenure was yet another indicator of the difficulties associated with implementing the recommendations of the 9/11 commission.[7]

The most controversial event of Panetta's tenure as DCI occurred on April 16, 2009, when President Obama ordered the release of secret memos detailing the use of torture as part of the CIA's interrogation practices during the Bush years. (For the sake of simplicity, and out of a belief in accuracy in language, the word "torture" will be used to characterize techniques such as waterboarding and sleep deprivation, or forcing Gitmo prisoners to listen to "Metallica," the latter of which strikes me as the contemporary equivalent of the medieval rack. I believe it is important to follow George Orwell's advice that precision in language is a critical element of political writing. In light of this, I have also chosen to retain the term "war on terror," despite the Obama administration's reluctance to use the term "war" and their preference for the term "violent extremism" over "terrorism.") Rebuffing Panetta's argument, and those of four of his predecessors, that releasing the memos would set a dangerous precedent regarding exposure of the agency's sources and methods, the president ordered their release and sharply criticized what he described as a "dark and painful chapter in our history."[8] After first suggesting that he might be open to some sort of independent inquiry, or "truth commission," to investigate possible Bush-era abuses, the president decided not to pursue such an option, despite strong support from Speaker Nancy Pelosi and Senate Judiciary Chairman Patrick Leahy. Apparently, officials in the Justice Department hoped that the release of the torture memos would lead the public to demand an independent inquiry. According to one source, the leadership at Justice believed that "if the public knew the details . . . there would be a groundswell of support for an independent probe." The source said these same officials "celebrated quietly [the decision to release the memos], and waited for the national outrage to begin."[9] Ultimately, the president stated that he would rather look forward than backward, and that the concept of such a commission "didn't seem altogether workable in this case."[10]

While the president decided against such a commission, his Justice Department has been somewhat aggressive in pursuing allegations of CIA abuses, although not aggressive enough for many of the president's supporters on the Left. An ongoing investigation involving the destruction of CIA videotapes depicting instances of torture appears to be coming to a head, with a focus on possible perjury charges against agency officials. In August 2009, Attorney General Holder ordered the federal prosecutor in the case, John Durham, to expand his inquiry to examine possible abuse of prisoners by CIA employees and contractors involved in interrogating terrorism suspects. Holder's decision to broaden the prosecutor's inquiry came despite the fact that two teams of Bush administration prosecutors had decided against such a probe, and that seven former CIA directors objected to the investigation. The federal prosecutor is approaching the end of his investigation, according to sources at the Justice Department, while at the same time the Senate Intelligence Committee is looking at the Bush administration's practice of rendition along with the use of torture in interrogations. As former CIA Director Michael Hayden has observed, "the agency is pretty much at capacity in responding to current inquiries," and this detracts from the agency's ability to "tak[e] the fight to the nation's enemies and tak[e] those enemies off the global battlefield." He added on another occasion, "intelligence officers need to know that someone has their back."[11]

There is no question that Attorney General Eric Holder sees terrorism as a law enforcement and judicial problem, a position that puts him distinctly at odds with the Bush administration, and, I would argue, at odds with traditional American practice. Barack Obama seemed to share this view, claiming in 2007 that "I was a constitutional law professor, which means unlike the current president [Bush] I actually respect the Constitution."[12] Both Holder and Obama are lawyers, and as such they embrace to varying degrees a new conception about war and national security that prevails in our increasingly legalistic society; a society where an almost religious devotion to international law and processes and procedures predominates among the elites. In some quarters, adherence to international law has superseded the national interest as the standard by which to measure American conduct. This was certainly true of Dawn Johnsen, whom the president nominated to be head of the Justice Department's Office of Legal Counsel. Johnsen had made a name for herself as a strident critic of the Bush OLC's "torture memos," whose legal arguments she found to be "outlandish" and "shockingly flawed."[13] Candidate Obama, a former University of Chicago law professor, was also in sync with the predominant opinion in the American legal community in believing that the courts, not the executive branch, are best equipped to determine the appropriate parameters of presidential emergency measures.

There is some evidence, however, that Obama has altered his position since becoming president.

The idea that the courts are the ultimate arbiter of what constitutes an emergency and in determining the limits of the nation's response is embraced by a majority of the Supreme Court, as they demonstrated in three cases growing out of President Bush's war on terror: *Rasul v. Bush* (2004), *Hamdan v. Rumsfeld* (2006), and *Boumediene v. Bush* (2008). In all of these cases, the Supreme Court awarded itself a role that throughout much of its history it had left to the elected branches of government. *Rasul*, as Jeffrey Toobin has observed, marked "the first time that a President ever lost a major civil liberties case in the Supreme Court during wartime." Writing for a six to three majority, Justice John Paul Stevens argues that "what is presently at stake is only whether the federal courts have jurisdiction to determine the legality of the Executive's potentially indefinite detention of individuals who claim to be wholly innocent of wrongdoing" and opened the door to detainees to challenging their imprisonment in the federal courts.[14] In *Hamdan*, Stevens wrote the opinion for a five to three majority that rejected President Bush's plan for military tribunals, plans that attempted to address the court's concerns in *Rasul*. Stevens objected to the administration's proposal partly on the grounds that the proposed military tribunals would violate the Geneva conventions. In his concurring opinion, Justice Stephen Breyer observed:

> Congress has denied the President the legislative authority to create military commissions of the kind at issue here. Nothing prevents the President from returning to Congress to seek the authority he believes necessary. Where, as here, no emergency prevents consultation with Congress, judicial insistence upon that consultation does not weaken our Nation's ability to deal with danger. To the contrary, that insistence strengthens the Nation's ability to determine—through democratic means—how best to do so. The Constitution places its faith in those democratic means. Our Court today simply does the same.[15]

Heeding Justice Breyer's reassuring words, Congress then attempted to address the Court's concerns as expressed in *Hamdan*, only to see this system overturned in *Boumediene v. Bush* (2008) by a 5-4 majority. Justice Stevens assigned the majority opinion to Anthony Kennedy, who wrote that the Constitution's guarantee of the right of habeas corpus applies to enemy combatants held on U.S. territory.[16] This was judicial activism at its worst: the court's "political questions doctrine," the idea of deferring to the elected branches of government on matters falling under their constitutional purview, is, for all practical purposes, dead. Simply put, according to the Constitution and to almost 220 years of tradition, Congress and the president are constitutionally empowered, among other things, to set the rules regarding the treatment of enemy combatants and the measures deemed necessary to gather intelligence and conduct a war.

Two recent cases reveal the extent to which the lower courts have followed the lead of the Supreme Court in assuming an activist stance on intelligence and national security matters. On March 30, 2010, U.S. District Judge Royce Lamberth asked Attorney General Eric Holder to inform him whether a case involving a $3 million settlement over alleged CIA misconduct involving a former agent for the Drug Enforcement Administration will be referred to internal inspectors for further investigation. Judge Lamberth and his peers no longer abide by the principles laid down by the Supreme Court in the case of *Totten v. United States* (1875), where the Supreme Court stated that matters of this nature were the prerogative of the executive branch, and that the courts were no place to resolve disputes of this kind.[17] The next day, on March 31, 2010, U.S. District Judge Vaughn R. Walker ruled that a Bush-era National Security Agency surveillance program was illegal, and that the government was liable to pay damages to a suspected Islamic charity based in Oregon, and to the organization's lawyers. The Judge rejected both the Bush and Obama administrations' claims that the lawsuit should be dismissed because allowing it to proceed would expose state secrets. The Judge claimed that the state secrets argument constituted "unfettered executive-branch discretion" that had "obvious potential for government abuse and overreaching." As the Islamic charity's lawyer noted approvingly, "The President, just like any other citizen of the United States, is bound by law. Obeying congressional legislation shouldn't be optional with the President of the United States." Instead of vigorously defending presidential prerogatives, the Obama Justice Department responded sheepishly to the judge's decision by noting that the administration had tightened its requirements for invoking the state-secret privilege, and that the privilege would be invoked only in extreme circumstances.[18]

This is no surprise, for this Justice Department sees all of these issues through the lens of the law professoriate. Politically, this approach has been a disaster. This became apparent with the administration's decision in November, 2009, to try 9/11 mastermind Khalid Sheikh Mohammed (KSM), and four other conspirators, in the civilian court system. The Justice Department made this decision despite the fact that a military tribunal was ready to try KSM and that the latter was prepared to plead guilty. Essentially the military tribunal would have consisted of a sentencing phase.[19] The initial Justice Department decision produced an outcry, but it was not until the arrest of Umar Farouk Abdulmutallab, the Christmas Day "Undie Bomber," that the outcry reached a crescendo. When it was revealed that Abdulmutallab had been read his rights after fifty minutes of interrogation, and that he exercised his right to remain silent after being Mirandized, administration critics pounced on the decision as an example of the president abandoning the war on terror and transforming it into just another legal matter. Former CIA Director Michael Hayden led the charge, claiming that "we got it wrong in Detroit on Christmas Day. We allowed an enemy combatant the protections of our Constitution before we had adequately interrogated him."[20] (The treatment of the Undie Bomber even became a factor in Scott Brown's upset win in the special Senate election in Massachusetts.) Under increasing pressure, the administration appears likely to back off its decision to try KSM in downtown Manhattan, just a few blocks from Ground Zero, although Eric Holder continues to defend the decision and recently stated that a trial in New York "is not off the table." As rumors began to circulate that his hold on the Attorney General's office may be slipping, Holder rejected the allegation that the Obama administration refused to acknowledge that the United States is at war. "We are at war, and we will use every instrument of national power—civilian, military, law enforcement, intelligence, diplomatic and others—to win. . . . We need not cower in the face of this enemy."[21]

The attempted May Day 2010 car bombing in Times Square brought all these issues to the fore once again. Thanks to the ineptness of the bomber, many lives were likely saved. The suspect, Faisal Shahzad, a Pakistani-born American citizen, was captured at Kennedy Airport and "Mirandized" by federal agents three to four hours after his arrest. By treating the Shahzad case as a criminal issue, the administration was again criticized for not treating Shahzad as an unlawful enemy combatant. In the wake of Shahzad's arrest, Attorney General Holder's commitment to dealing with terrorism as a criminal matter was brought into bold relief when he proposed an emergency exception to the 1966 Miranda decision. The emergency exception would allow investigators greater leeway to interrogate terror suspects before reading them their rights.[22] The debate over Holder's motives took a particularly ugly turn when former Vice President Cheney's daughter, Liz, and her organization *Keep America Safe* claimed that "the American people have a right to know whether lawyers who used to represent and advocate on behalf of terrorists" were now working for the Department of Justice.[23] Critics were not mollified when it was revealed that Neal Katyal, who represented Osama bin Laden's driver, Salim Hamdan, is now the Deputy Solicitor General, and Tony West, who defended John Walker Lindh, the American who joined Al Qaeda, is an Assistant Attorney General. However, most of the legal profession, including prominent conservatives such as Ted Olsen and Kenneth Starr, rallied to the side of these attorneys engaged in the time-honored tradition of pro bono work.[24]

It is increasingly apparent that there are deep divisions within Obama's administration over the best approach to conduct the war on terror, particularly regarding the status of detainees. This is especially true in the State Department, where former Yale Law School Dean Harold Koh, who was a harsh critic of Bush administration policies, now serves as the State Department's Legal Advisor. In 2004, Koh wrote that the United States' disregard for international law had placed it in "the axis of disobedience" along with North Korea and Saddam Hussein's Iraq.[25] Koh recently told the American Bar Association that the United States is now complying with domestic and international law recognizing "common and universal standards, not double standards. We are not saying we don't have to fight battles, we're just saying that we should fight those battles within the framework of law."[26] Koh has been at odds with the Department of Defense's top attorney, Jeh Johnson, who claims that the president has the discretionary authority to determine who can be detained and has argued against a strict interpretation of the laws of war.

For some critics on the Left, Obama's policies represent a continuation of the Bush policies, and they claim that whatever changes have occurred are merely "cosmetic." President Obama, to the extent that he has weighed into this ongoing debate, has reportedly stated that he does not want to embrace the kind of unrestrained view of presidential power that prevailed during the Bush years. This is not an esoteric legal debate; as the *New York Times* recently observed, the ultimate outcome of this debate "could reverberate through national security policies, ranging from the number of people the United States ultimately detains to decisions about who may be lawfully selected for killing using drones."[27] This view strikes me at once as both accurate and deeply disturbing, for it represents a remarkable ceding of presidential authority to executive branch lawyers and to their brethren in the judiciary who are playing a role they were never intended to play. Nonetheless, I believe many of President Obama's conservative critics, most prominently former Vice President Cheney, overstate their critique of Obama's national security policies, including some of his intelligence and counterterrorism policies. I do not believe this man is the second coming of Jimmy Carter; Eric Holder is perhaps, but as for Barack Obama, I am not convinced. For instance, the Obama administration placed an American citizen, Anwar al-Awlaki, a radical Islamic cleric, on its targeted killing list. This never happened during the Bush years, and represents a rejection of the views of those who approach the war in a legalistic fashion. Al-Awlaki has been linked to the terrorist act at Fort Hood that killed thirteen U.S. soldiers and to the Christmas Day Undie Bomber.[28] This action should be hailed by those who favor a robust execution of the war on terror. Unfortunately, the targeting of al-Awlaki raised concerns in some conservative blogs, who saw it as evidence of Obama's disregard for the Constitution, and in traditional legal and media circles as well, who see the war on terror as a criminal matter to be dealt with by traditional legal methods.[29] The absence of any "judicial review" of such a "kill" decision was upsetting to these observers. This sentiment can be seen in the comments of a former CIA lawyer, Vicki Divoll, who remarked that "Congress has protected al-Awlaki's cell phone calls, but it has not provided any protections for his life. That makes no sense." Congressman John Tierney of Massachusetts echoed Divoll's concerns, noting that the targeting of al-Awlaki "certainly raises the question of what rights a citizen has and what steps must be taken before he's put on the [kill] list."[30]

Evidence of Obama's pragmatic and robust approach can also be seen in his Afghan surge, his escalation of the Predator War in Pakistan, his refusal to release the torture photographs, his renewal of provisions of the Patriot Act that are the bane of the American Civil Liberties Union, and his appointment of solid mainstream realists (and Republicans) including Robert Gates, former marine General James Jones, and even Hillary Clinton and Leon Panetta. Panetta has presided over an escalation of the war on terror that has left what remains of Al Qaeda's leadership cowering in caves under Predator-filled skies in Pakistan. This escalation of the war on terror has led some conservatives, oddly enough, to criticize the president for being too aggressive in his pursuit of Al Qaeda and their Taliban allies. Marc Thiessen, a former Bush speechwriter, and Viet Dinh, a Georgetown University professor and one of the original authors of the Patriot Act, have both argued that the administration is killing too many Al Qaeda members and depriving the United States of valuable intelligence. They claim that the administration is pursuing an "execution" policy to avoid the touchy issue of what to do with detainees.[31]

President Obama has stayed true to his campaign pledge to draw down American forces in Iraq and transfer those resources to Afghanistan, and the CIA has been at the forefront of this intensified campaign against the Taliban and Al Qaeda. The agency controls the use of drone aircraft over Pakistan, and since President Obama took office fifty-five strikes have occurred (as of March 21, 2010) compared to only forty-five during the entire Bush era. Obama had only been in office for three days when he ordered his first drone strike.[32] Leon Panetta approves all of the drone strikes, and the devices are actually controlled from the agency's headquarters in Langley. Approximately 666 terrorists have been killed in these strikes in Pakistan during Obama's first fourteen months in office, compared to 230 in the Bush years. The biggest setback of the CIA's covert war in Pakistan, and one that has somewhat tarnished Panetta's reputation, involved the death of seven agency officers at a forward operating base in Khost, Afghanistan, on December 30, 2009. "We're in a war," Panetta was quoted as saying to his senior staff, and "we cannot afford to be hesitant. . . . The fact is we're doing the right thing. My approach is going to be to work that much harder . . . that we beat these sons of bitches."[33] Nonetheless, many former CIA operatives are critical of the agency's management for allowing an intelligence analyst to function as a covert operative and base chief in Khost.[34] This may be reflective of the fact that the operational side of the agency's house was depleted in the 1990s and has yet to recover.

Despite my admiration for the president's escalation of the war in Afghanistan and Pakistan, on a more fundamental level, I am concerned that his administration, and, more importantly, his allies in Congress, will take the nation's intelligence community in the wrong direction. While the pre-Church Committee CIA was noted for its "cowboy" swagger, the new CIA is excessively "lawyered up," although the Bush–Cheney administration tried desperately to change this ethos, particularly after it accepted George Tenet's resignation and replaced him with Porter Goss in 2004. Goss's efforts alienated many at the agency, who used their access to the media and Capitol Hill to undermine his tenure as DCI. Congressional micromanaging is primarily responsible for this new legalistic CIA, having transformed it from an agency willing to take risks, and act at times in a Machiavelllian manner, into just another sclerotic Washington bureaucracy. As mentioned, this risk-averse attitude was partially lifted during the Bush administration, but Congress is only willing to go so far, and only in times when the nation is, to be blunt, scared. Memories are short, and American memory is especially short. The CIA's cautious, legalistic attitude will not change unless the oversight committees of Congress acknowledge the uniquely executive character of intelligence and covert operations, and start to dismantle the cumbersome oversight apparatus erected during the past thirty-five years. In all honesty, the likelihood of this happening is on par with the likelihood that Paris Hilton will win the Nobel Prize in Physics.

In fact, the trend is in the opposite direction, with both the House and Senate Intelligence Committees seeking to enlarge their oversight responsibilities by tightening presidential notification requirements. Committee Democrats are once again trying to expand the number of members of Congress who would have to be notified about covert operations. House Democrats also attempted to include provisions that would have criminalized interrogation procedures that were deemed "cruel, inhuman, and degrading treatment."[35] To his credit, President Obama opposed many of the provisions of the impending intelligence authorization bill, which would allow the House and Senate Intelligence Committees a greater role in overseeing, and arguably, vetoing, some of the nation's most sensitive covert operations. In a chilling expansion of congressional power to micromanage the intelligence community, the administration ultimately agreed to a provision that allows the so-called Gang of Eight (the Speaker of the House, the House Minority Leader, the Senate majority and minority leaders, and the chair and ranking member of the House and Senate Intelligence Committees) to appeal the approval of an operation to the Director of National Intelligence. Also, the full intelligence committees of both Houses would be notified anytime there was a Gang of Eight notification, and the president would then be required to provide the committee members with "general information" about the proposed operation and provide updates on the need for continuing to limit access to details of an operation. The proposed legislation would require the president to record the date of a Gang of Eight briefing, so as to avoid a repeat of the Nancy Pelosi situation, where the latter denied that she had been briefed in 2002 regarding the use of torture. The authorization bill would also create an intelligence community-wide office of Inspector General, and perhaps water down the ability of the president to control the release of classified information by "whistleblowers." Additionally, the legislation would expand the authority of the Government Accountability Office to review intelligence community matters, which could dramatically expand Congress's micromanagement propensities.[36]

The current debate over these issues would be enhanced by an understanding that expansive notions of presidential power, particularly in the national security arena, are as old as the American Constitution. Our founding document vests the president with "the executive power," a power fraught with national security significance; establishes him as the Commander in Chief; gives him the authority to "take care" that the laws are faithfully executed; and, unique among the three branches, requires him to take an oath to "preserve, protect, and defend" the Constitution. In light of these powers, the authors of The Federalist Papers argued for an "energetic executive" characterized by "decision, activity, secrecy, and dispatch."[37] This view of presidential power was widely shared by our key founders; for instance, Thomas Jefferson's conception of executive power would have inflamed the editorial writers at the New York Times: "On great occasions every good officer must be ready to risk himself in going beyond the strict line of the law," and he added that there were "extreme cases where the laws become inadequate to their own preservation, and where the universal recourse is a dictator, or martial law."[38] Lincoln suspended habeas corpus and deprived hundreds of thousands of Americans who fought for the Confederacy of due process, and deported a former member of Congress from Ohio who objected to his policies. Teddy Roosevelt derided the view that the president could not act "unless he could find some specific authorization for it. My belief was that it was not only his right but his duty to do anything that the needs of the nation demanded. . . . I did not usurp power, but I did greatly broaden the use of executive power."[39] Franklin Roosevelt created military tribunals for Nazi saboteurs, who were tried and executed in rapid fashion. Captured during the second week of June, 1942, six of them died in the electric chair by August 8, including one who was an American citizen, while the latter's parents were convicted of treason for not turning their son into the authorities and ultimately deported to Germany. At the same time the territory of Hawaii was subjected to a form of martial law not seen since the Civil War. As historian Greg Robinson has noted:

> Army courts were part of the military government that took power in the then Territory of Hawaii following the Japanese attack on Pearl Harbor in December 1941. Commanding General Walter Short (who browbeat the civilian governor into approving unlimited martial law) declared himself military governor, dissolved the elected legislature and suspended the U.S. Constitution. The military regime proceeded over the following weeks to issue decrees regulating all aspects of civilian life. Meanwhile, the army closed down all civilian courts. When the courts reopened one week after Pearl Harbor, they were restricted to considering civil cases; a network of military commissions and provost courts was established to try all criminal cases. . . . Juries were forbidden and lawyers discouraged or even barred. . . . Of the 22,480 trials conducted in provost court in Honolulu in 1942–1943, 99 percent ended in convictions. . . . Judges frequently issued severe sentences, including imprisonment and hard labor, for trivial offenses, and no machinery existed for appeals.[40]

The Supreme Court, as was their traditional practice, waited until after the conflict concluded, overturning the practices of Hawaii's military government in 1946.[41] Since the founding of the nation, the courts and Congress had deferred to the executive branch on these issues, abiding by the Constitution and historical tradition. This tradition began to erode in the 1960s and 1970s, as the Courts expanded their role in the national security arena, frequently allying themselves with Congress to check the executive branch. These trends reached fruition for the Courts in the aforementioned detainee cases from the Bush presidency, while an incomplete but persistent congressional attempt by both Republicans and Democrats to wrest control of the nation's intelligence community continues apace.

President Obama genuinely believes that America's standing in the world was damaged during the Bush years, and there is ample evidence to support his belief. America's enemies could not have been given a greater gift than the series of images that emerged from Abu Ghraib, and fair or not, those images are forever linked with President Bush's treatment of detainees and in a sense to the larger war on terror. On top of this, America's friends believed their views were ignored, and that our nation was no longer committed to the rule of law and to international organizations such as the United Nations. This is Obama's and Holder's view as well, and it is a principled view, albeit in the latter's case, an excessively rigid view.[42]

Barack Obama strikes me as enough of a realist to see the world as it is, but not so when it comes to the war on terror. His refusal to acknowledge that this is a war, and secondly, a war against radical Islam, affects the execution of that war. Words matter, and how you view a challenge, how you define it, affects how you deal with that challenge. Unfortunately, the Obama administration seems to believe that softer semantics will help defuse the conflict between the United States and radical Islamists.[43] Perhaps it is no surprise then that the president seems unwilling to vigorously defend executive prerogatives in the realm of national security and emergency powers. This renders him politically vulnerable, and should, God forbid, another 9/11 occur the president would be remarkably exposed, in part due to the attacks of former Vice President Cheney and others who have criticized him from the start. But some of the blame would rightly belong to the president to the extent that he philosophically supports a legalistic and deferential approach to the war on terror. To paraphrase Alexander Hamilton: ambivalence in the executive is a leading character in the definition of dysfunctional government. Perhaps this is unfair, but Americans celebrate those presidents who push the boundaries of their office, especially in the national security realm. This is not an "imperial presidency" but an activist presidency that energetically executes its prerogatives and adheres to the practices of its predecessors in a manner that is constitutionally sound and frequently more coherent and effective.

One wishes that, as only Nixon could go to China, Obama would transform his party to accept the importance of an energetic executive who operates with secrecy and dispatch, and reject the encroachments of an imperial judiciary. Unfortunately for his country and his party, this is unlikely to happen. Wielding executive power, never a vocation for the pure and faint-hearted, is preferable to government by judicial fiat. Short of this we might as well sandblast Mount Rushmore and replace Abraham Lincoln and his friends with Justice John Paul Stevens and his colleagues.

Notes

1. "Transcript, Barack Obama's Inaugural Address," *New York Times*, January 20, 2009, www.nytimes.com/2009/01/20/us/politics/20text-obama.html (accessed June 29, 2010).

2. Mark Mazzetti and William Glaberson, "Obama Issues Directive to Shut Down Guantánamo," *New York Times*, January 21, 2009, www.nytimes.com/2009/01/22/us/politics/22gitmo.html?_r=1&scp=1&sq=Obama%20Issues%20Directive%20to%20Shut%20Down%20Guantanamo,%94%20The%20New%20York%20Times,%20January%2022,%202009&st=cse (accessed June 29, 2010).

3. Mark Mazzetti and Carl Hulse, "Panetta Is Chosen as C.I.A. Chief, in a Surprise Step," *New York Times*, January 5, 2009, www.nytimes.com/2009/01/06/us/politics/06cia.html (accessed June 29, 2010).

4. Jake Tapper, "Did Brennan Withdraw His Name from Consideration for CIA Post Before Obama Could Withdraw It For Him?" *ABC News*, Political Punch Blog, November 26, 2008, http://blogs.abcnews.com/politicalpunch/2008/11/did-brennan-wit.html (accessed June 29, 2010).

5. Bobby Ghosh, "CIA Chief Panetta Winning over Doubters at the Agency," *Time*, November 24, 2009, www.time.com/time/nation/article/0,8599,1942514,00.html (accessed June 29, 2010).

6. CIA Officer, in discussion with the author, March 17, 2010. The size of the DNI bureaucracy is approximately 1,500 employees.

7. "Dennis Blair's Replacement has Problems to Solve," *Washington Post*, May 22, 2010, www.washingtonpost.com/wp-dyn/content/article/2010/05/21/AR2010052104488.html (accessed June 2010).

8. Nicholas Lemann, "Terrorism Studies: Social Scientists Do Counter-insurgency," *New Yorker*, April 26, 2010, www.newyorker.com/arts/critics/books/2010/04/26/100426crbo_books_lemann?currentPage=all (accessed June 29, 2010); Mark Mazzetti and Scott Shane, "Interrogation Memos Detail Harsh Tactics by the C.I.A.," *New York Times*, April 17, 2009, www.nytimes.com/2009/04/17/us/politics/17detain.html (accessed June 29, 2010). The four former DCIs who opposed the release of the memos were George Tenet, John Deutch, Porter Goss, and Michael Hayden. See "Ex-CIA Chiefs Slowed 'Torture Memos' Release," *Associated Press*, April 17, 2009, www.msnbc.msn.com/id/30270759/ (accessed June 29, 2010).

9. Michael Hayden, "Time for CIA to Move Ahead, Not Back," *Washington Times*, August 20, 2009, www.washingtontimes.com/news/2009/aug/20/hayden-time-for-cia-to-move-ahead-not-back/?feat=home_columns (accessed June 29, 2010).

10. Shailagh Murray, "A Commission on Enhanced Interrogation? Obama Rebuffs Idea," *Washington Post*, April 23, 2009, http://voices.washingtonpost.com/44/2009/04/23/a_commission_on_enhanced_inter.html (June 29, 2010).

11. Carrie Johnson and Julie Tate, "CIA Videotape Investigation Appears to be Nearing a Close," *Washington Post*, March 24, 2010, www.washingtonpost.com/wp-dyn/content/article/2010/03/24/AR2010032402041.html (accessed June 29, 2010); Hayden, "Time;" Michael V. Hayden, "Obama Administration Takes Several Wrong Paths in Dealing with Terrorism," *Washington Post*, January 31, 2010, www.washing-tonpost.com/wp-dyn/content/article/2010/01/29/AR2010012903954.html (accessed June 29, 2010).

12. Ben Smith and Lisa Lerer, "44 to Reverse 43's Executive Orders," *Politico*, January 13, 2009, www.politico.com/news/stories/0109/17365.html (accessed June 29, 2010).

13. Jake Tapper, "Dawn Johnsen Withdraws her Nomination," *ABC News*, Political Punch Blog, April 9, 2010, http://blogs.abcnews.com/politicalpunch/2010/04/dawn-johnsen-withdraws-her-nomination.html (accessed June 29, 2010). Johnsen withdrew in the face of heated Republican opposition in the Senate, which delayed her confirmation for months. This delay was due in part to what Johnsen had written during the Bush years, including the following: "I'm afraid we are growing immune to just how outrageous and destructive it is, in a democracy, for the President to violate federal statutes in secret. . . . Incredibly, we still don't know the full extent of our government's illegal surveillance or illegal interrogations (and who knows what else)—despite Congress's failed efforts to get to the bottom of it." Johnsen later compared the Bush torture memos and the nation's reaction to them by drawing comparisons with the genocide in Rwanda. "The same question, of what we are to do in the face of national dishonor, also occurred to me a few weeks ago, as I listened to President Bush describe his visit to a Rwandan memorial to the 1994 genocide there. . . . President Bush spoke there . . . of the power of the reminder the memorial provides and the need to protect against recurrences there, or elsewhere. That brought to mind that whenever any government or people act lawlessly, on whatever scale, questions of atonement and remedy and prevention must be confronted. And fundamental to any meaningful answer is transparency about the wrong committed. . . . We must resist Bush administration efforts to hide evidence of its wrongdoing through demands for retroactive immunity, assertions of state privilege, and implausible claims that openness will empower terrorists. . . . Here is a partial answer to my own question of how should we behave, directed especially to the next president and members of his or her administration but also to all of us who will be relieved by the change: We must avoid any temptation simply to move on. We must instead be honest with ourselves and the world as we condemn our nation's past transgressions and reject Bush's corruption of our American ideals." Quoted in Glenn Greenwald, "Obama's Impressive New OLC Chief," *Salon*, January 5, 2009, www.salon.com/news/opinion/glenn_greenwald/2009/01/05/olc (accessed June 29, 2010).

14. Jeffrey Toobin, "After Stevens: What Will the Supreme Court Be Like Without Its Liberal Leader?" *New Yorker* 86, no. 5 (March 2010): 45–46, www.newyorker.com/reporting/2010/03/22/100322fa_fact_toobin (accessed June 29, 2010); *Rasul v. Bush*, 542 U.S. 466 (2004).

15. *Hamdan v. Rumsfeld*, 548 U.S. 557 (2006).

16. *Hamdan v. Rumsfeld*, 548 U.S. 557 (2006); Toobin, "After Stevens;" *Boumediene v. Bush*, 553 U.S. 723 (2008).

17. *Totten v. United States*, 92 U.S. 105 (1875); see also Stephen F. Knott, *Secret and Sanctioned: Covert Operations and the American Presidency* (New York: Oxford University Press, 1996), 148–49.

18. Charlie Savage and James Risen, "Federal Judge Finds N.S.A. Wiretaps Were Illegal," *New York Times*, March 31, 2010, www.nytimes.com/2010/04/01/us/01nsa. html (accessed June 29, 2010).

19. "Top 9/11 Suspects to Plead Guilty," *BBC News*, December 8, 2008, http:// news.bbc.co.uk/2/hi/7770856.stm (accessed June 29, 2010).

20. Hayden, "Obama Administration." The Director of National Intelligence, Dennis Blair, also criticized the handling of the Abdulmutallab case.

21. Charlie Savage, "Holder Won't Rule Out N.Y. 9/11 Trial," *New York Times*, April 15, 2010, www.nytimes.com/2010/04/15/us/politics/15holder.html (accessed June 29, 2010); "Holder Defends Decision to Try Accused 9/11 Terrorists in New York," *CNN Politics*, November 18, 2009, www.cnn.com/2009/POLITICS/11/18/ holder.new.york.trial/index.html (accessed June 29, 2010). The *New York Times* has been a leading proponent of the notion that the 9/11 terror suspects should be tried in the federal courts, although they note that trying "Mr. Mohammed [KSM] in a military court is at least explainable by the attack on the Pentagon." This is a rather cramped understanding of the nature of conflict; taken to its logical conclusion it seems to insist that only in cases of attacks on U.S. military installations does the military have a role to play in the war on terror, or in any nonstate on state conflict. See "The KSM Files," *New York Times*, April 15, 2010, www.nytimes. com/2010/04/15/opinion/15thu1.html (accessed June 29, 2010).

22. Charlie Savage, "Holder Backs a Miranda Limit for Terror Suspects," *New York Times*, May 9, 2010, www.nytimes.com/2010/05/10/us/politics/10holder.html (accessed June 29, 2010).

23. Quoted in Jonathon Chait, "Lawyer Up, Liz Cheney: Guilty 'til Proven Innocent," *New Republic*, March 17, 2010, www.tnr.com/article/politics/lawyer-up (accessed June 29, 2010).

24. Chris McGreal, "Liz Cheney Accused of McCarthyism over Campaign against Lawyers," *Guardian*, March 11, 2010, www.guardian.co.uk/world/2010/mar/11/liz-cheney-keep-america-safe (accessed June 29, 2010).

25. Robert Mackey, "Drone Strikes Are Legal, US Official Says," *New York Times*, March 29, 2010, http://thelede.blogs.nytimes.com/2010/03/29/drone-strikes-are-legal-u-s-official-says/ (accessed June 29, 2010).

26. Ibid.

27. Charlie Savage, "Obama Team Is Divided on Tactics Against Terrorism," *New York Times*, March 28, 2010, www.nytimes.com/2010/03/29/us/politics/29force. html (accessed June 29, 2010).

28. Scott Shane, "U.S. Approves Targeted Killing of American Cleric," *New York Times*, April 6, 2010, www.nytimes.com/2010/04/07/world/middleeast/07yemen. html (accessed June 29, 2010). A Republican congressman from Pennsylvania, Charles Dent, introduced a resolution on April 21, 2010, urging the Obama administration to strip al-Awlaki of his American citizenship. "Congressman Wants Radical Cleric's Citizenship Revoked," *Fox News*, April 21, 2010, www.foxnews.com/poli tics/2010/04/21/congressman-wants-radical-clerics-citizenship-revoked/ (accessed June 29, 2010).

29. For an example of conservative criticism of the Obama administration's decision to target al-Awlaki, see John McCormack, "Assassinating Awlaki," *Weekly Standard*, April 8, 2010, www.weeklystandard.com/blogs/assassinating-awlaki (accessed June 29, 2010).

30. Scott Shane, "U.S. Approval of Killing of Cleric Causes Unease," *New York Times*, May 13, 2010, www.nytimes.com/2010/05/14/world/14awlaki.html (accessed June 29, 2010).

31. Steven Benen, "Thiessen's Thesis Spreads," *Washington Monthly*, February 20, 2010, www.washingtonmonthly.com/archives/individual/2010_02/022506.php (accessed June 9, 2010).

32. Anthony Loyd, "US Drone Strikes in Pakistan Tribal Areas Boost Support for Taliban," *Times online*, March 10, 2010, www.timesonline.co.uk/tol/news/world/asia/article7055965.ece (accessed June 29, 2010); Tim Reid, "President Obama Orders His First Drone Attacks," *Times online*, January 23, 2009, www.timesonline.co.uk/tol/news/world/us_and_americas/article5575883.ece (accessed June 29, 2010).

33. Peter Finn and Joby Warrick, "Under Panetta, a More Aggressive CIA," *Washington Post*, March 21, 2010, www.washingtonpost.com/wp-dyn/content/article/2010/03/20/AR2010032003343.html (accessed June 29, 2010); "Statement on CIA Casualties in Afghanistan," *Central Intelligence Agency*, December 31, 2009, www.cia.gov/news-information/press-releases-statements/cia-casualties-in-afghani stan.html (accessed June 29, 2010).

34. Jeff Stein, "Ex-Spies Still Agitated over CIA's Afghan Losses," *Washington Post*, March 22, 2010, http://blog.washingtonpost.com/spy-talk/2010/03/nearly_four_months_after_an.html (accessed June 29, 2010).

35. Susan Crabtree, "Intel Bill Pulled over Controversial Added Interrogation Provision," *Hill*, February 25, 2010, http://thehill.com/homenews/house/83817-gop-cries-foul-over-amendment-to-intel-bill (accessed June 29, 2010).

36. Walter Pincus, "House Votes to Revise Intelligence Disclosure Rules for President," *Washington Post*, March 2, 2010, www.washingtonpost.com/wp-dyn/content/article/2010/03/01/AR2010030103310.html (accessed June 29, 2010); Mark Ambinder, "A Wrinkle in the Intelligence Debate," *Atlantic online*, February 25, 2010, www.theatlantic.com/politics/archive/2010/02/a-wrinkle-in-the-intelligence-debate/36620/ (accessed June 29, 2010); President, Statement of Administration Policy, "H.R. 2701—Intelligence Authorization Act for Fiscal Year 2010," July, 2010.

37. Alexander, Hamilton, James Madison, and John Jay, *The Federalist Papers*, ed. Clinton Rossiter (New York: Mentor, 1999), no. 70.

38. Paul Leicester Ford, ed., *The Works of Thomas Jefferson* (New York: G. P. Putman, 1898), 9:211.

39. Theodore Roosevelt, *An Autobiography* (New York: The Library of America, 2004), 614.

40. Greg Robinson, "The Tyrannical History of Military Tribunals for Civilians," *History News Network*, October 5, 2009, hnn.us/articles/117429.html (accessed June 29, 2010).

41. Ibid.

42. Holder's zealous devotion to civil liberties and civil rights is undoubtedly a principled, and hard-won, stance. His sister-in-law, Vivian Malone, was the woman who desegregated the University of Alabama in the famous schoolhouse door showdown with Governor George Wallace in 1963.

43. Examples of the Obama administration's unilateral semantic retreat include its rejection of the term "War on Terror" or the "Long War" in favor of the more rhetorically uninspired and inoffensive "Overseas Contingency Operation." See Scott Wilson and Al Kamen, "Global War on Terror is Given New Name," *Washington Post*, March 25, 2009, www.washingtonpost.com/wp-dyn/content/article/2009/03/24/AR2009032402818.html (accessed June 29, 2010). See also Attorney General Holder's testimony before the House Judiciary Committee, May 13, 2010, in which he was reluctant to use the term "radical Islam" or the word "terrorism" in attributing a motive to the Times Square bomber, the Fort Hood shooter, and the Christmas Day "Undie Bomber." *Oversight of the U.S. Department of Justice*, 111th Cong., 2nd sess., judiciary.house.gov/hearings/pdf/Holder100513.pdf (accessed June 29, 2010). See also the Defense Department's January 2010 report on the Fort Hood shootings, *Protecting the Force: Lessons from Fort Hood*, which examined the killing of thirteen Americans by an Army psychiatrist. The eighty-six-page report never mentioned the gunman's links to Anwar al-Awlaki or radical Islam as a possible motivation. See www.defense.gov/pubs/pdfs/DOD-ProtectingTheForce-Web_Security_HR_13Jan10.pdf (accessed June 29, 2010). The Secretary of the Department of Homeland Security, Janet Napolitano, achieving new heights of Orwellian excellence, prefers the term "man-caused disasters" instead of "terrorism." Cordula Meyer, "Interview with Homeland Security Secretary Janet Napolitano: 'Away from the Politics of Fear,'" *Spiegel Online International*, March 16, 2009, www.spiegel.de/international/world/0,1518,613330,00.html (accessed June 29, 2010).

CHAPTER SEVEN

The End of Small Politics?

Barack Obama and the Progressive Movement

David Alvis

In an interview with Oprah Winfrey near the conclusion of his first year of office, President Obama graded his performance a solid B-plus.[1] That score, argued Obama, would inevitably improve once Congress passed the proposed health care bill. "Affordable Health Care for all Americans" finally made its way through Congress and was signed by the president, but the passage of the legislation has not been accompanied with the kind of enthusiasm that the president hoped for. While I would generally be disinclined to grade presidential performance, it would be especially difficult for anyone to assign a precise score for Obama. During both the primaries and the presidential contest, Obama often spoke of his disdain for ideologies and his preference for results-oriented pragmatism. Yet, his message of pragmatism was commonly couched in terms of a visionary rhetoric that would reportedly transport his supporters into a near frenzy. By pragmatic standards, Obama would in fact deserve high marks. He convinced Democrats to compromise with their most virulent opponents in Congress and to pass a bill that did not contain the heavily advertised "public option." But, health care reform was also touted by Obama as a major landmark for his effort to change the general direction that American politics had taken since the presidency of Ronald Reagan and reinvigorate a public that had grown increasingly cynical about politics since the Reagan years. By this standard, Obama's accomplishments would probably deserve a much lower mark. One wonders why a president would hold himself to such conflicting standards of judgment, but Obama's attempt to synthesize pragmatism with his visionary rhetoric is not without precedent in American history.

During the Progressive era of American politics, reformers called upon their fellow citizens to substitute discretionary administrative government and the newly acquired discoveries of scientific management for the traditional features of American government. At the same time, the Progressives framed their argument in nearly religious tones; for instance Herbert Croly outlined the mission of Progressive reformers in the following way: "Like all sacred causes, it must be propagated by the Word and by the right of the Word, which is the Sword."[2] Despite its many intellectual and political leaders, the Progressive movement never succeeded in garnering sufficient support among the general public to change effectively the course of American politics. I believe that the reason for the failure of the Progressive movement rests in the political incompatibility of its fundamental ingredients and the impossible synthesis of its pragmatic means and its idealistic promises for the future. In so far as Obama's intellectual make-up borrows from these strands of Progressive thought, his political future may take the same course.

In his Inaugural Address, Obama offered the following formula for the successful conduct of a presidential administration: "The question we ask today is not whether our government is too big or too small, but whether it works."[3] The reason for past failures of reform, Obama explained, lies in the ideological rigidity on both the left and the right both outside but particularly inside of Washington, D.C. It is this ideological polarization of the nation on both sides, according to Obama, that accounts for the cynicism that many Americans now feel toward their government. Though Obama often blamed George Bush and Republicans for what he called their "can't do" philosophy of limited government, he also blames Democrats for their indifference to matters of fiscal responsibility.[4] In contrast to the majority of politicians who identify themselves as liberal or conservative, Obama prefers the label "pragmatist," meaning that he takes his cue from experience and a practical assessment of current economic and political conditions rather than "abstract ideologies."[5]

Obama's pragmatism is often hard to appreciate, particularly when he is criticized by members of his own party for being too idealistic as when he decided to place health care on the legislative agenda ahead of more pressing economic-stimulus concerns. Despite the criticism, I believe that if Obama had chosen a more expedient route in the early part of his presidential term, he would probably have alienated many supporters who were initially enthralled by a candidate who campaigned on the explicit promise that his presidency would transcend the mean and ornery debates of the past. What was most memorable about Obama's campaign was how he defined himself as anything but a hackneyed politician, vowing that as president he would not only change the policies of the Bush administration but he would change the tone of politics that had staled the air of Washington, D.C. well before Bush. As Cass Sunstein, in an aptly entitled piece "The Visionary Minimalist," assured readers of the *New Republic* who feared that a pragmatic Obama was simply another Bill Clinton with a little more class:

> From health care to assistance for low-income families to education to environmental protection, he emphasizes that Americans have duties to one another, and that government should be taking active steps to provide equal opportunity and to help those who need help. But, by nature, he is also an independent thinker, and he listens to all sides. One of his most distinctive features is that he is a minimalist, not in the sense that he always favors small steps (he doesn't), but because he prefers solutions that can be accepted by people with a wide variety of theoretical inclinations.[6]

Unlike Clinton, who generally spent more time triangulating than fighting for Progressive reform, Obama knows that the path to a realignment in American politics requires an indomitable commitment to an ambitious legislative program that can alter the current political landscape.[7]

Yet this landmark legislative accomplishment in health care reform has not been embraced with the kind of enthusiasm that would presage the fulfillment of a Messianic promise, nor did the final passage indicate the evidence for a developing realignment under Obama's leadership of the party. Aside from a growing tide of opposition to Obama's ambitious legislative agenda, what is most striking is that his own supporters seem to have regarded the whole thing as rather anticlimactic. What should have been a euphoric "moment" for those who eagerly anticipated such a landmark achievement under Obama's leadership now turns out to seem rather bathos. In fact, the only people who greeted the final passage of the legislation with anything like a toast were the maudlin members of the tea party who believed that the passage of this legislation was the beginning of the demise of the republic.

Given the level of accomplishment achieved by the successful passage of the legislation, why have Obama's popularity ratings suffered so much? One of the most obvious explanations for the lukewarm reception of the health care bill among many Obama supporters was the ugly spectacle of the process that accompanied this legislation. The legislation did not so much bring together an otherwise politically disenchanted nation as it actually reaffirmed what political scientists call "Beltway Partisanship." As Sidney Milkis explains, the battle over programmatic liberalism begun under the Reagan administration has not resulted "in a challenge to national administrative power," but has only moved the field of conflict to a contest for control of the administration and its services. Today, argues Milkis, government is "dominated by a politics of entitlements which [tends] to belittle efforts by Democrats and Republicans alike to define a collective purpose with a past and a future and [yields] instead a partisanship joined to a form of administrative politics which relegates electoral conflict to the intractable demands of policy advocates."[8] In the case of the health care bill, the whole ambit of the process with its logrolling, deal-making, and compromising with special interests indicated that even such a momentous piece of legislation as health care reform was *destined* to be produced in the arena of what Obama himself has pejoratively termed "small politics." Obama believed that his pragmatic statesmanship would move us beyond the politics of entitlements and special interests, but the spectacle of the health care bill clearly indicates that we have not. In addition to the seeming pettiness of the process, many supporters also felt nonplussed about the substance of the legislation. When opposition to the bill forced Democrats to discard the promise of a public option, many supporters lost confidence in their belief that Obama could really deliver on his promise to generate "change that we can believe in."

The Democratic primaries of 2008 were not for Obama just a bid for the Democratic ticket but an attempt to tender himself as the candidate that would restore America's confidence in their politicians and in government as a whole. Aside all of the talk of pragmatism was another standard offered by Obama and imbued throughout the tone of the campaign. Even more memorable than Obama's appeals to pragmatism was what I would call a messianic type of rhetoric—visionary appeals to the public that went beyond even the normal pale of fluffy campaign rhetoric. George H. Bush's "thousand points of light" seems modest now in contrast to Obama's "We are the ones we have been waiting for" or the "Audacity of Hope"—a Christian theological virtue now coined into a political shibboleth. As he boldly explained in his famous "Super Tuesday" speech: "Change will not come if we wait for some other person or if we wait for some other time. *We are the ones we've been waiting for. We are the change that we seek.* We are the hope of those boys who have so little, who've been told that they cannot have what they dream, that they cannot be what they imagine. Yes, they can" (emphasis added).[9] If the health care legislation of March 2010 was supposed to be the long-anticipated fulfillment of a foretold prophecy, it failed to rally supporters to declare "Church Triumphant!"

In light of these two diametrically opposed criteria and the very different grades that we might assign them respectively, how are we to finally assess Obama's performance? Perhaps we could average the two grades but that would seem to do injustice to one and give too much credit to the other. The problem resides in how incompatible are the expectations set by each— pragmatism, on the one hand, requires a slow, plodding course of measuring ideas and practices in light of experience, while the visionary rhetoric would appear to accept nothing less than the consummate happiness of the democratic whole.[10] Frustrated by the difficulty of pinning Obama down, opponents have labeled him extreme left or more perniciously, a socialist. Obama, by contrast, prefers to call himself a "Progressive." Looking back in American history, I believe that this label is more accurate because so much of his thinking resonates with the reformers of the early twentieth century who first coined the name. Obama is a Progressive and the polar strands of his governing philosophy reflect precisely the character of that period. I also believe that his presidency already suffers from the same problems as those that retarded the success of the original Progressive intellectual movement.

The Progressive era marks a notable period of intellectual thought in America in which many leading intellectuals and commentators began to rethink seriously the foundations of democratic politics. Following the industrial revolution, the nation had become a much more complicated organism of interconnected economic and political relations. By the early twentieth century, enormous interstate corporations had begun to limit the opportunities for newcomers to the market to strike out on their own enterprise. In light of this national economic growth local government seemed to matter less as the interests of the country were becoming increasingly national. The essential question posed by all of this economic development was whether democracy could successfully continue to be a desirable form of government as the issues that affected individuals across the nation became both more complicated and more distant from the provincial arena of local and state politics. Among the leading public intellectuals of this period was Herbert Croly, author of two well-known books on reform, including *The Promise of American Life* (1909) and *Progressive Democracy* (1912), and founder of the Progressive circulation *The New Republic*. Croly believed that America's traditional institutions of democratic government were no longer in step with the dynamic changes taking place in the national economy. In his first book, *The Promise of American Life*, Croly assails America's institutions of limited government because he thinks that their inherent tendency is to promote irresponsible leadership and ineffectual public policy. Constitutional government, according to Croly, was adopted for the purposes of maximizing individual freedom and self-determination; both of which were secured by imposing severe restrictions on the powers of government. This arrangement made sense at a time when most business transactions were no more extensive than that of a customer purchasing from his local grocer. But these limitations on government no longer comported with the needs of individual citizens at a time when the chief threats to freedom came from powerful national corporations that controlled a large share of the market from whom most consumers were forced to buy. What average citizens needed now was protection from unscrupulous robber barons rather than freedom from government.

Progressives were particularly concerned that Americans might lose faith in democratic government altogether under the pressure that had been exerted by these economic forces. There were already clear signs, thought Croly, that indicated Americans were beginning to lose their confidence in democratic government. As the nation's public policies were proving ineffective in restraining the consolidation of economic power, many Americans had grown cynical about the possibility that government could provide a solution. For Croly, the problem of the present is really the problem of the nation's past. Americans are skeptical about the contribution that government can make to the welfare of the nation because, thanks to the influence of Thomas Jefferson's extreme individualism, they conceive of democratic politics as a license for the selfish pursuit of their own interests.

> He [Jefferson] conceived a democratic society to be composed of a collection of individuals, fundamentally alike in their abilities and deserts; and in organizing such a society, politically, the prime object was to provide for the greatest satisfaction of the individual members. . . . It was unnecessary, moreover, to make any artful arrangements, in order to effect an equitable distribution. Such distribution would take care of itself, provided nobody enjoyed any special privileges and everybody had equal opportunities. Once these conditions were secured, the motto of a democratic government should simply be "Hands Off." . . . The vitality of a democracy resided in its extremities, and it would be diminished rather than increased by specialized or centralized guidance. Its individual members needed merely to be protected against privileges and to be let alone, whereafter the native goodness of human nature would accomplish the perfect consummation.[11]

Having imbibed Jefferson's vision of democratic government, Americans assume that when their self-interests are endangered by forces outside of their control, someone in government must be abusing their power. Consequently, the average American never seriously considers the possibility that government could play a positive role in the welfare of the country.

Croly's diagnosis of American Politics in the early 1900s is particularly relevant to our understanding of the premise behind much of the intellectual gist of the Obama campaign. In fact, it is interesting to note how similarly

Obama sees the challenges of governing at the dawn of the twenty-first century. In an early speech during the campaign in which he outlined his distinctive claim for the Democratic Presidential nominee, Obama explains:

> I remember when I first ran for the state senate—this was my very first race— back in Chicago . . . people would say, you seem like a nice young man. They would look over my literature. They would say, you have a fancy law degree, you teach at a fine law school, you've done fine work, you've got a beautiful family—why would you want to go into something dirty and nasty like politics?
>
> And the question is understandable and it bears on today because even those of us who are involved, even those of us who are active in the political process and in civic life, there are times where all of us feel discouraged some-times, where we get cynical about the prospects for politics because it seems as if sometimes that politics is treated as a business and not a mission, and that power is always trumping principle, and that we have leaders that are some-times long on rhetoric but short on substance, and so we get discouraged.[12]

There is nothing unique about a presidential candidate who professes to have the cure for the electoral blues, but, as the quote above illustrates, the stakes are much higher for Obama who claims to be engaged in a program of restoring the whole body politic rather than the more modest goal of waging a programmatic campaign that merely heals a particular wound or disease. Moreover, Obama's proposals for change are directly linked to fostering a new tone of politics. The right policy changes will flow from right changes in the manner in which we approach politics as a whole. Like Croly and the Progressives, Obama argues that the cynicism of today the result of a failure on the part of government to keep up with the evolutionary development of society. Hence, the real problem is not the failure of any particular political officer but the failure of the nation as a whole to revisit its most fundamental ideas and adapt democratic institutions to meet the challenges of a new century.

> The sweeping changes brought by revolutions and technology have torn down the walls between business and government and people and places all over the globe. . . . But while the world has changed around us, unfortunately it seems like our government has stood still. Our faith has been shaken, but the people running Washington haven't been willing to make us believe again. Now, it's the timidity, *it's the smallness of our politics* that's holding us back right now— the idea that there are some problems that are just too big to handle, and if you just ignore them that sooner or later they'll go away. (emphasis mine)[13]

Critical to the Progressive case for reform was the argument that we were now living at a world historic moment in which the rules that defined political

life in the past were no longer applicable to the economic and social conditions that currently prevailed. In terms very similar to the language of the Progressive era, Obama argued during the course of the campaign that the country
was standing at a momentous point in history where environmental conditions
have evolved to such a point that the old ways of governing now seemed obso-
lete. At this critical juncture, we face a momentous choice between continuing
the now discredited economic theories of the past or embracing the need for
greater regulation and public stewardship of the economy.[14]

In his acceptance speech in Denver, Obama called particular attention
to the way that the Bush administration fostered this outmoded understanding of government: "In Washington, they call this the Ownership Society,
but what it really means is—you're on your own. Out of work? Tough luck.
No health care? The market will fix it. Born into poverty? Pull yourself
up by your own bootstraps—even if you don't have boots. You're on your
own. Well it's time for them to own their failure. It's time for us to change
America." I find it unlikely that many members of the audience in Denver
immediately understood the reference to the programmatic campaign of the
Bush administration entitled the "Ownership Society;" a fact that is telling
about the horizon of Obama's intellectual ambitions.[15] In fact, Obama did
not merely refer to a bygone slogan of the Bush administration but elsewhere
he compared the Bush administration's domestic policy to the so-called
"laissez faire" attitude of the early twentieth century. In terms almost apro-
pos of an academic lecture, Obama explained: "But, you know, historically
there has been another name for it [the ownership society]; it's called "social
Darwinism"—the notion that every man or woman is out for him- or herself,
which allows us to say that if we meet a guy who has worked in a steel plant
for 30, 40 years and suddenly has the rug pulled out from under him and can't
afford health care or can't afford a pension, you know, life isn't fair." I suspect
that "social Darwinism" is not a household name among the general public
and Obama's use of the term suggests that he is also attempting to address
a very sophisticated audience. If my interpretation of his remarks is correct,
I think these observations demonstrate how serious Obama is in trying to
effect a full-scale realignment in American politics forging a new cleavage
between free market conservatives and those who see government as a desirable vehicle for social and economic change.[16]

Social Darwinism was of course an influential school of public thought
during the Progressive era and a lightning rod for the political alignment
of the day. Social Darwinists like Herbert Spencer argued that a free market was the ideal economic arrangement for separating the chaff from the
wheat—for just as natural selection weeds out the unfit from the fit so a

free economy selects the industrious and rational from the quarrelsome and contentious. Rather than rebel against capitalism's harsh treatment of certain portions of the population and the advantages gained by others, we should embrace the results just as natural organisms inevitably surrender to their better-adapted successors. As Richard Hofstadter describes the mood of the nation in the wake of the industrial revolution: "Understandably Darwinism was seized upon as a welcome addition, perhaps the most powerful of all, to the store of ideas to which solid and conservative men appealed when they wished to reconcile their fellows to some of the hardships of life and to prevail upon them not to support hasty and ill-considered reforms."[17] In *The Promise of American Life*, Croly does not actually use the term social Darwinism to describe this "laissez-faire" economic policy because he believes that the substance of social Darwinists is really no different from the traditional individual rights philosophy of the American Founding. For Croly, the most stubborn obstacle to reform is not the work of Herbert Spencer but the parameters of liberalism that have been inherited from the inception of the nation. Consequently, change for Progressives like Croly required gaining some critical distance from the very foundations of American politics.

At the beginning of his work, Croly complains about America's mixture of "optimism, fatalism, and conservatism."[18] Americans, according to Croly, conceive of their future as a self-fulfilling destiny in which individual self-interest will naturally lead to growth and prosperity. "The higher American patriotism . . . combines loyalty to historical tradition with the imaginative projection of an ideal national Promise."[19] Hence Americans are not only optimistic but they are also fatalistic in that they believe as a matter of unconditional faith that if individuals are left to their own devices each will necessarily contribute to the common good. "This better future," writes Croly, "is understood by him as something which fulfills itself. He calls his country, not only the Land of Promise, but the Land of Destiny." Like many Progressives, Croly adopted the following narrative why reform is a more pressing concern now despite the fact that the problems for reform date back to the Founding. According to this narrative, an unqualified faith in individual freedom and democracy was plausible during the eighteenth and nineteenth centuries when our national economy was highly dispersed, and beleaguered urban laborers could always strike out for the West where virgin land offered an outlet for individual ambition. However, with the close of the western frontier and the growing interdependence of the nation's economy, the beginning of the twentieth century marked a significant moment where individual freedom and democracy were no longer complementary. The captains of industry stood to benefit at the expense of labor under a system that favored individual self-determination and the average individual, alienated from his labor, was also becoming disaffected with politics.

The beginning of the twentieth century was therefore a momentous juncture in American political life for Progressives like Croly that presaged the following alteration in the way Americans think about their political life:

> The transformation of the old sense of a glorious national destiny into the sense of a serious national purpose will inevitably tend to make the popular realization of the Promise of American Life more explicit and serious. As long as Americans believed they were able to fulfill a noble national Promise merely by virtue of maintaining in tact a set of political institutions by the pursuit of private ends, their allegiance to their national fulfillment remained more a matter of words than of deeds, but now that they are being aroused from their patriotic slumber, the effect is inevitably to disentangle the national ideas and to give it more dignity.[20]

While it might appear that Croly's criticism of the founding principles requires a wholesale departure from the past, he in fact argues that abandoning the fundamental elements of rights and constitutional limitations on government is necessary to realize the true meaning of the founding. We can only realize the original "promise of American life" by rejecting the traditional restraints on government that have been cherished since the founding.

The difficulty facing Croly at the turn of the century was to explain how a nation could live up to its most fundamental obligation while dissolving the obligations imposed by the social contract. Croly hoped that his readers would see that America's fatal conservatism—its patriotic loyalty to traditional doctrines of right and equality—can no longer guarantee this ideal national Promise. "The fault in our vision of our national future possessed by the ordinary American," argues Croly, "does not consist in the expectation of some continuity of achievement. It consists rather in the expectation that the familiar benefits will accumulate automatically."[21] Progressive reform in America would depend upon the reformers' ability to reshape the public mind by distinguishing the Promise from the doctrines of the past. In the American mind, argued Croly, "the ideal Promise is identified with the processes and conditions which hitherto have very much simplified its fulfillment, and he (the average American) fails sufficiently to realize that the conditions and processes are one thing and the ideal Promise quite another." If Americans could see that a different set of processes were better than the ones currently embodied in law, they might be more receptive to the fundamental changes necessary to realize "the promise."

Croly finds his answer to the dilemma above in what he hopes will be the attraction of the mere notion of reform. The American Founding was an experiment; an experiment that put into practice modern liberalism and an experiment in a new form of government. What Americans ought to admire about the Founding is not the ideas that were fixed into law but rather the founders' courage demonstrated in their willingness to be innovators. To emulate them, we too must be open to reform. Rather than attempt to dissuade his fellow Americans from treating the founding as sacrosanct, Croly actually hoped to utilize this reverence for the past as a justification for inspiring more dramatic reforms in the future.

I believe that Obama's approach to the challenges of reform today is actually quite similar to that of Croly. Obama wants to inspire among the people a desire for change as an end in itself and he speaks highly of the courage that the American founders exhibited in their time when they too pushed for change. The most nebulous feature of Obama's campaign was the content of his most commonly used phrase, "Change." In what does the meaning of "change" consist for Obama? To get an understanding of what he means, we need to turn to his understanding of the fundamental features of American politics. In a chapter on the Constitution in his book, *The Audacity of Hope*, Obama makes his case for the "living constitution" thesis while at the same time praising the original Constitution for its enduring wisdom and virtue. In fact, the essential features of the Constitution, according to Obama, constitute something that all conservatives and liberals can agree on—the founders provided a "blueprint." "As with our understanding of the Declaration, we debate the details of constitutional construction, we may object to Congress' abuse of the expanded commerce clause powers to the detriment of the states, or to the erosion of Congress' power to declare war. But we are confident in the fundamental soundness of the Founders' blueprints and the democratic house that resulted. Conservative or liberal, we are all constitutionalists."[22] Indeed, at the opening of the chapter, Obama decries the fact that most legislators spend more time arguing over what the law "is" rather than what laws "ought to be." Faced with these manifold interpretations of fundamental and statutory law in Congress, Obama reports that he went back to read the Constitution at the beginning of his first term as a U.S. senator. He describes what a great boon it is in America that we can so easily return to our first principles because they are so accessible. In fact, he even confesses to his reader a certain sympathy for what he calls Justice Scalia's "strict constructionist" interpretation of the Constitution. "I understand the

strict constructionists' reverence for the Founders; indeed, I've often wondered if the Founders themselves recognized at the time the scope of their
accomplishment. I appreciate the *temptation* on the part of Justice Scalia and
others to assume our democracy should be treated as fixed and unwavering;
the fundamentalist faith that if the original understanding of the Constitution is followed without question or deviation, and if we remain true to the
rules that the founders set forth, as they intended, then we will be rewarded
and all good will follow" (emphasis mine).[23] Obama's account of strict-
constructionism reminds me of that strange mixture of optimism, fatalism,
and conservatism which Croly decries in *The Promise of American Life*—all of
which Obama seemingly endorses—until strikingly a few lines later he states:
"Ultimately, though, I have to side with Justice Stephen Breyer's view of the
Constitution—that it is not a static but rather a living document, and must
be read in the context of an ever changing world." But even here Obama
offers a rather uncontroversial interpretation that would or should be acceptable to anyone knowledgeable about Constitutional law on the Left or the
Right. In siding with Breyer's living constitution thesis against what Obama
calls the simple mindedness of the strict constructionists—he also says that
he cannot side with the apostates and relativists who conclude that because
there were differences over original intent among the founders themselves
therefore we are free to make up whatever constitutional meaning we want.
Comparing himself to creation scientists, he says that he himself feels like
those who reject Darwin in favor of intelligent design, "I prefer to assume
that someone's at the wheel." Having then set up the argument between
strict construction on one side and relativism on the other, Obama makes a
case for the pragmatic middle: "The answer I settle on requires *a shift in meta-
phors*, one that sees our democracy not as a house to be built, but a conversation to be had. According to this conception, the genius of Madison's design
is not that it provides us a fixed *blueprint* for action, the way a draftsman plots
a building's construction. It provides us with a framework and with rules, but
fidelity to these rules will not guarantee a just society or assure agreement on
what is right" (emphasis mine).[24] Hence the function of the Constitution,
according to Obama, is to force us into a conversation, "a "deliberative democracy" in which all citizens are required to engage in a process of testing
their ideas against an external reality." Now one might think that Obama is
simply saying that the Constitution sets the rules or procedures for policy-
making but does not determine the outcome. But what constitutional law
professor would need such an elaborate argument for this unobjectionable
contention, and, moreover, if this were his point, there would be little reason
for criticizing Justice Scalia whose jurisprudence reflects precisely this kind of

reasoning. Finally, if the Constitution merely set procedures which left each generation free to determine the policies which best suited them, why side with Breyer's living constitution thesis since there is really no reason to object to the original intent of the framers? Or alternatively, why does Obama think that we should we admire the Founders? Towards the end of his treatment of the Constitution in *The Audacity of Hope*, Obama explains: "The Founders may have trusted in God, but true to the Enlightenment spirit, they also trusted in the minds and senses that God had given them. They were suspicious of abstraction and liked asking questions, which is why at every turn in our early history theory yielded to fact and necessity."[25] As a philosophical movement, Pragmatism means the rejection of the kind of abstraction that characterizes Enlightenment thought in favor of testing theories according to the experience of fact and necessity. Obama, consciously or not, praises the Enlightenment of the founders for rejecting the Enlightenment. The "conversation" Obama must have in mind constitutes more than simply the right to freely determine policy goals under the Constitution's prescribed rules of procedure; it must mean finding a substitute in pragmatism for the narrow strictures of constitutionalism.

If there were a blueprint for Obama's constitutional jurisprudence, Croly's work would be the most likely candidate. Reflecting on the contribution of the Federalists to American Politics, Croly writes:

> Without their help there might not have been any American nation at all, or it might have been born under a far darker cloud of political suspicion and animosity. The instrument which they created, with all its faults, proved capable of becoming both the organ of an efficient national government and the fundamental law of a potentially democratic state. It has proved capable of *flexible* development both in function and in purpose, and it has been developed in both these directions without any sacrifice of integrity. (emphasis mine)[26]

For Croly, what turns out to be good about the Constitution is how flexible or malleable it has proven to be in practice. In the hands of the Federalist it proved to be a useful thing—bringing a disordered and disparate nation into a unified whole. But there were also elements of the Constitution, which, though appropriate to the time in which it was written, have proven to be impediments to national prosperity as times change. For instance, Croly cites the Constitution's protection of property in the form of the contract clause in the original document and the due process clause of the Fifth Amendment. At the time of the founding, it was useful to have an absolute protection on the right of contract, but as times have changed and our economy is in greater needed of active intervention by the federal government in the form of regulation than it is in need of individual entrepreneurship—the desirability of a constitutional protection on contracts and private property has declined. If we are true to the original intent of the founders—we should be flexible in our interpretation of the Constitution—thus resisting, in Obama's words, the "temptation," to side with a strict constructionist view that would commit us to useless abstractions such as contract rights or property rights.

Croly refers to America as a "promise"—hence, the title of the book— because a promise constitutes a very different and for Croly a more desirable foundation for political life than that of the liberal notion of a social contract. A contract demarcates the obligations of two respective parties in very precise terms in order to make clear what is required from each and consequently what is not required of either. A contract therefore is fixed at one point in time regardless of the circumstances that arise (unless of course those circumstances are themselves defined by the contract). Hence contracts are convenient to those parties that value their freedom from undefined obligations because it allows each party to protect their respective self-interests. A promise is a very different arrangement among two parties. A promise aims at achieving a certain end such that the obligations must always adapt to a changing environment in order to realize the final end. A promise looks to the future whereas a contract is narrowly defined by an action in the past and the realization of a promise often relies on individual sacrifice rather than limited consent. Unlike contracts, promises require common effort and are endangered by selfish individualism.

I am not suggesting that Obama directly borrowed this slogan from the work of Herbert Croly, but it is revealing how much his use of this term reflects that of Croly's. Obama uses the term "promise" with far greater emphasis and meaning than has been used by other presidential figures and it appears to me that his meaning is quite close to that of Croly. In his Democratic convention acceptance speech in Denver entitled "The American Promise," Obama used the word thirty-one times. More importantly, the term promise did not merely function in the speech as the justification for policy positions that Obama would push in the campaign, rather, he argued that "promise" is the antidote to the individualism of the past, an alternative understanding of America's history which emphasizes each citizens' obligations to his fellow citizens and not just to himself. The following selected quotations from the speech illustrate this point:

1. That's the *promise* of America—the idea that we are responsible for ourselves, but that we also rise or fall as one nation; the fundamental belief that I am my brother's keeper; I am my sister's keeper.

2. This too is part of America's *promise*—the promise of a democracy where we can find the strength and grace to bridge divides and unite in common effort.
3. Instead, it is that American spirit that American *promise*—that pushes us forward even when the path is uncertain; that binds us together in spite of our differences; that makes us fix our eye not on what is seen, but what is unseen, that better place around the bend.
4. And finally, Individual responsibility and mutual responsibility—that's the essence of America's *promise*. (emphasis mine)[27]

As the term figures in Obama's speech, "promise" restructures political life by cultivating a common bond and sense of purpose whereas abstract convictions sow seeds of faction and discontent. To realize a promise we must abandon more than just our individualistic habits—we need to surrender any claim that one set of ideas is absolutely right. Thus Obama praises the founders' concept of ordered liberty which, according to him, "implied a rejection of absolute truth, the infallibility of any idea or ideology or theology or 'ism,' any tyrannical consistency that might lock future generations into a single, unalterable course."[28]

In this light, Obama's emphasis on pragmatism makes sense and we can also see how closely his governing philosophy is reminiscent of the Progressives. Like Obama, Croly believes that the fulfillment of the Promise of American Life requires that we proceed pragmatically—utilizing what is good from our past in light of our experience of the present. The substantial discontent of the many throughout the nation with their political and social condition in the early twentieth century portended a loss of faith in democracy altogether—a cynicism witnessed particularly among labor that government exists for the advantage of the few rather than the many. Now, argues Croly, "the Promise of American Life is to be fulfilled, not merely by a maximum amount of economic freedom, but by a certain measure of discipline; not merely by the abundant satisfaction of individual desires, but by a large measure of individual subordination and self-denial."[29] Croly believes that average Americans will have to learn to live with a much larger regulatory state managed by individuals who possess superior knowledge and talent. Saving democracy therefore will require a revaluation of the past and a more pragmatic approach to politics.

Croly's famous formula for the reform of American politics is: "We need Hamiltonian means to Jeffersonian ends." During Croly's time, Jefferson and Hamilton were the symbolic figures for two different visions of democratic politics and the role of the national government. Reformers like

Theodore Roosevelt who wanted to extend the scope of federal regulatory power under the scientific management of individuals with substantial intellectual expertise and financial experience invoked the legacy of Alexander Hamilton. Others, like William Jennings Bryan, however, appealed to Jefferson for his patronage to the common man, in an attempt to once again restore democratic equality from the oppressive reign of consolidated economic power and political elitism. Appeals to Jefferson romanticized the ideal of self-government: individual citizens living unaffected by the economic power of avaricious tycoons and innocent of the corruption in political bossism. To Croly, Jefferson represents one desirable feature of American politics—"the democratic idea," meaning for Croly a fundamental belief in the equality of human beings and their common right to pursue a life of happiness unimpeded by the interference of others. Hamilton, on the other hand, represents what Croly calls "the national idea," the practical need to harness the collective powers of the nation under a central government led by the country's elite. A Hamiltonian, according to Croly, is a hard-nosed pragmatist, while a Jeffersonian is a romantic idealist. The enduring struggle between their ideas, argues Croly, constitutes the defining feature of American politics since the founding political debate. Where our nation's political development has gone wrong, argues Croly, is in putting these features in strict opposition to one another. Croly proposes that we seek a pragmatic alternative to the current ideological rigidity separating these two sets of ideas:

> We must seek to discover wherein each of these sets of ideas was right, and wherein each was wrong; in what proportions they were subsequently combined in order to form "our noble national theory," and what were the advantages, the limitations, and the effects of this combination.[30]

Croly's didactic account of historical inquiry here is revealing because it shows the extent to which he believes that pragmatism departs from the customary mode of thinking in American political life. The parties tend to be parochial because citizens conceive of nationalism or democracy, Jeffersonianism or Hamiltonianism, as if they were absolute truths that permanently obliged them to conduct politics in one way or another. Croly, on the other hand, believes that if we accept the idea that democracy is really an ongoing process of reform aimed at realizing a common promise, we can be more selective about the ideas of the past and judge them on their true merits—"whether they worked" to the benefit of the nation. Since Croly believes that both Jefferson and Hamilton had their virtues, we should be dedicated to reconciling the benefits among these two strands of thought.[31] Croly does not offer a set of measurements in the abstract for the appropriate combination because he thinks it is impossible to do so in the abstract. Certain periods of time require greater exercise of power among the elites and other times require greater deference to the will of the majority. Pragmatism, by contrast, requires calculating the effects of ideas on the operation of political life. By experimenting with political ideas and institutions in practice we can continually adjust government to the particular needs of the time while respecting the historical limitations of our circumstance.

To prepare citizens for this pragmatic politics of ongoing experimentation, Croly argues toward the end of his book that national politics as a whole must become like a school in which average citizens also engage and learn from this process of ongoing reform. "The process of educating men of moral and intellectual stature sufficient for the performance of constructive work cannot be disentangled from the process of fulfillment by means of intelligent collective action."[32] But even at the conclusion of his work, Croly is still groping for a way of including all citizens in this project. Toward the final pages, Croly hopes that he has found this in a religious form of inspiration:

> The laborious work of individual and social fulfillment may eventually be transfigured by an outburst of social enthusiasm—one which is not the expression of a mood, but which is substantially the finer flower of an achieved experience and living tradition. If such a moment ever arrives, it will be partly the creation of some democratic evangelist—some imitator of Jesus who will reveal to men the path whereby they may enter into the spiritual possession of their individual and social achievements, and immeasurably increase them by virtue of personal regeneration.[33]

What might have culminated in the rather dull life of dependence on an administrative state—for instance, Alexis de Tocqueville's soft-despotism—suddenly becomes an inspirational mission—a "religion of humanity." In his final statement in *The Promise of American Life*, Croly prophesizes: "The common citizen can become something of a saint and something of a hero, not by growing to heroic proportions in his own person, but by the sincere and enthusiastic imitation of heroes and saints, and whether or not he will ever come to such imitation will depend upon the ability of his exceptional fellow-countrymen to offer him acceptable examples of heroism and saintliness."[34] It may seem odd that a book devoted to making the case for pragmatic politics concludes on a note sounding near religious fervor. Croly was indeed the first child in America consecrated to August Comte's "Religion of Humanity," with its weird combination of science and religion.[35] But regardless of this biographical detail, I think there is a more logical explanation for the introduction of this religious tone. Croly argues in his book that Americans believe in a national destiny but lack a clear national purpose—hence their "optimism, fatalism, conservatism." However, as a proponent of pragmatism, Croly must avoid defining this purpose lest he too appear ideological or dogmatic. Since ideas can really only be measured by experience for the pragmatist—we can never precisely articulate what the end or purpose is.[36] For the average citizen, one suspects and Croly I think knows—that experimentation with no clear end or purpose is uninspiring and without either an anchor of fixed ideas in the past or clear knowledge of where we are going—Croly must resort to religious inspiration. The problem of Croly's thought and the problem of the Progressive movement as a whole can be summed up in the word "progress;" it never answers the question "from where; to where?" Without a fixed star to navigate the ship of state, Croly's vision of American politics seems both too dull and too grandiose.

Similarly, Obama hopes that our nation can be a school, what he calls a "deliberative democracy" where "all citizens are required to engage in a process of testing their ideas against external reality."[37] But what are they testing for? The lack of clarity about the ends tends to obscure the public's ability to assess reasonably the choice among the means. The problem is neatly illustrated by Obama's chief slogan: "Change We Can Believe In." But the question here is the same as that we asked of Progressivism: "from what; to what?" In so far as Obama avoids answering the question, he can both succeed in claiming to be pragmatic and he can inspire. But this kind of excitement without a clear purpose invites supporters to ascribe all of their individual convictions to Obama. The consequence, as illustrated by the passage of the health care bill, is that their hopes and aspirations will inevitably have to succumb to the normal democratic process of reconciling interests in legislation passed on the lowest common denominator.

I think Obama faces the same problem as the Progressive movement. Progressivism never achieved its goal of mounting a wholesale revision of the nation's political institutions because its reform efforts were always divided among a multiplicity of irreconcilable demands. Pragmatic leadership simply proved incapable of mustering a coherent program of reform.[38] I'm not sure that Obama's confrontation with Republicans who immediately threatened to campaign for the repeal of the health care legislation marks the end of his pragmatism, but his subsequent resort to language like "Bring it on!" suggests that he may be coming to terms with the fact that the nation is really looking for its president to provide strong principled leadership. Unfortunately for Obama, those battles are always fought on the field of "small politics."

Notes

1. The interview ran as follows:

Obama: Good solid B-plus. I think that we have inherited the biggest set of challenges of any president since Franklin Delano Roosevelt. We stabilized the economy, prevented the possibilities of a great depression, or a significant financial meltdown. The economy is growing again, we are on our way out of Iraq, I think we've got the best possible plan for Afghanistan, we have reset our image around the world, we have achieved an international consensus around the need for Iran and North Korea to disable their nuclear weapons, and I think that we're gonna pass the most significant piece of social legislation since social security and that's health insurance for every American.

Oprah: So B-plus—what could you have done better?

Obama: Well, B-plus because of the things that are undone. Health care is not yet signed. If I get health care passed, we tip into A-minus.

"Oprah Winfrey Interview with President Barack Obama," *ABC News*, December 14, 2009, http://blogs.abcnews.com/politicalpunch/2009/12/president-obama-grades-self-a-good-solid-bplus.html.

2. Herbert Croly, *The Promise of American Life* (Boston: Northeastern University Press, 1989), 21.

3. Barack H. Obama, "Inaugural Address," 2009 Presidential Inaugural, Capitol Building, Washington, DC, January 20, 2009.

4. Barack Obama, *The Audacity of Hope: Thoughts on Reclaiming the American Dream* (New York: Crown Publishers, 2006), 38.

5. Ibid., 93.

6. Cass Sunstein, "The Visionary Minimalist," *New Republic*, January 30, 2008.

7. Charles Kesler, "The Audacity of Barack Obama: Review of *The Audacity of Hope: Thoughts on Reclaiming the American Dream*, by Barack H. Obama," *Claremont Review of Books* 8, no. 4 (2008), www.claremont.org/publications/crb/id.1579/article_detail.asp (accessed July 16, 2010).

8. Sidney M. Milkis, *Political Parties and Constitutional Government: Remaking American Democracy* (Baltimore: Johns Hopkins University Press, 1999), 156.

9. "Barack Obama's Feb. 5 Speech," *New York Times*, February 5, 2008, sec. U.S./Politics, www.nytimes.com/2008/02/05/us/politics/05text-obama.html (accessed July 16, 2010).

10. James Ceaser has neatly explained this tension in the following terms: the 2008 campaign was an event that unfolded on an entirely different plane from ordinary politics. It signaled the emergence on a worldwide scale of the "Religion of Humanity," for which Obama became the symbol. What Americans have discovered is that being the representative of this transpolitical movement does not fit easily, if it fits at all, with serving as president of the United States. James Caeser, "The Roots of Obama Worship: Auguste Comte's Religion of Humanity Finds a 21st-century Savior," *Weekly Standard* 15, no. 18 (January 25, 2010), www.weeklystandard.com/articles/roots-obama-worship.

11. Croly, *Promise*, 43.

12. Remarks of Senator Barack Obama: Take Back America 2007, Washington, DC, June 19, 2007, http://obamaspeeches.com/077-Take-Back-America-Obama-Speech.htm (accessed July 16, 2010).

13. Ibid.

14. Caesar makes the interesting observation that the chief challenge for Obama is to keep his supporters "yearning" for a world historic individual in himself rather than identifying himself as a world historic individual. "When the history of this period is written, the 2008 campaign will almost certainly be seen as a watershed event in cultural history, above and beyond any connection it had to American politics, when a world-wide movement congealed to display its enthusiasm for Barack Obama. This perspective will also require a reassessment of the place of Obama. To be sure, the campaign will continue in one respect to be regarded as being all about Obama. This has been Obama's perception, and understandably so. Only the most rare of persons, after being the object for over a year of such unrelenting adulation, could have resisted the temptation to think that the world revolved around him. Barack Obama is clearly not that person. His speeches and remarks are filled with references to himself in a ratio that surpasses anything yet seen in the history of the American presidency. But in another respect, the 2008 campaign was about something much larger than Barack Obama. The character of the event will not be grasped until the focus begins to shift from Barack Obama to the yearning for Barack Obama. It is in the thoughts and actions of those who adored him that the most interesting and important dimension of the campaign took place." www.weeklystandard.com/articles/roots-obama-worship.

15. Admittedly, Hillary Clinton also mentioned this catchphrase of the Bush administration in a May 2007 address entitled: "Modern Progressive Vision: Shared Prosperity." There she explained: "They call it the ownership society. But it's really the 'on your own' society." Available at www.presidency.ucsb.edu/ws/index.php?pid=77051 (accessed July 16, 2010). However, I am unaware of any continued reference to the Ownership Society by Clinton once the formal campaign was underway.

16. Kesler, "The Audacity of Barack Obama."

17. Richard Hofstadter, Social Darwinism in American Thought (Boston: Beacon Press, 1992), 5.

18. Croly, Promise, 7.

19. Ibid., 6.

20. Ibid., 21.

21. Ibid., 6.

22. Obama, Audacity of Hope, 88.

23. Ibid., 90.

24. Ibid., 88.

25. Ibid., 93.

26. Croly, Promise, 34.

27. Remarks of Senator Barack Obama: The American Promise (Democratic Convention) Denver, CO, August 28, 2008, www.barackobama.com/2008/08/28/remarks_of_senator_barack_obam_108.php (accessed July 16, 2010).

28. Obama, *Audacity of Hope*, 93.

29. Croly, *Promise*, 22.

30. Ibid., 28.

31. Ibid.

32. Croly, *Promise*, 405.

33. Ibid., 453–54.

34. Ibid., 454.

35. David W. Levy, *Herbert Croly of the New Republic* (Princeton, NJ: Princeton University Press, 1985), 36–38.

36. James H. Nichols, Jr., "Pragmatism and the U.S. Constitution," in *Confronting the Constitution*, ed. Allan Bloom (Washington, DC: The AEI Press, 1990).

37. Obama, *Audacity of Hope*, 92.

38. See Daniel T. Rodgers "In Search of Progressivism," *Reviews in American History* 10, no. 4 (1982): 113–32. See also Peter G. Filene, "An Obituary for 'The Progressive Movement,'" *American Quarterly* 22, no. 1 (Spring 1970): 20–34.

CHAPTER EIGHT

~

Presidential Masks

Barack Obama and FDR

Marc Landy

Franklin Delano Roosevelt is the president who most readily invites comparison with Barack Obama. Both became president in the midst of economic collapse, replacing discredited Republican incumbents. Media commentators harped on the similarities between the two and voiced their expectations that Obama would unleash a torrent of policy initiatives bold enough to match the New Deal's epochal "hundred days." Nature endowed both of them with a calm temperament and a cool, unruffled demeanor. This chapter will seek to understand the Obama presidency better by exploring both the similarities and the differences between these two men.

Even the most coincidental of similarities prove meaningful. Both hail from Hyde Park.[1] At first glance, Hyde Park, Chicago, could not be more different from Hyde Park, New York. The former is an academic enclave surrounded by ghetto poverty while the other, especially in FDR's day, was a rural ghetto of the great houses of the wealthy and the prominent. Yet, the two Hyde Parks share a critical common trait. Both are patrician bastions. Hyde Park, New York patricians were primarily the descendants of what cousin Teddy Roosevelt termed "the malefactors of great wealth," who forged the industrial and transportation revolutions of the nineteenth century.[2] Hyde Park, Chicago is a capital of the contemporary patriciate, which is no longer grounded in race, religion, and family background, but rather on education, profession, style, and ideology. Obama is a member in good standing of the "new class" of law and business school professors, economists, foundation executives, think tankers, congressional staffers, and media pundits who have melded with the captains of industry, finance, and politics to form the patriciate of our times. FDR went to Harvard and Columbia. So did Obama, albeit in reverse order. As mentioned above, both carry themselves with the dignity and composure of a patrician. FDR was jauntier and more ingratiating. But that was typical of the patriciate of his day. Obama's more somber bearing and clipped, humorless speaking style is in keeping with the current patrician manner.

Indeed, it is Obama's patrician air that makes him susceptible to the same charge levied at FDR, that he is a traitor to his people. FDR's wealthy peers famously referred to him as "that man." They viewed him as a traitor to his class. Obama has been accused of being a traitor to his race. In March 2000, Illinois State Senator Donne Trotter told the *Chicago Reader* newspaper:

> Barack is viewed in part to be the white man in blackface in our community. You just have to look at his supporters. Who pushed him to get where he is so fast? It's these individuals in Hyde Park, who don't always have the best interests of the community in mind.[3]

Such qualms did not evaporate even after he had been president for almost a year. In December of 2009, Congressional Black Caucus Chair Barbara Lee (D-Calif) criticized Obama for neglecting his promise not to ignore the critical relationship between race and poverty.

> With more than 24 percent of African Americans living below the poverty line and African Americans 55 percent more likely to be unemployed than other Americans, the existence of racial disparities is undeniable. As a candidate, President Obama said in his speech on race during the Democratic primary, "race is an issue that I believe this nation cannot afford to ignore right now." The facts speak for themselves. The Congressional Black Caucus recognizes that behind virtually every economic indicator you will find gross racial disparities.[4]

As befits their ambiguous political identities, FDR and Obama have complex relationships to the Democratic Party. They do not fit the stereotype of either insider or outsider. FDR began his political career as an outsider. He was a "dry," rural, Protestant in a state party that was overwhelmingly "wet," Catholic, and urban. He came in from the cold as a result of his strong and highly public support for the greatest Catholic politician of the first half of the twentieth century, Al Smith. FDR's first major public appearance after he came down with polio was at the 1924 Democratic National Convention where he gave a nominating speech for Smith. Thus, he distanced himself from his fellow "dry," Protestant Democrats who were mobilizing to defeat Smith, which they managed to do after 102 ballots. FDR gave another nominating speech for Smith in 1928. His reward was to earn Smith's support, and with it the backing of most party regulars, for his gubernatorial nomination in 1928.

Obama was very much a Chicago Democratic insider. He neatly balanced his liberal Hyde Park support with the backing he obtained from Mayor Richard Daley and the Cook County Democratic organization. His closest political confidant, Valerie Jarrett, was also one of the mayor's closest aides and advisors. Daley did not actively support Obama's unsuccessful candidacy for Congress. But the mayor could hardly have thought less of the young State Senator for trying to defeat the man, Bobby Rush, who had had the audacity to challenge him in the previous mayoral election. Obama's apostasy came when he decided to challenge Hillary Clinton for the presidential nomination. Clinton was the candidate of the party establishment as her early endorsements by many U.S. senators, congresspersons, and governors, as well as such powerful party coalition members as AFSCME, AFT, NOW, and ADA. Obama was only a first-term senator in the middle of his term. Even Warren Harding, the only other first-term senator to be nominated for president, finished his senatorial term before becoming president. Powerful pressure was exerted on Obama to wait his turn. Hillary Clinton's attacks on Obama were so bitter and trenchant that it was widely believed that they provided the Republicans with more than sufficient ammunition to defeat Obama should he obtain the nomination.

Both Obama and FDR endured difficult first-term nomination battles followed by easy general election victories. FDR was the front runner in 1932 but his path was obstructed by the party's two-thirds rule. With victory in November virtually assured, several rivals hoped to gain the nomination not so much by bringing themselves forward as by stymieing his effort to obtain two-thirds of the delegate votes. They knew that much of his delegate support was at best lukewarm. They were sure that if the balloting went on too long, those unenthusiastic supporters would tire of the tedium of the repeated vote tallies and seek to look elsewhere. The strategy almost worked. Although FDR obtained clear majorities in each of the three rounds of voting, he was still far from of a two-thirds margin. He gained the needed votes only because his lieutenants were able to convince William Randolph Hearst, who controlled the California and Texas delegations, that Newton Baker would be the nominee if FDR did not win on the next ballot. Baker, an outspoken internationalist, was anathema to Hearst. FDR had muted the internationalist sentiments he had espoused when he ran for vice president in 1920 and was, therefore, barely, acceptable to Hearst, who had been backing John Nance Garner of Texas.

FDR cruised to victory in the general election. Even though there was no public consensus on the causes of the Depression, the blame was borne by the incumbent. FDR offered no credible prescription for curing the nation's economic woes. Indeed his pledge to balance the budget in the midst of such a precipitous deflation would have added to those problems had he put it into effect. But his energy was infectious and his cheerful optimism offered a refreshing alternative to Hoover's downbeat solemnity.

According to the polls, Obama was in a virtual tie with McCain as of early September. But McCain's choice of Sarah Palin did not wear well with the voters, nor did his quixotic response to the economic crisis. As the election neared, Obama's victory became a virtual certainty.

Confident of victory, FDR and Obama played it safe. The promises of "a new deal for the American people," and "hope and change," on which they based their campaigns, gave little concrete guidance as to how they would actually govern. FDR took office without having shed the widespread impression that he was an amiable lightweight. Likewise Obama's very brief political career coupled with his moving but unspecific campaign rhetoric provided little insight into his real political persona. Therefore, more than most presidents, both needed to establish their political persona after their election. In both cases, the public wanted to know who is he really: a plutocrat; a democrat; black or white?

In response to the economic catastrophes they faced, both offered a grab bag of diverse policy proposals. FDR's early efforts included purchasing silver, declaring a bank holiday, cartelizing industry, the Tennessee Valley Authority, as well as public works and jobs programs. As Morton Keller remarks:

> The (Obama's) stimulus bill was a 1,071-page dog's breakfast: a long wish list of liberal projects (such as negating a portion of Bill Clinton's 1996 welfare reform act), and local pork, seasoned by $300 billion in tax cuts.[5]

More important than happenstance similarities or even than those resulting from aspects of personality and temperament are the ideological similarities. Both FDR and Obama are Progressives. Although FDR preferred to call himself a liberal, a term he reinvented, he fully shared Obama's commitment to fundamental Progressive tenets. Government is a useful and necessary engine of progress. Progress should involve not only technological and economic

improvement but the proper deployment and distribution of those improve-
ments to bring about greater political, economic, and social equality. FDR
proclaimed those commitments in his famous New Deal Speech with which
he accepted the 1932 Democratic Party nomination.

> Ours must be a party of liberal thought, of planned action, of enlightened
> international outlook, and of the greatest good to the greatest number of our
> citizens. . . . My program, of which I can only touch on these points, is based
> upon this simple moral principle: the welfare and the soundness of a Nation
> depend first upon what the great mass of the people wish and need; and sec-
> ond, whether or not they are getting it.[6]

In his 1941 "State of the Union Address" he declared that government
had a responsibility to guarantee four freedoms: freedom of speech, religion,
freedom from fear, and freedom from want. Whereas the first three comport
with the eighteenth-century liberal principles of the Constitution, the latter
requires the sort of positive, economically interventionist government that
Progressivism championed.

Senator Obama echoed similar sentiments in his celebrated address at the
2004 Democratic National Convention.

> I believe we can give our middle class relief and provide working families with
> a road to opportunity. I believe we can provide jobs to the jobless, homes to
> the homeless, and reclaim young people in cities across America from violence
> and despair.[7]

And again in his 2006 "Take Back America Speech,"

> I've had enough of our kids going to schools where the rats outnumber the
> computers. I've had enough of Katrina survivors living out of their cars and
> begging FEMA for trailers. And I've had enough of being told that all we can
> do about this is sit and wait and hope that the good fortune of a few trickles
> on down to everyone else in this country.[8]

President Obama's eagerness to involve the federal government in matters
as diverse as healthcare, climate change, and energy development reveals
that the president has not departed from the senator's Progressive outlook
and ambition.

In order to maximize support for their most important Progressive policies,
both FDR and Obama misinformed the public about how their signature policies would operate. FDR described his Social Security program as an insurance

program in which each person maintained his or her own account. But, in fact, the program operated on a pay-as-you go basis. Each year, the money raised in FICA tax is used to pay the pensions and other benefits of Social Security recipients. No one has an account and there is no effort made to calculate payments on an actuarial basis. One is taxed on the basis of one's wage income.

President Obama repeatedly assured the public that his health care plan was revenue neutral, meaning it would not cost the taxpayers any additional monies. The savings needed to cover the costs of the tens of millions of new health insurance beneficiaries would come from purported savings in Medicare costs that he must have known would never be realized. Because the Congressional Budget Office (CBO) was not willing to call the president a liar, it confirmed that his plan as presented was revenue neutral.

Both FDR and Obama were labeled by some of their conservative critics as socialists. The charge is untrue. They both rejected calls from leftwing allies, Rexford Tugwell and Paul Krugman respectively, to nationalize the banks.[9] The Tennessee Valley Authority (TVA) was as close to socialism as FDR ever got and he made clear that this experiment in federally provided electricity was intended only as a "yardstick" by which to judge private providers. The public option originally backed by Obama had a similar yardstick rationale. It would set rates sufficiently low to pressure the private insurers to keep their prices down. TVA was never emulated. The public option may not have been a good idea but it hardly constituted socialism. Those who pin the "red" label on FDR or Obama need a crash course in Progressivism, which is committed to government oversight and intervention but not government ownership.

The Mask of Command

These important similarities notwithstanding, the two presidents differ about perhaps the most critical of all aspects of executive leadership, what the great contemporary military historian John Keegan calls "the mask of command."[10] Keegan likens a commander to an actor in a Greek amphitheatre. To be seen and comprehended by the audience he must wear a mask. The purpose of the mask is not disguise but amplification. The mask is larger, bolder, and cruder than a real face. It is necessary because the audience cannot see and grasp the nuances and subtleties of facial expression. Likewise an actor does not speak in a normal voice nor gesticulate normally. Theatrical diction is artificially crisp, full throated, and loud. Theatrical gestures are exaggerated. Obama has a countenance suitable for molding into a mask of command. Obama's face is impassive and dignified; his speech sonorous and stern. His physical composure is ideal for television which, unlike a Greek Amphithe-atre, exaggerates and distorts motions and gestures. But the analogy should not be taken too far. The mask of command is made up of more than looks, voice, and gesture. It is composed of words and deeds that convey a sense of confidence, steadfastness, strength, patience, wisdom, and courage. Obama's public displays of ambivalence; his occasional inability to repress politically embarrassing private sentiments; his lack of appreciation for protecting the dignity of his office; and his impatience have conspired to prevent him from devising a mask as magisterial and commanding as the one FDR wore.

Most surprising, considering Obama's well-deserved reputation for dignified self-control, have been the politically damaging gaffes he has committed and his seeming offhand insult of an important ally. During the primaries, he ratio-nalized his inability to gain support among white working-class voters thusly:

> You go into these small towns in Pennsylvania and, like a lot of small towns in the Midwest, the jobs have been gone now for twenty-five years and noth-ing's replaced them. And it's not surprising, then, they get bitter, *they cling to guns or religion* or antipathy to people who aren't like them or anti-immigrant sentiment or anti-trade sentiment as a way to explain their frustrations (my italics).[11]

This was a double gaffe. First, he equated something that so many people revere—religion—and something so many people treat as right—gun own-ership—with xenophobia and parochialism. Second, he implied that people who worship and hunt do so not from conviction or for pleasure but as a means for coping with resentments. Hillary Clinton immediately pounced on Obama's statement, "The people of faith I know don't 'cling' to religion because they're bitter. . . . People embrace faith not because they are materi-ally poor but because they are spiritually rich."[12]

Upon learning that the noted African American Harvard Professor Henry Louis Gates, Jr., had gotten into an altercation with a Cambridge, Mas-sachusetts police officer at his Cambridge home, Obama told the press that the "Cambridge police acted stupidly in arresting somebody when there was already proof that they were in their own home."[13] When he made the state-ment, he lacked full knowledge of what had actually transpired. Over the next several days facts emerged that undermined Obama's criticism of the officer and put Gates in a less-than-flattering light. The official police report made clear that the police had ample cause to investigate what was going on at Gates' house. A neighbor called the police to tell them that two black men with what appeared to be backpacks were attempting to break into the house.

It later turned out that Gates had returned from Europe, had misplaced his key, and had used his shoulder to force the door open. When police officer James Crowley arrived Gates was already inside. When Crowley asked him to step outside onto the porch, Gates refused. Crowley then informed Gates that he was investigating a report of a break-in, to which Gates replied, "Why, because I am a black man in America?"

In response to further questions about who else was in the house, Gates began yelling and accused Crowley of being a racist who "had no idea who he was messing with." Gates repeatedly demanded that Crowley state his name but continued to yell so loudly that he did not hear Crowley give his name as well as explain that he was there in response to a citizen reporting a break-in. When Crowley started to return to his car, Gates pursued him, calling him a racist, and threatening retribution for the incident. At that point, the officer informed Gates that he was being disorderly. He repeated the warning and still Gates refused to stop screaming. At that point, the officer arrested him.[14] Gates never disputed these facts.

Crowley did not conform to the stereotype of a racist cop. In 1993, when the celebrated African American Boston Celtic star Reggie Lewis was undergoing cardiac arrest, Crowley had given him mouth-to-mouth resuscitation.[15] He had also co-taught a course on racial profiling at the Lowell Police Academy with a black police officer for five years.[16]

As a gesture of solidarity in the wake of 9/11, the British Government lent George W. Bush a bust of Winston Churchill by the great British sculptor Sir Jacob Epstein. Bush accorded it a prominent place in the Oval Office. When Britain offered to extend the loan for the duration of Obama's term, Obama refused and returned the bust. The only explanation offered was that each incoming president puts his own stamp on Oval Office decor.[17] In one fell swoop, Obama snubbed an ally and revealed disdain for someone who is perhaps even more highly regarded and revered in the United States than in Britain.[18]

These two gaffes and the insult to Britain share something in common. They accurately reflect deep-seated sentiments. Like so many Ivy League liberals, Obama believes that resentment and bitterness are what drive blue-collar people to hunt and pray. Henry Louis Gates, Jr., was his friend as well as a fellow African American so, naturally, he assumed that if Gates had a confrontation with a white policeman, the policeman was at fault. Obama's image of Churchill is not that of a savior of Western Civilization but of an imperialist who presided over the torture of Kenyan freedom fighters, including his grandfather.

It is unthinkable that FDR would have made gaffes of this magnitude. This is not to say either that he had perfect political pitch, nor that he harbored no private resentments and prejudices. Obama has yet to take any political initiative as wrongheaded and politically damaging as FDR's court-packing scheme. In private, at least before he became president, FDR was heard to utter the sorts of anti-Semitic and anti-Catholic remarks that were fully acceptable in his social circles. But he never did so in public. He kept his private feelings securely hidden behind his mask. Unlike FDR, Obama lacks the self-discipline to repress such impolitic sentiments.

A similar weakness is revealed by a major lapse in Obama's efforts to maintain the dignity of his office. At the behest of his political allies in Chicago, Obama made a trip to Copenhagen to lobby the International Olympic Committee to award the Olympic Games to his home city. Of course, the president of Brazil went to Copenhagen with the game goal. His is a nation on the rise, not yet secure in its standing on the world stage. Hosting the Olympic Games may do much to improve Brazil's global prestige. But the United States is the world's superpower. It cannot improve its standing in the world by engaging in the sort of competition that the effort to host the Olympic Games represents. If it wins, that merely reinforces its reputation as a bully. If it loses, it merely provides an occasion for lesser nations to gloat. Therefore it should do what only the most powerful nation in the world can do. It should stand aloof, as if the mere act of competing with lesser nations was beneath its dignity. Obama's eagerness to act as a shill for Chicago demeaned his nation and, as its executive, himself as well. The fact that his effort failed was of only secondary consequence.

Obama's impatience has proved far more politically damaging than his gaffes or even his debacle as an international traveling salesman. His haste to pass signal pieces of legislation is seen as comparable to FDR's efforts during "the 100 days" but the analogy is misleading. FDR understood that the only mandate he received from the election was to conquer the Depression and that, pace contemporary conservative critics such as Amity Shlaes, he did.[19] He recognized that he had no mandate from the public to enact transformative policy such as Social Security, which he did not press Congress to pass until the third year of his term, in 1935. He recognized that he needed to project a single-minded devotion to restoring prosperity. He was, as he later described himself, Doctor New Deal. He devoted virtually all his efforts in his first year in office to programs and policies whose sole aim was to boost the economy.

The sole exception was passage of the TVA, a project he supported, the impetus for which came from Senator Norris of Nebraska, who had been fighting for it for a decade. With regard to the TVA, FDR was not expending political capital but rather striving to increase it by placating the old Progressive warhorses like Norris for whom its creation was the fulfillment of a long and lovingly held ambition. He also went to great lengths to show that the huge outflows of spending that he was authorizing were devoted solely to the emergency and therefore temporary. He distinguished between the regular budget, which he was pledged to balance, and the emergency budget which would shrink once the Depression was alleviated. Among the earliest of the "100 days" statutes was the Economy Act, which drastically reduced government spending by cutting the salaries of government employees and reducing World War I veteran pensions.[20] While this action was counterproductive from a macroeconomic standpoint, it was strong proof of FDR's resolve to treat the Depression as a temporary emergency, not as an excuse to permanently expand the federal government. FDR would wait until he had the public firmly behind him before he embarked upon his broader project of federal government aggrandizement. Toward that end, FDR asked his Labor Secretary, Frances Perkins, to organize and lead a public education campaign aimed at building political support for Social Security. Perkins embarked upon a nationwide speaking tour, giving one hundred speeches in support of old-age pensions in 1933 alone.[21]

Obama took the opposite tack. He chose to make his number one legislative priority something that was not directly related to economic recovery, health care reform. Although many of his advisors, including Chief of Staff Rahm Emanuel, urged him to defer health care until later in the term, Obama refused. He had promised the voters that he could make Washington work and the best way of fulfilling that promise was to take on the most important problem facing the country and fix it permanently. He proclaimed to a joint session of Congress: "I am not the first president to take up this cause (health care), but I am determined to be the last."[22] Putting the best face on a decision he had opposed, Rahm Emmanuel told a *Wall Street Journal* conference of top corporate chief executives that "you never want a serious crisis to go to waste—this is an opportunity to treat what used to be long term problems be they in the healthcare area, the energy area . . . as immediate and must be dealt with."[23] Thus Obama was planning to exploit the crisis atmosphere generated by the economic collapse to enable him to pass other programs, including health care and energy reforms. Unlike FDR, he did not deem it wise to garner political capital first from a successful attack on the crisis to then use in pursuit of his broader goals. In the event, his strategy was successful. Despite the embarrassing defeat in the special election to fill the late Ted Kennedy's seat, and the consequent loss of a filibuster-proof majority in the Senate, he succeeded in convincing the House to pass the existing Senate bill unaltered, thus foregoing the need for a conference and thus forestalling the opportunity for a filibuster. And so the most ambitious policy reform in half a century was passed by straight party vote. In contrast to Social Security, the bill is not popular with the public.

War Command

Economic collapse is not the only critical circumstance these two presidents share. They are both war presidents, commanders as well as chief executives. It is no coincidence that the term "mask of command" was coined by a military historian. However important the crafting of the appropriate mask is in peacetime, it is even more critical to the conduct of war. In a stable regime such as the United States, domestic policy disputes mostly boil down to money—who pays and for what purpose. Such conflicts are real and hotly contested but they do not raise the same terrible question that war does: is the cause really worth the deaths of young American men and women? This is the question that the commander-in-chief must be prepared to answer convincingly. The question has two parts. Is the cause of sufficient moment to require such sacrifice? And, are we sufficiently certain of victory to ensure that the sacrifice is not in vain? The first part requires cogent reasoning skillfully conveyed. This plays to Obama's talents as a rhetorician. His speech in Oslo on the occasion of his being awarded the Nobel Peace Prize is a wonderfully cogent and moving explanation of why war is a necessary aspect of foreign policy and why the United States' efforts to combat worldwide terror are justified and necessary.[24]

Rhetoric is also necessary to address the second part of the question, but more than fine words are required to win the public's trust. In an effort to separate himself and his administration from what he takes to be the excessive moralism, triumphalism, and zealousness of his predecessor, Obama has chosen to display publicly his ambivalences about many critical aspects of American national security including: its status as a superpower, the nature of the conflict, the character of the enemy the United States is fighting, and the depth of U.S. commitment to the most active theater of that war, Afghanistan.

At a press conference ending the Nuclear Security Summit held in the Spring of 2010, Obama gave vent to his mixed feelings about the America's dominant role in world affairs: "Whether we like it or not, we remain a dominant military superpower."[25] Such ambivalence stands in marked contrast not only to presidents Obama might dismiss as triumphalists, such as George W. Bush and Ronald Reagan, but also to his immediate Democratic predecessor,

Bill Clinton. In his Second Inaugural Address Clinton proudly announced that "American stands alone as the world's indispensable nation."[26]

Bush clearly defined the nature of the conflict that emerged from 9/11, declaring a "War on Terror." The Obama administration has stricken that phrase from its official vocabulary. It removed the term "Islamic radicalism" from its National Security Strategy document. These deletions have not been replaced with cogent and meaningful alternative locutions. Thus, the public is left uncertain as to how the conflict should be understood and who is involved.

Obama does not deny that the United States has enemies but, like the conflict itself, he defines them ambiguously. Bush called North Korea, Libya, and Iran "the axis of evil."[27] He then eliminated Libya from the list when it agreed to abandon its efforts to acquire nuclear weapons. Obama has not only abandoned that epithet, in the Nuclear Posture Review Report issued in April 2010, he has also abandoned the term "rogue states," a term employed by Bill Clinton.[28] Instead, the former axis of evil nations are referred to as "outliers."[29] Use of this term obliterates any distinction between them and the other states that have refused to sign the Nuclear Non Proliferation Treaty such as Israel, India, and Pakistan.[30]

Similar ambivalence obscures the Obama administration's approach to captured illegal enemy combatants. Initially it chose to deviate from its predecessor's policy of trying all illegal enemy combatants in military tribunals and announced it would try 9/11 defendant Sheikh Mohammed and five other terror suspects in civilian court.[31] The administration has also chosen to treat both the so called Christmas Bomber, Umar Farouk Abdulmutallab, and the "Times Square Bomber," Faisal Shahzad, as ordinary criminals. Both were arrested, read their Miranda rights, indicted in civilian court, and allowed to meet with counsel. On the other hand, the administration has not abandoned the use of military tribunals. Five other illegal enemy noncombatants are scheduled to be tried by those entities.[32] The administration has offered no cogent rationale for choosing to try some terror suspects as civilians and others as wards of the military. While defending its decision to extend Miranda rights to would-be bombers, it has also proposed that a terror exception be established that would permit the government to interrogate suspected terrorists without informing them of their rights.[33]

Obama's most ostentatious display of ambivalence was his lengthy and highly public reconsideration of his pledge to fully prosecute the war in Afghanistan. Such a pledge had been a centerpiece of his critique of Bush foreign policy during the 2008 campaign. He accused Bush of over committing to the "wrong war," Iraq, and stinting on the "right war," Afghanistan.

During a visit to Afghanistan in July of 2008, he said, "I think one of the biggest mistakes we've made strategically after 9/11 was to fail to finish the job here, focus our attention here. We got distracted by Iraq."[34]

As president, he reiterated his commitment. In March of 2009, he ordered four thousand more troops to Afghanistan, pledging to "disrupt, dismantle and defeat" the terrorist al-Qaida network in Afghanistan and neighboring Pakistan.[35] He reiterated his commitment in the months following his inauguration and made a big point of sending his own emissary, General Stanley McChrystal, to Afghanistan to report back to him about what was necessary to make good on that pledge. Yet when McChrystal returned from Afghanistan recommending forty-five thousand additional troops, Obama hesitated.[36] He then spent the next nine weeks conducting a series of high-level meetings devoted to reconsidering his Afghan commitments.[37] In the end, he did agree to a thirty thousand troop increase but he also pledged to begin withdrawing U.S. troops by mid 2011.[38]

Obama had many good reasons for reconsidering his Afghan commitment. The Afghan president, Mohammed Karzai, was proving to be a weak leader who abetted pervasive corruption among his subordinates, including his own brother. The U.S. military was experiencing great difficulty in training and motivating its Afghani counterpart. And, Obama well knew that many of those who voted for him did not approve of the Afghan war. They had chosen to interpret his bellicose campaign statements as nothing more than an expediency, a gesture demonstrating that he was "tough" but one that would prove empty once he gained power.[39] In order to retain the trust and support of such supporters, Obama deemed it necessary to show them that a decision to escalate U.S. military support for Afghanistan would be taken only after the most deliberate and painstaking review of all the plausible options.

But such a lengthy display of uncertainty incurs tremendous costs. It reveals to friends and enemies alike that you are not fully committed to pledges you have made in the past and therefore they should discount any pledges you make in the future. Friends recognize they cannot count on the United States for the long haul. Those forced to choose between supporting the Afghan government or the Taliban readjust the calculus of that choice based on the diminished certainty of sustained U.S. involvement. The Taliban readjusts its strategy in response to Obama's signal that the United States is not in this struggle for the long run. A powerful regional power, India, is forced to reconsider its strategy for coping with the threat posed by the return to power of a radical Islamic regime on its border by diminishing its reliance on the United States as it formulates its own anti-Taliban policy.[40] This array of difficulties is a powerful reminder that an American president's mask of command is worn as much to impress his international audience as his domestic one.

In the same speech in which he announced his decision to send thirty thousand more troops to Afghanistan, Obama explained his pragmatic national security policy.

> As president, I refuse to set goals that go beyond our responsibility, our means or our interests. And I must weigh all of the challenges that our nation faces. I do not have the luxury of committing to just one. Indeed, I am mindful of the words of President Eisenhower, who—in discussing our national security— said, "Each proposal must be weighed in the light of a broader consideration: the need to maintain balance in and among national programs."[41]

These are the words not of a commander but of a policy analyst. The essence of the contemporary practice of policy analysis is the continual reordering of priorities in the light of the changing costs and benefits, risks and opportunities, associated with various policy alternatives.[42] It is all about flexibility. This is a laudable practice when one is indeed dealing with policy—health care, pollution control, etcetera. But war is not merely policy. Waging war is only partly about the efficient allocation of resources. Flexibility is a desirable tactical element of warfare but a dubious strategic one. Success is far more about those qualities that the mask of command is designed to project—resolution, confidence, courage.

Instead of quoting Eisenhower on the virtues of pragmatism, Obama would have done better to heed Ike's criticism of Truman's excessive flexibility regarding Korea. "To vacillate, to hesitate—to appease even by merely betraying unsteady purpose—is to feed a dictator's appetite for conquest and to invite war itself." In the same speech, Ike stressed that one thing he would not do was pledge an end to war in Korea by any exact date.[43]

The circumstances surrounding FDR's war leadership were far different than Obama's. He did not have to cope simultaneously with economic collapse and an ongoing war. He could more readily shed the mask of "Doctor New Deal" in favor of Doctor Win the War.[44] On the other hand, he could not claim to be constrained by his predecessor's military commitment. He had to inspire a reluctant public and Congress to prepare for war and to help the British and Russians who were already fighting Hitler. One will never know whether in the absence of Pearl Harbor and the consequent declaration of war against the United States by the Germans FDR would have succeeded in bringing the United States fully into the war. But, at a minimum, his relentless efforts to alert the American public to the dangers at hand greatly enabled the United States to prepare for war and to provide essential aid to Russia and Britain. Those efforts also greatly enhanced FDR's credibility when indeed the fight did become necessary. In the wake of the Japanese sneak attack on Pearl Harbor and the German declaration of war, the public well remembered both his prescient warnings as well as the false hopes provided by congressional and other appeasers and isolationists.

During the war the inevitable strategic and tactical disagreements were kept private. FDR's public face was one of radiant confidence and certainty of victory. As early as 1943 he and Churchill issued a statement demanding unconditional surrender by the Axis, a position from which they never deviated.[45] This unambiguous statement of war aims clarified the expectations of friend and foe alike. It reinforced FDR's continual claim that this was not a war about territory or power but about the irreconcilable principles of freedom and slavery and that the defense of freedom left no room for compromise. Unlike in Afghanistan, soldiers fighting in North Africa, Italy, or France knew precisely what they were fighting for.

LBJ

As the foregoing argues, Obama's combination of impatience regarding domestic policy and ambivalence regarding foreign policy is profoundly different from FDR's impeccable sense of timing and his resoluteness. In these crucial regards, Obama more closely resembles another Progressive Democratic president, Lyndon Johnson. Like Obama, Johnson felt compelled to exploit a crisis to push ambitious policy proposals that did not have deep public support and were hastily crafted. Rather than economic collapse, LBJ's crisis resulted from the assassination of JFK. His windfall was the massive Democratic landslide that ensued a year later. The "War on Poverty" was curtailed in 1966 and survived Nixon's 1968 victory in truncated form.[46] LBJ was not unaware of the risk he took in proceeding so precipitously with such lightly tested major innovations. But his eagerness to make sure that the nation's crisis did not go to waste rested on his pessimism about the U.S. electorate. He doubted that his overwhelming congressional majority would survive long, or that he would be reelected. Therefore, he felt it necessary to exploit his very temporary advantage. Like the Obama administration, he was captivated by the FDR "100 Days" precedent, even though he did not properly understand it.

LBJ prosecuted the War in Vietnam with the same marked ambivalence that has characterized Obama's words and actions about fighting terror. He told his biographer, Doris Kearns, that he would not copy FDR by abandoning domestic reform to concentrate all his and the nation's attention and effort on fighting the war. He would insist on remaining Doctor War on Poverty even as he became Doctor Win the War. His task was therefore to maintain public enthusiasm for domestic reform even as it took on the rigors of a foreign war. To do so he determined that he could not make those rigors too onerous. Unlike Bush in Iraq and Afghanistan, he did not call up the reserves. He did not ask for a tax increase. His efforts to stem draft evasion were half-hearted at best.[47] He did not order up an extensive and well-orchestrated propaganda blitz devoted to selling the war to the public. At the same time, he was unstinting in his efforts to bring the enemy to the bargaining table.

Although LBJ did offer cogent defenses of the war, in the face of the half-hearted mobilization and the ostentatious eagerness for peace, his words could not overcome an increasingly pervasive sense that the whole thing was not worth the trouble. As Vietnam War historian Herbert Schandler put it, "Having never been built, it could hardly be said that the national will collapsed."[48]

Conclusion

This chapter holds up FDR as the gold standard for commanders. And yet in critical respects his task was simpler and easier than the one Obama confronts. World War II was the greatest international military challenge the United States has ever faced. But even if one includes the years leading up to the war, as FDR tried to impress the American people with the need to prepare and perhaps fight, the war was of relatively short duration. The battle against international terrorism has already lasted longer and it shows no signs of abating. The Depression of the thirties was far more devastating than the circumstances the United States currently confronts, but that very severity made FDR's leadership task easier. Destitute Americans of that era were far more ready to accept radical remedies than are contemporary Americans, a majority of whom opposed the bailouts and whose fears about the uncertain impact of Obamacare exceed their hopes.[49] FDR's medicine was easy to swallow—deficit spending, public jobs, and old-age pensions. So far, Obama has prescribed similarly palatable cures—fiscal stimuli, job creation, and entitlement expansion. But far more bitter-tasting pills will soon be required. If the European debt crisis seems too remote to convince Americans that their day of fiscal reckoning is close at hand, they have only to observe California's dire straits to recognize that current levels of entitlement spending and debt dependency are unsustainable.

No modern American president has ever tried to preach peacetime austerity. Reagan and JFK cut taxes. LBJ and Obama launched massive new spending initiatives with no commensurate tax increases. George W. Bush outdid them all by coupling major tax cuts with a massive new entitlement program, Medicare Prescription Drugs. To be fair, Bush also embarked upon the only serious attempt at entitlement reform, but his Social Security privatization was unsuccessful even at capturing the imagination and support of his own party. Thus, there is no precedent for the task Obama must soon confront or risk sending his country into serious and perhaps irremediable economic and political decline. He and his successors will need to address the overspending crisis with the same resolve and persistent call for self-control and sacrifice that only the greatest American war presidents, FDR and Lincoln, have so far attempted. They must wear a mask of command sufficiently sturdy and fearsome to impress Americans to work longer into old age, care more for their elderly relatives with fewer health care services, and, more broadly, develop levels of self-abnegation and public spiritedness previously reserved for war.

Notes

1. Comparing a contemporary person with one from the past creates great awkwardness regarding verb tense. For the sake of narrative flow, I use the present tense when making comparisons between them in the same sentence despite the obvious, and therefore harmless, factual inaccuracy of so doing.

2. This epithet was a favorite of TR's. Its first documented use was in a speech at Provincetown, Massachusetts, on August 20, 1907.

3. Kenneth T. Walsh, "Obama's Years in Chicago Politics Shaped His Presidential Candidacy: Two Decades in the Windy City Produced the Obama We Know Today," posted April 11, 2008, https://therealbarackobama.wordpress.com/2008/04/11/rezkowatch-hotlist-041108/ (accessed July 18, 2010).

4. Glenn Thrush, "Black Caucus Reminds Obama of Pledge Not to 'Forget' Race," *Politico*, December 8, 2009, www.politico.com/blogs/glennthrush/1209/Black_Cau cus_urges_Obama_to_not_to_forget_race.html (accessed July 17, 2010).

5. Morton Keller, "Fixing the Economy: The New Deal and the New Foundation," unpublished manuscript, 14.

6. Franklin Roosevelt, Nomination Address, July 2, 1932, http://newdeal.feri.org/speeches/1932b.htm (accessed July 19, 2010).

7. Barack Obama, "Keynote Address at Democratic National Convention," July 27, 2004, www.washingtonpost.com/wp-dyn/articles/A19751-2004Jul27.html (accessed July 19, 2010).

8. Barack Obama, "Take Back America" speech, June 14, 2006, http://obama speeches.com/077-Take-Back-America-Obama-Speech.htm (19 July, 2010).

9. Keller, "Fixing the Economy," 14.

10. John Keegan, *The Mask of Command* (New York: Penguin, 1987).

11. "Barack Obama's 'Guns and Religion' Blunder Gives Hillary Clinton a Chance," *Times*, April 14, 2008, www.timesonline.co.uk/tol/news/world/us_and_americas/us_elections/article3740080.ece (accessed July 17, 2010).

12. Ibid.

13. Michelle McPhee and Sara Just, "Obama: Police Acted 'Stupidly' in Gates' Case," July 22, 2009, http://abcnews.go.com/US/story?id=8148986&page=1 (accessed July 17, 2010).

14. Incident Report 9005 127, Cambridge Police Department, Cambridge, MA, 7/16/09, 13:21:34, www.foxnews.com/projects/pdf/Gates_Arrest.pdf (accessed July 17, 2010).

15. Laurel J. Sweet, Marie Szaniszlo, Laura Crimaldi, Jessica Van Sack, and Joe Dwinell, "Officer in Henry Gates Flap Tried to Save Reggie Lewis: Denies He's a Racist, Won't Apologize," *Boston Herald*, July 23, 2009, www.bostonherald.com/news/regional/view.bg?&articleid=1186567&format=&page=2&listingType=Loc#articleFull (accessed July 17, 2010).

16. O'Ryan Johnson, "Crowley Teaches Racial Profiling at Police Academy," July 23, 2009, *Boston Herald*, www.bostonherald.com/news/regional/view/20090723crowley_teaches_racial_profiling_class_at_academy/srvc=home&position=0 (accessed July 18, 2010).

17. Tim Shipman, "Barack Obama Sends Bust of Winston Churchill On Its Way Back to Britain: Barack Obama Has Sent Sir Winston Churchill Packing and Pulse Rates Soaring Among Anxious British Diplomats," *Daily Telegraph*, February 14, 2009, www.telegraph.co.uk/news/worldnews/northamerica/usa/barackobama/4623148/Barack-Obama-sends-bust-of-Winston-Churchill-on-its-way-back-to-Britain.html (accessed July 18, 2010). *Newsweek*, "Obama Returns Churchill Bust To England: British Press Sees Snub," February 22, 2009, *Huffington Post*, www.huffingtonpost.com/2009/02/22/obama-returns-churchill-b_n_168919.html (accessed July 18, 2010).

18. For a comprehensive account of Churchill's reputation and his persistent popularity, see John Ramsden, *Man of the Century: Winston Churchill and His Legend Since 1945* (New York: Columbia University Press, 2002). Regarding Churchill's remarkable fame and popularity in the United States, see especially xiv, 325–70.

19. Amity Shlaes, *The Forgotten Man: A New History of the Great Depression* (New York: Harper Collins, 2007). Shlaes uses wrong unemployment numbers—the major thing FDR did to fight the Depression was to create public jobs—those real jobs for which people were paid real money and which for the most part they did real work were not counted as jobs—those who held them were for purposes of the unemployment statistics considered unemployed. If these workfare Americans are considered to be employed, the Roosevelt administration reduced unemployment from 25 percent in 1933 to 9 percent in 1936, up to 13 percent in 1938 (due largely to a reversal of the fiscal activism which had characterized FDR's first term in office), back to less than 10

percent at the end of 1940, to less than 1 percent a year later when the United States was plunged into the World War II at the end of 1941. GDP figures, after falling precipitously under Hoover, rose impressively every year during the New Deal, on the order of 10 percent, except in 1937 when FDR cut the budget. When spending increased in 1938, the economy bounced back. See Tim Lacono, *Real GDP Since 1930, Seeking Alpha*, February 4, 2009, http://seekingalpha.com/article/118349-real-gdp-since-1930 (accessed July 18, 2010). Gross National Product or Expenditure, 1929–1946, National Income Supplement to Survey of Current Business, July 1947, 19. Bureau of Economic Analysis Digital Library, reference this document with: http://library.bea.gov/u?/ SCB,3197, http://library.bea.gov/cdm4/document.php?CISOROOT=/SCB&CISOPT R=3197&REC=8&CISOSHOW=3161 (accessed July 18, 2010).

20. James E. Sargent, "FDR and Lewis Douglas: Budget Balancing and the Early New Deal," *Prologue* 6 (1974): 33–43.

21. Frances Perkins, *The Roosevelt I Knew* (New York: Harper Colophon Books, 1964).

22. Remarks by the President to a Joint Session of Congress on Health Care, September 9, 2009, The White House: Office of the Press Secretary, Washington, DC, www.whitehouse.gov/the_press_office/remarks-by-the-president-to-a-joint-session-of-congress-on-health-care (accessed September 9, 2009).

23. Rahm Emanuel on the Opportunities of Crisis, WSJDigitalNetwork, November 19, 2008, viewed on You Tube, www.youtube.com/watch?v=_mzcbXi1Tkk (accessed July 18, 2010).

24. Remarks by the President at the Acceptance of the Nobel Peace Prize, December 10, 2009, Oslo City Hall, Oslo, Norway, The White House: Office of the Press Secretary, www.whitehouse.gov/the-press-office/remarks-president-acceptance-nobel-peace-prize (accessed July 18, 2010).

25. President Barack Obama, Closing Remarks, Press Conference at Nuclear Summit, April 13, 2010, The White House, Office of the Press Secretary, America.gov, www.america.gov/st/texttrans english/2010/April/20100413195648ihecuor8.89 9653e-02.html (accessed July 18, 2010).

26. President William Jefferson Clinton, Second Inaugural Address, January 20, 1997, reproduced on Bartleby.com, www.bartleby.com/124/pres65.html (accessed July 18, 2010).

27. George W. Bush, State of the Union Address, January 29, 2002, archives.cnn.com/2002/ALLPOLITICS/01/29/bush.speech.txt/ (accessed July 18, 2010).

28. William Jefferson Clinton, "Statement Announcing the President's Signature of the National Missile Defense Act of 1999," in *Pushing the Limits: The Decision of National Missile Defense* (Washington, DC: Council to Reduce Nuclear Dangers, 2000), 55.

29. David E. Sanger and Peter Baker, "Obama Limits When U.S. Would Use Nuclear Arms," *New York Times*, April 5, 2010, www.nytimes.com/2010/04/06/world/06arms.html (accessed July 18, 2010).

30. "Outliers Urged to Join Nonproliferation Regime, Global Security Newswire," May 7, 2010, NTI, May 17, 2010, http://gsn.nti.org/gsn/nw_20100507_7585.php (accessed July 18, 2010).

31. "Accused 9/11 plotter Khalid Sheikh Mohammed Faces New York Trial," November 13, 2009, 2:01 p.m., *CNN Justice*, www.cnn.com/2009/CRIME/11/13/khalid.sheikh.mohammed/index.html (accessed July 18, 2010). As of this writing it is still not clear whether in fact Sheikh Mohammed will actually be tried in civilian court; the decision is being reconsidered by the Attorney General.

32. Ibid.

33. Charlie Savage, "Holder Backs a Miranda Limit for Terror Suspect," *New York Times*, May 9, 2010, www.nytimes.com/2010/05/10/us/politics/10holder.html (accessed July 18, 2010).

34. "Obama Calls Situation in Afghanistan 'Urgent,'" CNN Politics.com, Election Center 2008, July 21, 2008, www.cnn.com/2008/POLITICS/07/20/obama.afghanistan/ (accessed July 18, 2010).

35. "Obama Unveils Afghanistan Plan President Says U.S. Must 'Disrupt, Defeat and Dismantle' al-Qaida," *Associated Press*, March 27, 2009, MSNBC.com, www.msnbc.msn.com/id/29898698/.

36. Eric Schmitt and Thom Shanker, "General Calls for More U.S. Troops to Avoid Afghan Failure," *New York Times*, September 20, 2009, www.nytimes.com/2009/09/21/world/asia/21afghan.html; see also "Is It Amateur Hour in the White House?—Analysis: The Leak of Gen. McChrystal's Report Shows the Obama Administration is Mishandling Afghanistan," *Newsweek*, September 22, 2009, www.newsweek.com/id/215991.

37. Dean Nelson, "Analysis: Obama's Troop Surge Won't Solve Karzai Problem," *Telegraph*, December 5, 2009, www.telegraph.co.uk/news/worldnews/northamerica/usa/barackobama/6703655/Analysis-Obamas-troop-surge-wont-solve-Karzai-problem.html (accessed July 18, 2010).

38. Sheryl Gay Stolberg and Helene Cooper, "Obama Adds Troops, but Maps Exit Plan," *New York Times*, December 1, 2009, www.nytimes.com/2009/12/02/world/asia/02prexy.html (accessed July 18, 2010).

39. Christina Lamb, "Democrats in Revolt Over Barack Obama's Troop Surge," *Sunday Times*, November 29, 2009, www.timesonline.co.uk/tol/news/world/us_and_americas/article6936327.ece (accessed July 18, 2010).

40. Chidan Rajghatta, "Stay the Course in Afghanistan, PM Manmohan Singh Urges US," TNN, November 24, 2009, *Times of India*, http://timesofindia.indiatimes.com/world/us/Stay-the-course-in-Afghanistan-PM-Manmohan-Singh-urges-US/articleshow/5262957.cms (accessed July 18, 2010). G Parthasarath, "Uncertainty in India-US Ties," *The Pioneer*, New Delhi, April 15, 2010, www.dailypioneer.com/249212/Uncertainty-in-India-US-ties.html (accessed July 18, 2010).

41. Barack Obama, Speech on Afghanistan, December 1, 2009, http://abcnews.go.com/Politics/full-transcript-president-obamas-speech-afghanistan-delivered-west/story?id=9220661 (accessed July 19, 2010).

42. For a classic exposition of policy analysis, see Edith Stokey and Richard Zeck-hauser, *A Primer for Policy Analysis* (New York: Norton, 1978).

43. Dwight D. Eisenhower, "I Shall Go to Korea" speech, October 25, 1952, *Documents of American History II M2010*, http://tucnak.fsv.cuni.cz/~calda/Documents/1950s/Ike_Korea_52.html (accessed July 18, 2010).

44. Excerpts from the Press Conference, December 28, 1943, *American Presidency Project*, www.presidency.ucsb.edu/ws/index.php?pid=16358 (accessed July 18, 2010).

45. Churchill–FDR Joint Statement, Casablanca, Morocco, January 24, 1943, and January 24, 1943, *American Presidency Project*, www.presidency.ucsb.edu/ws/index.php?pid=16408&st=&st1= (accessed July 18, 2010).

46. Daniel Patrick Moynihan, *Maximum Feasible Misunderstanding* (New York: Free Press, 1966).

47. Bruce J. Shulman, *Lyndon Baines Johnson and American Liberalism*, 2nd ed. (Boston: Bedford St. Martin's, 2007), 147.

48. Herbert Y. Schandler, *The Unmaking of a President: Lyndon Johnson and Vietnam* (Princeton, NJ: Princeton University Press, 1977), 8.

49. As of May 17, 2010, a majority of Americans opposed the new health care law. "56% Still Want to Repeal Health Care Law, Political Class Disagrees," May 17, 2010, *Rasmussen Report*, www.rasmussenreports.com/public_content/politics/current_events/healthcare/march_2010/health_care_law (accessed July 18, 2010).

CHAPTER NINE

~

Barack Obama's Postracial Presidency

A New Joshua for a New Civil Rights Era

Carol McNamara

Barack Obama's 2008 presidential campaign raised the prospect of a postracial society for the United States. The campaign called on Americans to put the legacy of racial division behind them and to judge Obama's candidacy on the basis of his merit and character, regardless of the color of his skin.[1] In Obama's breakthrough 2004 Democratic Convention speech, he called to mind the integrationist civil rights movement of Martin Luther King, Jr., by rejecting what he considered the efforts of "the spin masters and negative ad peddlers" to slice up America. Instead, he argued for the essential unity and racial integrity of the country: "There's not a black America and white America and Latino America and Asian America; there's the United States of America."[2] The message of Barack Obama on the day he announced his candidacy for President of the United States was one of unity, unity in the quest for justice and opportunity, for better schools, better jobs, and health care for every American, and, above all, unity in the belief that "beneath all the differences of race and region, faith and station, we are one people."[3]

And yet, as a presidential candidate, Obama could not avoid racial controversy. In mid-campaign, Obama was compelled by the political storm caused by the divisive and racially charged comments of his Chicago pastor, Reverend Jeremiah Wright, accusing white people of endemic racism, to deliver his account of race in America and in his own life. During the campaign, many sought to understand who Barack Obama was.[4] In his so-called race speech, "A More Perfect Union," Obama reiterates briefly his biography in order to establish the grounds for his claim to a unique perspective on American political life. He is "the son of a black man from Kenya and a white woman from Kansas." He was raised with the help of his World War II–generation white grandparents. He attended "some of the best schools in America" but he also lived in one of the world's poorest nations—Indonesia. Obama reminds us that he is "married to a black American who carries the blood of slaves and slave owners" and he has "brothers, sisters, nieces, nephews, uncles and cousins, of every race and every hue, scattered across three continents." And perhaps most importantly, he knows that "in no other country on Earth" is his story even possible. We also know that before entering Harvard Law School, Obama worked as a community organizer in Chicago, returning after graduation to work as a civil rights lawyer and as a lecturer at the University of Chicago, before his entry into political life as a state senator in Springfield and, then, as the U.S. senator from Illinois in Washington D.C. Obama's argument is that it is his biracial, multicultural background and his community service in African American neighborhoods that give him a distinctive understanding of the American people in all their diversity. Obama's message in the campaign and beyond is an ambitious one—that he is uniquely positioned as president to create a heretofore unattainable unity that would overcome racial and ethnic boundaries in the United States.

Even as Obama introduced himself in this manner during the campaign, something about him remained elusive or difficult to pin down. As Joan Walsh writes in her review of David Remnick's *The Bridge*, Obama demonstrated "his slightly not-there quality: Supporters could love their own Obama, whether the one in the Shepard Fairey posters and Will-i-am songs, or the guy who talked about his white family's Kansas values,' praised Ronald Reagan, and reached out to make Republicans 'Obamacons.'"[5] Obama spoke to black America as one who had chosen blackness.[6] Princeton political scientist Melissa Harris-Lacewell told Remnick that she didn't think "Obama could have been elected if he had married a white woman. . . . Had he married a white woman he would have signaled that he had chosen whiteness, a consistent visual reminder that he was not on the African-American side."[7] And when Obama spoke to white Americans, Joan Walsh explains, he made them "feel better about themselves for liking him."[8] Or, as Shelby Steele explains it, Obama gave white America "the benefit of the doubt" on racial matters.[9] Obama's biracial identity and his ability to develop a relationship with black and white Americans were meant, it seems, to symbolize the racial unity he believed he could advance in the United States.

In his "A More Perfect Union" speech, Obama seeks to build on his message of racial unity through the promise of the Constitution. He reminds his audience that the answers to the racial challenges with which Americans still struggle, lie, as they always have, in the words of the Constitution: "a Constitution that had at its very core the ideal of equal citizenship under the law; a Constitution that promised its people liberty, and justice, and a union that could be and should be perfected over time."[10] In an effort to explain the context of Reverend Wright's comments, Obama tells the story of American racism in his speech. He argues, "That so many of the disparities that persist in the African American community today can be directly traced to inequalities passed on from an earlier generation that suffered under the brutal legacies of slavery and Jim Crow." To move beyond the "racial stalemate we've been stuck in for years," Obama calls on Americans to work together to combat the inequities remaining from past racial discrimination, to heal and transcend "the old racial wounds." Yet, while Obama notes in passing that African Americans must continue "to insist on a full measure of justice in every aspect of American life," his chief focus is the effort to connect the particular grievances of African Americans "for better health care, and better schools, and better jobs—to the larger aspirations of all Americans."[11] Thus, the latter part of Obama's speech on race focuses on the economic challenges he argues are common to all Americans: education, health care, and employment. The suggestion seems to be that for candidate and now President Obama, while legal challenges remain, the chief civil rights issues for African Americans and other minorities are social and economic, and the most effective way to address them is through the development of social and economic policies that promote equality, integration, and prosperity across the wide swath of American life.

Historically, the American presidency has supplied ambivalent leadership in racial politics. When Barack Obama was elected in 2008, he became the first African American President of the United States. In the end, 52.9 percent of all Americans and 96 percent of African American voters supported President Obama. The tension between black America and the American presidency would appear to have been resolved prior to and solidified by this historic election. Expectations in the African American electorate were certainly high that President Obama would devote himself directly to what African American civil rights leaders call the "black agenda."[12] Differences within the African American community arose quickly, however, with some leaders arguing that President Obama is not targeting sufficiently the chronic problems in black America concerning health care, education, and unemployment, but, instead, addressing them only "as part of a wider economic, educational or other policy."[13] It may be possible to explain this gap between expectations and the actions of the president by taking into account the unusually high hopes that many held for the transformative powers of Obama's presidency. It is equally plausible to argue that expectations of presidential actions in the realm of civil rights have more often been disappointed than fulfilled, and while this disappointment frequently has had something to do with the convictions or courage of particular presidents, they are just as often attributable to the complexities of presidential leadership within the system of federalism and the separation of powers.

In order to understand more fully why the presidency has often fallen short with regard to moral and political leadership on matters of race, this chapter will consider what the role of the presidency has been in the African American quest for equal civil rights during the founding, pre- and postcivil war periods, and into the time of the modern presidency. Is the presidency endowed with the constitutional powers to address the issues of racial politics? What powers, constitutional or extraconstitutional, have presidents exercised to expand black civil rights in America? The obstacles to presidential leadership with regard to racial matters are many: limited constitutional powers, federalism, party politics, and moral and intellectual courage, are among them. A fuller understanding of the president's role in racial matters up to this point will put the expectations, goals, and early accomplishments of the Obama campaign and administration in the context of the presidency's history on race as a whole. Then, we can consider the following: does President Obama have a specific "black agenda"? What is the place of civil rights in President Obama's Progressive policy agenda? Is it possible for a president to maintain the pursuit of a "black agenda" or the agenda of any specific group or faction, and to serve the national agenda of the American people without creating at least a difficult, if not an unsustainable, tension?

The Presidency, Race, and Politics

The responsibilities of the American President are, according to his oath of office, to preserve and protect the Constitution of the United States, and to see that the laws are faithfully executed. At the foundation of those laws are, of course, the principles articulated in the Declaration of Independence—that all men are created equal in their rights to life, liberty, and the pursuit of happiness. These fundamental principles and legal requirements were immediately compromised by the continued practice of slavery under the Constitution, during the initial ninety years of the Republic. American presidents often stood ineffectually in the face of slavery and what after the Civil War came euphemistically to be called "Southern Democracy." Though many pre–Civil War presidents expressed a private abhorrence of slavery, all publicly approached slavery, not in the context of principle and morality, but through the lens of practical politics. Many asked themselves what would bring about the end of slavery but few took an active role in hastening its demise. What, then, were the efforts of American presidents prior to the era of the modern presidency to preserve the promise of the Declaration and the Constitution as they apply to African Americans? What efforts did early presidents make to address slavery and secure civil rights for African Americans?

Although many early presidents expressed moral repugnance for slavery on a personal level, and even believed in the eventual necessity of emancipation, most believed that the president had little legal power within the constitutional order to bring about abolition, and some, who may have aimed to limit the duration of slavery through their actions, unintentionally prolonged it. George Washington is a case in point. Washington was personally opposed to slavery on two counts: the economic inefficiency and backwardness of the slave-labor system and his own moral repugnance to it, both of which led him to advocate abolition privately and to free his own slaves in his will. Yet, the chief obstacle to leading the public or political challenge against southern slavery was most likely Washington's conception of the presidency as "a unifying force for the new nation." He believed that his ability as the first president to stand as a symbol of American unity was essential to holding the fabric of the fragile new nation together. As such, he was unwilling to risk the division an early challenge to slavery would pose to the precarious constitutional experiment.[14] Similarly, Thomas Jefferson openly advocated the abolition of slavery in his *Notes on the State of Virginia*, because he believed slavery was a moral evil, but perhaps even more so because he was convinced it undermined the republican virtue necessary to ensure the success of the American Constitution.[15] As candidate and as president, however, Jefferson cautiously avoided the topic of emancipation as intolerable to his Southern constituents. Did Presidents Washington and Jefferson miss an early opportunity to resolve an issue that would plague the United States for hundreds of years to come? Would the moral authority of Washington and Jefferson have provided the leadership necessary for the timely abolition of slavery and a more solid foundation for American republicanism? Or, would the effort to challenge the South have precipitated a Civil War, endangering the entire American experiment in republican government, as the two presidents feared? Surely, it was appropriate to argue, as Washington did, that the only "proper and effectual mode" by which to accomplish abolition was through legislative authority, but what, then, was the appropriate place for presidential leadership in the struggle for emancipation and civil rights?

The pre–Civil War presidencies did, if anything, less to address the problem of slavery.[16] Jefferson's postpresidential support for the expansion of slavery into the territories prolonged the problem of slavery rather than diffused it, as Jefferson argued it would.[17] In fact, every president after Jefferson and until Abraham Lincoln made a similarly flawed judgment, believing that the expansion of settlement into the vast American-Western territories would maintain sectional balance and diffuse the tension created by slavery, allowing it to fall gradually into disuse. None until Lincoln, including Jefferson I would argue, understood fully that because slavery was valued in the South as the foundation for a way of life rather than merely an economic institution, the question concerning whether the new territories would be slave or free would intensify, rather than diminish, the division caused by slavery.

Abraham Lincoln and Franklin Delano Roosevelt are, in fact, the presidents Barack Obama has most praised and most sought to emulate in his presidential leadership in pursuit of equality in economic and civil rights in the United States. Like Lincoln, Obama seeks to end divisions among the American people; like FDR, he seeks to do so through Progressive public policy. Obama admits that the circumstances of his presidency are profoundly different than those of his predecessors. Both Lincoln and FDR found their political goals thwarted by Southern politics, slavery in the case of Lincoln, and Jim Crow segregation in the case of FDR. As a result, both were compelled by circumstances to take on the South and to reach out to bring African Americans into their political parties.

Abraham Lincoln was the first president to provide moral and political leadership with regard to slavery and civil rights. Whereas other candidates and presidents sought to support or avoid slavery by deferring the issue, Lincoln recognized that the institution of slavery presented a moral crisis that would divide the nation perpetually until it was resolved either in favor of slavery or against it.[18] He was also unwilling to concede that the practice of slavery in the United States' territories should be subject to what his 1858 Illinois Senate opponent Stephen Douglas promoted as the democratic principle of popular sovereignty. In Lincoln's "Cooper Union Address," which he delivered as an unannounced aspirant for the Republican presidential nomination, Lincoln made a strong argument supporting the authority of the federal government to control slavery in the Federal Territories.[19] It is fashionable but not entirely correct to argue, as Senator Obama did in a *Time* magazine article, that Lincoln's wartime Emancipation Proclamation "was more a military document than a clarion call for justice,"[20] or, as Melissa

V. Harris-Lacewell contends, that Lincoln "was often acting more for the Union than for racial equality."[21] For, as Lincoln's prewar and war speeches and his correspondence make clear,[22] he was persuaded not only that slavery is wrong, but that union and emancipation were ultimately inseparable objectives. Lincoln capitalized on the Civil War to exercise his executive power more energetically than any other president had, to secure Civil War victory and a Union "dedicated to the proposition that all men are created equal" and to "a new birth of freedom," under government "of the people, by the people, for the people."[23] Lincoln also supported vigorously the passage of the Civil War amendments to the Constitution in order to codify the civil rights gains of African Americans. Harris-Lacewell argues that Lincoln's actions earned him in the black imagination, "the role of an Old Testament prophet," who delivered them out of bondage. This affection for Lincoln tied black Americans to the Republican Party until the presidency of FDR.[24] Lincoln provided a model for the moral and practical exercise of presidential leadership necessary to end discrimination and obtain civil rights for African Americans under the Constitution. He demonstrated that the president had the legal constitutional authority to uphold the principles of the Declaration and the Constitution if he was willing to exercise the necessary political and moral leadership.

Post–Civil War presidents receded into the background, however, in enforcing the hard-won victory against racial inequality. They argued that the required deference to states' rights, in particular, the belief that presidents had no federal authority to enforce the Civil War amendments in the states, the Whig idea of legislative supremacy, and raw political necessity left presidents powerless to confront Jim Crow segregation and "Southern Democracy." Because the black vote remained largely Republican until the election of 1936 when the FDR Democrats deliberately courted their vote in an effort to undermine the power of the conservative Southern wing of the Democratic Party, post–Civil War Republican presidents made small efforts to guarantee a free ballot for African Americans. Presidential leadership of this era proved inadequate to the task of confronting Southern Democracy, however; in particular, the most egregious and unchecked crime of lynching. Even the Progressive presidencies of Theodore Roosevelt, Woodrow Wilson, and Franklin Roosevelt sacrificed African American civil rights for their own reform agendas.[25]

FDR's presidential legacy in civil rights is notably mixed. Much is written about Roosevelt's personal insensitivity on the subject of race and his initial reluctance to rock the proverbial political boat of the Democratic Party coalition between Northern Progressives and Southern Conservatives.[26] Kevin

J. McMahon concedes that FDR's initial impulse was to tailor New Deal legislation to southern preferences in order to win the support of Southern Democrats in Congress. But Southern intransigence on New Deal legislation led FDR to look for new Democratic voters in the North to liberate himself from the constraints of a southern–conservative-led Democratic Congress. In the 1936 election, Roosevelt successfully courted the black vote in the North. McMahon's argument is that when FDR failed to achieve his goal of undermining Southern conservatives in his notorious 1938 purge campaign, he began his pursuit of liberal transformation through progressive appointments to the federal bench and the Supreme Court, which led all the way to *Brown v. Board of Education*.[27] New Deal legislation, political attention, and the changes in the Court are largely credited with acquiring the African American vote for FDR and the Democratic Party. President Obama clearly sought to emulate FDR's success in his 2008 electoral strategy by rebuilding an electoral Democratic majority through the activation and integration of African Americans and Latinos voters. The chief lesson Obama takes from the FDR years in *The Audacity of Hope*, however, is that Roosevelt's willingness to exercise the power of the national government energetically saved "capitalism from itself through an activist federal government that invests in its people and infrastructure, regulates the marketplace, and protects labor from chronic deprivation."[28] Obama argues that Progressive New Deal policies produced a redistribution of wealth that created greater equality, prosperity, and security for all Americans, including minorities.[29]

The Civil-Rights-Era Presidency

The four civil-rights-era presidents (Truman, Eisenhower, Kennedy, and Johnson) confronted the continuing challenge of Southern segregationists, as well as increasing pressure from civil rights groups, with varying degrees and categories of executive initiative, but it is not until the presidency of Lyndon Johnson that Progressive social and economic policies are reintroduced as a deliberate means to completing the civil rights campaign. President Truman unilaterally initiated an important civil rights reform, desegregation of the U.S. military, promptly after World War II. By proceeding through executive order, he avoided congressional roadblocks. Truman was "motivated by his personal revulsion to reports that decorated African-American veterans, in uniform, had been dragged from buses in the South and beaten only hours after being discharged."[30] Presidents Eisenhower and Kennedy both supported desegregation but preferred gradual and low profile progress towards securing civil rights for African Americans. Sidney Milkis argues that Kennedy had the additional political problem endemic to the Democratic Party of "having to nurture a fragile liberal consensus."[31] Both presidents favored private persuasion to bring about integration but both were compelled to resort to the use of force to ensure compliance with court-ordered desegregation of schools and universities and federal supremacy.[32] In the end, Kennedy was also pushed by the activists in his Justice Department to use the administrative tools of the executive branch "to take affirmative action to enhance minority employment opportunities" in the government.[33] Like Truman, he could proceed unilaterally on certain matters, such as government employment policies, which enabled him to make some "progress" on civil rights by avoiding the obstacles posed by Democratic Party politics.

It is Lyndon Johnson, however, who is the first president to seize the leadership of the civil rights movement. He made history by passing through the Senate the 1964 Civil Rights Act and the Voting Rights Act of 1965, with the objective of establishing "first class citizenship" for African Americans.[34] Racial justice was for Johnson a necessary but insufficient foundational step toward what he understood as a fully just and good society. Johnson's grand ambition was to improve on the New Deal with his own Progressive vision of a "Great Society," in which all Americans "can come to live the good life." To implement his Great Society vision, Johnson's administration devised and pushed through Congress a set of social welfare policies under the umbrella of what he called the "War on Poverty," the signature legislation of the "Great Society." In his 1964 University of Michigan Commencement address, Johnson explained that the goal of the "Great Society" was "to advance the quality of our American civilization," starting with "an end to poverty and racial injustice," but ultimately aiming at "abundance and liberty for all." The Great Society would be a place where every child can find knowledge to enrich his mind and to enlarge his talents. It is a place where leisure is a welcome chance to build and reflect, not a feared cause of boredom and restlessness. It is a place where the city of man serves not only the needs of the body and the demands of commerce but the desire for beauty and the hunger for community.[35]

Milkis argues that Johnson's ambition was "to treat the deeper causes of the country's maladies," which included the problem of racial injustice, by expanding liberal politics beyond the economic programs of the New Deal to include "quality-of-life" social reforms, both through the power of the presidency and the mobilization of community action.[36] While Eisenhower and Kennedy understood civil rights chiefly in terms of law and order issues, Johnson sought to harness the "the idealistic zeal of the civil rights movement as the potential source of a new political order."[37] Milkis has high praise for Johnson's personal desire to accomplish civil rights reform and his ability to "take advantage of the opportunity that civil rights direct action provided" in order to pass "the landmark laws of 1964 and 1965."[38] Harris-Lacewell even suggests that "Lyndon B. Johnson could arguably be understood as equivalent to Abraham Lincoln in terms of the sheer impact of his presidency on African American citizenship." Like Lincoln, "Johnson took on the mantle of an Old Testament prophet," according to Harris-Lacewell, demanding that the nation "face the challenge of racial inequality in order to save its own democratic promise."

Of course, history would not judge LBJ on his civil rights leadership alone. Harris-Lacewell explains that the war in Vietnam led Martin Luther King, Jr., to become a critic of Johnson, despite his unwavering support for African American civil rights. She concludes that Johnson's failed leadership on Vietnam turned him into "a forgotten prophet."[39] Milkis concludes that Johnson was unable to sustain both his alignment with the particular cause of the civil rights movement and to "manage all the other responsibilities that the modern presidency pulls in its train," including the broad coalition necessary to support his ambitious Great Society programs and foreign policy agenda.[40] Furthermore, Milkis contends, Johnson employed contradictory means to accomplishing his objectives: the highly centralized exercise of executive power in the White House and Community Action Programs (CAPs), which paradoxically fostered insurgency and a more decentralized participatory democracy. According to Milkis, Johnson's ambitious exercise of executive power both demonstrated the potential and the limits of the modern presidency in leading the country to support specific social causes. But, in the end, the decentralization of the CAPs developed a base for protest groups against Johnson's policies, particularly the war in Vietnam.[41] Nevertheless, despite their failings, it is the Progressivism of FDR's New Deal vision and Johnson's Great Society that truly set the stage for Barack Obama's approach as president to integrating civil and economic rights for African Americans into mainstream American politics and policy.

The civil-rights-era presidents differed from earlier presidencies in that the expectations and pressure to make progress on civil rights for African Americans mounted during this time period, as Martin Luther King, Jr.'s civil rights movement gained momentum and as court decisions demanded government action. Nevertheless, many of the obstacles to civil rights reform remained in place to varying degrees: the constitutional limitations imposed on executive action by the legislature, the obstacles encountered by the raw politics of Southern Democracy, and the necessity of forming a national agenda that addressed the needs of the American people as a whole, while attending to the needs of a particular constituency, were persistent political challenges to the exercise of executive power. Even Lyndon Johnson, whose civil rights' goals were the grandest, ultimately met the limits of his political talent and ambition when he lost southern support as a result of his civil rights legislation, while, at the same time, he lost the support of civil rights leaders who could not support the war in Vietnam. And yet, despite the obstacles and setbacks these presidents faced, their actions raised expectations for executive leadership, that a president willing to exercise moral and political leadership and accept the inevitable costs could and should bring about further change in the realm of civil rights.

Barack Obama's Postracial Presidency

The day following the 2008 presidential election, Adam Nagourney proclaimed in the *New York Times* that on November 4, "Barack Hussein Obama was elected the 44th president of the United States . . . sweeping away the last racial barrier in American politics with ease as the country chose him as its first black chief executive."[42] Was this the glorious end of the civil rights era, or its real beginning? Obama clearly sees his election as a new stage or step in the civil rights movement. Certainly, in the context of his historic election, the expectations for the Obama presidency were high and the responsibilities extensive. Obama was elected president of the entire United States and yet as the first black president, he seemed also to have special responsibilities for forwarding the black agenda of the civil rights groups who had supported him so enthusiastically during the campaign. Conditions with regard to civil rights have changed significantly since the Johnson years when African Americans in the South were prevented from exercising their fundamental civil rights to vote, to live and eat and ride buses side by side with white Americans. But is Obama's challenge of meeting the expectations of his particular constituency, while addressing the needs of the nation as a whole, altogether different from that of Lyndon Johnson? Is it possible to connect seamlessly the particular grievances of African Americans with the larger aspirations of all Americans, which Obama asserted was his intention? Or will such tensions always afflict the presidency, even the first black president, from whom the country expects so much?

Barack Obama's writings and speeches, and, of course, his actions as president provide guidance on his understanding of the current circumstances and demands of the civil rights agenda, and how he intends to lead both African Americans and the nation as a whole on that agenda. Essentially, his approach prior to and during the campaign followed two tracks. First, he made a dedicated effort to assure African Americans of his full membership in their community in order to secure their political support. Then, on the national stage, in his writings and policy speeches, Obama reached out beyond the African American community to present himself to mainstream America as a biracial candidate, who could move the country beyond race. He would "make his biracial ancestry a metaphor for his ambition to create a broad coalition of support, to rally Americans behind a narrative of moral and political progress."[43] On the campaign trail, he explained his belief that the real remaining civil rights issues are what he categorizes in his precampaign book, *The Audacity of Hope*, as "Opportunity" or economic rights issues that, he argues, are national in scope.

The initial challenge of Barack Obama's campaign for the Democratic Party presidential nomination was to persuade the African American community to support his candidacy. David Remnick explains in *The Bridge* that many in the black community were either wary of another "symbolic black candidacy," or still loyal to the Clintons.[44] Obama's answer to this challenge was, Remnick argues, "to nominate himself as the inheritor of the most painful of all American struggles, the struggle of race." Because his exotic name and mixed racial background raised questions about his authenticity, Obama had to establish his credentials as a member of the African American community.[45] In appealing directly for African American support, Obama, like others who have assumed leadership of the civil rights movement in varying capacities, from Frederick Douglass and Abraham Lincoln to Martin Luther King, Jr., and Lyndon Johnson, sought the mantle of Old Testament prophet in the black community, as he embarked on his presidential campaign. As James Ceaser, Andrew Busch, and John Pitney make clear in their account of the 2008 election, *Epic Journey*,[46] he could not hope to win the Democratic nomination for president without African American support.

Early on in his quest for the Democratic nomination in 2007, Obama paid an unannounced visit to Union Missionary Baptist Church in Des Moines, Iowa, where he "cast himself . . . as a natural and necessary heir to the civil rights greats, appealing to black worshippers to show the courage of their forerunners and back his candidacy for president." Invoking the tradition of the black church as the starting point for African American culture, community, and political activism, Obama "cast his campaign in historic and even divine terms," according to reporters Mike Allen and Carrie Budoff Brown. Obama insisted that "he was there mainly to worship," and that he didn't "want to get too political," but few doubted his political purpose at the church during the early Iowa political season.[47]

Obama presented himself to his African American audience as the candidate who identified with and could best forward the black civil rights agenda. In the Iowa church, according to the reporters, he reproduced the "rising, rhythmic, repetitive intonation," reminiscent of "the civil rights pioneers," who "like Moses" "had been to the mountain top but did not reach the Promised Land." Instead, Obama recounted, they left it to their successors, the Joshua generation, to complete their mission. Obama acknowledges his debt and that of his contemporaries to those of the Moses generation who sacrificed and suffered through beatings, unjust incarceration, the attacks of dogs and fire hoses, to achieve their objectives. And yet although Obama acknowledges progress in civil rights, he wonders whether the inheritors of the Moses generation, "the Joshuas among us are willing to stand up, are willing to be counted, are willing to vote, are willing to organize, are willing to mobilize, are willing to get going."[48]

The Joshua generation is clearly the theme Obama uses to establish his legitimacy with African American voters, to indicate his reverence for the civil rights founders, and to engage young and old black voters in his story and his campaign. The first of the Joshua Generation speeches was delivered at the Brown Chapel in Selma, Alabama, commemorating the Selma Voting Rights March.[49] Here, Obama addresses the Joshua generation, his contemporaries, directly as the successors of the founding generation of civil rights giants, to remind them of their inheritance and responsibility. In Selma and in Iowa, Obama confronted a challenge that had implications for the contemporary civil rights movement, and for his own narrative. He acknowledges the success of the civil rights movement on the one hand, but he also says that "society's disparities between black and white remain as large as ever."[50] This latter argument may be necessary for establishing his identification with the black agenda. The question is how the two arguments fit together.

Obama argues in black churches and on the national stage that the chief terrain of the civil rights battle today is for economic rights to address what he calls "structural inequalities."[51] The call for greater economic rights in the Selma and Iowa speeches is a means to explaining how his leadership will address economic inequities for African American voters. On the theme of economic rights, Obama adopts the hallowed language of Franklin Roosevelt's *Fourth Inaugural Address*, in which he calls for "a second Bill of Rights under which a new basis for security and prosperity can be established for all—regardless of station, race or creed."[52] Obama echoes FDR's enumeration of these economic rights in the Selma speech and in *The Audacity of Hope*. In the Selma speech, Obama reminds the Joshua generation that although the civil rights movement has achieved much, "we've still got a lot of economic rights that have to be dealt with." These rights include: a right to adequate health care, adequate funding for education, a right to a higher minimum wage, retraining and adequate government support for the unemployed. In every case, Obama also calls for personal responsibility from African Americans but also "a government that is as responsive as the need that exists all across America" to address the difficulties afflicting the black community.[53]

It is with the expansion of the understanding of civil rights to include economic rights that Obama also tries to integrate his civil rights agenda into a broad national Progressive policy agenda. Obama's economic vision is not new: in addition to reviving Roosevelt's economic bill of rights, his assimilation of racial and economic equality is reminiscent of Johnson's Great Society objectives.[54] In an effort to demonstrate a foundation for racial unity on economic issues, Obama argues that African Americans are helped most by government programs that are not race specific and that assimilate the black agenda with the concerns of the mainstream of American politics and economics. "Ultimately," Obama contends,

> the most important tool to close the gap between minority and white workers may have little to do with race at all. These days, what ails working-class and middle-class blacks and Latinos is not fundamentally different from what ails their white counterparts: downsizing, out sourcing, automation, wage stagnation, the dismantling of employer-based health-care and pension plans and schools that fail to teach young people the skills they need to compete in a global economy. . . . And what would help minority workers are the same things that would help white workers.[55]

Obama's argument is that a rising economic tide lifts all boats, including minority boats. This is the civil rights message of unity that Obama seeks to advance: that all the American people benefit from an economy led by a government that aims at creating greater economic equity and security.

Identity Politics and Reverend Wright

Of course, as I note at the beginning of this chapter, Barack Obama was unable to avoid divisive racial controversy during the campaign. Obama's long and close association with Jeremiah Wright exposed him to the suspicion that he was in covert agreement with Wright's criticism of white America. As T. Denean Sharpley-Whiting of Vanderbilt African American Studies Professor wrote:

Wright's homiletics had the effect of coloring Obama a bit too darkly; his damning of American racism and genocides at home and abroad diminished Obama's averred gift of "second sight" into both black and white worlds, marred his claim to authenticity and a new politics.[56]

To address the real questions his association with Jeremiah Wright raised for the country, Obama delivered the "A More Perfect Union" speech. One of the chief objectives of the speech is to explain the difference between what Obama describes as Wright's static, hopeless image of a racist America and his own idea of a union, founded on the promise of the Constitution, that is in the process of perfecting itself morally and politically, and moving toward a greater unity of purpose. Obama received both praise and criticism for his speech from both mainstream and African American audiences. Henry Louis Gates, Jr., believed that the speech "rescued the Obama candidacy," showing that "he is our ultimate figure of mediation, standing tall above quarrels that most of us assume to be irreconcilable."[57] But, according to David Remnick, not all African Americans, even those who would disagree with Wright, were so pleased with this speech or subsequent speeches on the subject of race. Princeton Professor Cornell West was, and continues to be, critical of Obama for equating "the oppression of blacks with white resentment." Other black intellectuals and activists argued that when Obama asks African Americans to take responsibility on issues of family and fatherhood, he is "patronizing his audiences and minimizing the themes of institutionalized racism." Remnick reports that Glenn Loury, a prominent black economist, commented that Obama "was talking over the audience (in this case at the Apostolic Church of God on Chicago's South Side) to the rest of the country."[58] While the vast majority of African Americans continues to approve of his job performance, several black leaders who gave Obama the benefit of the doubt prior to his election, such as activist and PBS talk show host Tavis Smiley, have charged that "the nation's first African American president has failed to help black communities hit hard by the downturn" through "targeted aid" for minorities. Perhaps ironically, it is Al Sharpton, a man with a reputation for radical protest on race issues, who has become the president's defender in the black community. He tells civil rights leaders that they can't expect "Mr. Obama to become a 'black exponent of black views,'" and that they are applying a "double standard" to Obama, expecting "more from a black president than they would demand of a white Democratic president."[59] But is it surprising that they do?

President Obama has responded to the criticism of black leaders by repeating his insistence that African Americans will benefit most through his universalization of economic rights. Indeed, since taking office, Obama has clearly pursued a Progressive policy agenda which he argues expands government investment in the American people as a whole, including minorities. A list of his liberal policy initiatives and successes in the first eighteen months of his administration supports Obama's claims: liberal appointments to the Supreme Court and the National Labor Relations Board; stimulus spending and the government rescue of the auto industry; the overhaul of the student loan lending program—putting the federal government firmly in control of the program; education reform, in particular the "Race to the Top," a competitive grant program for state education reform; and, of course, the passage of health care and financial reform. On the table remain environmental legislation as well as immigration reform. These programs and proposals might not achieve the economic objectives Progressives believe they will, but they are perfectly consistent with the civil rights policy approach Obama trumpeted in *The Audacity of Hope* and during his campaign. So, why would African American leaders be dissatisfied with Obama's approach as president to civil rights issues? And are they correct that Obama's agenda is too detached from the black agenda?

Two summer incidents, the first in 2009 and another in 2010, raise questions concerning whether President Obama and his administration are as race-neutral and free from association with identity politics as President Obama's explicit policies and rhetoric suggest. The first event occurred in the summer of 2009 in an episode involving African American Harvard Professor Henry Louis Gates, Jr., which is well documented by Marc Landy in this volume. As Landy explains, upon learning that Mr. Gates had been involved in an altercation with a Cambridge, Massachusetts police officer at his home, Obama told the press that the Cambridge police had "acted stupidly" in arresting Gates in his own home. Obama took the opportunity raised by the question about the Gates' incident at the press conference to remind the country that, although he did not know the facts of the case,

> What I think we know, separate and apart from this incident, is that there is a long history in this country of African-Americans and Latinos being stopped by law enforcement disproportionately. And that's just a fact." He added later that the incident was "a sign of how race remains a factor in this society."[60]

Obama's hasty assumption that this was a case of racial profiling backfired politically when it became apparent that Cambridge police Officer James Crowley "did not conform to the profile of a racist cop," as Landy tells us. In fact, he instructed other policemen on how to avoid racial profiling. President Obama attempted to relieve the tensions created by his interference in the incident by inviting both Gates and Crowley to the White House for what has come to be called the "Beer Summit," an awkward effort at what James Ceaser calls, also in this volume, "tonal populism." One explanation for Obama's unguarded remarks is that Gates is the president's friend. But as Shelby Steele observed at the time, Mr. Obama's rash assumption that white racism was involved in the episode may reveal a "reflexive racialism" characteristic of the sort of "identity politics" that belies the promise of the president's postracialism "to operate outside of tired cultural narratives."[61]

Others have accused the Obama administration of using race for political purposes. In the summer of 2010, another incident arose involving President Obama's Department of Justice and the New Black Panther Party. According to J. Christen Adams, a veteran Justice Department voting-rights lawyer, the Obama Justice Department, led by Attorney General Eric Holder, inappropriately dropped charges of voter intimidation against the New Black Panther Party.[62] Justice Department officials ordered the lawyers pursuing the charges stemming from election day, 2008, to dismiss the claims, arguing that the "facts and law did not support the case." Adams contends that the real reason the charges were dropped in what he considers a case of indisputable voter intimidation against both black and white voters is "the profound hostility by the Obama Civil Rights Division in the Justice Department towards a race-neutral enforcement of civil rights laws."[63] The Justice Department issued a reply expressing regret that "a former department attorney" would distort the facts and make "baseless allegations to promote his or her agenda."[64]

Abigail Thernstrom, Vice Chair of the U.S. Commission on Civil Rights, also counters that the New Black Panther Party's violation of the Voting Rights Act might not, in fact, meet the very high legal standard set for prosecution in section 11(b) of the act for proving voter intimidation. She notes that "after months of hearings, testimony and investigation—no one produced actual evidence that any voters were too scared to cast their ballots." Her conclusion is that the New Black Panther Party is "a lunatic fringe group that is clearly into racial theater" and that there are more pressing voting rights issues before the Department of Justice, notably, her concern that the Holder Department of Justice will interpret the Voting Rights act to require race-conscious redistricting. Thernstrom contends the current political reality does not support the idea that African Americans and other minorities require extraordinary federal protection to ensure fair representation.[65] But if Adams' broader accusation that the official policy of Holder's Department of Justice is to avoid "bringing civil rights cases against nonwhite defendants on behalf of white victims" is substantiated, then, this, together with Thernstrom's redistricting concerns, might suggest an administration that speaks of a policy for the nation but practices racial politics through preferences.[66] This might indicate that the old, divisive side of the Progressive civil rights agenda that promoted racial preferences as a chief means to addressing racial inequality remains a part of the Obama administration approach to civil rights.

Conclusion

Presidential ambitions in racial politics have always confronted the constitutional limitations of executive power imposed sometimes by the legislature, often by politics. Because the president represents all the people of the United States, he must formulate policies that serve the public good as a whole, and avoid advancing policies that promote divisions. Public expectations for presidential action have become very high and public standards for the president's leadership, especially on legal and moral issues like civil rights, are equally high. President Obama's rhetorical leadership with regard to civil rights points toward an America in which old wounds will be healed and ancient divisions transcended. His chief practical solution to the remaining civil rights issues is to integrate them with what he considers the economic rights of all Americans by introducing policies that create greater equality of conditions across the nation. But like presidents before him, and perhaps more so given the historic proportions of his Presidency and the expectations his own candidacy and campaign raised, President Obama finds himself caught between the expectations of the African American minority that supported his electoral victory and his own vision of a unified policy for the whole country. A case in point might be the controversy in July, 2010 surrounding the edited remarks of Shirley Sherrod, an African American and former Georgia Director of rural development for the United States Department of Agriculture, which seemed to indicate that she had discriminated against white farmers. Sherrod was quickly asked to resign by the Agriculture Department, only to be offered an apology and reemployment when her full remarks proved to be a story of overcoming discrimination. Once again, the administration found itself caught up in a racial controversy; trying to demonstrate it would not tolerate racial discrimination in any form, even black against white, it rushed to judgment and, as in the Crowley affair, found itself in trouble with its African American constituency. In her response, Sherrod seemed to separate herself in terms of race and experience from the president. She suggested that President Obama "is not someone who has experienced what I have experienced through life, being a person of color."[67]

President Obama emphasizes that his biracial and multicultural background place him above the tired old cultural divisions of black and white in America and make it possible for him to create new solutions to the old problems of "structural inequality" and economic rights that unite the concerns of African Americans with the concerns of mainstream America. Because the president of the United States wields considerable power, especially with a supportive Congress, to establish the economic policy direction of the country, it is possible President Obama's new civil–economic rights agenda for the nation as a whole will yield more comprehensive results than previous presidencies in establishing a postracial society. Perhaps in the end, then, President Obama's success in civil rights will be judged more by the quality and success of his economic policies. But much will also depend on whether he can avoid problems similar to those that beset President Johnson's Great Society programs. Ultimately, President Johnson was unable to hold his political coalition of African Americans and Southern Democrats together. In the Spring of 2010, President Obama launched the November mid-term election campaign with an appeal to his voters: first time voters in 2008, African Americans, Latinos and women, who powered his presidential victory in 2008.[68] Will President Obama be able to satisfy both his narrow and broader constituencies, the African American and minority communities, and the American public at large without falling back on the identity politics he has publicly rejected? Will his Progressive agenda of securing economic rights create new kinds of social divisions? Is Barack Obama still in the model of a civil rights Old Testament prophet or is he truly a new postracial Joshua? If the success of his administration is judged ultimately by the success of his Progressive agenda and his economic policies, then, perhaps that would be the truest sign that Americans live in a postracial society.

Notes

1. Barack Obama, *The Audacity of Hope: Thoughts on Reclaiming the American Dream* (New York: Vintage Books, 2006), 275.

2. Barack Obama, "Democratic Convention Speech," July 28, 2004, www.command-post.org/2004/2_archives/013937.html (accessed June 28, 2010).

3. Barack Obama, "Senator Obama's Announcement for President," February 10, 2007, www.nytimes.com/2007/02/10/us/politics/11obama-text.html?_r=1&ref=politics&pagewanted=print (accessed July 14, 2010).

4. Interestingly, it is a question that observers, even supporters, continue to ask. See Richard Cohen, "Who is Barack Obama?" July 20, 2010, *Washington Post*, www.realclearpolitics.com/articles/2010/07/20/barack_obama_introduce_yourself_106374.html (accessed July 20, 2010).

5. Joan Walsh, "Barack Obama: The Opacity of Hope," April 5, 2010, *Salon*, www.salon.com/news/opinion/joan_walsh/politics/2010/04/05/david_remnick_the_bridge (accessed April 4, 2010).

6. The *Washington Times* reported that President Obama marked "African American" on his U.S. census form, without indicating that he was multiracial. Joseph Curl, "Obama's Census Mark Reveals Race Views," *Washington Times*, April 30, 2010, www.washingtontimes.com/news/2010/apr/30/checked-box-offers-window-into-obamas-views-on-rac/ (accessed July 19, 2010).

7. David Remnick, *The Bridge: The Life and Rise of Barack Obama* (New York: Alfred A. Knopf, 2010), 502.

8. Walsh, "Barack Obama: The Opacity of Hope."

9. Shelby Steele, *A Bound Man: Why We Are Excited About Obama and Why He Can't Win* (New York: Free Press, 2008), 104.

10. Barack Obama, "Barack Obama's Speech on Race: A More Perfect Union," *New York Times* Transcript, March 18, 2008, www.nytimes.com/2008/03/18/us/politics/18text-obama.html?_r=2&pagewanted=r (accessed June 18, 2010).

11. Ibid.

12. Jesse Washington, "PBS Host Smiley Calls Meeting to Urge Black Agenda," March 4, 2010, www.google.com/hostednews/ap/article/ALeqM5jXCd4lj_G6Njgcjj Sb4nUhnBQim-w (accessed March 4, 2010).

13. Lola Adesioye, "Should Obama Do More for Black America?" *Guardian*, March 3, 2010, www.guardian.co.uk/commentisfree/cifamerica/2010/mar/02/barack-obama-black-america/print (accessed June 18, 2010).

14. Dorothy Twohig, "That Species of Property: Washington's Role in the Controversy Over Slavery," *The Papers of George Washington*, 1997, http://gwpapers.virginia.edu/articles/twohig_2.html (accessed June 21, 2010).

15. Jefferson also argued that after emancipation, colonization of the manumitted slaves should be required to avoid miscegenation. He was persuaded by his own "scientific" conclusions of the inferiority of the black race. John Chester Miller, *The Wolf by the Ears: Thomas Jefferson and Slavery* (New York: The Free Press, 1977), 55, 58–59.

16. Melissa V. Harris-Lacewell, "African Americans, Religion, and the American Presidency," in *Religion, Race, and The American Presidency*, ed. Gastón Espinosa (Lanham, MD: Rowman & Littlefield, 2008), 209.

17. Miller, *The Wolf by the Ears*, 36, 247–48.

18. Abraham Lincoln, "House Divided Speech," Springfield, Illinois, June 16, 1858, http://showcase.netins.net/web/creative/lincoln/speeches/house.htm (accessed June 23, 2010).

19. Abraham Lincoln, "Cooper Union Address," New York, February 27, 1860, http://showcase.netins.net/web/creative/lincoln/speeches/cooper.htm (accessed June 24, 2010).

20. Barack Obama, "What I See in Lincoln's Eyes," June 26, 2005, *Time*, www.time.com/time/magazine/article/0,9171,1077287,00.html (accessed June 24, 2010).

21. Harris-Lacewell, "African Americans, Religion, and the American Presidency," 211.

22. Initially, Lincoln feared that racial harmony between the races would be impossible and he favored voluntary (never forced) postemancipation colonization. When he realized, however, that African Americans were hostile to colonization, as were the Latin American countries he envisioned as their destination, the president's desire began to decrease. Participation of blacks in the armed forces, starting in 1863, and "an ill-fated attempt to colonize blacks in Haiti," led Lincoln to abandon the idea of colonization altogether. See George Sinkler, *The Racial Attitudes of American Presidents: From Abraham Lincoln to Theodore Roosevelt* (New York: Double Day & Company, 1971), 44–53.

23. Abraham Lincoln, "The Gettysburg Address," November 19, 1863, http://showcase.netins.net/web/creative/lincoln/speeches/gettysburg.htm (accessed June 24, 2010).

24. Harris-Lacewell, "African Americans, Religion, and the American Presidency," 211–13.

25. Theodore Roosevelt believed that he "set the same standard for the black man and for the white" . . . but he "did not feel he was in a position to be a racial statesman, not in public at any rate." Sinkler, *The Racial Attitudes of American Presidents*, 345.

26. "Getting to Know the Racial Views of Our Past Presidents: What about FDR?" *The Journal of Blacks in Higher Education* 38 (Winter 2002/2003), 44–46. FDR was unwilling even to support antilynching legislation to avoid provoking Southern Democrats. See Kevin J. McMahon, *Reconsidering Roosevelt on Race: How the Presidency Paved the Road to Brown* (Chicago: University of Chicago Press, 2004), 12.

27. McMahon, *Reconsidering Roosevelt on Race*

28. Obama, *The Audacity of Hope*, 183.

29. Ibid., 291.

30. Ronald D. Sylvia, "Presidential Decision Making and Leadership in the Civil Rights Era," *Presidential Studies Quarterly* 25, no. 3 (Summer 1995): 396–97.

31. Milkis adds that Kennedy was also "riveted by the heightened tensions of the Cold War." Sidney Milkis, "The Modern Presidency, Social Movements, and the Administrative State: Lyndon Johnson and the Civil Rights Movement," in *Race and American Political Development*, ed. Joseph Lowndes, Julie Novkov, and Dorian T. Warren (New York: Routledge, 2008), 257.

32. Sylvia discusses the Eisenhower handling of Little Rock and Kennedy's use of force in the desegregation of the University of Mississippi; Sylvia, "Presidential Decision Making," 398–403.

33. Sylvia argues that "scholars of equal opportunity trace the origins of the term, affirmative action to President Kennedy's Executive Order 10925;" Ibid., 401.

34. Ibid., 403.

35. Johnson first outlined his vision for the "Great Society" in a 1964 University of Michigan Commencement Address, "Remarks at the University of Michigan,"

May 22, 1964, Lyndon Baines Johnson Library and Museum, www.lbjlib.utexas.edu/
johnson/archives.hom/speeches.hom/640522.asp (accessed June 28, 2010).

36. Sidney M. Milkis, "Preface" and "Introduction: Lyndon Johnson, the Great
Society, and the 'Twilight' of the Great Society," in *The Great Society and the High
Tide of Liberalism*, ed. Sidney M. Milkis and Jerome M. Mileur (Amherst: University
of Massachusetts Press, 2005), xii, 12, 16.

37. Ibid., 272, 274.

38. Ibid., 274.

39. Harris-Lacewell, "African Americans, Religion, and the American Presidency," 222–24.

40. Milkis, "Modern Presidency," 274.

41. Ibid., 271–74.

42. Adam Nagourney, "Obama Elected President as Racial Barrier Falls," *New
York Times*, November 5, 2008, www.nytimes.com/2008/11/05/us/politics/05elect.
html (accessed April 5, 2010).

43. Remnick, 4.

44. Ibid., 14.

45. Ibid., 3–4, 15.

46. James Ceaser, Andrew E. Busch, and John J. Pitney, *Epic Journey: The 2008
Elections and American Politics* (Lanham, MD: Rowman & Littlefield, 2009), 26.

47. Mike Allen and Carrie Budoff Brown, "Obama Casts Himself as Civil Rights
Successor," November 25, 2007, *Politico*, www.politico.com/news/stories/1107/7026.
html (accessed April 6, 2010).

48. Ibid.

49. Barack Obama, "Selma Voting Rights March Commemoration," Selma,
Alabama, March 4, 2007, www.barackobama.com/2007/03/04/selma_voting_rights_
march_comm.php (accessed July 1, 2010). The march followed the March 7, 1956,
events of "Bloody Sunday," the day African Americans marching from Selma to the
capital in Montgomery were beaten down by Alabama state troopers when they tried
to cross the Edmund Pettus Bridge. See Remnick, *Bridge*, 9.

50. Ibid.

51. Barack Obama, "Remarks by the President to the NAACP Centennial
Convention," July 17, 2009, www.whitehouse.gov/the_press_office/Remarks-by-the-
President-to-the-NAACP-Centennial-Convention-07/16/2009/ (accessed July 11,
2010).

52. Franklin Roosevelt, "Fourth Inaugural Address," January 20, 1945, http://
millercenter.org/scripps/archive/speeches/detail/3337 (accessed July 4, 2010).

53. Obama, "Selma Voting Rights March Commemoration."

54. Shelby Steele argues in *A Bound Man: Why We Are Excited About Obama and
Why He Can't Win* that although people said that Obama was "'fresh,' 'new,' and
unconventional . . . his truest problem is . . . that he is so utterly conventional," both
on racial and economic issues (126).

55. Obama, *The Audacity of Hope*, 291.

56. Remnick, *The Bridge*, 520.

57. Ibid., 525.

58. Ibid., 526, 534.

59. Peter Wallsten, "Obama's New Partner: Al Sharpton," *Wall Street Journal*, March 17, 2010, http://online.wsj.com/article/SB1000142405274870458840457512 3404191464126.html (accessed July 7, 2010).

60. Katharine Q. Seelye, "Obama Wades into a Volatile Race Issue," *New York Times*, July 23, 2009, www.nytimes.com/2009/07/23/us/23race.html (accessed July 7, 2010).

61. Shelby Steele, "From Emmitt Till to Skip Gates," *Wall Street Journal*, August 1, 2009, http://online.wsj.com/article/SB10001424052970204619004574322054186 035002.html (accessed July 8, 2010).

62. Adams resigned in protest in July, 2010, in order to testify in front of the Commission on Civil Rights. The DOJ has prohibited attorneys from complying with requests from the Commission to have lawyers testify.

63. J. Christian Adams, "Unequal Law Enforcement Reigns at Obama's DOJ," *Pajamas Media*, June 28, 2010, http://pajamasmedia.com/blog/j-christian-adams-you-deserve-to-know-%E2%80%94-unequal-law-enforcement-reigns-at-obamas-doj-pjm-exclusive/ (accessed July 5, 2010).

64. Kevin Ferris, "Back Channels: Panther Case Dismissal Needs Explanation," *Philadelphia Inquirer*, July 4, 2010, www.philly.com/inquirer/currents/20100704_ Back_Channels__Panther_case_dismissal_needs_explanation.html (accessed July 5, 2010).

65. Abigail Thernstrom, "The New Black Panther Case: A Conservative Dissent," *National Review*, July 6, 2010, http://article.nationalreview.com/437619/the-new-black-panther-casebr-a-conservative-dissent/abigail-thernstrom (accessed July 15, 2010).

66. Adams, "Unequal Enforcement."

67. George Stephanopolos, "George's Bottom Line," *ABC News*, July 22, 2010, http://blogs.abcnews.com/george/2010/07/shirley-sherrod-obama-is-not-someone-who-has-experienced-what-i-have-experienced-through-life.html (accessed July 24, 2010).

68. David Chalian, "Obama Launches DNC 'Vote 2010' Midterm Election Effort," *ABC News*, April 26, 2010, http://blogs.abcnews.com/politicalpunch/2010/04/obama-launches-dnc-vote-2010-midterm-election-effort.html (accessed July 15, 2010)

CHAPTER TEN

~

The Changing Face of Barack Obama's Leadership

James W. Ceaser

From charisma to populism—this has been the trajectory of Barack Obama's leadership over the past two years. Obama started out running a hard-hitting campaign, strongly criticizing the Bush administration for its economic policies, its "failure of leadership," and, especially, its "tragic mistake" in invading Iraq.[1] Yet as the race proceeded, Obama became best known for something that transcended his policy stances. Combining a high-minded oratory with a compelling personal appeal, he was able to excite, elevate, and at times even mesmerize his audiences, attracting crowds on a scale never previously seen in American politics. The emphasis in his speeches shifted to promote two broad and unifying themes: change and postpartisanship. Obama captured the imagination of millions, not just among Americas, but all around the world. His supporters so believed in his goodness and powers that he could describe his own nomination, without embarrassment or irony, as "the moment when the rise of the oceans began to slow and our planet began to heal."[2]

Obama's support continued to climb throughout the transition period and into the early months of his presidency, with his approval rating with the American public reaching nearly 70 percent in March of 2009. Faced thereafter with the inevitable trials and tribulations of governing, and determined to push a vast agenda that proved less popular than he thought, his support began to fade, falling to 45 percent by the summer of 2010.[3] In an effort to counter the decline, Obama sought increasingly to shore up support by rougher methods. He targeted opposition symbols ("the insurance industry," "dishonest doctors," "speculators," "a bunch of fat cat bankers on Wall Street," and the oil companies), called out and assailed individual opponents (Rush Limbaugh and the Republican leaders Mitch McConnell and John Boehner), and referred disparagingly to Republicans in general ("this crowd") and to those in the Tea Party movement.[4] Along with these attacks, he tested the old populist mantra of rallying the people—"I won't stop fighting for you"—and in April (six months before the mid-term election) called for the reconstitution of his 2008 electoral base of "young people, African Americans, Latinos, and women."[5]

By engaging in these campaign-style appeals outside of the normal campaign season, President Obama has emerged as practitioner-in-chief of what Alexander Hamilton referred to in *The Federalist Papers* as the "little arts of popularity."[6] These arts, as Hamilton well knew, are an inevitable feature of democratic politics, but their spread from the province of electoral politics, where the presidential-selection system in recent times has already degenerated into a nursery of populism and demagoguery, into the "normal" conduct of the presidency, represents a dramatic reversal of the founders' design. The Constitution was crafted to prevent a populist presidency; Obama today is in the midst of creating one.

Since the terms used to characterize the popular arts—charisma, populism, and demagoguery—are notoriously imprecise and value-laden, there is always a risk that a discussion of leadership style may seem unduly provocative. But leaving the exact words aside, the general direction in which Obama has been heading can hardly be disputed. In January of 2010 the friendly *Huffington Post* ran a headline: "President Takes Populist Message on the Road."[7] Even some of his staunchest and most serious supporters, among them *Washington Post* columnist E. J. Dionne, noted (approvingly) Obama "turning toward populism" early in 2010, a move Dionne thought was "imperative." Dionne's only advice was that Obama should ramp up the effort, which he clearly has done.[8] No one in the White House is embarrassed or dismayed at this turn of presidential style.

What the president's supporters add by way of explanation, if excuses for employing the "little arts" are still thought to be needed, is that he is only responding to an unprecedented series of vitriolic attacks, some with racial undertones, coming from detractors at Fox News and in the Tea Party movement. The President of the United States is a victim. But this explanation, whether or not it accurately characterizes the opposition (or whether the treatment of the president is all that unusual), misses the main point. The founders' concern was for the norms and standards of the presidency, not the behavior of the president's opponents. Many past presidents, including Washington and Lincoln, endured stinging criticisms from the press and from popular movements of the day, but never responded in kind. Besides, a president today does not want for other means to get his message across, having at his beck and call a staff of highly paid professional spokespersons, not to mention the usual array of flacks working on his behalf in the press corps. Does a president who has become his own chief point man put at risk an asset that is helpful to his standing and vital for the nation's political system: the dignity that attaches to the presidential office?

The drift toward a more charged rhetoric generated enough consternation by the spring of 2010 that the president himself decided temporarily to backtrack. In a commencement address at the University of Michigan, Obama, clad in academic regalia, adopted a more statesmanlike tone, deploring the lack of "civility" that is "starting to creep into the center of our discourse." He went on: "We can't expect to solve our problems if all we do is tear each other down. You can disagree with a certain policy without demonizing the person who espouses it. You can question somebody's views and their judgment without questioning their motives." To emphasize his fairness, he positioned himself above the fray, making a point of decrying the excesses "practiced by both fringes of the ideological spectrum, by the Left and the Right."[9] Yet Obama's lofty tone served only to grate on those who saw in the president's words the repetition of his by now all-too-familiar tactic of preaching earnestly what he does not practice. This tendency, they point out, has been especially evident in the areas in which "fair processes" and "good government" are most at issue, like public finance of campaigns (which Obama supported and then exempted himself) and the practice of bipartisanship (which Obama touted publicly but largely ignored in practice.) However nice the speech sounded, no one is being fooled.

The Popular Arts

The "popular arts," as that phrase was conceived by the authors of *The Federalist Papers*, referred to the various methods of boosting public support: dazzling (if one can), practicing an easy familiarity, promising and offering generous benefits, raising energy and anger by targeting and dividing, and blaming convenient scapegoats. Gaining approval by these methods stood in contrast, in the founders' analysis, to winning support by achieving stature. Stature comes from public recognition of having performed good service, or having displayed admirable qualities, or having demonstrated sound judgment. It is manifest when a political leader establishes himself "in the esteem and confidence" of a considerable portion of the public, so that public standing includes a dimension of "looking up" to a figure.[10]

Stature is one of the most elusive and precious qualities in political life, and it is almost always in short supply. Executives (governors) and public servants (including military leaders, like General Powell or General Petraeus), who build records of service, are in a better position to acquire stature than are legislators, whose main activity is expressing a point of view, about which there may always be a difference of opinion. Still, some legislators have managed to win a measure of stature by a career of championing important measures. Being elected to the presidency itself usually confers an initial measure of stature, not just because running a successful presidential campaign is a kind of accomplishment, but because the office of the presidency brings with it a certain dignity and distinction. But how a president acts in office affects whether he adds to this stature or diminishes it. Slipping approval ratings may tempt some presidents to try to revive their fortunes by indulging in the popular arts. What few presidential advisors bother to tell their clients, however, is that approval ratings are not a measure of stature. Efforts to "bump up the positives" by the popular arts can push up approval ratings, but very often come at the expense of losing stature.

The practice of the popular arts is as old as democratic politics. Only the names that designate its various techniques have changed. The founders were partial to the expressions of "playing the favorite," "popular leaders," "sycophants," and "demagogues." The last term connected their thought back to the classical treatments of popular government found in the works of Thucydides, Plato, Aristotle, and Plutarch.[11] Demagoguery, as the founders understood it, referred not only to the activity of lowly and mean rabble rousers who appealed to anger and fear—the likes of Cleon, described by Thucydides—but also to the more dashing figures, like Alcibiades or Julius Caesar, who appealed to positive emotions and fueled larger visions of hope and glory.

The terms used most frequently in contemporary discussions of the popular arts, charisma and populism, both originated after the founding. Charisma, meaning the "gift of grace" in its New Testament usage, was coined for political analysis by the German sociologist Max Weber around the turn of the twentieth century. Weber defined it as "a certain quality of an individual personality, by virtue of which one is 'set apart' from ordinary people and treated as endowed with supernatural, superhuman, or at least specifically exceptional powers or qualities." These qualities, Weber went on, are "regarded as divine in origin or as exemplary, and on the basis of them the individual concerned is treated as a leader."[12] While Weber meant the term to be a clear scientific concept, it has turned out to be anything but, and even Weber himself, when he used it in the context of modern politics, found that he had to relax the maximalist criteria. (What, after all, does it mean to have "exceptional powers or qualities"?) The term in common parlance today often is invoked to describe not only political figures, but also movie stars, sports figures, and performers. It is not always easy to distinguish it from celebrity.

In trying to confront the phenomenon of Obama's charisma, dubbed "Obamamania," during the 2008 campaign, it almost seemed as if John McCain's staff had been studying Weber's writings. A McCain campaign ad, released in the early summer of 2008, sought to pull down Obama's exalted image to mere celebrity by beginning with photo snapshots of Britney Spears and Paris Hilton before turning to Obama, who the narrator called "the biggest celebrity in the world."[13] A companion ad entitled "The One," by contrast, all but acknowledged Obama's charisma, ending with a scene from movie *The Ten Commandments*, where Moses (played by Charlton Heston) parts the waters of the Red Sea. The ad ends, "Barack Obama may be the one, but is he ready to lead?"[14]

For all of its imprecision, charisma seems to capture that certain "something" about a leader about which it might be said that you know it when you see it. Barack Obama *circa* 2008–2009 had it, Mitch McConnell does not. To take Weber's thought a bit more on its own terms, the leader who would come closest to being charismatic is the one who has a religious-like hold over his followers. This aspect of Obama's appeal during the campaign was palpable, as evidenced in the following personal account by Ezra Klein, a writer for *The Washington Post*:

> Obama's finest speeches do not excite. They do not inform. They don't even really inspire. They *elevate*. They enmesh you in a grander moment, as if history has stopped flowing passively by, and, just for an instant, contracted around you, made you aware of its presence and your role in it. He is not the Word made flesh, but the triumph of word *over* flesh, over color, over despair. . . . Obama is, at his best, able to call us back to our highest selves, to the place where America exists as a glittering ideal, and where we, its honored inhabitants, seem capable of achieving it, and thus of sharing in its meaning and transcendence.[15]

Weber's concept of charisma adds a further dimension to an understanding of leadership by stressing the aspect of a *relationship* between followers and leaders. Charisma depends not just on the qualities of the charismatic figure from above, but on a willingness to follow from below, which may stem from a deep-seated need on the part of the adherents. Whether charisma is ultimately driven more from the supply side than the demand side is difficult to determine; both, at any rate, are necessary. In the case of Obama's charisma, the importance of the demand side was already evident in the antiwar movement in 2004, before Obama appeared on the scene. But the person who stepped forward as the leader at that time, Howard Dean, whatever his other qualities, was small, unattractive, and snarly. In a similar vein, George McGovern, who led the antiwar movement in 1972 at a moment when its adherents seemed to be crying out for a charismatic figure, could never provide personal electricity. The chance for a charismatic leader disappeared with the assassination of Bobby Kennedy in 1968.

Although the founders lacked the term to describe a person anointed in the eyes of his followers, who rides to power on an enticing message of hope, they were not wholly oblivious to the phenomenon. In one of the more elegant and insightful passages of *The Federalist Papers*, John Jay identified a form of high demagoguery, in which the public might be "deceived by those brilliant appearances of genius and patriotism, which, like transient meteors, sometimes mislead as well as dazzle."[16]

In the many accounts written so far of Obama's meteoric rise in 2008, insufficient attention has been given to the demand side of the relationship and in particular to the peculiar yearning at that moment for a great leader. Barack Obama came to the fore in American politics in a period that was not only charismatically challenged, but also strikingly lacking in its supply of active political leaders of stature or even, more modestly, of political heft. Take the Senate. Who were the grand names in 2008 that stood out as substantial figures, other than John McCain and perhaps Ted Kennedy? Was it Chris Dodd, or Harry Reid? The same held true for the House of Representatives. A deficit of stature in this case is more to be expected, for the simple reason that most "stars" leave the House to move up the political ladder. Still, in the past there were representatives who enjoyed national recognition as substantial figures, like Sam Rayburn, or Tip O'Neill, or, more recently, Richard Gephardt. In 2008—and still today—there was no one in the House who even approached having this kind of standing. Barney Frank is evidently intelligent, but he often presents himself as a kind of prankster or clown. As for the governors, there were no doubt competent individuals in 2008, Mitt Romney among them, but there were few who were known nationally. The exception was Arnold Schwarzenegger, who even today is still best remembered as a barbarian or a terminator.

What was (and is) true of politics on the American scene was truer of the world as a whole. Who among the still active leaders qualified as a significant statesperson or even a person of enormous standing, someone whom the public could name, like a Tony Blair, a Nelson Mandela, or a Mikhail Gorbachev? Instead, the video photo ops of the world figures taken at those innumerable summits, in which the world leaders were invariably displayed against a light blue backdrop, showed a barely recognizable Gordon Brown, conspicuous by his dourness, Nicholas Sarkozy, bounding like a nervous little ferret, and Angela Merkel (perhaps in fact the most gifted of the group). Otherwise, it was a total blank. Almost no one could name the prime minister of Japan or say who's Hu in China. The only personages who in some sense were known to Americans in 2008 were two obvious populists or demagogues, Hugo Chavez and Mahamoud Ahmadinejad, both on the verge of turning into tyrants. Next to all of these insignificant (or contemptible) personages appeared a new and attractive figure, unsullied by any previous political activity, whom many could only imagine or hope would fill this dreary void. For that moment, Obama looked to be a Brobdingnagian among Lilliputians.

A touch of charisma (or something like it) is a nice thing for a president to have. There is no doubt that Harry Truman and Gerald Ford—men who made no pretense, because they could not, to possessing the "gift"—may have been disadvantaged for the want of it—though the same could surely have been said in another era of two great men, and credible presidents, John Adams and James Madison. In the final analysis, however, charisma sits uneasily with a republican form of government. There is no doubt a place for the wholesome expression of enthusiasm in a democracy, which is what so many analysts claimed that Obama's campaign engendered. But there is a fine line between a healthy enthusiasm and a dangerous form of hero worship.

One alarming aspect of charismatic politics that was on full display in the 2008 campaign was the obsequious performance of the leading journalists in the major newspapers and television networks. These vaunted pillars of what was once called the Fourth Estate by and large abandoned even the pretense to objectivity to fall into line behind Barack Obama, first in the primary campaign against Hillary Clinton and then in the final election campaign against John McCain. One of Obama's best jokes, funny only because it was so true, came at the White House correspondents' dinner in 2009, when Obama told his audience: "Most of you covered me; all of you voted for me. Apologies to the Fox table."[17] A failure of a similar kind, again in the context of charismatic politics, occurred when so many historians and journalists succumbed to the charms of John Kennedy to paint a mythical image of his presidency that was likened to Camelot.

Judgments about charisma will always be subjective. But looking over the past half century, it seems plausible to argue that while Ronald Reagan and Bill Clinton both possessed great popular allure and charm, only John Kennedy (especially after his tragic death) and Barack Obama (during the campaign) can lay claim to enjoying charismatic moments. The link between these two men therefore merits special attention. In one of the most highly covered events of the 2008 Democratic primary campaign—a day that for Hillary Clinton still lives in infamy—the major wing of the Kennedy family, including Ted Kennedy and Caroline Kennedy, gathered at a rally to endorse Barack Obama. Caroline told the audience that Obama would be able to make people "feel inspired and hopeful about America the way people did when my father was president."[18] The rally resembled nothing so much as a ceremony in which the priestly keepers of the power of charisma, held as an amulet, were now at last prepared to bestow it on another figure.

Charisma poses a deeper challenge to constitutional government: the temptation of its bearer to try to guard it at all cost, which is only a natural human reaction. This reaction becomes more worrisome, however, when the maintenance of the leader's charisma is regarded as an asset that the nation cannot afford to lose. Obama supporters regularly insist that his standing in the world is vital to changing perceptions about America and to winning concessions or favors from foreign powers. Obama himself reportedly expressed this point when he met in 2008 with Democratic members of Congress: "I have become a symbol [abroad] of the possibility of America returning to our best traditions."[19] The nation's foreign policy has arguably become hostage to the president's charisma.[20] Some of Obama's foreign policy speeches, in which he took public issue with his predecessor and questioned American motives—positions that might ordinarily be thought to be un-presidential or dishonorable—have been justified as necessary to sustain the President's image, which, it is promised, can be leveraged at some point for the nation's interest.

Perhaps so, although the record to date has yet to show many concrete returns. But this kind of realism hardly bespeaks a foreign policy conducted with "a decent respect to the opinions of mankind," where principles are set down as markers, designed one day to open eyes and convince others. It represents instead a foreign policy based on an indecent pandering to an evanescent infatuation with a person.

Tonal Populism

Populism is another term used to designate the popular arts. It was adopted as the name of a political party in the 1890s (also known as the People's

Party). Not only has the content of the term been vague, but also the evaluation placed on it has shifted and continues to shift. At the outset, followers of the Populist Party and the larger movement obviously saw the term in a positive light. Opponents, especially those in the Progressive movement, managed not only to neutralize it, but eventually to turn it into term of opprobrium. Populism came to be seen as backward and xenophobic. Later on, Progressive and liberal historians regularly associated it with most dangerous kinds of reactionary popular movements, from fascism to McCarthyism.[21] Sometime thereafter, however, the term made a partial comeback. While it still occasionally has the negative connotation, it is frequently used today descriptively and often with a positive connotation. For a time, when John Edwards was running for the presidency in 2004 and 2008, he was regularly described in the press as having a "positive populist message," and, as noted, today many commend President Obama for his turn to populism.

The term is so ambiguous in its content that it can only be saved for analytic use by breaking it down into two different components: "tonal populism" and "political populism." Tonal populism refers to a dimension of meaning that has become mainstream in American political life. Populist here refers to the claim that a person (or a party or movement) is without pretention. Populism is an emanation of the plain people. A person is a guy like all others, someone you could have a beer with, or a gal like all the others, someone whom you could be frank with, if not go moose hunting with. Populism in this sense may once have been thought vulgar, at least from an aristocratic or upper-class point of view, but the democratic character of American mores made it inevitable that it would eventually take its place as an acceptable, even respectable, part of American politics. Tonal populism is nonelitist, but without any special policy message. A typical example was found in the opening line of Scott Brown's stump speech in his 2010 senate campaign in Massachusetts: "Friends and fellow citizens, I'm Scott Brown, I'm from Wrentham, I drive a truck and I'm asking for your vote."[22]

Tonal populism is often said to have originated in American politics with Andrew Jackson, the first president from a western state (Tennessee), who made no bones about his common origins or tastes. But populism only achieved full mainstream status when it became bipartisan in the presidential campaign of 1840, which John Quincy Adams described as marking "a revolution in the habits and manners of the people." The Whig Party invented the notion of the campaign as a mass spectacle by mobilizing party faithful to hold rallies, sing songs, and enact dramatic skits, all to celebrate the downhome virtues of "Old Tip" (William Henry Harrison), whose simple ways were captured in the campaign's symbols of the log cabin and hard cider. The

Whigs managed to out-Jackson Jacksonianism, a feat that was all the more impressive because it was achieved by a political party that, only four years earlier, had rejected party organization altogether as demagogic and prided itself on representing the more respectable elements of society, too proud to truckle after votes. All this changed when, as one Whig observer remarked at the time, "men of the highest culture did not disdain at times to 'go down to the people.'"[23]

While tonal populism is now accepted, even favored, in American politics, not everyone can successfully claim it. There are only just so many country lawyers to go around. For a politician to try to force himself into the mold of an ordinary guy when it does not fit can make him look not only phony but ridiculous. Just ask John Kerry, who campaigned for the presidency in 2004 in a leather jacket, meanwhile returning to one of his several mansions to drink green tea and go windsurfing. It never worked. Fortunately for American politics, even though claiming tonal populism may be an asset, it is not the only way to rise to prominence. There are other avenues, including demonstrating competence, achieving stature, and possessing charisma. Neither John F. Kennedy nor Barack Obama, for example, made tonal populism the basis of their claim to distinction.

If claiming tonal populism is not essential for an American political leader, it is nevertheless important not to be viewed as an "elitist," which is the bane of tonal populism. It is a frequent ploy of tonal populism, and perhaps its worst aspect, to play the game of labeling someone "out of touch," sometimes merely by pointing to the "objective" indicators of an old family name, wealth (especially inherited), and a high educational status at a prized institution. Each of these indicators can present challenges to an aspiring political leader, although in most instances adept individuals have found ways to escape or neutralize the charges. Americans can be remarkably tolerant today even of wealth and privilege. What they cannot excuse, however, is an attitude that shows disdain of the average person. John Edwards, who ran for the presidency as the self-proclaimed people's candidate, survived his multimillionaire fortune, huge mansion, and four-hundred-dollar haircuts; what he could never have survived, and what only became known later, was his comment to an aide that he hated attending state fairs where "fat rednecks try to shove food down my face. I know I'm the people's senator, but do I have to hang out with them?"[24]

It is clear today, and conceded by political analysts from both parties, that Democrats have run afoul of tonal populism more than Republicans. Despite the fact that Republicans suffer slightly more from the disadvantages of family name and wealth, though probably no longer of educational status, intellectual spokespersons on the Democratic side have been more open in letting slip their disdain for the "average" American, as in their initial reaction to the selection of Sarah Palin as the vice-presidential nominee of the Republican Party in 2008. But such generalizations about the parties do not govern every individual case. Bill Clinton remains the prime example of the Democrat who, despite holding a Yale law degree, winning a Rhodes Scholarship, and befriending many liberal intellectual elites, had no trouble claiming to be a tonal populist. It was not just the fact that he came from a dirt-poor background in Arkansas and a troubled family, or that he spoke naturally with a Southern intonation (although he would often annoyingly dial up the twang before certain audiences). Bill Clinton was also saved by his vices. Any man who was known for gobbling down two Big Macs in one sitting, who could count among his girlfriends Gennifer Flowers and Paula Jones, and who had a nickname of Bubba, was beyond all suspicion of elitism.

On the Republican side, the most interesting cases are the two Bushes, George and George W. Both of them carried the triple burden of family name, wealth (some inherited), and educational status. These damaged George somewhat, especially when they were added to a government career in which he served in the "elite" services of the diplomatic corps and the CIA. George was often accused of being a blue-blood, with a long resume. He succeeded nonetheless in being elected president. But the old ghost came back to haunt him in 1988, when, during a visit to a supermarket, he reportedly expressed astonishment at the device of a price scanner, which by that time had become fairly common. Bush was accused of being a man out of touch with the plight of the average American, a charge that stuck during tough economic times.

The case of George W. is even more intriguing. On the scale of objective factors, W. stood in certain respects in a worse position than his father, as he was a son of a president and doubly inflicted with degrees from Yale and Harvard. He was very nearly sunk in the 2000 election for this reason alone, when Texas Governor Ann Richardson uttered, in as elongated a drawl as the nation had ever heard, the most memorable line of the 2000 Democratic convention: "Poor George, he can't help it. He was born with a silver foot in his mouth." George W. managed to survive and by the end to efface entirely any connection with elitism. He was helped partly by his own down-home demeanor and his Texas connections, but what truly saved him was the smugness of his detractors. They so relentlessly attacked his mannerisms, tastes, and intelligence and ridiculed his evangelical faith that they denied themselves any possibility of depicting him as out of touch with the average American.

Barack Obama has had a peculiar and troubled relation to tonal populism. He made virtually no attempt in the 2008 campaign to claim it or establish himself as a "familiar" figure, with the rare exceptions being his appearances before African American audiences, where he would sometimes slip into a more popular African American tone and cadence. Obama could afford to eschew making an appeal to tonal populism because he had more compelling qualities. Not only did he have his charisma, but he displayed an impressive intellectual bearing in his famous Philadelphia oration on race in March (responding to the questions of his relations with Reverend Wright) and a remarkable "coolness" and sobriety during the financial crisis that struck the nation in September. Obama during the campaign did not have to be of the people, because he was evidently above them and in a way that his supporters admired.

Obama was, and in most ways remains today, conspicuously nonpopulist in the tonal sense. At the same time, it also should have been easy for Obama to escape the trap of offending the populist spirit. He had little in the way of objective status to indict him, coming from a broken family without wealth or status, and being from a race that has been on the outside, and so unjustly treated, in American life. All Obama had to do was live down his Harvard law degree and his position as a professor at the University of Chicago, hardly an insurmountable task for such a talented politician. Nevertheless, in one of his major weaknesses as a political leader, he has repeatedly blundered into situations of being plausibly accused of elitism, from which he has had difficulty extracting himself. All have come from mistakes of his own making. There was an early issue in the campaign when he stopped wearing a flag pin on his lapel, which it had appeared that he took off deliberately in criticism of a certain kind of strong or populist patriotism. He later succumbed and put it back on, largely denying the significance of the whole matter.[25] Far more important, in what nearly cost him the nomination, Obama in a supposedly closed speech to a highly liberal audience in San Francisco, explained away some of the opposition to him from Midwestern workers: "They get bitter, they cling to guns or religion or antipathy to people who aren't like them . . . as a way to explain their frustrations." Hillary Clinton pounced on this comment as "elitist," a charge that was repeated across the spectrum. Obama tried to deflect the criticism by going back to the objective factors: "I am amused about this notion of elitist, given that when you're raised by a single mom, when you were on food stamps for a while when you were growing up, you went to school on scholarship."[26]

Since becoming president he has continued to struggle on this point. In one highly visible and controversial incident in which a white police officer,

James Crowley, arrested his friend, Harvard English professor Henry Lewis Gates, Jr. (an African American), Obama sided with his friend and accused Crowley of "acting stupidly." Without having checked the facts of the incident, Obama classified it as a race issue, whereas many saw it as a class matter, with an elite professor disrespecting a police officer. Obama later partly backtracked, offering a half apology. The elitism issue was brought further front and center when Obama called Crowley and Gates together to the White House for the so-called "beer summit." There is nothing in principle more populist in America than guys "having a beer." Yet when the summit took place and the photo-ops were released, the only guy who looked truly at ease with his beer was officer Crawley. On a larger note, it is conspicuous that no one working for President Obama could publicly utter an "Aw Shucks" without it looking phony.

Finally, there was President Obama's ill-advised encounter with Scott Brown's truck, in which Obama, campaigning for Brown's opponent, gently ridiculed Brown for his campaign ads, telling his audience, "everybody can buy a truck." He missed the iconic status of trucks. Except perhaps in Cambridge, where the Prius rules, average Americans, even in Massachusetts, cling stubbornly to their large vehicles. The blogs had a field day decrying the president's elitism.

Tonal populism, though it is widely accepted and has become part of the fabric and even fun of American politics, is still occasionally subjected to criticism. Critics no longer object to it, of course, from an aristocratic view that dismisses openly the very idea of democracy and scoffs, like Coriolanus, at "the beast with many heads"; they instead argue that the populist point of view goes too far in celebrating popular common sense, which can sometimes hide popular prejudice and put into question the legitimate role of experts. This criticism would have far greater merit than it does if it were not for the fact that it is so often used to protect experts from trying to claim more authority than the knowledge they possess warrants.

Political Populism and Demagoguery

Populism has another meaning, designated here as "political populism." Its principal form involves pitting one part of the community against another in order to generate energy and boost popularity. It speaks in one way or another of a popular "us" ("the people"), representing the good, and an oligarchic "them" (the elite or the interests), representing the bad. In contrast to tonal populism, which is content to try to establish sympathies and associations, political populism generally promises to make important policy changes, such as punishing the big interests, spreading the wealth around, or stripping government of certain functions.

There is both a Leftist and a Rightist version of political populism. The Left speaks of an economic power elite that is manipulating the system to its advantage, oppressing the people. The Right speaks of a class of experts bent usually on using public authority in one way or other to transform their morals and run people's lives. The Left will resolve the problem by taking on Big Capital, the Right by confronting Big Government. Both versions are powerful in their appeal, which is one reason they are used so frequently. It is arguable that the Left recently has had a tougher rhetorical case to make, for the reason that the public today is not always aware that it is oppressed by the wealthy. The wealthy have found ways to fool people, which require leaders on the Left to wake them up and make them aware of their false consciousness. Leaders on the Right, too, have to make people aware of plots directed against them, which are hidden under the supposed neutrality of academic reports ("studies show that . . .") or theoretical doctrines (a "living constitution"). But once the challenge becomes clear, there is usually little problem stirring those on the Right, so palpable and obvious is the disdain displayed by elites on the Left.

These two versions of populism reflect parts of the genuine public philosophies of liberalism and conservatism. It is only to be expected, therefore, that aspects of the two populisms would appear in public discourse as genuine arguments and that in any political campaign there would be expressions of populism. But political populism in the fuller sense occurs when the populist themes become the core of the presentation and when it is deployed as a self-conscious technique, replacing argument, to gin up support, and solidify and boost opinion. Politicians clearly know when they are "going populist," and the tone and character of their presentation usually leave little doubt of what they are doing. White House advisors signaled in January that the president was about to launch a populist campaign, and Obama quickly followed with an attack on the Supreme Court decision of *Citizens United v. FEC*, which struck down certain limitations on campaign ads by corporations: "It is a major victory for big oil, Wall Street banks, health insurance companies and the other powerful interests that marshal their power every day in Washington to drown out the voices of everyday Americans."[27] Subtlety has never been a part of populism.

One of the best examples of a political populist appeal in American history was William Jennings Bryan's "Cross of Gold Speech" delivered at the Democratic convention in 1896. Bryan, known as the "Great Commoner" (one can't get more populist than that), was probably the greatest campaign orator in American history, at least until Barack Obama. His speech was so powerful that it won him the party's nomination a few days later. Bryan made sure early on in the speech to cover his tonal populist base by invoking Andrew Jackson: "What we need is an Andrew Jackson to stand as Jackson stood, against the encroachments of aggregated wealth." He then went on vividly to set the city, which was the symbol of finance and the gold standard, against the farms, where the true people resided:

> I tell you that the great cities rest upon these broad and fertile prairies. Burn down your cities and leave our farms, and your cities will spring up again as if by magic. But destroy our farms and the grass will grow in the streets of every city in the country. . . . Having behind us the producing masses of this nation and the world . . . we will answer their demand for a gold standard by saying to them: You shall not press down upon the brow of labor this crown of thorns, you shall not crucify mankind upon a cross of gold.

Populism as a technique is often contrasted with "statesman-like" rhetoric, which aims to appease conflict, tone down division, and appeal to reason. Of course statesmanship in its highest sense is the management of affairs for the public good, which may sometimes require an approach that divides. But the statesman would follow this path only when necessary and not for mere political gain. The usual tone of the statesman will be calming and deliberate, and it was the aim of those who created the presidential office to promote statesmanship. Indeed, in usual parlance today, the terms "statesman-like" and "presidential" are used synonymously. To engage in populism or parallel demagogic tricks, to blame others, to show so little magnanimity—all of these actions necessarily appear un-presidential.

Political populism has been the technique of choice of many candidates for the presidency, especially during contested races for party nominations. Still, even in presidential campaigns, there are choices about how far and in what degree to take a populist stance. An internal debate on this question took place inside the Gore campaign in the late summer of 2000, as the Democratic Party convention approached. The issue was whether Gore would adopt a more moderate or statesmanlike pose, defending the record of achievement of the Clinton years and stressing his own experience as a mature leader, or appear as a populist, "fighting" for the people. The answer appeared almost the second Gore appeared on the stage, when he launched into his speech delivered with a hyped-up mountain accent, promising to take on every big interest and, repeatedly, to "fight for you." Many Democrats to this day have never forgiven him for what some called a flaming populist oration.

Gore's populist appeal was later refined to a more polished form by his vice-presidential nominee John Edwards in his "two Americas" campaigns of 2004 and 2008. The two Americas were the rich and the poor or, in a simpler version, "the super rich and everyone else." Today, more has been learned about John Edwards than most probably ever care to know. But the unwillingness of so many political commentators to condemn his cheap populism, which was so evident at the time, reveals a blind spot in seeing demagoguery whenever it takes the form of defending the "poor" and inciting class warfare.

A look at Barack Obama's speeches during the 2008 campaign shows no shortage of political populist rhetoric. Yet this part of his campaign so clearly took a back seat to the articulation of his grander themes and to the attraction of his person that it is impossible to justly describe the core of his appeal as populist. Now that his themes have dissipated into thin air and the charisma has worn off, it is more and more the technique of political populism that characterizes Obama's leadership. But coming from a president, rather than a candidate, it appears at the wrong time and in the wrong place.

The Presidential Office

The modern president is at once a policy advocate (or party leader) and a constitutional officer. These two roles at some point must come into conflict, and one of the challenges every president must confront is to find a proper balance between the two. Today, Barack Obama is on the brink of abandoning the presidential role.

The presidential part of the office, while suggested by the Constitution, is in reality more the creation of George Washington, who made it one of his primary tasks to "fill in the blanks" of the Constitution and establish the norms and expectations appropriate to the office.[28] Washington invented presidentialism. One of those norms is for the president to appear as president of all the people, even when others may not choose to accept him as such. His advocacy, no matter how strong, must respect a set of limits and be characterized by a certain forbearance. Because the president is not like everyone else, he must respond differently to criticism and react with a formal magnanimity even beyond what his opponents might deserve. For a president to wage a populist campaign outside of the campaign season, for a president to call out directly by name another citizen, for a president to pose himself as "fighting for you," pulls the office down and the occupant with it. This is the behavior of a candidate, and an ordinary one at that, not the comportment of the chief executive.

With his commanding voice, his elegant presence, and his intelligence and command of the language, Barack Obama has more personal tools to be presidential than any president since Dwight D. Eisenhower, who had a different set of skills. But, with the exception of Bill Clinton, Obama has shown less inclination than any of these presidents to be so. The loss to him has been incalculable. With the decline of his charisma, which anyone could have foreseen, the logical, and politically astute, course of action would have been to gradually replace charisma with presidentialism. Obama has taken just the opposite path. His political counselors do not have the slightest clue of the damage they have done to him, because they have no conception of what the office of the presidency is all about. They coach their prince to be presidential on one day and populist on the next, oblivious to the obvious fact that if "presidentialism" appears as a mere pose it inevitably produces the opposite effect of what is intended.

To be presidential, a president must practice it daily, to the point that others have no choice but to view it as sincere. Then and only then can a president on rare occasion break from the mold. Obama has professed to regard George Washington and Abraham Lincoln as his models, but there is no indication that he has studied, or if studied taken to heart, the manner in which either man conducted himself as president. They jealously guarded the dignity of the office; he is heedlessly frittering it away.

Notes

1. "Obama Declares He's Running for President," CNN, May 2, 2007, www.cnn.com/2007/POLITICS/02/10/obama.president/index.html (accessed July 11, 2010).

2. Barack Obama, speech delivered on June 3, 2008 in Minneapolis, Minnesota, www.breitbart.com/article.php?id=d912vd200&show_article=1 (11 July 2010).

3. Gallup Tracking Poll, "Obama Job Approval" (January 1, 2009–July 1, 2010), www.gallup.com/poll/113980/Gallup-Daily-Obama-Job-Approval.aspx (accessed July 11, 2010).

4. See Weekly Address: "Taking the Insurance Companies on Down the Stretch," October 17, 2009; "Obama Slams 'Fat Cat Bankers,'" December 12, 2009, www.google.com/hostednews/afp/article/ALeqM5g2J-qjM_z5yfHUp4moR-3S-IvSuA; "Remarks by the President on the Economy at Carnegie Mellon University," June 2, 2010, www.whitehouse.gov/the-press-office/remarks-president-economy-carnegie-mellon-university (accessed July 24, 2010).

5. Alister Bull, "Obama Talks Tough in Ohio," Reuters, January 22, 2010, www.reuters.com/article/idUSTRE60L4MC20100122 (July 11, 2010); "Obama Jumps into Race . . . ," Fox News, April 26, 2010, www.foxnews.com/politics/2010/04/26/obama-jumps-race-appeal-latinos-african-americans-women-youth/ (accessed July 11, 2010).

214 ⁓ James W. Ceaser

6. Alexander Hamilton, John Jay, and James Madison, *The Federalist Papers*, ed. Charles Kesler (New York: Penguin Books, 2003), no. 68.

7. Phillip Elliott, "Obama Town Hall in Ohio: President Takes Populist Message on the Road," *Huffington Post*, January 22, 2010, www.huffingtonpost.com/2010/01/22/obama-takes-populist-push_n_432749.html (accessed July 11, 2010).

8. E. J. Dionne, Jr., "Supreme Court Ruling Calls for a Populist Revolt," *Washington Post*, January 25, 2010, www.washingtonpost.com/wp-dyn/content/article/2010/01/24/AR2010012402298.html (accessed July 11, 2010).

9. "Remarks by the President at University of Michigan Spring Commencement, Big House," University of Michigan, Ann Arbor, Michigan, May 1, 2010, www.whitehouse.gov/the-press-office/remarks-president-university-michigan-spring-commencement (accessed July 11, 2010).

10. Hamilton, Jay, and Madison, *The Federalist Papers*, no. 78 and no. 57.

11. Ibid., no. 49 and no. 66.

12. Max Weber, *The Theory of Social and Economic Organization* (New York: Oxford University Press, 1947), 358–59.

13. JohnMcCain.com, "Celeb," video, 2008, www.youtube.com/watch?v=oHXYsw_ZDXg&feature=player_embedded (accessed June 26, 2010).

14. JohnMcCain.com, "The One," video, 2008, www.youtube.com/watch?v=mopkn0lPzM8 (accessed June 26, 2010).

15. Ezra Klein, "Obama's Gift," *The American Prospect*, January 3, 2008, www.prospect.org/csnc/blogs/ezraklein_archive?month=01&year=2008&base_name=obamas_gift (accessed July 11, 2010).

16. Hamilton, Jay, and Madison, *The Federalist Papers*, no. 64.

17. Richard Leiby, "Obama Delivers the Zingers at Journalists' Dinner," *Washington Post*, May 10, 2009, www.washingtonpost.com/wp-dyn/content/article/2009/05/09/AR2009050902802.html (accessed July 11, 2010).

18. Caroline Kennedy, "A President Like My Father," *New York Times*, January 27, 2008, www.nytimes.com/2008/01/27/opinion/27kennedy.html (accessed July 11, 2010).

19. Jonathan Weisman, "Obama's Symbolic Importance," *Washington Post*, July 30, 2008, http://blog.washingtonpost.com/the-trail/2008/07/29/obamas_symbolic_importance.html (accessed July 11, 2010).

20. "President More Popular Abroad than at Home," Pew Foundation Survey, June, 2010, http://pewresearch.org/pubs/1630/obama-more-popular-abroad-global-american-image-benefit-22-nation-global-survey (accessed July 11, 2010).

21. Margaret Canovan, *Populism* (New York: Harcourt Brace, 1981), 183–85.

22. Matt Viser, Eric Moskowitz, and Martin Finucane, "Obama Stumps for Coakley," January 17, 2010, *Boston Globe*, www.boston.com/news/local/breaking_news/2010/01/a_long_line_wai.html (accessed July 11, 2010).

23. Robert Gunderson, *The Log Cabin Campaign* (Lexington: University of Kentucky Press, 1957), 7.

24. From Andrew Young's *The Politician*, as cited in *USA Today*, January 27, 2010, "Book Tells of John Edwards' Affair, His Disdain for 'Fat Rednecks,'" http://content. usatoday.com/communities/ondeadline/post/2010/01/book-tells-of-john-edwards-affair-his-disdain-for-fat-rednecks-/1 (accessed July 11, 2010).

25. Jay Newton-Small, "Obama's Flag Pin Flip-Flop?" *Time*, May 14, 2008, www. time.com/time/politics/article/0,8599,1779544,00.html (accessed July 11, 2010).

26. Ellen Wulfhorst, "Obama Calls Elitism Attack 'Political Silly Season,'" Reuters, April 15, 2008, www.reuters.com/article/idUSN1516902320080415 (accessed July 11, 2010).

27. Arthur Delaney, "Supreme Court Rolls Back Campaign Finance Restrictions," *Huffington Post*, January 21, 2010, www.huffingtonpost.com/2010/01/21/ supreme-court-rolls-back_n_431227.html (accessed July 11, 2010).

28. See Mark Rozell, "Washington and the Origins of Presidential Power," and Gary L. Gregg II, "The Symbolic Dimensions of the First Presidency," in *Patriot Sage: George Washington and the American Political Tradition*, ed. Gary L. Gregg II and Matthew Spalding (Wilmington, DE: ISI Books, 1999).

CHAPTER ELEVEN

~

Federalism under Obama

Ryan J. Barilleaux

Shortly after Barack Obama assumed the presidency, the *New York Times* published a report outlining a "new view of federalism" being promoted by his administration. Under a headline suggesting openness to "a broader role for the states," the *Times* explained that the new administration appeared to embrace an idea known as "progressive federalism," by which "Washington will look to the states for new ideas and even a measure of guidance" on issues related to the environment, consumer protection, and other regulatory matters. It was, the *Times* proclaimed, "a states' rights movement that a liberal could love."[1]

Before the end of that year, however, Barack Obama's commitment to federalism was called into question. In November, Gene Healy of the Cato Institute denounced what he characterized as Obama's "phony federalism," arguing that the president really wanted centralization and uniformity and would accept state diversity only when states pursue policies that "please blue team sensibilities."[2] Other critics of the Obama administration also charged the president with commitment to enhancing the power of the federal government. They pointed to his health-care reform plan and other policies to claim that Mr. Obama wanted to centralize all governmental decision-making in Washington. Columnist George Will attacked what he called "coerced federalism" being practiced by the Obama Administration, arguing that it was nothing more or less than further centralization of power in

217

Washington.[3] In one extreme example, the tabloid *Weekly World News* even warned its readers in July 2011: "Obama to Write New Constitution." According to the story, the president said of the Constitution "the document is so outdated, that it is now becoming a hindrance to governing the country." Further, he supposedly signed an Executive Order voiding the Constitution, because "We need to move forward. We need change."[4] In this view, Obama is hostile to federalism.

These competing interpretations of Obama's policies—that he is committed to federalism; that he is opposed to it—highlight the enigma of the president's view of federalism and its place in the constitutional order. On one hand, his administration has adopted policies that seem to demonstrate respect for state self-determination: e.g., granting California a waiver from federal auto emissions standards in 2009 to enable that state to see higher standards or reversing the Bush Administration's policy of prosecuting medical marijuana cases in states that have legalized that type of use.[5] On the other hand, the Obama Administration has taken other actions to expand federal power at the expense of the states: the signal action here was the individual mandate on purchasing health insurance that was a central feature of the health-care reform bill, because it intrudes on states' power to regulate citizens' health and safety and because it embraces an essentially unlimited understanding of the Commerce Clause.[6]

Which of these interpretations best explains Obama's approach to federalism? This chapter suggests that the answer is neither one. Barack Obama has neither embraced a philosophy of "progressive federalism," nor has he practiced a cynical kind of "phony federalism." Rather, the evidence of his presidency supports a third interpretation of federalism under Obama: that he takes an instrumental view of federalism, one which gives primacy to other principles and shapes administration actions according to other priorities.

Other analysts, particularly Conlan and Posner,[7] have examined the role of federalism in the policies of the Obama Administration, but none has effectively placed Obama's approach to federalism within his overall understanding of the constitutional order. Most analyses have been policy-specific, content-oriented, or even focused on the constitutionality of particular policies; none has really considered how federalism under Obama is part of a larger view of the American political system. To understand President Obama's approach to federalism, this chapter examines his view of the constitutional system, surveys his administration's record on issues related to federalism, and examines the means he has used to promote his policy agenda. This evidence not only demonstrates Obama's instrumental approach to federalism, but also shows how the president's approach to federalism illuminates his overall view of the American regime.

Barack Obama and the Constitutional System

Barack Obama came to the presidency with limited service at the national level, but with experience as a community organizer in Chicago, nearly eight years in the Illinois Senate, and more than a decade teaching constitutional law at the University of Chicago. This resume led many observers, especially those interested in federalism, to hope that Mr. Obama would be sympathetic to the interests and needs of subnational governments. For example, shortly after Obama's election in 2008, one prominent Democratic consultant told the *Washington Times*, "Obama seems by instinct to understand that not everything important in this country happens in Washington. Anybody who's been a community organizer kind of gets that most government is at the state and local level."[8]

When Mr. Obama addressed issues of federalism in 2008, he suggested that he did get it that state and local government really matters in the United States. In remarks to the National Governors Association that December, Obama expressed solidarity with state chief executives:

> It always feels like a bit of a homecoming when I meet with governors. Because while I stand here today as President-elect, I will never forget the eight years I served in the state Senate in Illinois. It is in state and local government that the rubber hits the road. Of all our elected leaders, you are the ones people count on most to solve the problems in their communities and to help them get by in difficult times. And it's your state governments that bear some of the toughest burdens when an economic crisis strikes.[9]

In the same speech, he invoked Justice Brandeis on how the federal system enables a state to serve as a laboratory, calling this fact "one of the blessings of our democracy."[10] He said he wanted to see states "testing ideas." It is not surprising that some observers be optimistic about the new president's commitment to the principle of federalism. Even Republican Governor Mark Sanford of South Carolina said, "I'm certainly hopeful he will indeed push for states to be the laboratories for change."[11]

Obama's message at the outset of his administration certainly suggested a president who would be very supportive of federalism, but his view of federalism must be considered within the context of his overall constitutionalism. Obama's constitutionalism was expressed fairly consistently in his writings and major speeches and is marked by a few core principles.

Obama's constitutional interpretation: Barack Obama discussed his understanding of American constitutional government in his second book, *The Audacity of Hope*. In his discussion of constitutional controversies and competing theories of constitutional interpretation, Obama made it clear what mattered most to him in any discussion of constitutional issues. As he put it then, "If we're honest with ourselves, we'll admit that much of the time we are arguing about results."[12] Constitutional process is less important than policy outcomes. To emphasize this point, a few sentences later he stated,

> More often than not, if a particular procedural rule—the right to filibuster, say, or the Supreme Court's approach to constitutional interpretation—helps us win the argument and yields the outcome we want, then for that moment at least we think it's a pretty good rule. If it doesn't help us win, then we tend not to like it so much.[13]

Furthermore,

> On the truly hard cases, the truly big arguments, we have to take context, history, and the practical outcomes of a decision into account . . . the Founding Fathers and original ratifiers have told us *how* to think but are no longer around to tell us *what* to think. We are on our own, and have only our own reason and judgment to rely on.[14]

For Obama, results are what matter most, and constitutional principles are things we use if they support the results we want. Theories of constitutional interpretation are not unimportant, but Obama chooses a constitutional theory that allows him to focus on outcomes. Considering the debate between Justice Scalia's originalism and Justice Breyer's view of the Constitution as a "living document," Obama declared his choice: "Ultimately, though, I have to side with Justice Breyer's view of the Constitution—that it is not a static but rather a living document, and must be read in the context of an ever-changing world." [15]

This "living document" view does not mean that Obama regards everything in the Constitution as evolving; on the contrary, some things are fixed and explicit. As Obama put it, "much of the Constitution's language is perfectly clear and can be strictly applied. We don't have to interpret how often elections are held, for example, or how old the president must be. . . . "[16] But anything that is not "perfectly clear and strictly applied," which Obama said is the case for "many of its most important provisions,"[17] is open interpretation and an understanding that evolves over time.

This distinction between what is clear-cut in the Constitution and what can or must be interpreted is similar in concept to what Alexander Bickel called the "manifest constitution" and the "constitution of open texture."[18] Bickel likewise saw some constitutional provisions (e.g., terms of office) as leaving room for little or no interpretation; other provisions (such as the Commander-in-Chief clause, due process, or the Elastic Clause) invite interpretation. But unlike Obama, Bickel did not see the "constitution of open texture" as an invitation to engage in a results-oriented constitutionalism. On the contrary, in his approach to constitutional interpretation Bickel explicitly invoked Edmund Burke and recommended careful legal reasoning and a moral calculus to prevent the Constitution from becoming little more than legal window-dressing for political positions and policy preferences. For example, Bickel (a liberal Democratic in politics, while a conservative in constitutionalism) criticized both Brown v. Board of Education and Roe v. Wade for being illicit exercises in social policy-making by judges.[19]

In contrast to Bickel, Obama supports a results-oriented form of constitutional interpretation. He supports both Brown and Roe because he agrees with their outcomes. He disagrees with the original understanding of the Fourteenth Amendment because it is "an understanding of equality to which few of us would want to return."[20] Obama's view of federalism must be understood in the larger context of his constitutionalism.

Principles and Priorities in Obama's America: If Barack Obama's constitutionalism is primarily about interpretation to promote certain principles and achieve certain outcomes, what principles does he hold up as central to American government? The answer can be found in his most important speeches.

In his address to the 2004 Democratic National Convention, the speech that propelled Obama onto the national stage, Obama identified three principles as most important in America: unity, freedom, and opportunity. He famously said that there are no real divisions in the United States: "there is not a Black America and a White America and Latino America and Asian America—there's the United States of America."[21] This unity is important because it means that government policies that affect one affect all. Likewise, America stands for freedom, and Obama referred to "constitutional freedoms" and "basic liberties" as important principles to be promoted and protected. Finally, America is about opportunity, and Obama repeatedly invoked the United States as special and admirable because it provided opportunities to all.

Four years later, while running for president, Obama gave a speech on "A More Perfect Union" at the National Constitution Center in Philadelphia.

In this address, he returned to the theme of an evolving Constitution that he had reviewed in his second book. He characterized the Constitution as "ultimately unfinished" because it failed to resolve the issue of slavery. Nevertheless, he found in the charter valuable principles: "a Constitution that had at its very core the ideal of equal citizenship under the law; a Constitution that promised its people liberty, and justice, and a union that could and should be perfected over time."[22] Returning to themes from 2004, he talked about America in terms of unity, equality, and opportunity.

When he accepted the 2008 Democratic nomination for president, Obama spoke primarily about policy, but some of his remarks linked government policies to their constitutional foundations. Again, the themes of unity and opportunity were prominent: government "should ensure opportunity" and we "rise or fall as one nation." Obama did not mention federalism, although many of the issues he raised (education, jobs, welfare, urban crime) are ones involving state and local governments. To the contrary, through his theme of unity he spoke of all problems as essentially national problems, although not all required governmental solutions: "government can't turn off the television and make a child do her homework."[23]

Finally, in his 2009 Inaugural Address, President Obama made only vague and general references to "our founding documents." He proclaimed that what really matters in government are results: "The question we ask today is not whether our government is too big or too small, but whether it works." The Constitution that forms the basis of our republic is more a set of ideals than a framework for governing: "Our Founding Fathers, faced with perils that we can scarcely imagine, drafted a charter to assure the rule of law and the rights of man, a charter expanded by the blood of generations. Those ideals still light the world, and we will not give them up for expedience's sake."[24] Federalism was not mentioned explicitly; the president's attention was focused on the problems he intended to solve and the goals he wanted the nation to achieve.

As this review demonstrates, Barack Obama's constitutionalism is centered on an expansive reading of the Constitution with an eye toward promoting national unity, equality, and opportunity. He accepts the "manifest constitution" (as Bickel called it) as a set of explicit rules, but is more interested in the "constitution of open texture" that allows the national charter to be a living document to be measured by how well it enables government to promote the principles he values most. Where is federalism in this understanding? To the extent that the Constitution is "perfectly clear" (e.g., equal representation for states in the Senate), it must be obeyed; where it provides us with "general principles" (one supposes on most issues of federal-state relations), "We are on our own, and have only our own reason and our judgment to rely on."[25]

The Obama Administration's Record on Issues Related to Federalism

Some presidents come to the White House making federalism-related proposals that are prominent aspects of their political agendas. Lyndon Johnson's Great Society was an explicit enlargement of the powers and responsibilities of the federal government and a diminution of the states. His successor, Richard Nixon, convinced Congress to adopt a program of revenue sharing by which the national government would give states funds to pursue their own goals. Ronald Reagan extolled the virtues of government close to the people—in the states and localities—and wanted to reduce the power of Washington. In 2001, George W. Bush assembled the nation's governors at a roundtable discussion at the White House at which he announced a "new federalism initiative" that would decentralize power from the federal government to the states, but by the end of his presidency Bush was regarded as "one of the most hostile of recent presidents in his dealings with states, cities, and counties."[26] Federalism has been a key theme in the policies of several recent administrations.

What of the Obama Administration? The answer is more complex than just looking for a single federalism initiative. Despite the promise implied by the *New York Times* story in January 2009 about "progressive federalism," this administration has not pronounced one overarching policy or program related to federalism. Rather, the administration's record on issues related to federalism is contained in its various policies and proposals on specific issues. What follows is not a comprehensive review of Obama Administration policies, but a sample of key measures that illuminate the place of federalism under Obama.

2009 stimulus: To combat the economic downturn that began with the collapse of the housing market in 2008, President Obama persuaded Congress to pass a $787 billion stimulus package (American Recovery and Reinvestment Act) to be spent in 2009 and 2010. According to the Rockefeller Institute of Government, one-third of the stimulus ($246 billion) went to or through the states. About eleven percent ($87 billion) assisted states in keeping their Medicaid programs operating, while another $63 billion (about 8.5 percent) went to infrastructure projects, and a range of state-operated safety net programs (including workforce investment funds, food stamps, Head Start, and other programs) also received an infusion of stimulus funding.[27] This money enabled states and local governments to make up for revenue losses due to the recession, keep Medicaid patients on their rolls, and avoid layoffs of teachers and other public employees. In that sense, the stimulus assisted state and local governments. But state legislators found that the funds came with significant strings attached. As *State Legislatures* magazine reported in 2010,

> States could not change their Medicaid eligibility laws. They had to follow so-called "maintenance of effort" rules on education as well, meaning they couldn't reduce their level of existing spending once they accepted the federal help. And the entire package, from road construction to weatherization, was predicated on states meeting unprecedented transparency and accountability requirements.[28]

States were required not only to cut funding (e.g., in Medicaid), but also they also had to spend stimulus money quickly and meet other federal requirements. Because the size and scope of the stimulus package, as well as the requirements it imposed on the states, one analyst characterized the measure as "Reagan in reverse."[29]

Cap-and-trade: One key Obama Administration initiative, albeit unsuccessful, was the proposal to set ambitious limits on carbon emissions (cap) and establish a national market whereby business and industry could buy and sell rights to emit such gases (trade). The plan met fierce opposition and was attacked on the grounds that it would drive up prices for gasoline, electricity, food, and nearly everything else, destroy jobs, and further damage an economy already weakened by the Great Recession that started in 2008. One critic, Representative Rob Bishop (R-UT), argued that the bill attempted to impose a uniform national solution to a problem that could be addressed more effectively at the state level. Invoking the theme of states as laboratories, Rep. Bishop made the case for allowing state experimentation before attempting a national policy: "There are regions of this country where cap-and-trade policies may be popular. Some people residing in the Northeast, urban areas, and certain coastal regions appear to support cap-and-trade policies. At least the Congressional representatives in these areas seem eager to implement strict carbon regimes on their citizens."[30] While the potential effect of the proposal on jobs and prices likely had more to do with the fate of the bill than federalism issues, cap-and-trade reflected the Obama Administration's approach to it top policy priorities.

Health-care reform: President Obama's central policy initiative has been health-care reform, and the bill that was signed into law has key implications for federalism. The most important of these lies in the individual mandate to purchase health insurance, which was included in the bill to help secure the support of health insurance companies.[31] By establishing a federal mandate for all citizens to purchase health insurance, the act has stimulated a constitutional controversy over whether it constitutes an unconstitutional infringement on state power by the federal government. Shortly after the act was passed in 2010, thirteen state attorneys general filed suit against it (eventually, twenty-six attorneys general would be named plaintiffs in the suit), alleging that the mandate exceeds the powers delegated to Congress in Article I of the Constitution.[32] They argued that the mandate infringes on state police powers (powers to regulate health and safety of citizens, established in constitutional law as reserved to the states).[33] In reply, proponents of the mandate argue that it is a reasonable and precedent-based extension of Congress's constitutional powers.[34]

No matter the outcome of the legal challenge to the health-care reform law, the Affordable Care Act, the measure and its defense by the administration reflects President Obama's constitutionalism and the place of federalism in it. For example, the White House website contains a major section on health care reform, including a defense of the new law:

> The Affordable Care Act, passed by Congress and signed into law by the President in March 2010, gives you better health security by putting in place comprehensive health insurance reforms that hold insurance companies accountable, lower health care costs, guarantee more choice, and enhance the quality of care for all Americans.[35]

From nearly all of the website's pages on health care, a visitor can an interactive map of the states called "50 States, 50 Stories," to "Find out what's happening in your state and listen to stories from people across the country who are benefitting from the new law."[36] The states are featured as places where reform is taking place; they are important as concrete places in which the national goals of health-care reform are taking place.

Environmental policy: One area in which Barack Obama promised to take a much more progressive line than the preceding Bush Administration was in environmental policy, and his administration's record has both pleased and frustrated environmental activists. At the outset, Obama seemed to be pursuing a course set by the idea of "progressive federalism." In June 2009, his Environmental Protection Agency (EPA) granted a waiver for California and thirteen other states to set tighter standards for automobile ozone emissions than allowed under federal law, a sharp reversal from the no-waiver emissions standards approach of the Bush Administration.[37] At the same time, the EPA initiated a formal process to review the ozone standard set in 2008 by the Bush EPA.[38] Lisa Jackson (Obama's Administrator of EPA), pressed by environmental and public health groups, wanted to adopt a stricter standard. For nearly two and a half years, she and her agency conducted a process of review and revision. Administrator Jackson understood that a tougher rule would encounter significant opposition from business, conservative groups, and other critics. To offset problems, she met three times in June 2011 with White House Chief of Staff William Daley, and subsequently revised the proposed rule to make it more acceptable to critics and the White House.

Despite this attempt to smooth the way for tougher ozone standard, opponents made a strong case against it to Chief of Staff Daley and Cass Sunstein, the administration's "regulatory czar."[39] Particularly important in arguing against the rule were current and former governors. John Engler, former Governor of Michigan and president of the Business Roundtable, argued that the rule would burden state and local officials. Likewise, Governor Bev Perdue of North Carolina (a Democrat, in a state that Obama had narrowly won in 2008) also opposed the rule. Her representative told White House officials that it could lead to "lack of employment, loss of health care, and in some cases, loss of a home"[40] for citizens of her state. John Engler told the New York Times that "the governors were very helpful"[41] in making the case against the rule.

Supporters of the rule almost attempted to make a strong case for it, but found that they were not receiving the warm welcome they expected. Daley and Sunstein were skeptical of the rule, but for different if related reasons. Daley seemed most concerned about unemployment and the state of the economy, and the effect that a potentially job-killing regulation would have on President Obama's reelection prospects. Sunstein opposed it because it would be subject to review again in 2013 (possibly by a different administration, if Obama were not reelected) and because about half of the EPA's own studies showed that the costs of the rule exceeded its benefits.

Shortly before Labor Day 2011, the president announced that he was killing the proposed rule. Unlike every other rule turned down by the Obama White House (about 130 as of November 2011), only the ozone rule was publicly rejected. According to the New York Times, the president's decision was influenced by deference to state governors in the interest of Obama's reelection.

Federal preemption of state laws: Another aspect of relations between the national government and the states is preemption, which refers to invalidation of state laws that conflict with federal law. Preemption can and has led to disputes between the national and subnational governments over appropriate areas of authority, and in 2009 President Obama took action to give greater deference to states in framing federal policy than the Bush Administration had done. He signed a memorandum for agency heads that directed them to include statements of preemption in regulations "only when such statements have a sufficient legal basis" and to review existing rules to make sure they met this standard.[42]

The Obama memorandum was seen as much friendlier to "progressive federalism" than had been the policy of the Bush Administration, which invoked preemption to keep states from engaging in more aggressive (and business unfriendly) regulation on the environment, consumer protection, and other issues on the progressive agenda.[43] One device used under Bush, and now banned by Obama, was to include claims of preemption in the preambles of regulations, where they could be used to affect changes in policy beyond the scope of the specific regulation to which these preambles were attached.[44]

The upshot of the Obama memorandum on preemption was what Conlan and Posner call "one-tail devolution," because it devolved authority from the federal government to the states only to the extent of allowing states with progressive policy agendas greater flexibility.[45] At the same time, in assessing the substantive impact of this new policy, Conlan and Posner concluded that it "remains to be seen."[46] The Obama Administration has made some allowances for state flexibility in regulation—e.g., a California law on carbon dioxide emissions from automobiles and state rules on financial institutions—but there has not been some sweeping new era in federal-state relations brought on by the memorandum.

The Obama Administration's record on preemption, like its record on other issues related to federalism, is not one easily summarized as friendly or hostile toward federalism. What is just as important as this record, however, has been the various means that the administration has used to advance its agenda. The next section takes up the various means that the administration has employed to advance the president's agenda.

Carrots, Sticks, and Other Methods of Advancing the Obama Agenda

Barack Obama and his administration have employed a variety of methods for inducing states to cooperate in advancing the president's policy goals. These methods include incentives to stimulate state action (call them carrots), measures to discourage or prevent states from going their own way (call them sticks), and other techniques to advance Obama's agenda.

Several of the methods of the Obama Administration are based on a structural fact of the contemporary American political scene: in the wake of the Great Recession that began late in the Bush presidency, most American states face fiscal crises and are heavily reliant on the federal government to keep them from financial ruin. This reliance increased measurably after President Obama took office: "In 2008, federal funds accounted for about 26.3 percent of state government spending, according to the National Association of State Budget Officers. In 2009, that figure jumped to about 30 percent and in 2010, to 34.7 percent, because of Recovery Act funds."[47] Despite claims by several Republican governors in 2009 that they would refuse to accept stimulus funds, massive debts in state budgets persuaded all states to accept aid from the federal government. This fact helped the Obama Administration to promote its policy agenda.

Carrots: The Obama Administration has employed three major types of measures to induce states to assist in promoting its agenda. First are waivers that enable states to deviate from federal law in order to pursue their own approaches to policy areas. These waivers can be explicit, as in the 2009 waivers granted to fourteen states allowing them to adopt stricter ozone emissions standards than allowed under federal law, or they can be de facto waivers that result from an administration decision not to enforce a federal law.

One of the best examples of a de facto waiver was the Attorney General's announcement in October 2009 that the Justice Department would not interfere with the use of medical marijuana in states that allowed it. This announcement marked a reversal of the policy pursued by the Bush Administration, which held that federal law prohibiting marijuana sale or use trumped state attempts to legalize marijuana use for medical reasons. Attorney General Eric Holder told reporters gathered for the announcement that "it will not be a priority to use federal resources to prosecute patients with serious illnesses or their caregivers who are complying with state laws on medical marijuana."[48] The result was a *de facto* waiver for any state, such as California, to adopt its own rules in this area.

A second type of carrot used by the president to induce state support for his policies has been the special deal. In order to win support from senators whose votes he badly needed to pass his health-care reform bill, in 2009 the president agreed to give special deals to several states. The most infamous arrangement was "a permanent exemption from the state share of Medicaid expansion for Nebraska, meaning federal taxpayers have to kick in an additional $45 million in the first decade."[49] This arrangement was dubbed the "Cornhusker Kickback" because it provided a unique reward to Nebraska in exchange for the vote of its Senator Ben Nelson. Other special deals included $300 million in extra federal support for Medicaid for Louisiana (dubbed the "Louisiana Purchase"),[50] an exemption from a federal excise tax for non-profit insurers in Nebraska and Michigan, and protection from cuts in benefits for Medicare Advantage recipients in Pennsylvania, New York, and Florida.[51] The upshot of these deals is to carve out special arrangements for particular states in order to secure passage of the president's reform plan.

Finally, the Obama Administration has used competitive grants to states to induce them to comply with national goals. The best example in this regard comes in the area of education, in which the administration has used its Race to the Top grant program to alter state policies. As *State Legislatures* magazine reported in 2010,

> The criteria for the Race to the Top fund—a $4.35 billion pot of grant money left largely to the discretion of U.S. Education Secretary Arne Duncan—led at least 10 states to change their laws in hopes of winning some of the money. Last November, Obama and Duncan visited Madison to talk about education. Duncan was particularly harsh, calling Wisconsin's laws antiquated, unacceptable and even "ridiculous." Rather than take offense, both chambers of the Legislature the next day passed a package of four bills mean to appease him. "There's no question those of us in Wisconsin want to have as strong an application as we can to get at the $4.35 billion," Senator John Lehman, who chairs the Education Committee, said during floor debate. "It is true that a big carrot got people thinking."[52]

Sticks: Most of the sticks employed by the Obama Administration have been corollaries of the carrots. As shown in the 2009 stimulus package and the Race to the Top grant program, the funds allocated by the administration come with a set of standards and mandates designed to induce state compliance with national goals. The health-care reform act likewise puts new limits on states. As *State Legislatures* reported, "Now states will have a lot less choice about how they spend their health care money—and certainly less choice about limiting their expenditures."[53] The health care law also prohibits states from lowering eligibility requirements for Medicaid or the Children's Health Insurance Program, or else risk losing all Medicaid funding (in 2009, federal funding accounted for at least 40 percent of the Medicaid budget in thirty-six states[54]).

Another type of stick is the refusal to tolerate variation from federal law; in effect, this is the reverse of a waiver. In 2010, the Obama Administration entered a legal challenge to block Arizona's new immigration enforcement law, which the Attorney General said violated the federal government's jurisdiction over immigration: "Setting immigration policy and enforcing

immigration laws is a national responsibility. . . . Seeking to address the issue through a patchwork of state laws will only create more problems than
it solves."[55] The law in question, while highly controversial, did not attempt
to alter federal law, but gave Arizona law-enforcement officers the power to
detain anyone they suspected of being in the country illegally. Other states
passed similar measures, and the Justice Department has gone to court to
block all of these laws.[56]

Other Means for Advancing the Obama Agenda: In addition to these
governmental actions, President Obama has weighed in with rhetoric and
political support in controversies over state laws involving organized labor.
When in 2011 Wisconsin and other states adopted laws to diminish the bargaining power of public employee unions, protests broker out against these
measures (the Wisconsin protest was especially large). President Obama
defined this issue as one that transcended states' control over their own
workforces:

> Obama accused Scott Walker, [Wisconsin's] new Republican governor, of
> unleashing an "assault" on unions in pushing emergency legislation that would
> change future collective-bargaining agreements that affect most public em-
> ployees, including teachers. The president's political machine worked in close
> coordination Thursday with state and national union officials to get thousands
> of protesters to gather in Madison and to plan similar demonstrations in other
> state capitals. Their efforts began to spread, as thousands of labor supporters
> turned out for a hearing in Columbus, Ohio, to protest a measure from Gov.
> John Kasich (R) that would cut collective-bargaining rights. By the end of
> the day, Democratic Party officials were organizing additional demonstrations
> in Ohio and Indiana, where an effort is underway to trim benefits for public
> workers.[57]

In a related incident, in June 2011 the National Labor Relations Board
sued to block the Boeing Corporation from opening a factory in non-union
South Carolina, arguing that the company was acting in retaliation against
unions for strikes at the company's facilities in Washington State. Controversy ensued, with South Carolina officials and Republicans charging that
the administration was trying to dictate state labor laws. Asked about the
matter, the President said that companies should be able to relocate anywhere in the country as long as they followed the law, but refused to criticize
the Board for its action and thus gave priority to organized labor over South
Carolina's labor laws. [58]

President Obama and his administration have thus employed a range of
methods to pursue his goals. As Paul Posner of George Mason University has

put it, "This is an administration that doesn't take the states and locals as it finds them. It has an agenda."[59] It is precisely this point—that the Obama agenda is what matters most to the president—that explains Obama's approach to federalism.

Obama's Agenda-Driven, Instrumental Approach to Federalism

Many epithets have been applied in an effort to characterize Barack Obama's approach to federalism. It has been called "progressive federalism," "crazy quilt federalism," "coerced federalism," "cooperative federalism," and "phony federalism." But none of these labels captures what is really going on in this administration.

A more accurate understanding of Obama's approach to federalism is one rooted in his constitutionalism. Barack Obama sees the Constitution as divided between those elements that are "perfectly clear" and everything else, where "we are on our own, and have only our own reason and our judgment to rely on." Within that framework, he is committed to advancing his agenda by the most effective means available.

The agenda he pursues is most accurately identified as the Obama Agenda. It is committed to a set of progressive policy goals *and* to the political success of Barack Obama. It is not strictly a progressive agenda; if it were, President Obama would not have killed the EPA's proposed ozone standard in 2011 and he would have continued fighting for the so-called "public option" on health-care reform (a government health-care insurance plan to be offered in addition to private insurance, dropped from the bill to help win support from moderate Democrats). If President Obama were committed to federalism as a principle, as was Ronald Reagan, then his administration would not be suing to block state immigration laws, attempting to block Boeing's move to South Carolina, or insisting on such strict standards and mandates for states receiving federal stimulus funds and grants.

It is the Obama Agenda because it mixes progressive policy goals—stricter environmental and consumer-protection rules, greater uniformity in national education standards, protection of organized labor—with adjustments, compromises and concessions intended to bring Barack Obama political and electoral success. Progressives wanted President Obama to fight for a more progressive health-care reform bill, even if it might not pass, rather than compromise and accept a more incremental reform act. Likewise, they wanted him to stand firm on tough environmental protection standards, arguing that these would be popular as well as good policy. But Barack Obama wanted to be able to claim victory in the health-care reform fight and was not willing to allow an ozone standard to jeopardize his reelection.

Barack Obama is not Woodrow Wilson. Wilson took on the central political institutions of his day—at home, the checks-and-balances system he saw as a recipe for political gridlock; abroad, the balance-of-power system he saw as a recipe for war—and was willing to challenge them even at the cost of his own political fortune. To that end, he expanded presidential power in order win support for his New Freedom program and waged a nationwide campaign to force the Senate to accept the League of Nations. The effort ruined his health and nearly destroyed his presidency. Obama appears to be more interested in success than fights over principle. He pursues a progressive agenda, but not at the cost of political or electoral victory.

What is the place of federalism in the Obama Agenda? It subordinates federalism to Obama's twin goals. To that extent, the title of this chapter is deliberate: federalism is *under* Obama because he is committed to his progressive policy agenda and his own political success more than he is to the idea of the states as laboratories. As one federalism analyst put it, the Obama Administration does not see "states being the laboratories of democracy in and of themselves," but under Obama "some of them will become the federal government's laboratories of democracy."[60]

Notes

1. John Schwarz, "Obama Seems to be Open to a Broader Role for the States," *New York Times*, January 30, 2009. www.nytimes.com/2009/01/30/us/politics/30federal .html. Accessed November 18, 2011. "Progessive federalism" has also been called "blue state federalism." See David J. Barron, "Blue State Federalism at the Crossroads," *Harvard Law and Policy Review* 3-1 (2009): 1-7.

2. Gene Healy, "Obama's Phony Federalism," www.cato.org. www.cato.org/pub_display.php?pub_id=10971. Accessed November 18, 2011.

3. George Will, "Coercive Federalism: A Wolf in Sheep's Clothing," *Deseret Morning News*, October 2, 2011. www.deseretnews.com/article/700183949/Coercive -federalism-a-wolf-in-sheeps-clothing.html. Accessed November 21, 2011.

4. Frank Lake, "Obama to Write a New Constitution," *Weekly World News*, July 19, 2011. weeklyworldnews.com/headlines/35813/obama-to-write-new-u-s-constitution/. Accessed November 21, 2011.

5. Healy, loc. cit.

6. See, for example, Ilya Somin, "Regulating Inactivity: A Radical Constitutional Departure," *Jurist*—Forum, July 1, 2011. jurist.org/forum/2011/07/ilya-somin-sixth -circuit-ruling.php. Accessed November 21, 2011.

7. Timothy J. Conlan and Paul L. Posner, "Inflection Point? Federalism and the Obama Administration," *Publius* 41(October 2011): 421-446.

8. David Osborne, quoted in Stephen Dinan, "Obama Sees Strength in States; Federalist Message to Governors Appeals to Republicans," *Washington Times*, December 3, 2008, p. A1.

9. Barack Obama, "Remarks at the National Governors Association Meeting in Philadelphia," December 2, 2008. www.presidency.ucsb.edu/ws/index.php?pid=84941#axzz1eMDl60th. Accessed November 21, 2011.

10. Ibid.

11. Dinan, "Obama Sees Strength in States."

12. Barack Obama, *The Audacity of Hope* (New York: Random House, 2006), p. 136.

13. Ibid.

14. Ibid., p. 138.

15. Ibid., p. 139.

16. Ibid., p. 139.

17. Ibid., p. 139.

18. Alexander Bickel, *The Morality of Consent* (New Haven, Conn.: Yale University Press, 1975), p. 29.

19. See Bickel, *The Morality of Consent*, p. 28, on *Roe v. Wade*. On *Brown*, see Bickel, *The Supreme Court and the Idea of Progress* (New Haven, Conn.: Yale University Press, 1978).

20. Obama, *Audacity*, p. 139.

21. Barack Obama, "2004 Democratic National Convention Keynote Address," July 27, 2004, *American Rhetoric.com*. www.americanrhetoric.com/speeches/PDFFiles/Barack%20Obama%20-%202004%20DNC%20Address.pdf. Accessed November 21, 2011.

22. Barack Obama, "A More Perfect Union," March 18, 2008, *American Rhetoric.com*. www.americanrhetoric.com/speeches/barackobamaperfectunion.htm. Accessed November 21, 2011.

23. Barack Obama, "Democratic Convention Presidential Nomination Acceptance Address," August 28, 2008, *American Rhetoric.com*. www.americanrhetoric.com/speeches/PDFFiles/Barack%20Obama%20-%20Democratic%20Nomination%20Acceptance.pdf. Accessed November 21, 2011.

24. Barack Obama, "Inaugural Address," January 20, 2009. www.presidency.ucsb.edu/ws/index.php?pid=44&st=&st1=#axzz1eMDl60th. Accessed November 21, 2011.

25. Obama, *Audacity*, p. 138.

26. Peter Harkness, "Obama and the States," *Governing*, January 2009, p. 18.

27. Data on stimulus spending and requirements taken from Thomas L. Gais, "Federalism During the Obama Administration," The Nelson A. Rockefeller Institute of Government, Presentation to the Annual Conference of the National Federation of Municipal Analysts, Santa Ana Pueblo, New Mexico, May 7, 2010. www.rockinst.org/pdf/federalism/2010-05-07-federalism_during_obama_administration.pdf. Accessed November 17, 2011.

28. Alan Greenblatt, "Federalism in the Age of Obama," *State Legislatures*, July/August 2010, pp. 27-28.

29. Geoffrey Garrett, "Stimulus is Reagan in Reverse," *Weekend Australian*, February 7, 2009, p. 22.

30. Rob Bishop, "When It Comes to Cap-and-Trade, Give Federalism a Chance," *Daily Caller*, January 15, 2010. dailycaller.com/2010/01/15/when-it-comes-to-cap-and-trade-give-federalism-a-chance/. Accessed November 21, 2011.

31. See transcript for "Obama's Deal," PBS-Frontline, April 13, 2010. www.pbs.org/wgbh/pages/frontline/obamasdeal/etc/script.html. Accessed November 21, 2011.

32. A website created by the plaintiffs can be found at www.healthcarelawsuit.us/. Accessed November 21, 2011.

33. For example, see Randy A. Barnett, "Commandeering the People: Why the Individual
Health Insurance Mandate is Unconstitutional," Georgetown Public Law and Legal Theory Research Paper No. 10-58. scholarship.law.georgetown.edu/facpub/434. Accessed November 22, 2011.

34. Mark A. Hall, "The Constitutionality of Mandates to Purchase Health Care," Legal Solutions in Health Reform, O'Neill Institute for National and Global Health Law, Georgetown University. www.law.georgetown.edu/oneillinstitute/national-health-law/legal-solutions-in-health-reform/Papers/Individual_Mandates.pdf. Accessed November 22, 2011.

35. www.whitehouse.gov/healthreform/healthcare-overview#healthcare-menu. Accessed November 22, 2011.

36. www.whitehouse.gov/healthreform/map#healthcare-menu. Accessed November 22, 2011.

37. Andrew Cline, "Obama's Crazy Quilt Federalism," *The American Spectator*, July 13, 2010, spectator.org/archives/2010/07/13/obamas-crazy-quilt-federalism. Accessed November 16, 2011.

38. What follows is largely based on John M. Broder, "Re-Election Strategy is Tied to a Shift on Smog," *New York Times*, November 16, 2011, p. A1.

39. Sunstein's actual position is director of the Office of Information and Regulatory Affairs in the Office of Management and Budget. In that capacity, he oversees the process of reviewing proposed rules from all federal agencies. The *New York Times* and others have called him the "regulatory czar."

40. Broder, loc. cit.

41. Broder, loc. cit.

42. "Memorandum for the Heads of Executive Departments and Agencies," May 20, 2009. www.whitehouse.gov/the-press-office/presidential-memorandum-regarding-preemption. Accessed November 22, 2011.

43. See Conlan and Posner, pp. 431-432.

44. See Catherine M. Sharkey, "Preemption by Preamble: Federal Agencies and The Federalization of Tort Law," *DePaul Law Review* 56 (April 2007): 227-259.

45. Conlan and Posner, p. 432.

46. Conlan and Posner, p. 432.

47. "States Addicted to Federal Spending? Rhetoric Against Spending Far From Reality," ABC News.com, April 14, 2011, abcnews.go.com/Politics/federal-spending-states-addiction/story?id=13360706#.TtENoluHjYY. Accessed November 26, 2011.

48. Quoted in Cline, "Obama's Crazy Quilt Federalism," loc. cit.

49. "Payoffs to States Get Harry Reid to 60 Votes," POLITICO.com, December 19, 2009, www.politico.com/news/stories/1209/30815.html. Accessed November 26, 2011.

50. "Pork Greased Reform's Passage," POLITICO.com, December 22, 2009, www.politico.com/news/stories/1209/30877.html. Accessed November 26, 2011.

51. "Payoffs to States," loc. cit.

52. Greenblatt, p. 28.

53. Greenblatt, p. 28.

54. www.kff.org/medicaid/upload/8205.pdf. Accessed November 26, 2011.

55. Quoted in Cline, "Obama's Crazy Quilt Federalism," loc. cit.

56. "Justice Department Sues to Block Utah Immigration Law," POLITICO.com, November 22, 2011, www.politico.com/news/stories/1111/68992.html. Accessed November 26, 2011.

57. "Obama Joins Wisconsin's Budget Battle, Opposing Republican Anti-Union Bill," *Washington Post*, February 18, 2011, www.washingtonpost.com/wp-dyn/content/article/2011/02/17/AR2011021705494.html. Accessed November 26, 2011.

58. "Obama Declines to Criticize NLRB for Boeing Ruling But Says Companies Should Be Free to Relocate Factories Within the U.S.," *Los Angeles Times*, June 29, 2011, latimesblogs.latimes.com/money_co/2011/06/obama-nlrb-boeing-south-carolina-factory-union-workers-lawsuit.html. Accessed November 26, 2011.

59. Greenblatt, p. 28.

60. Marcia Howard, quoted in Greenblatt, p. 28. Emphasis added.

CHAPTER TWELVE

~

President Obama, Commander-in-Chief

Melanie M. Marlowe

As a candidate for president, Barack Obama made reversing what he saw as the excessive claims of executive power made by President Bush a central feature of his campaign. Candidate Obama made especially clear his distaste for Bush-era war policies such as indefinite detention at Guantanamo Bay, rendition, and aggressive interrogation. Over and over again on the campaign trail and during the transition period, he promised transparency in policymaking and to end those programs and establish a course of action more in line with American values.[1]

But the president has conceded ground in places where his supporters might wish he had not[2]: Guantanamo is still open, he has continued the Bush-era surveillance program, he has expanded claims of state secrets, and his administration has prosecuted more leakers of national security information than have all previous administrations combined.

Upon accepting the Nobel Peace Prize in 2009, the president gave a speech which outlined some of the principles that guide his thinking about war.[3] Even at this event celebrating peace, the president did not shy away from the obvious: the United States was a nation at war, and he was the commander-in-chief. As the American president, he "reserved the right to act unilaterally if necessary to defend" the United States. War can be just, he noted, if it is fought in "self-defense; if the force used is proportional; and if, whenever possible, civilians are spared from violence." He stated that war may sometimes be necessary to save lives and can be "justified on humanitarian grounds." Diplomacy would not stop Hitler, and may not prevent genocide today. He observed that civil war has become as troublesome as wars between nations, and that international institutions play an invaluable role in maintain peace.

In the last three years, President Obama has a number of wartime accomplishments, his most prominent being the capture and killing of Osama bin Laden.[4] His supporters are grateful he kept his promise to end the war in Iraq and that he is drawing down troops from Afghanistan. In 2011, the United States intervened in domestic conflict in Libya, protecting civilians and helping to oust the four-decades-old dictatorship there. The president has implemented a policy of targeted killing which has resulted in the elimination of leaders of various terrorist cells.

This chapter will review the U.S. involvement in Libya and the president's ongoing drone program. While President Obama inherited many war issues from the Bush administration, the Libyan intervention was a conflict which began and ended during his tenure. Drones were used in the War on Terror during the previous administration, but they were not utilized anywhere near the degree they are today. Examining these issues helps us to understand how the president views his responsibility as commander-in-chief. We will mainly consider the constitutional implications of these issues, but we will briefly address the policy consequences as well.

Military Action in Libya

In early February 2011, protesters in the cities of Benghazi and Zentan called for the removal of Muammar Qaddafi,[5] the dictator who had ruled Libya for more than forty years. The demonstrations gained momentum and reached the capital of Tripoli, where they were quickly met with violence by Qaddafi's forces. On February 23, President Obama publicly condemned Qaddafi's actions against his own people and called upon his administration officials to "prepare the full range of options we have to respond to this crisis," including how we might work with allies.[6] But some worried that his emphasis on moving carefully and coordinating responses with other nations meant the dictator would have more time to organize his forces and put the uprising to a violent end. After the president's speech, the *Washington Post* editorial page noted that the leaders of Britain, Germany, Italy, and France had all condemned Qaddafi's violence against his own people, and that until that day, "only one major Western leader had failed to speak up on Libya: Barack Obama."[7] *Washington Post* editorial writer Eugene Robinson argued that the President's words calling for Qaddafi to refrain from violence were not enough; he must work with NATO to establish a no-fly zone that would be enforced.[8]

Administration officials were reluctant to intervene in what had become a civil war. Secretary of Defense Robert Gates stated that although rebels had not officially asked the United States for military assistance, his department was considering "a lot of options and contingencies." He warned that any military action would consume scare defense resources and would have an effect on American military operations elsewhere in the world. Secretary Gates also wondered if a military presence in Libya, even to protect civilians, might be perceived as an American attack upon a Muslim country, and if it might draw the United States into a long conflict.[9] Bill Daley, the White House Chief of Staff, criticized those who were eager to establish a no-fly zone: "Lots of people throw around phrases like 'no-fly zone,' and they talk about it as though it's just a video game. Some people who throw that line out have no idea what they're talking about."[10] James R. Clapper, Jr., the Director of National Intelligence, went so far as to tell the Senate Armed Services Committee it was very likely that over the long term "the [Qaddafi] regime will prevail."[11]

On February 26, the United Nations Security Council passed Resolution 1970, expressing concern for the safety of civilians, demanding an end to the violence, supporting an investigation of human rights violations, implementing an arms embargo against Libya, and calling for the assets of the Qaddafi family to be frozen. Congress also took action. On March 1, the United States Senate passed by unanimous consent a resolution calling for action to protect civilians and supporting diplomatic efforts to resolve the crisis.[12] Democratic Senators Kerry and Lieberman, and Republic Senator John Mc-Cain, called for the imposition of a no-fly zone, although other members of Congress, including Democratic Senator Jim Webb and Republican Richard Lugar, cautioned against entering into a military commitment lightly.[13]

President Obama was under domestic and international pressure to take action, but was restrained.[14] The State Department spokesman, P.J. Crowley, refused to characterize Qaddafi as a "dictator."[15] After one of Qaddafi's sons said his family would "fight to the last minute, until the last bullet," the United States government said it was "analyzing the speech of Seif al-Islam Qaddafi to see what possibilities it contains for meaningful reform."[16] When the press asked why the president had not mentioned Libya in several public messages, press secretary Jay Carney said the president and Secretary of State had had a "scheduling issue," but that they would be meeting soon and making a statement.[17]

In spite of minor victories the rebels' situation deteriorated quickly in the first weeks of March. Cities which had been taken by the rebels were reclaimed by Qaddafi's forces in violent battles. Regime loyalists, who had superior air defenses, were now within 100 miles of the rebel stronghold of Benghazi.[18] The situation for the opposition was desperate.

On March 12, the Arab League asked the United Nations Security Council to establish a no-fly zone over Libya.[19] Observers recognized that should several Western nations come to the rebels' aid, this would diminish claims of American aggression against a Muslim country.

Around this time, Hillary Clinton began pushing for a tougher administration position. She was able to enlist the help of Samantha Power, a senior National Security Council aide, and Susan Rice, United States Ambassador to the United Nations, who believed she could get a stronger resolution from the UN Security Council—so strongly, that she had written an "American wish list" resolution a week before the president gave her the go-ahead to submit one. In debates described as "healthy," they pushed Gates, Brennan, National Security Advisor Tom Donilon, and the president himself to reconsider military action.[20]

On March 17, the Obama administration requested that the United Nations authorize other actions that might be necessary to protect civilians, should the United States decide to intervene. That same day, the United Nations Security Council passed Resolution 1973,[21] expressing grave concern for civilians in harm's way and insisting that Qaddafi leave occupied cities and cease all hostilities against his people. The resolution permitted Member States, "acting nationally or through regional organizations or arrangements" "to take all necessary measures . . . to protect civilians." The resolution made clear that while a no-fly zone could be established and that attacks might take place from the air or nearby ships, "a foreign occupation force of any form on any part of Libyan territory" would not be allowed.[22]

Left unresolved was what nations would take the lead in the case of military action. The United States already had significant military resources in the region, but worries about being dragged into another extended conflict in that part of the world, and concern that American troops would be seen as occupiers of a Muslim nation gave American officials doubts as to whether the United States should be in front of any operation.

On March 18, President Obama met with congressional leaders and told them that any kinetic military activity the United States might be involved in would last only "days not weeks."[23] That evening, he addressed the situation in Libya to the nation. He condemned the violence Qaddafi had unleashed on his own people and reviewed the actions of the United Nations, including the requirements of Resolution 1973. President Obama stated that the terms of the resolution were "not negotiable." Should Qaddafi refuse to comply, "the international community will impose consequences, and the resolution will be enforced through military action."[24]

It was. On March 21, the President issued a letter to the Speaker of the House and President Pro Tempore of the Senate, notifying them that two days earlier "U.S. military forces commenced operations" as part of an international effort authorized by UN Security Council Resolution 1973. It was done "to prevent a humanitarian catastrophe and address the threat posed to international peace and security by the crisis in Libya."[25] In Operation Odyssey Dawn, American and allied forces would be undertaking a "series of strikes on air defense systems and military airfields" in order to enforce a no-fly zone and protect civilians. The strikes, the president noted in the first paragraph, were to be "limited in their nature, duration, and scope." Emphasizing the restricted nature of American involvement, he assured Congress that ground forces had not been introduced, and that he anticipated handing leadership of the operation to a coalition force shortly. He stated he was working under this "constitutional authority to conduct U.S. foreign relations and as commander-in-chief and chief executive," and concluded that the letter was "part of my efforts to keep the Congress fully informed, consistent with the War Powers Resolution."[26] Administration officials reiterated that Qaddafi was not a specific target of the allies' action, although they hoped that the economic sanctions, arms embargo, and travel ban on the family would leave him isolated and unable to continue as head of government.[27]

Just a few days into the operation, cracks were appearing the coalition. Allies were expressing differences of opinion on when NATO would take command and what, precisely, that would mean. There was some grumbling that of all the Arab states only Qatar had offered to send fighter jets for the campaign.[28] At the end of the first week of the operation, President Obama, British Prime Minister Cameron, and French President Sarkozy were able to iron out their differences. NATO would promptly take control of enforcing the no-fly zone and be responsible for protecting civilians, which included launching airstrikes against regime forces on the ground. Operation Unified Protector would be run by Canadian Lt. General Charles Bouchard. The United Arab Emirates offered twelve warplanes, leaving twenty Arab League which would not take part in combat operations.[29]

In mid-July, the United States formally recognized the rebel organization, the Transitional National Council, as the official government of Libya.

Qaddafi was caught by rebels in the town of Sirte on October 20 and killed that same day.[30] President Obama thanked American soldiers and diplomats who worked on behalf of the Libyan people, and congratulated all coalition forces for their efforts.[31] Noting a promise kept, he stated that the Qaddafi regime had ended "without putting a single U.S. service member on the ground." In the eyes of the administration the operation was successful, but was it legal?

The Legal Question

Congressional Authorization and the War Powers Resolution
Congress passed the War Powers Resolution (WPR) over President Nixon's veto in 1973.[32] The timing of the law's enactment cannot be overlooked; this was a period when Congress, nearing the end of the Vietnam War and still investigating Watergate, sought to restrain what was perceived as an imperial presidency. The WPR's stated purpose is to

> fulfill the intent of the framers of the Constitution and ensure that the collective judgment of both the Congress and the President will apply to the introduction of United States Armed Forces into hostilities, or into situations where imminent involvement in hostilities is clearly indicated by the circumstances, and to the continued use of such forces in hostilities or in such situations.[33]

Section 1541(c) states that when introducing troops into actual or imminent hostilities, the president is only acting pursuant to his constitutional commander-in-chief powers when war has been declared or other clear authorization has been given, or when there has been an "attack upon the United States, its territories or possessions, or its armed forces." Section 1542 requires the president, when "possible," to "consult with Congress" prior to placing troops in a hostile situation, and to "consult regularly with Congress" until the hostilities have ceased.

If troops have been or are likely to be introduced into hostilities or a potentially-hostile situation and there has been no declaration of war, the president is required, by Section 1543(a), to submit a report to Congress within forty-eight hours of troop movement. In this report he must explain why the use of troops is necessary, under what constitutional and legislative authority he acted, and what he judges the scope and duration of involvement to be.

Finally, for our purposes, sixty days after the submission of the report, the president must withdraw troops unless Congress 1) has declared war or clearly authorized force in that circumstance, 2) has acted to extend the sixty-day limit, or 3) is unable to act as a result of an attack. The president may extend the deadline by an additional thirty days if he reports to Congress that the time is necessary to complete a safe removal of forces.[34]

Two of the main players in the Libyan action were strong supporters of a prominent congressional role in military operations—when they were Senators. In an interview while on the presidential campaign trail in 2007, candidate Obama told reporter Charlie Savage that "the president does not have power under the Constitution to unilaterally authorize a military attack in a situation that does not involve stopping an actual or imminent threat to the nation." He also volunteered that he had recently sponsored legislation that would have required "any offensive military action taken by the United States against Iran" to be "explicitly authorized by Congress."[35]

Presidential candidate Hillary Clinton told the same reporter that

The president has a solemn duty to protect our nation. If the country is under truly imminent threat of attack, of course, the President must take appropriate action to defend us. At the same time, the Constitution requires Congress to authorize war. I do not believe that the president can take military action—including any kind of strategic bombing—against Iran without congressional authorization.[36]

In early April, the Office of Legal Counsel of the Department of Justice submitted a written opinion on the legality of the intervention in Libya.[37] The opinion reviewed the president's words to the public and his messages to Congress before and during American involvement in the military campaign. The opinion first asserted that if he is protecting vital national interests, the president may engage in military operations "without specific prior authorization from Congress."[38] Because the president is "responsible for the conduct of our foreign relations,"[39] he has independent constitutional authority to secure the foreign policy objectives and national security of the nation. The president, unlike Congress, is able to act with the secrecy and decisiveness that military operations often require.

Furthermore, the opinion claimed, "the 'historical gloss' placed on the Constitution by two centuries of practice" provides dozens of examples of "presidential uses of military force abroad in the absence of prior congressional approval."[40] This is important, the opinion noted, because it helps us evaluate how the president and Congress understand "their respective roles and responsibilities" under the Constitution.[41] The Constitution does not require Congress to formally approve every military operation,[42] but, depending on circumstances, it would need to authorize "prolonged and substantial military engagements, typically involving exposure of U.S. military personnel to significant risk over a substantial period."[43]

Applying what we might call the "national interest" and "substantial military engagement" standards to the Libyan intervention, the OLC memo defended President Obama's actions. Similar to arguments other presidents have made, President Obama "reasonably" asserted that it was in the interest of the United States to maintain "regional stability and support the UNSC's credibility and effectiveness."[44] These are "sufficiently important national interests to fall within the President's constitutional power." And his promise that the engagement in Libya would be of "limited nature, duration, and scope" meant that what "the President anticipated directing" was not a "'war' in the constitutional sense necessitating congressional approval under the Declaration of War Clause."[45]

Executive-Congressional Action
In a letter to Congress on May 20 (coincidentally, apparently, the day the sixty-day clock expired), the president emphasized that NATO had officially been in full control of the operation since April 4, that the United States was playing a supporting role, and that there was little danger to troops (remotely controlled drone attacks on specific targets were a large part of the American function).[46] He asked for congressional backing, as that would "demonstrate a unity of purpose on an important national security matter." He concluded, "it has always been my view that it is better to take military action, even in limited action such as this, with Congressional engagement, consultation, and support." If Congress wanted to get on board, fine. If not, that was okay, too.

While the president's letter to Congress in March noted that his report was "consistent" with the War Powers Resolution, the May letter made no mention of it nor did it allude to the law in any way. While he invited Congress to support what he had already done, Section 1544(b) of the WPR clearly indicates that the president requires explicit permission, not simply a message of encouragement, to continue the operation. Otherwise, he must plead "unavoidable military necessity" as an obstacle to bringing troops home, in which case he has an additional thirty days to conclude action and begin withdrawal of troops.

Members of Congress noticed the deadline. Authorities on the WPR noted that never before had an American president ignored the sixty-day deadline and continued a military campaign without any congressional funding or authorization.[47] Some Republican members asked the president to clarify his position on the WPR, while others urged him to seek congressional authorization.[48]

In mid-June, a bipartisan group of ten members of the House of Representatives, led by Congressman Dennis Kucinich of Ohio, sued the Obama administration in federal court for its "circumvention of Congress and its use of international organizations such as the United Nations and the North Atlantic Treaty Organization to authorize the use of military force abroad."[49] Members sought, among other things in a rather expansive list of claims, a declaration that the Libyan intervention was a "war" under Article I, and therefore unconstitutional without a declaration from Congress; a declaration that a UN resolution is not a constitutional substitute for a congressional declaration of war; and an injunction stopping all U.S. military involvement in Libya (unless Congress declared war).

On October 20, the day Qaddafi was killed, Judge Reggie Walton dismissed the lawsuit on the grounds that "plaintiffs have not demonstrated they are without a legislative remedy," and they therefore lack standing.[50] Because he was able to dismiss the case on this ground, he did not proceed to rule on whether plaintiffs sought resolution for a nonjusticiable political question.[51]

In a June 14 letter to President Obama, Speaker of the House John Boehner reminded him that as President, he had a constitutional obligation to ensure the laws were "faithfully executed"—including the law that is the War Powers Resolution. As the ninety-day clock was about to strike and the President still had not formally asked for authorization, Speaker Boehner noted that "the House is left to conclude that you have made one of two determinations: [that] the War Powers Resolution does not apply to the mission in Libya, or you have determined that the War Powers Resolution is contrary to the Constitution."[52]

The administration took the first approach in a June 15 report detailing military and diplomatic activity in Libya and executive-congressional engagement at home. The thirty-two-page public report contained a one-paragraph explanation of the administration's legal view of the operation to that point, finding that the action was legal and "consistent with the War Powers Resolution . . . because U.S. military operations are distinct from the kind of 'hostilities' contemplated by the Resolution's sixty-day termination provision."[53]

Harold Koh, the State Department's Legal Advisor, further explained this "hostilities" argument in a hearing before the Senate Foreign Relations Committee shortly after the ninety-day bell had rung.[54] First, he asserted, the "mission is limited" to supporting NATO in the restricted role of protecting civilians. While NATO forces are more "deeply engaged" in the mission than are American forces, the WPR termination provision only applies to U.S. troops.[55] Second, American troops have limited exposure to enemy fire or confrontation with hostile forces. There have been no American casualties, and the limited nature of the mission does not cause concern that there will be a large number of American casualties.[56] Third, there is very little chance this operation will develop into "a broader conflict characterized by a large U.S. ground presence, major casualties, sustained active combat, or expanding geographical scope."[57] Finally, we are using limited means—"modest in terms of its frequency, intensity, and severity." Most of the sorties are being flown by allies to whom we are simply offering intelligence and refueling capabilities. This is not an aggressive bombing campaign; the few American strikes have only been to enforce the no-fly zone, and drones are being used to strike against targets where there is a need to protect civilians.[58]

Senator Webb strongly disagreed with Koh's analysis:

When you have an operation that goes on for months, costs billions of dollars, where the United States is providing two-thirds of the troops, even under the NATO fig leaf, where they're dropping bombs that are killing people, where you're paying your troops offshore combat pay and there are areas of prospective escalation—something I've been trying to get a clear answer from with this administration for several weeks now, and that is the possibility of a ground presence in some form or another, once the Qaddafi regime expires—I would say that's hostilities.[59]

Other administration officials disagreed with Koh's views as well. It was reported that Jeh Johnson, General Counsel at the Pentagon, Caroline Krass, Acting Head of the Office of Legal Counsel, and Attorney General Eric Holder also objected to the "hostilities" reasoning. Krass and Johnson argued that the WPR required the president to "terminate or scale back" the operation after the sixty-day clock had run out.[60] Johnson thought that if the drone strikes were stopped, the administration would have a stronger case that there were no "hostilities" under the WPR. President Obama took the unusual step of overruling the OLC and going with the advice of White House counsel Bob Bauer and the State Department's top legal advisor, Harold Koh, in coming to his conclusion that America's involvement in Libya did not amount to "hostilities" under the WPR.[61]

On June 24, the House of Representatives overwhelmingly rejected a bill authorizing the use of American forces in Libya, 123–295. In better news for the administration, on the same day, the House defeated a bill that would have limited funding for military operations there.[62] An energetic president might be inclined to invoke the House's votes that day as a clear example of why Congress cannot be safely trusted with all war powers.

Analysis

The public arguments defending the legality of the intervention in Libya are weak and somewhat conflicting. The April OLC opinion depended upon the operation being "limited in nature, duration, and scope." By May 20, the cost of U.S. involvement was thought to be around $750 million and estimated to reach over $1 billion by September.[63] Between early April, when the United States gave control of the operation to NATO, and June 20, American forces had fired approximately ninety missiles on regime targets.[64] The United States was doing more than just refueling planes and providing intelligence, so the "limited nature" argument was not valid. By June, when the operation hit the ninety-day mark, the operation had exceeded what could reasonably be called "limited duration," another one of the criteria the president had used to justify military engagement without congressionally authorization. On several after March 20 the administration had demanded that Qaddafi give up political power, possibly stretching the scope of the operation to regime change.

The claim that the action in Libya did not amount to hostilities under the WPR is also difficult to take seriously. It appears that the administration tacitly acknowledged that American forces were initially involved in WPR-covered hostilities, but after the handoff of the mission to NATO, it didn't understand the WPR to apply to the operation. But United States military personnel remained there, some in fighter jets, drawing combat pay, others serving in different capacities. People on the ground were being killed and other targets destroyed. When American forces weren't firing directly, they were making it physically possible for other nations' troops to do so. It is quite certain that if Libya sent armed unmanned aerial vehicles over Philadelphia and fired on American targets, the United States would consider that "hostilities."

Instead of relying on the tenuous legal claims noted above, the president and his advisors would have been on stronger ground to do one of two things: comply with the WPR and get authorization from Congress, or go on the record stating the WPR is an infringement on the president's constitutional powers, and have that debate with Congress and the public.

Presidents are understandably reluctant to get authorization for military action from Congress. Members of Congress have their own constituencies, and the president may have to spend valuable time to win them over to his side. Restrictions on the president's authority to use force may be written into the authorization, or, in the worst case for the president, Congress may simply reject the operation. Perhaps President Obama really thought the engagement wouldn't last more than a few weeks, and didn't think congressional support would be worth the trouble. But it can be politically-wise to have Congress on board. When things go wrong, as they almost always do, a president who has acted alone is more exposed to public scorn than is someone who had the representatives of the people supporting him. Of course, one may also agree that it is legally-required to have the explicit backing of Congress before engaging in military action.

The WPR has a long and controversial history.[65] When following its guidelines, presidents have generally only acknowledged they are acting "consistent" with the law and not that they are legally bound by its provisions. Members of Congress can hardly be said to be models of integrity when it comes to enforcing the WPR; they are frequently in favor of or oppose the law based on which party holds the White House. The June 24 votes demonstrate that even Congress can't decide what it thinks about its wartime responsibilities.

This being the case, if President Obama believed the WPR unconstitutionally restricted his authority, it would have been good to have this discussion with Congress and the American public instead of clouding the issue with dubious legal theories. In this instance, he could have taken his argument from President Nixon who, in the message explaining his veto of the WPR, stated that the law would endanger America's ability to act as "a force for peace," including in humanitarian operations in nations where there is domestic turmoil.[66]

Finally, it is very difficult to square the constitutional views of presidential candidates Obama and Clinton with their arguments during the Libyan campaign. As senators and candidates for president, both stated that the president would need Congress's consent before launching a strike on an Iranian nuclear facility, something that would have a limited objective and plainly serve a vital national security interest. They were unequivocal in their views that any military action outside of a response to an imminent attack could only be undertaken with congressional approval. But once in the executive branch, both made public arguments that in what was clearly a conflict of choice did not require prior authorization by Congress.

It may be that for humanitarian operations, because there is no apparent threat to the nation, it will be harder to get the approval of Congress, but if one believes that congressional authorization is required for military action, one must get it even when the military is being used for "nonaggressive" reasons. The administration instead relied on authorization from the UN Security Council. While it may have been especially smart in this case to go to a Muslim country with international support, the United States Constitution gives Congress, not the United Nations, a share of responsibility for American troops. The UNSC and U.S. Congress are not interchangeable.

It is evident that the president did not want to send troops to Libya. He was eventually pushed into the operation by members of his own administration, prominent members of Congress, the press, and the international community he had so often committed to working with. Once he made the decision to engage, he minimized public expectations (he went on a trip to Central and South America, and he did not directly address the nation until March 28, nine days after hostilities began) and the role of the United States. The American government apparently was so anxious to transfer the operation to NATO that there was a deadly lapse between the time the United States let it go and when NATO picked it up.[67]

One might wonder, if the national security interest in preserving stability in the region was so important, as the justification claimed, why didn't the United States didn't go in earlier, when momentum was on the side of the rebels and international support had coalesced? And why, if the United States had "unique capabilities" that were essential to the protection of civilians, weren't these resources used more aggressively to ensure that goal?

In June 2012, the crisis in Syria is front-and-center, and the same reluctance the administration had toward engagement in Libya is seen again. As with the situation in Libya, it appears that the president has left much of the handling of the problem to Hillary Clinton and Susan Rice.[68] It was Clinton addressed the Houla massacre, in which 108 civilians were killed, and in the president's absence, it is she who has declared that there is no meaningful international opposition to Assad's tactics.[69] In Libya, Qaddafi ignored repeated warnings to stop the violence against his people. It is unlikely that Bashar Assad, a man who is willing to permit the slaughter of at least 10,000 people, will respond favorably to any plan proposed by Kofi Annan, or that he is threatened by President Obama's creation of an Atrocities Prevention Board. As in Libya, members of Congress and heads of governments are beginning to see intervention in Syria as inevitable.[70]

But there are different between the two situations, and if he does decide to intervene in Syria, President Obama may find he has a more difficult situation than he found in Libya. The international community is divided. Over the last year, Russia has solidified its opposition to any intervention on behalf of civilians as it continues to arm Assad and his loyalists. Europe is directing its attention to its own currency crisis, so there are fewer allies willing to shoulder the work. An intervention couldn't be considered a success without ensuring the Assad regime were replaced with a government that respected basic human rights and would work with the United States and Europe on national security matters, but the opposition in Syria is divided and possibly full of al Qaeda forces. Iran, which has considerable influence over Assad, would have to be confronted. With the presidential election five months away, the unpredictability of events in the part of the world and the possibility of getting dragged into a long and costly conflict, intervention must seem like a very unattractive option.

The president's rhetoric on the campaign trail and during the Libyan conflict put him in an uncomfortable situation today. In his March 28 speech on Libya, the president asserted that he would not "wait for the images of slaughter and mass graves before taking action." He appealed to Americans' patriotism to encourage support for the intervention, indicating there is something special about Americans that must support democracy around the world.[71] "Wherever people long to be free, they will find a friend in the United States." While many presidents make these kinds of statements, Barack Obama campaigned on the premise that he was going to be different; that there was something about him more deserving of trust; that the "international community" would be responsive to him. Whatever a president's ideals, this is a risky policy for a president to have. It makes intervention the default policy of the administration, so the president must explain why we aren't going to support democratic aspirants, not why it is in our national security interest to do so.

Drones

In a Democratic presidential primary debate in June 2007, Senator Barack Obama explained why he would use a Hellfire missile to eliminate Osama bin Laden, even if he knew the attack would also take innocent lives: "I don't believe in assassinations, but Osama bin Laden has declared war on us, killed 3,000 people, and under existing law, including international law, when you've got a military target like bin Laden, you take him out. And if you have twenty minutes, you do it swiftly and surely."[72]

When it comes to the use of missiles to kill suspected terrorists, the president has remained true to his word, taking out individuals through strikes at a much faster clip than did his predecessor. When George W. Bush left office, he handed over control of thirty-four drones or unmanned aerial vehicles (UAVs) to the new commander-in-chief. Today, there are fifty-seven UAVs[73] engaging in targeted killing in countries such as Afghanistan, Pakistan, Yemen, and Somalia. The New America Foundation estimates that in the last year of the George W. Bush administration, there were 33 strikes in Pakistan, where the Central Intelligence Agency has traditionally carried out hits. That number rose to 53 in 2009 and 118 in 2010, President Obama's second year in the White House.[74] There were two strikes in Yemen in 2009; in the first five months of 2012, there were 22.[75] The Joint Special Operations Command may work with the CIA in that and other countries.

Those who support the use of drones make several arguments in their favor. Drones provide an effective way for Americans to eliminate suspected terrorists without having to arm large numbers of troops or risk special operations forces who must physically enter a country and work in extremely remote places. Compared to the cost of training, equipping, and moving troops to a terrorist hideout, UAVs are inexpensive and may have greater mobility in difficult terrain.[76] There is little risk of harm to Americans, since drones are operated from safe bases, and because the planes have defined targets, civilians are not likely to be drawn into a fight and harmed. Leaders of nations where terrorists train and hide may not be able to overtly support the United States. Insofar as they remain covert, drone operations do not damage the legitimacy cooperative governments have with their own people. Finally, the United States doesn't have to worry about a long legal process in which defendants use the judicial system to tie up resources or make a case for their cause.[77]

While the use of drone technology to target individuals for elimination is effective, it has opponents. Arguments have been made that if the United States has prohibited the torture of individuals as a tool of war, picking out individuals for execution is surely worse.[78] Of course, as with many military operations, there is concern about "collateral damage"—harm that might come to innocent civilians who happen to be passing through the vicinity of a target or who might be the victim of faulty intelligence.[79] Targeted killing might cross the line from justifiable killing in self-defense to assassination, which the United States has banned.[80] Decisions have to be made about who will be killed. Should only high-level al Qaeda leaders be subject to strikes, or should low-level followers be targeted as well? How does one get classified as a target, and by whom?[81] There are constitutional questions, revolving around when, where, and to whom the protections of the Bill of Rights must apply. Must the strikes take place on or near a recognized battlefield, or is all the world a war zone for this purpose? Some argue that strikes are not good policy; we should instead focus our efforts on capturing terrorists who might be interrogated for information to use against enemies of the United States.[82]

A possible lack of accountability is also disturbing. Different degrees of oversight apply to CIA and military activities and the organizations carry out, and the CIA and military have different but sometimes overalapping kill lists and mission procedures.[83] This could be especially troubling in a case where a strike resulted in civilian deaths.[84] There are also concerns about whether CIA drone operators, because they are not members of regular armies, could be tried by other nations if caught.[85]

The Program in Practice

In April 2010, it was reported that Anwar al-Awlaki, a Muslim cleric and suspected terrorist, was added to a list of individuals the CIA was permitted to kill. He had previously been on the JSOC target list, but because he was born in New Mexico, and was thus an American citizen, the White House had to approve the move to the CIA roll.[86] Awlaki, a leader of the growing terrorist organization al Qaeda in the Arabian Peninsula (AQAP), was believed to be residing in Yemen, where he had earlier faced but escaped Americans seeking to kill him.[87] The White House did not confirm or deny this information.

Response to the news of Awlaki's placement on the list distressed civil libertarians. Glenn Greenwald protested that the president's claim "not merely to imprison, but to assassinate far from any battlefield, American citizens with no due process of any kind."[88] Jacob Sullum complained that the Obama administration is essentially claiming "unreviewable authority to kill enemies that it unilaterally identifies anywhere in the world."[89] The American Awlaki, though possibly involved in anti-American activity, had not been charged in any court with any crime, and therefore not had not been convicted of any wrongdoing. Could the United States Government proceed to lawfully execute him?

In August 2010, the ACLU and the Center for Constitutional Rights sued the United States government on behalf of Nasser al-Awlaki, the father of Anwar al-Awlaki.[90] The ACLU, seeking to have Awlaki removed from the rumored "kill list" because he was not an "imminent threat" to national security, argued that "outside of armed conflict, both the Constitution and international law prohibit targeted killing except as a last resort to protect against concrete, specific, and imminent threats of death or serious physical injury."[91] Without confirming or denying that Awlaki was on such a list, the government argued that if Awlaki turned himself in to the proper legal authorities, he would no longer be in danger of a possible use of force against him. Simply because had chosen not to avail himself of the normal legal process did not confer standing upon someone acting on his behalf.

The government further claimed that the case should be dismissed under the "political questions" doctrine, which calls for certain issues to be resolved by the branches of government elected by the people.[92]

Agreeing with the government that Mr. Awlaki did not have standing to sue on behalf of his son, Judge John D. Bates dismissed the case on December 7, 2010.[93] Judge Bates also concurred with the government on the political question issue, noting that while the matter of whether the United States government may target a citizen for execution is a grave question, his court was not the place for it to be resolved. He was careful, however, not to place all executive action outside the realm of judicial review, stating that "This Court does not hold that the executive possesses unreviewable authority to order the assassination of any American whom he labels an enemy of the state," but conceded that in this type of situation, judges are "functionally ill-equipped" to make the policy determinations necessary for adjudication.[94]

While the judicial branch did not settle the legal question of when the government could target an individual, the executive branch was wrangling with that question as well. Jeh Johnson and Harold Koh disagreed about the legal authority of the president to strike at targets in Yemen and Somalia. The outcome of this debate would have practical effects on the operations the United States was pressing against al Qaeda in the Arabian Peninsula (AQAP) and al Shabbab in those countries. The Pentagon maintained that the sweeping nature of the 2001 AUMF authorized striking at members of any anti-American group which has associated itself with al Qaeda, including individuals who are not fighting on a regular battlefield in a country where their activities are not suppressed. Koh, on the other hand, took a more restrictive view. He argued that in order for the United States to lawfully kill targets outside the Afghan battlefield, the government must be able to make a legitimate claim of self-defense. Therefore, only those who are actively involved in operations aimed at imminently harming the United States may be targeted.

On September 30, 2011, while traveling in a convoy with other al Qaeda members in Yemen, Anwar al-Awlaki was was killed in a drone strike carried out by the CIA and JSOC. Another American citizen, Samir Khan, was also killed, although he was not a target of the hit. Khan edited Inspire, al Qaeda's online magazine, in which he declared he was "proud to be a traitor to America."[95] Awlaki had been under surveillance for several days, but fear of civilian casualties caused officials to delay the strike.[96] Commenting on the news of Awlaki's death at a ceremony for outgoing Joint Chiefs of Staff Chairman Mike Mullen and incoming Chairman Martin Dempsey, President Obama outlined some of Awlaki's terrorist activities and said that

"The death of Awlaki is a major blow to al Qaeda's most active operational affiliate." Without directly admitting the role of the United States in the attack, he called the operation "a tribute to our intelligence community and to the efforts of Yemen and its security forces," and warned that the United States "will be determined, we will be deliberate, and we will be resolute in our commitment to destroy terrorist networks that aim to kill Americans."[97]

Abdulrahman al-Awlaki, the teenage son of Anwar al-Awlaki, was one of nine men killed in another strike in Yemen two weeks following his father's death.[98] The younger Awlaki was not a target of the hit, which claimed the lives of at least two high-value targets.

Following the strike on Anwar al-Awlaki, a government official reviewed for the press more specifics of Awlaki's history of anti-American activity.[99] He was especially known for recruiting Americans to act against the United States, and the title of his last Inspire article, "Targeting the Populations of Countries That Are at War with Muslims," makes it clear that he was interested in devising plots to kill civilians.[100] He had recruited Umar Farouk Abdulmutallab, the Nigerian-born militant who attempted to blow up a plane bound for Detroit on Christmas Day in 2009, and it is believed he inspired and communicated with Major Nidal Hasan, an Army psychiatrist charged in the November 2009 Ft. Hood massacre in which thirteen people were killed and thirty-two wounded. He conspired with a British Airways employee to blow up a plane on its way to the United States. (The plot did not succeed.) Another admitted follower, Faisal Shahzad, attempted to detonate his explosive-laden vehicle in Times Square in May 2010. It is believed he mailed bombs from Yemen to Chicago, with the expectation the bombs would detonate in the sky. They did not.[101]

For some civil libertarians, the understanding that Awlaki had been involved in these activities was not enough to justify execution. Conor Friedersdorf recalled mistakes the government had made by fingering the wrong person for recent high-profile national security crimes. He maintained that the administration could have at least given Awlaki counsel, tried him in absentia, and then, if a guilty verdict were returned, he could be targeted at that point.[102]

Andrew Cohen complained that the judicial branch had not taken hold of the situation. The Supreme Court, he argued, should answer what is possibly "the most important legal question . . . of the decade": does the president's program of targeting American citizens for elimination violate the Fifth Amendment's due process clause? Cohen argued that Judge Bates, in deferring to the elected branches, made things worse. During the Bush administration, the Supreme Court adjudicated several cases dealing with individual rights and the War on Terror[103]. Here, he argued, Bates gave the government a blank check it promptly cashed on September 30.

Following the Awlaki killing, more concern was also expressed about "collateral damage." Administration officials repeatedly brushed aside questions about civilian casualties. In June 2011, counterterroism chief John Brennan stated that "there hasn't been a single collateral death because of the exceptional proficiency, precision of the capabilities that we've been able to develop."[104] When members of the press and human rights organizations expressed disbelief, he later restated the government's position: "Fortunately, for more than a year, due to our discretion and precision, the U.S. government has not found credible evidence of collateral deaths resulting from U.S. counterterrorism operations outside of Afghanistan or Iraq, and we will continue to do our best to keep it that way."[105]

The death of Awlaki brought more demands from civil libertarians, law professors, members of the George W. Bush administration, and members of Congress of both parties, for fuller disclosure about who is on the government's strike list and how one gets on that list.[106] Rumors of a memo from the Justice Department's Office of Legal Counsel defending the legality of the strike against Awlaki were met by the White House with silence as to whether such a document even existed.

But such a document had been completed in June 2010, and its contents were leaked to Charlie Savage, who published a summary of the approximately 50-page memo in the *New York Times*. The memo, according to Savage, indicates that Awlaki had become a leader of AQAP, specializing in planning attacks that would kill Americans. AQAP was a "cobelligerent" with al Qaeda, so a hit on Awlaki would be lawful under the 2001 Authorization for the Use of Military Force.[107] If capturing Awlaki were not practicable, he could be killed by the United States in self-defense. Even though he was found in Yemen, not on the "hot" battlefield of Afghanistan, he was a legitimate target because he was participating in "armed conflict." The fact that he was engaged in an "armed conflict" with the United States also exempted him from the government's ban on assassination. The Yemeni president had quietly authorized the United States to fire on someone in his country, so there was no violation of sovereignty. Citing various Supreme Court cases, the memo concluded that the Fourth Amendment's protection against "unreasonable searches and seizures" and the Fifth Amendment's protection of "due process" did not apply because Awlaki is not a typical criminal. While he may have begun his political life as a source of violent written and spoken propaganda, he had moved to planning attacks—some successful—to be carried out by al Qaeda militants.

The *Washington Post*, which supported the government's action in Yemen, editorialized that the al-Awlaki memo should be released because questions raised by the killing, such as whether individuals who are not in a recognized war zone may be targeted, and what kind of process American citizens are due before being killed by their own government, are difficult and deserving of response. Additionally, failure to confront these legal questions might lead some to conclude that President Obama has the same contempt for domestic and international law that the *Post* saw in President Bush's wartime measures.[108]

The *New York Times* was less patient. After editorializing about the lack of information provided by the administration to the press[109] and being denied information about the killing of Awlaki through Freedom of Information Act requests, the paper filed a lawsuit against the Department of Justice to get the OLC memo defending the strike against him.[110]

Even members of the Obama administration were having doubts about whether the program was going too far. Cameron Munter, the United States Ambassador to Pakistan, protested that "he didn't realize his main job was to kill people." Chief of Staff Bill Daley wondered if all the strikes were really necessary. "One guy gets knocked off, and the guy's driver, who is No. 21, becomes No. 20? At what point are you just filling the bucket with numbers?"[111]

The Administration Comes Clean—Sort Of

It was clear that the White House could no longer manage to keep from addressing the public secret of the drone program. But how should an explanation of policy and legality be done? For months, key players in national security policy had been debating how much and when to divulge more information to the American people.[112] While the CIA was naturally reluctant to expose the program to public (including international) eyes, Director David Petraeus and Director of National Intelligence Clapper eventually came to the conclusion that limited disclosure of the legal reasoning behind strikes was acceptable. Janet Napolitano, head of Homeland Security, and Kathryn Ruemmler, the White House counsel, concerned about how it might affect pending lawsuits, continued to press for less disclosure. On the other side was Koh, who wanted to provide the public with the most information.[113] It was decided that the Attorney General, Eric Holder, would deliver an address in which he would disclose more than Napolitano and Ruemmler wanted, but less than Koh had hoped for.[114]

In his speech at Northwestern University School of Law in March 2012, Attorney General Holder had a difficult task before him. How would he explain and legally defend a program many of President Obama's supporters vehemently opposed,[115] while not appearing to support a kind of executive power and secrecy he and other government officials had been so critical of during the Bush administration?

Holder began by stating that "we are a nation at war," but "we do not have to choose between liberty and security." The Obama administration would carefully follow the law in making any national security decisions, he said, but the threat to the United States requires the use of tools such as surveillance, detention, and even targeted killing. To ensure that the national security organizations observe legal procedures and protect individual rights, some congressional, judicial, and executive oversight is available. However, he asserted, according to the Constitution, "the conduct and management of national security operations are core functions of the executive branch," and the president does not need judicial permission to "use force abroad against a senior operational leader of a foreign terrorist organization with which the United States is at war—even if that individual happens to be a U.S. citizen."[116] The president may act without knowing "when then precise time, place, and manner of an attack become clear"—something that might be close to Bush-era claims of preemption without Bush-era discussion of it.

The attorney general noted that there is statutory authorization, in the form of the AUMF, as well as constitutional authority, for the president's actions. He must protect the nation against "imminent attacks." International law is also on the side of the president, he said, because we are fighting belligerents in an armed conflict and we may use lethal force in self-defense. To be justifiable force, United States must conform to the principles of necessity, distinction, proportionality, and humanity.[117] He alluded to the use of drones when he said that "the use of stealth or technologically advanced weapons" is not inconsistent with these principles, and may even further them by reducing civilian casualties.

Holder went on to distinguish between assassination and killing in self-defense, and noted that the government reserves the right to kill American citizens, should it determine the facts warrant it. This, too, would be a decision made largely by the executive branch, since "'Due process' and 'judicial process' are not one and the same, particularly when it comes to national security. The Constitution guarantees due process, not judicial process."

While the Attorney General's speech was considered "the good and right thing" to do,[118] it did not answer some serious questions. Who, precisely, is making a decision about whom, where, and when to strike? What kind of evidence is required to make the decision, and how sure are officials are of the veracity of the information? If we can target "associated forces," what is the precise definition of "associated"?[119] If the president may act to stop an "imminent threat of violent attack," what does *each* of those words mean?[120] What is "oversight"? And how much oversight, exactly, do the legislative and judicial branches have over the executive arm of government?

The *Washington Post* noted that shortly after taking office, the attorney general made public several controversial OLC memos written during the Bush administration. It again called on Eric Holder to release the OLC memos making the legal case for drone strikes.[121]

The following month, the administration was ready to more fully address the reasons for and legal status of the use of drones. John Brennan gave a speech at the Woodrow Wilson International Center for Scholars in which he publicly acknowledged the successful use of drone strikes, praised their effectiveness in eliminating many terrorist leaders, and congratulated President Obama for recent military successes, including the elimination of Osama bin Laden.

But there was more to the speech than adulation. Brennan admitted that although the administration believes the use of drones is "legal, ethical, and wise," it has still failed to explain to the American people how targets for strikes are approved. There must be some clarification on this point, since the United States is still "at war" and will continue to use this "critical tool."

Brennan described in general terms how government officials decide whether or not a particular individual will be a target of a drone strike.[122] He stated that there are "rigorous standards" to be met when placing a name on the target list. First, "the individual must be a legitimate target" under either international or domestic law. Federal courts have held that the 2001 Authorization for the Use of Military Force covers members of al Qaeda and those who are affiliated with it, including those who are not on a "hot" battlefield such as Afghanistan. Second, the strike must contribute to the nation's security. Will it stop individuals who want to carry out or support future attacks and have or can obtain the means to do so? Next, is the government able to capture the target instead of killing him? A live target might provide information that could save even more lives, but a ground operation could put American troops or foreign nationals (or our relationship with another government) in harm's way. Finally, are we acting with as much respect as possible for other states' sovereignty, and doing what we can to get the cooperation of heads of state?

This address, like the attorney general's, did not satisfy all listeners.[123] The actual process for deciding what names end up on the target list still was not disclosed, nor did he disclose who was involved in creating the list. Additionally, since some of the groups whose members are targeted were not in existence when the AUMF was passed, should these individuals be subject to strikes? How much of an effort is expended into capturing combatants? He did not reveal nations where strikes are taking place or from which bases where operations are conducted. No disclosure was made of numbers of targets hit, and he called civilian casualties "exceedingly rare." This was in line with a statement he made in late 2011, that "there hasn't been a single collateral death because of the exceptional proficiency [and] precision of the capabilities we've been able to develop."[124]

Finally, Stephen Preston, CIA General Counsel, gave a speech at Harvard noting the importance of strong intelligence capabilities in combating current threats to the national security of the United States.[125] He emphasized that his organization is dedicated to the rule of law, and therefore it must have regular lawful authorization to act. He stressed that although many of the agency's activities are secret, the organization is subject to different kinds of oversight, including judicial oversight. CIA operations must be careful to protect against civilian casualties.

Beginning around the time administration officials were planning speeches in which to make the legal and political arguments in favor of the drone policy, articles explaining various aspects of the program started appearing in major newspapers.[126] It was clear that the administration was selectively leaking information about the still-classified program to the press, hoping to frame it in a way that would preserve political and legal legitimacy and frame the president's actions in the way the administration wanted for the upcoming election.[127] The most telling of the articles, which was written with the cooperation of more than thirty-five former and current government officials, was published in the *New York Times* on May 29.[128]

The process of getting on the "kill list" was disclosed in "A Measure of Change." Targets are selected approximately once a week during meetings dubbed "Terror Tuesday" by participants. More than one hundred national security officials meet by teleconference to review the Power Point slides with biographies and activities of potential targets, coming up with lists of names to be recommended to the president for strikes. Searching questions are asked about each "candidate," and individuals who are no longer considered a threat to the United States may be removed from the consideration list. The list goes to the White House, where Brennan and the president against review each potential target, finally coming up with what is known as the "kill list." It was reported that a strike in which innocent civilians were killed prompted the president to implement a policy under which he personally approves hits with any possibility of civilian casualties. He also authorizes every strike in Yemen and Somalia, as well as all "signature strikes," hits which target unnamed individuals or clusters of people because of particular movements or communication activity.

It was revealed, in perhaps the most controversial part of the piece, that the administration has adopted a rather innovative method of counting civilian casualties. Unless there is explicit evidence to the contrary, all military-age males in a strike zone are counted as combatants: "people in an area of known terrorist activity, or found with a top Qadea operative, are probably up to no good." Thus, it was possible for Brennan to assert with a straight face that there had been zero or only a few civilian casualties in the previous year.

After the publication of the *New York Times* article, the administration's method of calculating civilian deaths came under fire. Civil libertarians skewered the administration's policy. Conor Friedersdorf took aim at the "Nobel Peace Prize-winning president":

[W]e've gone from his insistence, as a U.S. Senator, that it would be unjust to try accused terrorists in a military tribunal with an attorney, to his judgment, as president, that if one member of al Qaeda is someplace, every guy in vague physical proximity automatically meets the convenient 'innocent until probably up to no good' standard.[129]

Jay Carney, the White House press secretary, reiterated that the president's primary responsibility to the nation is to ensure the safety of American citizens, a job President Obama takes "enormously seriously." But when asked for specifics, he would not clarify the number of civilian casualties or explain how the U.S. government was working to minimize civilian deaths.[130]

The day after the Becker and Shane article was published, a *New York Times* editorial titled "Too Much Power for a President" called President Obama "thoughtful and farsighted" and congratulated him for studying the "just-war theories of Augustine and Thomas Aquinas." But, it argued, a politician who has the ability to "order the killing of American citizens or foreigners far from a battlefield" faces electoral pressures that might skew his judgment. A court should review the president's determinations to ensure that adequate evidence exists to warrant his conclusions. The editorial again called for the release of the OLC memo and for the publication of guidelines for future targeted killings.[131]

Analysis
In their offices in Washington, officials may be able to reduce or even eliminate collateral damage simply by classifying all the dead as combatants. On

the ground, however, the effect of strikes is not so easily dismissed. Reports in 2011 and 2012 indicated that strikes are being used as a recruiting tool for AQAP, whose numbers increased from around three hundred members in 2009 to approximately seven hundred in May 2012. Incidents, such as the December 2009 strike in which nearly three dozen women and children were mistakenly killed, fuel hostility against the United States. While most Yemenis don't join AQAP to actively fight against the United States, those who feel national or tribal sovereignty is disrespected may become sympathetic to the group, and may provide safe haven and other resources to AQAP militants.[132]

The administration may consider the growing antagonism to be simply a pesky side effect of an effective counterterrorism weapon. The success of strikes in taking out key militants, including Sakhr al-Tafi in late May 2012 and Yahya al-Libi in early June 2012, makes it a tool that is not easy to give up.[133] While drone attacks do not remove all threats, they remove some, which American national security advisors must see as a plus. With each kill, institutional knowledge evaporates, and eliminating those with particular expertise in bombmaking, financing, or arms acquisition prevents new adherents from learning those skills.[134]

Congress has just provided an additional $75 million for fighting terror cells such as AQAP, al Shabab, and Boko Haram in Yemen and East Africa. In spite of Secretary of Defense Panetta's assurances that "there is no consideration"[135] of the introduction of U.S. ground forces in Yemen, it has been reported that at least twenty American special operations forces are there, providing intelligence and coordination for targeted killing.[136] The president has given support to expanding signature strikes and a larger role for the CIA in Yemen. While traveling to Pakistan, Secretary Panetta dismissed demands from Pakistani officials who say that strikes violate their nation's sovereignty.[137] These developments strongly indicate that questions of why and how drones are used are not going to go away for the administration.[138] It must be prepared to address those issues.

Each national security speech made by an administration official emphasized that measures are taken to minimize collateral damage, that capture is almost always an option, that the president has legal authority to make these decisions, and that the process for naming targets is serious and deliberative. Each complimented the judiciary for knowing its institutional limits and staying out of national security matters it is incapable of resolving. The possibility of judicial intervention of the kind the *New York Times* advocates must certainly be of concern to administration officials. National security officials must convince judges outside of the courtroom that that a thoughtful, multilevel review process, supported by frank discussion and articulation of threat, is the process "due" these people, as the attorney general claimed in his speech.

Others must be convinced, too. Surely Obama administration officials recall the uproar against Bush administration war policies. (In many instances, they were leading the opposition.) The press, human rights groups, and current and former government officials demanded the administration explain some policies and change others. The public may not have well understood legal arguments about Bush-era policies, but commentary by elites and the inability of President Bush and his aides to make coherent arguments made the policies seemed ineffective, morally wrong, unconstitutional, or a combination of the three. President Obama must persuade prominent opinion makers that what he is doing is right as a matter of law and of policy. Otherwise, he will risk the same loss of domestic and international public support his predecessor suffered.

As in other administrations, President Obama's advisors have made assertions of secrecy when they don't want oversight of certain policies, but selectively leaked information in order to strategically promote and get support for those policies later. The willingness of officials to advertise many details of the program through a stream of leaks, some of them providing significant information about particular instances, shows that the serious national security argument for keeping everything under wraps is no longer valid.

In any explanation, intelligence should not be compromised. The public does not need information about kinds of weapons used, countries where strikes are taking place, who is carrying out the hits, or how intelligence is gathered to get someone on the kill list or to execute the mission (although those issues might be taken up separately for other purposes). A redacted version of the OLC memo or a separate document explaining the reasoning would support the most relevant arguments, which should be explained by the president. Most importantly, what does the president see as his legal authority for the strikes? Does he rely on provisions in Article II? How much and what groups does the AUMF cover? Does the administration think it needs to seek further congressional authorization to cover other individuals or groups? Is there a limit to his power when it comes to national security? How are the constitutional rights of American citizens understood in the review process? At different times, President Obama and the attorney general have made the case that terrorists could or should be tried in American courts. How can that be squared with execution? Does anyone speak on behalf of the targets? Are all associates of terrorist cells considered to be in armed conflict? What constitutes "armed conflict" outside a "hot" battlefield?

The revelation that the president is personally involved in approving so many strikes is likely also aimed at convincing the public in an election year that he is serious about national security matters. To those who supported him and are disappointed with what might look like illegal extrajudicial killing, he can argue that he is taking responsibility for the program and his superior moral judgment is brought to bear in each case. To those who might consider him a weak commander-in-chief, he can appear decisive and willing to take the fight to the terrorists. The revelation that David Axelrod, his primary political advisor, was a regular at the Terror Tuesday meetings, demonstrates the political importance the president sees in the smooth operation of the program.

The drone campaign is a significant innovation in counterterrorism strategy which also permits the president to minimize public expectations and disappointment, at least in the short term. How many Americans know who today's "Number Two al Qaeda operative" is, or what makes a hit a success? Targeted killing means no coffins unloaded at Dover AFB and no reporters standing by a pool of blood on the evening news. In the face of looming defense budget cuts, it gives the appearance of something effective being done. There is no discussion about Guantanamo being open when the issue of detention comes up. President Obama is free from having to deal with the politics and procedures of lengthy, expensive trials—in a military commission or civilian court?—where accused terrorists can make a case or publicize a cause. The advantages make the program, in the words of Leon Panetta, "the only game in town."[139]

In the long run, however, firing from the air is not always a substitute for engagement. "Dead men tell no tales and thus are no help in anticipating the next attack or informing us about broader terrorist activities."[140] Detention and interrogation are procedurally and legally difficult, but information is an essential weapon in war. "Exclusive reliance on drones and a no-capture policy spend down the investments in intelligence . . . without replenishing the interrogation-gained information needed to predict future threats."[141] And whether targeted killing meets the moral standards President Obama holds for American policy is still being debated.

Conclusion

President Obama appears to be a reluctant commander-in-chief. It seems he delays action unless he can clearly succeed, or be seen to succeed. He is comfortable leaving his department secretaries to see what they can do, without making it clear they are under his direction. He downplays the role the United States does or might play, even as he insists through words and force that dictators step down. When he uses force, he clearly wants to do so with as little oversight of his decision making as possible by Congress or the courts. He has implemented a counterterrorism effort using new, nimble, and what proponents claim is very effective technology, but he will not explain why it is a legal program and the best option. Although he speaks frequently about the success of the bin Laden raid, he does not go out of his way to talk about significant action in the Middle East or his general war doctrine. Perhaps this is because the adjustments from the Bush era are not as significant as supporters would have liked, or as much as he said he wanted. Some changes were made to Bush detention, interrogation, and rendition programs, but the new policies intentionally included "wiggle words" so the president could "maintain [his] options."[142] It seems as though there is a conflict between his ideals and political reality.

The president is the commander-in-chief and as such he has a responsibility to act according to the Constitution. President Obama may well have been within his constitutional rights to remain in Libya longer than sixty days without congressional approval, but the case he made for it was entirely unconvincing. Human rights groups, American and foreign government officials, and international bodies have questioned the legality and morality of the drone program,[143] but as much as it has been discussed by administration officials and the press, the public legal case is not satisfying. Future presidents will act based on the president's arguments in both cases.[144] If President Obama believes his actions to be lawful and necessary, they must be available to his successors. Legitimacy cannot rest on vague references to law, transient popularity ratings, or his perceived moral stature. The president must provide a *credible* defense grounded in the most enduring foundation, the Constitution and laws of the United States.

Notes

1. Associated Press, "Obama Makes Intel Picks, Vows No Torture," MSN.com, January 9, 2009, www.msnbc.msn.com/id/28574408/ns/politics-white_house/t/obama-names-intel-picks-vows-no-torture/ (accessed June 3, 2012).

2. See chapter three of this volume for a brief discussion of these matters.

3. Barack Obama, "Remarks by the President at the Acceptance of the Nobel Peace Prize," December 10, 2009, www.whitehouse.gov/the-press-office/remarks-president-acceptance-nobel-peace-prize (accessed May 23, 2012).

4. Scott Wilson, "Obama Strategy of Taking Credit for Osama bin Laden Killing Risky, Observers Say," *Washington Post*, April 30, 2012, www.washingtonpost

.com/politics/obama-strategy-of-taking-credit-for-osama-bin-laden-killing-risky-some
-observers-say/2012/04/30/gIQApuAxrT_story.html?hpid=z1 (accessed May 23, 2012).

5. The sources referenced in this chapter spell the Libyan dictator's name in different ways. I use "Qaddafi" throughout the chapter, except in article titles, so as to facilitate research. The same is true for Anwar al-Awlaki, who is discussed in the next section.

6. William Branigin, Mary Beth Sheridan, and Colum Lynch, "Obama Condemns Violence in Libya, Asks for 'Full Range of Options,'" *Washington Post*, February 23, 2011, www.washingtonpost.com/wp-dyn/content/article/2011/02/22/AR2011022206935.html (accessed May 22, 2012).

7. Editorial, "Why was President Obama Last to Speak Up on Libya," *Washington Post*, February 23, 2011, www.washingtonpost.com/we-dyn/content/article/2011/02/23/AR2011022305993.html (accessed May 22, 2012).

8. Eugene Robinson, "It's Time to Get Tough with Libya," *Washington Post*, February 25, 2011, www.washingtonpost.com/wp-dyn/content/article/2011/02/24/AR2011022406481.html (accessed May 22, 2012).

9. Karen DeYoung and Craig Whitlock, "U.S. Defense Leader Warn of No-Fly-Zone Risks," *Washington Post*, March 2, 2011, www.washingtonpost.com/wp-dyn/content/article/2011/03/01/AR2011030104406.html (accessed May 22, 2012).

10. MSN.com, Meet the Press transcript, March 6, 2011, www.msnbc.msn.com/id/41906285/ns/meet_the_press-transcripts/t/meet-press-transcript-march/#.T74it-sWgxE (accessed May 22, 2012).

11. Alex Spillius, "Libya: 'Gaddafi Will Prevail,' Says Barack Obama's Intelligence Chief," *The Telegraph*, March 10, 2011.

12. United States Senate, Senate Resolution 85, March 1, 2011, thomas.loc.gov/cgi-bin/query/z?c112:S.RES.85: (accessed May 22, 2012).

13. David A. Fahrenthold, "Congress Members Struggle to Define Message on Middle East, North Africa," *Washington Post*, March 3, 2011, www.washingtonpost.com/politics/congress-members-struggle-to-define-message-on-mideast-north-africa/2011/03/14/ABIJMJX_story.html (accessed May 22, 2012), Michael McGuire, "Lugar Warns against U.S. War in Libya," *Examiner.com*, March 8, 2011, www.examiner.com/article/lugar-warns-against-us-war-libya (accessed June 3, 2012).

14. Jonathan S. Landay, "Despite Reluctance," U.S. Could Be Forced to Act in Libya," McClatchy, March 2, 2011, www.mcclatchydc.com/2011/03/02/109737/despite-reluctance-us-could-be.html (accessed May 21, 2012).

15. When asked on February 16, 2011, whether Qaddafi was a dictator, Crowley did not at first respond. When asked the question again, he replied, "I don't think he came to office through a democratic process." Stephen F. Hayes, "An Administration Adrift," *Weekly Standard*, March 7, 2011, www.weeklystandard.com/articles/administration-adrift_552541.html (accessed May 22, 2012).

16. Gerri Peev and Tom Kelly, "Bloodbath as 300 are Massacred for Defying Gaddafi in Libya, while U.S. and UN Condemn Britain for Cosying up to Tyrant,"

Daily Mail, February 21, 2011, www.dailymail.co.uk/news/article-1359075/Libya
-protests-Gaddafi-massacres-300-UK-condemned-cosying-tyrant.html (accessed
June 3, 2012).

17. Hayes, "An Administration Adrift."

18. Karen DeYoung, Edward Cody and William Branigin, "Obama Concerned
About Gaddafi's Gains but Says Noose is Tightening on Libyan Leader," *Washington Post*, March 11, 2011, www.washingtonpost.com/world/us-to-send-aid-team-to
-eastern-libya-clinton-to-meet-rebel-representatives/2011/03/10/ABxH6ZQ_story
.html (accessed May 22, 2012).

19. Diaa Hadid, "Arab League Asks UN for Libya No-Fly Zone," *Huffington Post*,
March 12, 2011, www.huffingtonpost.com/2011/03/12/arab-league-asks-un-for-libya
-no-fly-zone_n_834975.html (accessed May 22, 2012).

20. Helene Cooper and Steven Lee Myers, "Obama Takes Hard Line with Libya
After Shift by Clinton," *New York Times*, March 18 2011, www.nytimes.com/
2011/03/19/world/africa/19policy.html?pagewanted=all (accessed May 2012).

21. United Nations Security Council, Resolution 1973, March 17, 2011, daccess-
dds-ny.un.org/doc/UNDOC/GEN/N11/268/39/PDF/N1126839.pdf?OpenElement
(accessed May 21, 2012).

22. Dan Bilefsky and Mark Landler, "As U.N. Backs Military Action in Libya, U.S.
Role Is Unclear," *New York Times*, March 17, 2011, www.nytimes.com/2011/03/18/
world/africa/18nations.html?pagewanted=all (accessed May 22, 2012).

23. Jake Tapper, "Obama to Members of Congress: Action Versus Libya to Last
'Days not Weeks,'" *ABCNews.com* Political Punch blog, March 18, 2011, abcnews
.go.com/blogs/politics/2011/03/obama-to-members-of-congress-action-versus-libya
-in-days-not-weeks/ (accessed May 22, 2012).

24. Barack Obama, Remarks by the President on the Situation in Libya, March 18,
2011, www.whitehouse.gov/the-press-office/2011/03/18/remarks-president-situation
-libya (accessed May 23, 2012).

25. Barack Obama, Letter from the President Regarding the Commencement of
Operations in Libya to the Speaker of the House of Representatives and President
Pro Tempore of the Senate, March 21, 2011, www.whitehouse.gov/the-press-office/
2011/03/21/letter-president-regarding-commencement-operations-libya (accessed
May 23, 2012).

26. Ibid.

27. Abby Phillip, "Pentagon: We're Not Hunting Qadhafi," Politico, March 20,
2011, www.politico.com/news/stories/0311/51620.html (accessed May 22, 2012),
Karen DeYoung, "Questions Raised about U.S. Goals and Role in Libya," *Washington Post*, March 20, 2011, www.washingtonpost.com/world/questions-raised-about-us
-role-and-goals-in-libya/2011/03/20/ABus9h3_story.html (accessed May 22, 2012).

28. Mark Landler and Steven Erlanger, "Obama Seeks to Unify Allies as More
Airstrikes Rock Tripoli," *New York Times*, March 22, 2011, www.nytimes.com/
2011/03/23/world/africa/23libya.html?pagewanted=all (accessed May 22, 2012).

29. Steven Erlanger and Eric Schmitt, "NATO Set to Take Full Command of Libyan Campaign," *New York Times*, March 25, 2011, www.nytimes.com/2011/03/26/world/africa/26libya.html?pagewanted=all (accessed May 21, 2012).

30. Associated Press, "Muammar Gaddafi Killed, Captured in Sirte," *Huffington Post*, October 20, 2011, www.huffingtonpost.com/2011/10/20/muammar-gaddafi-killed_n_1021462.html (accessed May 23, 2012).

31. Barack Obama, "Remarks by the President on the Death Of Muammar Qaddafi," The White House Office of the Press Secretary, October 20, 2011, www.whitehouse.gov/the-press-office/2011/10/20/remarks-president-death-muammar-qaddafi (accessed May 22, 2012).

32. U.S. Code 50 (1973) sec. 1541 et.seq. www.law.cornell.edu/uscode/text/50/chapter-33 (accessed May 23, 2012)

33. Ibid., sec. 1541(a).

34. Ibid., sec. 1544(b).

35. Charlie Savage, "Barack Obama's Q&A," *Boston Globe*, 20 December 2007, www.boston.com/news/politics/2008/specials/CandidateQA/ObamaQA/ (accessed May 23, 2012).

36. Charlie Savage, "Hillary Clinton's Q&A," *Boston Globe*, 20 December 2007, www.boston.com/news/politics/2008/specials/CandidateQA/ClintonQA/ (accessed May 23, 2012).

37. Office of Legal Counsel, United States Department of Justice, "Authority to Use Military Force in Libya," April 1, 2011, www.justice.gov/olc/2011/authority-military-use-in-libya.pdf (accessed May 22, 2012).

38. Ibid., 6.

39. Ibid.. 6. (Quoting *Youngstown Sheet & Tube Co. v. Sawyer*, 353 U.S. 579, 610-611 (1952) (Frankfurter, J., concurring.)

40. Ibid., 6.

41. Ibid., 7-8.

42. Ibid., 8.

43. Ibid.

44. Ibid., 10.

45. Ibid., 13.

46. Barack Obama, "President Obama's Letter about Efforts in Libya," *New York Times*, May 20, 2011, www.nytimes.com/2011/05/21/world/africa/21libya-text.html (accessed May 22, 2012).

47. Jake Tapper and Devin Dwyer, "President Obama's Libya Intervention Hits 60-Day Legal Limit," ABCNews.com, May 20, 2011, abcnews.go.com/Politics/libya-president-obama-congress-faces-questions-war-powers-act/story?id=13642002#.T7xQGkV8CFk (accessed May 22, 2012).

48. Ibid. See also Charlie Savage and Thom Shanker, "As NATO Claims Progress in Libya, a U.S. Deadline Is Put to the Test," *New York Times*, May 21, 2011, www.nytimes.com/2011/05/21/world/africa/21libya.html (accessed May 22, 2012).

49. Reid J. Epstein, "Lawmakers Sue Obama over Libya," *Politico*, June 15, 2011, www.politico.com/news/stories/0611/57032.html (accessed May 23, 2012).

50. Josh Gerstein, "Judge Zings Lawmakers, Dismisses Lawsuit over Libya Mission," *Politico*, October 20, 2011, www.politico.com/blogs/joshgerstein/1011/Judge_zings_lawmakers_dismisses_War_Powers_lawsuit_over_Libya.html (accessed May 23, 2012). Judge Walton chided the plaintiffs for wasting the resources of the court with a case they knew presented political questions which would not be resolved in that forum. *Kucinich v. Obama*, 11-1096 (D.D.C. 2011), 4. https://ecf.dcd.uscourts.gov/cgi-bin/show_public_doc?2011cv1096-14

51. Kucinich v. Obama, 23, n. 9.

52. Jonathan Allen, "Boehner gets into War Powers Act," *Politico*, June 15, 2011, www.politico.com/news/stories/0611/57014.html (accessed May 22, 2012).

53. "United States Activities in Libya," June 15, 2011, www.foreignpolicy.com/files/fp_uploaded_documents/110615_United_States_Activities_in_Libya_--_6_15_11.pdf (accessed May 22, 2012).

54. Harold Koh, Testimony on Libya and War Powers, Senate Foreign Relations Committee, June 28, 2011 www.foreign.senate.gov/imo/media/doc/Koh_Testimony.pdf (accessed May 22, 2012).

55. Ibid., 7-8.

56. Ibid., 8.

57. Ibid., 10.

58. Ibid., 11.

59. Jennifer Steinhauer, "Obama advisor Defends Libya Policy to Senate," *New York Times*, June 28, 2011, www.nytimes.com/2011/06/29/us/politics/29powers.html (accessed May 23, 2012).

60. Charlie Savage, "2 Top Lawyers Lost to Obama in War Policy Debate," *New York Times*, June 17, 2011, www.nytimes.com/2011/06/18/world/africa/18powers.html?pagewanted=all (accessed May 23, 2012).

61. As Savage notes in "2 Top Lawyers Lost to Obama," the OLC traditionally "decides what the best interpretation of the law is" without respect for particular policies, then submits that view to the president or attorney general. They may overrule the OLC opinion, "but it is extraordinarily rare for that to happen." In this case, President Obama accepted legal views from various agencies in a "less formal way," apparently by phone and in conversation (so without a hard paper trail), then made his decision. While it is acknowledged that the president always makes the final determination, it was noted that "This is not a process designed to produce a sound legal decision...When the president effectively decides the legal questionin the first instance based on the input of interested agencies, his legal judgment is inevitably skewed a great deal by wanting to uphold his policy." Jack Goldsmith, "President Obama Rejected DOJ and DOD Advice, and Sided with Harold Koh, on War Powers Resolution," *Lawfare* blog, June 17, 2011, www.lawfareblog.com/2011/06/president-obama-rejected-doj-and-dod-advice-and-sided-with-harold

-koh-on-war-powers-resolution/ www.lawfareblog.com/2011/06/president-obama
-rejected-doj-and-dod-advice-and-sided-with-harold-koh-on-war-powers-resolution/
(accessed June 2, 2012).

62. Jennifer Steinhauer, "House Spurns Obama on Libya but Does Not Cut Funds,"
New York Times, June 24, 2011, www.nytimes.com/2011/06/25/us/politics/25powers
.html (accessed May 22, 2012).

63. Tapper and Dwyer, "President Obama's Libya Intervention Hits 60-Day Legal
Limit."

64. Charlie Savage and Thom Shanker, "Scores of U.S. Strikes in Libya Followed
Handoff to NATO," *New York Times*, June 20, 2011, www.nytimes.com/2011/06/21/
world/africa/21powers.html (accessed May 23, 2012).

65. Richard F. Grimmett, "War Powers Resolution: Presidential Compliance,"
Congressional Research Service Report, March 25, 2011, fpc.state.gov/documents/
organization/159786.pdf (accessed May 31, 2012). See especially pages 11-16.

66. Richard Nixon,"Veto of the War Powers Resolution," *The American Presidency Project* October 24, 1973, www.presidency.ucsb.edu/ws/index.php?pid=
4021#axzz1vpPQ9L39 (accessed May 22, 2012).

67. C.J. Chivers and David D. Kirkpatrick, "Libyan Rebels Complain of Deadly
Delays under NATO's Command," *New York Times*, April 4, 2011, www.nytimes.
com/2011/04/05/world/africa/05libya.html (accessed May 31, 2012).

68. Scott Wilson, "On Foreign Policy, Obama Focuses on Economic Issues,
Not on Syrian Turmoil," Washington Post, June 2, 2012, www.washingtonpost
.com/politics/on-foreign-policy-obama-focuses-on-economic-issues-not-on-syrian
-turmoil/2012/06/02/gJQAVrSX9U_story.html (accessed June 3, 2012).

69. Michael Birnbaum, "European Voices Go Silent on Syria," Washington Post,
May 31, 2012 www.washingtonpost.com/world/europe/european-voices-go-silent
-on-syria/2012/05/31/gJQAbbXD5U_story.html (accessed June 2, 2012).

70. Jeremy Herb, "Obama Faces Tough Choices in Syria," The Hill DEFCON
Hill blog, April 21, 2012, thehill.com/blogs/defcon-hill/policy-and-strategy/222899
-obama-faces-tough-choices-in-syria (accessed June 3, 2012).

71. Barack Obama, "Remarks by the President in Address to the Nation on
Libya," March 28, 2011, www.whitehouse.gov/the-press-office/2011/03/28/remarks
-president-address-nation-libya (accessed May 23, 2012).

72. Adam Entous, "Special Report: How the White House Learned to Love the
Drone," *Reuters*, May 18, 2010 www.reuters.com/article/2010/05/18/us-pakistan
-drones-idUSTRE64H5SL20100518 (accessed May 22, 2012).

73. Micah Zenko, "How Many Civilians Are Killed by U.S. Drones?" Council on
Foreign Relations Power, Politics, and Preventive Action blog, June 4, 2012, blogs
.cfr.org/zenko/2012/06/04/how-many-civilians-are-killed-by-u-s-drones/ (accessed
June 4, 2012).

74. New America Foundation, "The Year of the Drone," June 4, 2012, counter-
terrorism.newamerica.net/drones (accessed June 4, 2012).

75. Bill Roggio and Bob Barry, "Charting the data for US air strikes in Yemen, 2002 – 2012," *Long War Journal*, May 28, 2012, www.longwarjournal.org/multimedia/Yemen/code/Yemen-strike.php (accessed June 4, 2012).

76. Victor Davis Hanson, "More Rubble, Less Trouble," *Defining Ideas*, May 3, 2012, www.hoover.org/publications/defining-ideas/article/116356 (accessed May 23, 2012).

77. Entous, "Special Report: How the White House Learned to Love the Drone."

78. Mary Ellen O'Connell, "Why Obama's 'Targeted Killing' Is Worse than Bush's Torture," *The Guardian*, January 20, 2012, www.guardian.co.uk/comment isfree/cifamerica/2012/jan/20/why-obama-targeted-killing-is-like-bush-torture (accessed May 22, 2012).

79. Ibid.

80. Entous, "Special Report: How the White House Learned to Love the Drone."

81. Karen DeYoung, "Secrecy Defines Obama's Drone War," *Washington Post*, December 19, 2011, www.washingtonpost.com/world/national-security/secrecy-defines-obamas-drone-war/2011/10/28/gIQAPKNR5O_story.html (accessed May 23, 2012).

82. Marc A. Thiessen, "Mr. President, Please Don't Kill This Terrorist," *Washington Post*, May 14, 2012, www.washingtonpost.com/opinions/mr-president-please-dont-kill-this-terrorist/2012/05/14/gIQAF8oxOU_story.html (accessed May 23, 2012).

83. Greg Miller, "Under Obama, An Emerging Global Apparatus for Drone Killing," *Washington Post*, December 27, 2011, www.washingtonpost.com/national/national-security/under-obama-an-emerging-global-apparatus-for-drone-killing/2011/12/13/gIQANPdILP_story.html (accessed May 31, 2012),

84. Charlie Savage, "U.N. Official to Ask U.S. to End C.I.A. Strikes," *New York Times*, May 27, 2012, www.nytimes.com/2010/05/28/world/asia/28drones.html (accessed May 22, 2012), Adam Serwer, "When the US Government Can Kill You, Explained," The Nation, March 6, 2012, www.motherjones.com/mojo/2012/03/eric-holder-targeted-killing (accessed May 22, 2012).

85. Savage, "U.N. Official to Ask U.S. to End C.I.A. Strikes."

86. Greg Miller, "Muslim Cleric Aulaqi is 1st U.S. Citizen on List of Those CIA Is Allowed to Kill," *Washington Post*, April 7, 2010, www.washingtonpost.com/wp-dyn/content/article/2010/04/06/AR2010040604121.html (accessed May 22, 2012).

87. Mark Mazzetti, Eric Schmitt and Robert F. Worth, "Two-Year Manhunt Led to Killing of Awlaki in Yemen," *New York Times*, September 30, 2011, www.nytimes.com/2011/10/01/world/middleeast/anwar-al-awlaki-is-killed-in-yemen.html?pagewanted=all (accessed May 23, 2012).

88. Glenn Greenwald, "Confirmed: Obama Authorizes Assassination of U.S. Citizen," *Salon.com*, April 7, 2010, www.salon.com/2010/04/07/assassinations_2/ (accessed May 22, 2012).

89. Jacob Sullum, "License to Kill," *Reason*, June 9, 2010, reason.org/news/show/obama-license-kill (accessed May 22, 2012). In this part of his article, Sullum is specifically objecting to comments made in a speech given by Harold Koh, legal advisor

at the State Department, defending drone strikes as legal under the principle of self defense. Speech at the Annual Meeting of the American Society of International Law, March 25, 2010, www.state.gov/s/l/releases/remarks/139119.htm (accessed May 23, 2012).

90. *Al-Aulaqi v. Obama*, 10cv1469 (D.D.C. 2010). Charlie Savage, "Suit over Targeted Killings is Thrown Out," *New York Times*, December 7, 2010, www .nytimes.com/2010/12/08/world/middleeast/08killing.html (accessed May 22, 2012).

91. ACLU, "Al-Aulaqi v. Obama: Lawsuit Challenging Targeted Killings," ACLU, www.aclu.org/national-security/al-aulaqi-v-obama (accessed May 22, 2012).

92. United States Department of Justice, "Opposition to Plaintiff's Motion for Preliminary Injunction and Memorandum in Support of Defendants' Motion to Dismiss," *Lawfare* blog, 2-3, www.lawfareblog.com/wp-content/uploads/2010/09/ usgbrief.pdf (accessed May 22, 2012).

93. *Al-Aulaqi v. Obama.*

94. Warren Richey, "Judge Dismisses Bid to Remove Anwar al-Awlaki from U.S. 'Kill List,'" *Christian Science Monitor*, December 7, 2010 www.csmonitor.com/ USA/Justice/2010/1207/Judge-dismisses-bid-to-remove-Anwar-al-Awlaki-from-US -kill-list (accessed May 22, 2012).

95. Mark Mazzetti, et. al., "Two-Year Manhunt Led to Killing of Awlaki in Yemen.

96. Charlie Savage, "Secret U.S. Memo Made Legal Case to Kill a Citizen," *New York Times*, October 8, 2011, www.nytimes.com/2011/10/09/world/middle east/secret-us-memo-made-legal-case-to-kill-a-citizen.html?pagewanted=all (accessed May 23, 2012).

97. David Jackson, "Obama: Terrorists Will Find 'No Safe Haven Anywhere,'" *USA Today*, Semptember 30, 2011, content.usatoday.com/communities/theoval/ post/2011/09/obama-terrorists-will-find-no-safe-haven-anywhere/1#.T8Gz49U WgxE (accessed May 22, 2012).

98. Peter Finn and Greg Miller, "Anwar al-Awlaki's Family Speaks Out Against His Son's Death In Airstrike," *Washington Post*, October 17, 2011, www.washington post.com/world/national-security/anwar-al-awlakis-family-speaks-out-against-his-sons -deaths/2011/10/17/gIQA8kFssL_story.html (accessed May 22, 2012).

99. Kimberly Dozier, "Obama: Anwar Al-Awlaki Death a Major Blow to Al Qaeda," *Huffington Post*, September 30, 2011, www.huffingtonpost.com/2011/09/30/ obama-anwar-al-awlaki-dead_n_988924.html (accessed May 22, 2012).

100. Thomas Joscelyn, AQAP Releases 7th Edition of Inspire," *Long War Journal*, September 27, 2011, www.longwarjournal.org/archives/2011/09/aqap_releases_ sevent.php (accessed May 22, 2012).

101. Perhaps to shore up the legal and political cases against Awlaki, on the day he was killed the U.S. Government gave him the title of "chief of external opera-tions." Greg Miller and Alice Fordham, *Washington Post* Checkpoint Washington blog, September 30, 2011, www.washingtonpost.com/blogs/checkpoint-washington/ post/aulaqi-gets-new-designation-in-death/2011/09/30/gIQAsbF69K_blog.html (accessed May 30, 2012).

102. Conor Friedersdorf, "President Obama, Executioner-in-Chief," *The Atlantic*, September 30, 2011, www.theatlantic.com/politics/archive/2011/09/president-obama-executioner-in-chief/245965/ (accessed May 22, 2012).

103. Andrew Cohen, "Where is the Judicial Branch on Targeted Killings?" *The Atlantic*, October 1, 2011, www.theatlantic.com/national/archive/2011/10/where-is-the-judicial-branch-on-targeted-killings/245979/ (accessed May 22, 2012).

104. Ken Dilanian, U.S. Counter-Terrorism Strategy to Rely on Surgical Strikes, Unmanned Drones," *Los Angeles Times*, June 29, 2011, articles.latimes.com/2011/jun/29/news/la-pn-al-qaeda-strategy-20110629 (accessed May 30, 2012).

105. Scott Shane, "C.I.A. Is Disputed on Civilian Toll in Drone Strikes," *New York Times*, August 11, 2011, www.nytimes.com/2011/08/12/world/asia/12drones.html?pagewanted=all (accessed June 3, 2012).

106. Peter Finn, "Political, Legal Experts Want Release of Justice Dept. Memo Supporting Killing of Anwar al-Awlaki," *Washington Post*, October 7, 2011, www.washingtonpost.com/world/national-security/political-legal-experts-want-release-of-justice-dept-memo-supporting-killing-of-anwar-al-awlaki/2011/10/07/gIQABCV9TL_story.html?wprss=rss_politics (accessed May 22, 2012).

107. Authorization for the Use of Military Force, Public Law 107-40 [S. J. RES. 23], September 18, 2001.

108. Washington Post Editorial Board, "Administration Should Do More to Defend the Awlaki Strike," *Washington Post*, October 7, 2011, www.washingtonpost.com/opinions/administration-should-do-more-to-defend-the-awlaki-strike/2011/10/04/gIQASHEbOL_story.html (accessed May 23, 2012).

109. Arthur S. Brisbane, "The Secrets of Government Killing," *New York Times*, October 8, 2011, www.nytimes.com/2011/10/09/opinion/sunday/the-secrets-of-government-killing.html (accessed May 22, 2012).

110. Justin Sink, "New York Times Sues Justice Department Over Targeted-Killing Memo," *The Hill* DEFCON Hill blog, December 23, 2011, thehill.com/blogs/defcon-hill/policy-and-strategy/201197-new-york-times-sues-justice-department-over-targeted-killing-memo (accessed May 22, 2012).

111. Jo Becker and Scott Shane, "A Measure of Change: Secret 'Kill List' Proves a Test of Obama's Principles and Will," *New York Times*, May 29, 2012, www.nytimes.com/2012/05/29/world/obamas-leadership-in-war-on-al-qaeda.html?_r=2&hp&pagewanted=all (accessed May 30, 2012).

112. Daniel Klaidman, "Obama Team to Break Silence on al-Awlaki Killing," *The Daily Beast*, www.thedailybeast.com/newsweek/2012/01/22/obama-team-to-break-silence-on-al-awlaki-killing.html (accessed May 23, 2012).

113. Ibid.

114. Eric Holder, Speech at Northwestern University School of Law," March 5, 2012, www.justice.gov/iso/opa/ag/speeches/2012/ag-speech-1203051.html (accessed May 22, 2012). Jeh Johnson gave a speech at Yale Law School which touched on targeted killings and executive authority during war. He discussed "associated forces" which might be legitimate targets under the still valid AUMF. While the president

does not have unlimited constitutional authority, Johnson agreed with Judge Bates that the courts are not able to make judicial determinations regarding targeted killing. "National Security Law, Lawyers, and Lawyering in the Obama Administration," Speech at Yale Law School, Lawfare blog, February 22, 2012, www.lawfareblog .com/2012/02/jeh-johnson-speech-at-yale-law-school/ (accessed May 22, 2012).

115. Spencer Ackerman, "When Your Friends Bless the Assassination of American Citizens without Due Process," Attackerman, October 9, 2011, spencerackerman.typepad.com/attackerman/2011/10/oh-marty.html (accessed May 22, 2012).

116. Perhaps to solidify his legitimacy as a target under the government's standards, upon his death, Awlaki was given the title "chief of external operations" for AQAP. Greg Miller and Alice Fordham, "Anwar al-Aulaqi Gets new Designation in Death," *Washington Post* Checkpoint Washington blog, September 30, 2011, www.washingtonpost.com/blogs/checkpoint-washington/post/aulaqi-gets -new-designation-in-death/2011/09/30/gIQAsbF69K_blog.html (accessed May 22, 2012).

117. Holder explained: "The principle of necessity requires that the target have definite military value. The principle of distinction requires that only lawful targets – such as combatants, civilians directly participating in hostilities, and military objectives – may be targeted intentionally. Under the principle of proportionality, the anticipated collateral damage must not be excessive in relation to the anticipated military advantage. Finally, the principle of humanity requires us to use weapons that will not inflict unnecessary suffering."

118. Deborah Pearlstein, "Holder's Speech," OpinioJuris blog, March 6, 2012, opiniojuris.org/2012/03/06/holders-speech/ (accessed May 22, 2012).

119. Ibid.

120. Andrew Cohen, "On 'Targeted Killing' Speech, Eric Holder Strikes Out," *The Atlantic*, March 6, 2012, www.theatlantic.com/national/archive/2012/03/on -targeted-killing-speech-eric-holder-strikes-out/254000/ (accessed May 22, 2012).

121. Washington Post Editorial Board, "It's Time to Release the Drone Memos," *Washington Post*, March 5, 2012, www.washingtonpost.com/opinions/its-time-to-release-the-drone-memos/2012/03/05/gIQA7jVXtR_story.html (accessed June 2, 2012).

122. John Brennan, "The Ethics and Efficacy of the President's Counterterrorism Strategy," Speech given at the Woodrow Wilson International Center for Scholars, April 30, 2012, www.wilsoncenter.org/event/the-efficacy-and-ethics-us-counterterrorism-strategy (accessed May 22, 2012).

123. Spencer Ackerman, "Pentagon Issues Drone War Talking Points," *Wired.com*, May 11, 2012, www.wired.com/dangerroom/2012/05/drone-talking-points/ (accessed May 22, 2012), Greg Miller, "Brennan Speech is First Obama Acknowledgement of Use of Armed Drones," *Washington Post*, April 30, 2012, www.washingtonpost.com/world/national-security/brennan-speech-is-first-obama-acknowledgement-of-use-of -armed-drones/2012/04/30/gIQAq7B4rT_story.html (accessed May 23, 2012).

124. DeYoung, "Secrecy Defines Obama's Drone War."

125. Stephen Preston, "CIA and the Rule of Law," Remarks at Harvard Law School, *Lawfare* blog, April 30, 2012, www.lawfareblog.com/2012/04/brennanspeech/ (accessed May 30, 2012).

126. DeYoung, "Secrecy Defines Obama's Drone War," Klaidman, "Obama Team to Break Silence on al-Awlaki Killing," Savage, "Secret U.S. Memo Made Legal Case to Kill a Citizen," Miller, "Under Obama, An Emerging Global Apparatus for Drone Killing," Daniel Klaidman, "The Obama Campaign Touts a Commander in Chief Who Never Flinches, But the Truth is More Complex. How the President Came to Embrace a New Way of War," *The Daily Beast*, May 28, 2012, www.thedailybeast .com/newsweek/2012/05/27/drones-the-silent-killers.html (accessed May 30, 2012).

127. Obama Strategy of Taking Credit for Osama bin Laden Killing Risky, Observers Say," Klaidman, "The Obama Campaign Touts A Commander in Chief Who Never Flinches."

128. Becker and Shane, "A Measure of Change: Secret 'Kill List' Proves a Test of Obama's Principles and Will."

129. Conor Friedersdorf, "Under Obama, Men Killed by Drones Are Presumed to be Terrorists," *The Atlantic*, May 29, 2012, www.theatlantic.com/politics/archive/2012/05/ under-obama-men-killed-by-drones-are-presumed-to-be-terrorists/257749/ (accessed May 31, 2012).

130. Carlo Munoz, "White House Under Fire for Aggressive Armed Drone Campaign," *The Hill* DEFCON Hill blog, May 29, 2012, thehill.com/blogs/defcon -hill/policy-and-strategy/229917-white-house-under-fire-for-aggressive-armed -drone-campaign- (accessed May 30, 2012).

131. *New York Times* editorial board, "Too Much Power for a President, *New York Times*, May 30, 2012, www.nytimes.com/2012/05/31/opinion/too-much-power-for -a-president.html?_r=2&ref=opinion (accessed May 30, 2012).

132. Sudarsan Raghavan, "In Yemen, US Airstrikes Breed Anger and Sympathy for al-Qaeda," *Washington Post*, May 20, 2012, www.washingtonpost.com/world/ middle_east/in-yemen-us-airstrikes-breed-anger-and-sympathy-for-al-qaeda/ 2012/05/29/gJQAUmKI0U_story.html (accessed May 31, 2012).

133. Declan Walsh and Eric Schmitt, "Drone Strike Killed No. 2 in al Qaeda, U.S. Officials Say," *New York Times*, June 5, 2012, www.nytimes.com/2012/06/06/ world/asia/qaeda-deputy-killed-in-drone-strike-in-pakistan.html?_r=1&hp (accessed June 5, 2012).

134. Robin Simcox, "Killing Key al Qaeda Leaders: It Works," *Los Angeles Times*, May 24, 2012, articles.latimes.com/2012/may/24/opinion/la-oe-simcox-targeted -killings-work-20120524 (accessed May 30, 2012).

135. Jim Garamone, "U.S. Trainers, Military Cooperation Return to Yemen," American Forces Press Service, May 8, 2012, www.defense.gov/news/newsarticle .aspx?id=116252 (accessed June 3, 2012).

136. Carlo Munoz: "US Wades Deeper into Counterterrorism Fight in Yemen and East Africa," *The Hill* DEFCON Hill blog, May 28, 2012, thehill.com/blogs/

defcon-hill/policy-and-strategy/229709-us-wades-deeper-into-counterterrorism
-fight-in-yemen-and-east-africa (accessed May 30, 2012).

137. Alissa J. Rubin, "Panetta Visits Afghanistan Amid Mounting Violence,"
New York Times, June 7, 2012, www.nytimes.com/2012/06/08/world/asia/panetta
-visits-afghanistan-amid-mounting-violence.html?_r=1&ref=world (accessed June
7, 2012).

138. Munoz, "White House under Fire for Aggressive Armed Drone Campaign."

139. Patrick B. Pexton, "Are Drone Strikes the Only Game in Town?" National
Journal National Security Experts blog, January 11, 2010, security.nationaljournal.
com/2010/01/are-drone-strikes-the-only-gam.php (accessed June 4, 2012). Panetta,
Clinton, and Brennan are, according to officials, "always ready to step on the accel-
erator." Miller, "Under Obama, an Emerging Global Apparatus for Drone Killing."

140. Daniel Byman, "Do Targeted Killings Work?", Brookings Institution, July
13, 2009, www.brookings.edu/research/opinions/2009/07/14-targeted-killings-byman
(accessed June 3, 2012).

141. John Yoo, "Obama, Drones and Thomas Aquinas," Wall Street Journal, June
7, 2012, online.wsj.com/article/SB1000142405270230366590457745227179431280
02.html?mod=WSJ_Opinion_LEADTop (accessed June 7, 2012).

142. Becker and Shane, "A Measure of Change."

143. Shane Harris, "Are Drone Strikes Murder?" National Journal, January 9, 2010,
www.nationaljournal.com/member/magazine/are-drone-strikes-murder--20100109
(accessed June 5, 2012).

144. Ackerman, "When Your Friends Bless the Assassination of American Citizens without Due Process."

~

Bibliography

Adams, J. Christian. "Unequal Law Enforcement Reigns at Obama's DOJ." *Pajamas Media*, June 28, 2010. http://pajamasmedia.com/blog/j-christian-adams-you-deserve-to-know-%E2%80%94-unequal-law-enforcement-reigns-at-obamas-doj-pjm-exclusive/ (accessed July 5, 2010).

Adesioye, Lola. "Should Obama Do More for Black America?" *Guardian*, March 3, 2010. www.guardian.co.uk/commentisfree/cifamerica/2010/mar/02/barack-obama-black-america/print (accessed June 18, 2010).

Alexander, Matthew. "Torture's Loopholes." *New York Times*, January 20, 2010. www.nytimes.com/2010/01/21/opinion/21alexander.html (accessed June 29, 2010).

Allen, Mike, and Carrie Budoff Brown. "Obama Casts Himself as Civil Rights Successor." *Politico*, November 25, 2007. www.politico.com/news/stories/1107/7026.html (accessed April 6, 2010).

Amar, Akhil. *America's Constitution: A Biography*. New York: Random House, 2005.

Ambinder, Mark. "A Wrinkle in the Intelligence Debate." *Atlantic Online*, February 25, 2010. www.theatlantic.com/politics/archive/2010/02/a-wrinkle-in-the-intelligence-debate/36620/ (accessed June 29, 2010).

Associated Press. "Ex-CIA Chiefs Slowed 'Torture Memos' Release." April 17, 2009.

———. "Obama Slams 'Fat Cat Bankers.'" *Google News*, December 12, 2009. www.google.com/hostednews/afp/article/ALeqM5g2J-qjM_z5yfHUp4moR-3S-IvSuA (accessed June 26, 2010).

———. "Obama Unveils Afghanistan Plan." *MSNBC.com*, March 27, 2009. www.msnbc.msn.com/id/29898698/ (accessed June 26, 2010).

———. "Text of Obama's Speech Tuesday." *Breitbart*, June 3, 2008. www.breitbart.com/article.php?id=d912vd200&show_article=1 (accessed June 26, 2010).

277

Baker, Peter. "In Court Nominees, Is Obama Looking for Empathy by Another Name?" *New York Times*, April 25, 2010.

———. "Obama to Use Current Law to Support Detentions." *New York Times*, September 24, 2009. www.nytimes.com/2009/09/24/us/politics/24detain.html (accessed January 22, 2010).

———. "Obama's War Over Terror." *New York Times Magazine*, January 4, 2010. www.nytimes.com/2010/01/17/magazine/17Terror-t.html?pagewanted=all (accessed June 26, 2010).

Balkin, Jack M. "Original Meaning and Constitutional Redemption." *Constitutional Commentary* 24, no. 140 (2007).

Barabak, Mark Z. "Thousands Gather in D.C. to Protest Healthcare Overhaul Plan." *Los Angeles Times*, September 13, 2009. www.articles.latimes.com/2009/sep/13/nation/na-capitol-rally13 (accessed June 7, 2010).

"Barack Obama: The President's News Conference." The American Presidency Project, February 9, 2009. www.presidency.ucsb.edu/ws/index. php?pid=85728 (accessed March 24, 2009).

Barilleaux, Ryan J. "Venture Constitutionalism and the Enlargement of the Presidency." In *Executing the Constitution*, edited by Christopher S. Kelley. Albany, NY: SUNY Press, 2006.

Barnes, Fred. "He's No FDR." *Weekly Standard*, March 8, 2010. www.weeklystandard.com/articles/hes-no-fdr (accessed March 23, 2010).

Barry, John. "Is It Amateur Hour in the White House?" *Newsweek*, September 22, 2009. www.newsweek.com/2009/09/21/is-it-amateur-hour-in-the-white-house.html (accessed June 26, 2010).

Baumgartner, Jody C., and Jonathan S. Morris. "Who Wants to Be My Friend? Obama, Youth, and Social Networks in the 2008 Campaign." *Communicator-in-Chief*, edited by John Allen Hendricks and Robert E. Denton, Jr. Lanham, MD: Rowman & Littlefield, 2010.

BBC News. "Top 9/11 Suspects to Plead Guilty." December 8, 2008.

Benen, Steven. "Thiessen's Thesis Spreads." *Washington Monthly*, February 20, 2010. www.washingtonmonthly.com/archives/individual/2010_02/022506.php (accessed June 9, 2010).

Bessette, Joseph M., and Gary J. Schmitt. "The Powers and Duties of the President: Recovering the Logic and Meaning of Article II." In *The Constitutional Presidency*, edited by Joseph M. Bessette and Jeffrey K. Tulis. Baltimore, MD: Johns Hopkins University Press, 2009.

Bessette, Joseph M., and Jeffrey Tulis. "The Constitution, Politics, and the Presidency." In *The Presidency in the Constitutional Order*, edited by Joseph M. Bessette and Jeffrey Tulis. Baton Rouge: Louisiana State University Press, 1981.

Beyond the Dome. http://blogs.cqpolitics.com/ (accessed June 26, 2010).

Bird, Jeremy. "Organizing for America: Looking Back, Marching Ahead." *Huffington Post*, January 6, 2010. www.huffingtonpost.com/jeremy-bird/organizing-for-america-lo_b_413000.html (accessed June 6, 2010).

Blum, Justin. "Medical Marijuana Policy Eased by Justice Department." *Bloomberg.com*, October 19, 2009. www.bloomberg.com/apps/news?pid=newsarchive&sid=aZyHHGxOpwz0 (accessed January 19, 2010).

Blume, Howard. "Department of Education Targets L.A. Unified for Investigation." *Los Angeles Times*, March 9, 2010.

Blumenstein, James F. "Regulatory Review by the Executive Office of the President: An Overview and Policy Analysis of Current Issues." *Duke Law Journal* 51, no. 3 (December 2001).

Bravin, Jess. "Liberals Sketch Out Dreams and Limits for Supreme Court." *Wall Street Journal*, May 26, 2009.

Bresnahan, John. "Cash-poor Obama Says No to Reid." *Politico*, September 16, 2008. www. politico.com/news/stories/0908/13485.html (accessed June 5, 2010).

Bresnahan, John, and Josh Gerstei. "Rove Deposed in U.S. Attorney Probe." *Politico*, July 7, 2009. http://dyn.politico.com/printstory.cfm?uuid=578CDD0A-18FE-70B2-A87147E37EC2C3DB (accessed March 17, 2010).

Breyer, Stephen. *Active Liberty: Interpreting Our Democratic Constitution*. New York: Vintage, 2006.

Busch, Andrew E. "Constitutional Discourse and American Government." The Heritage Foundation, August 22, 2008. www.heritage.org/Research/Reports/2008/08/Constitutional-Discourse-and-American-Government (accessed June 29, 2010).

Bush, George W. "Executive Order 13,422: Further Amendment to Executive Order 12,866 on Regulatory Planning and Review." 72 *Federal Register* 2763 (January 18, 2007).

———. "State of the Union Address." January 29, 2002. http://archives.cnn.com/2002/ALL POLITICS/01/29/bush.speech.txt/ (accessed July 18, 2010).

Byrd, Robert C. "Letter to President Obama." February 23, 2009. www.eenews.net/public/25/9865/features/documents/2009/02/25/document_gw_02.pdf (accessed April 2, 2010).

Calabresi, Steven, and Saikrishna Prakash. "The President's Power to Execute the Laws." *Yale Law Journal* 104 (1994).

Campaign Finance Institute. "Reality Check: Obama Received About the Same Percentage from Small Donors in 2008 as Bush in 2004." November 24, 2008. www.cfinst.org/Press/Releases_tags/08-11-24/Realty_Check_-_Obama_Small_Donors.aspx (accessed June 3, 2010).

Canovan, Margaret. *Populism*. New York: Harcourt Brace, 1981.

Carter, Jimmy. "Executive Order 12,044: Improving Government Relations." *Code of Federal Regulations*, title 3, p. 152 (1979).

Caucus, The. http://thecaucus.blogs.nytimes.com/ (accessed June 26, 2010).

Ceasar, James W. *Presidential Selection: Theory and Development*. Princeton, NJ: Princeton University Press, 1979.

———. *Reforming the Reforms*. Cambridge: Ballinger, 1982.

———. "The Roots of Obama Worship: Auguste Comte's Religion of Humanity Finds a 21st-century Savior." *Weekly Standard* 15, no. 18 (January 25, 2010). www.weeklystandard.com/articles/roots-obama-worship.

Ceasar, James W., Andrew E. Busch, and John J. Pitney, Jr. *Epic Journey: The 2008 Elections and American Politics*. Lanham, MD: Rowman & Littlefield, 2009.

Ceasar, James W., Glen Thurow, Jeffrey Tulis, and Joseph M. Bessette. "The Rise of the Rhetorical Presidency." *Presidential Studies Quarterly* 11, no. 2 (Spring 1981): 158–71.

Central Intelligence Agency. "Statement on CIA Casualties in Afghanistan." Washington, DC: C.I.A., December 31, 2009. www.cia.gov/news-information/press-releases-statements/cia-casualties-in-afghanistan.html.

Chait, Jonathon. "Lawyer Up, Liz Cheney: Guilty 'til Proven Innocent." *New Republic*, March 17, 2010. www.tnr.com/article/politics/lawyer-up (accessed June 29, 2010).

Chalian, David. "Obama Launches DNC 'Vote 2010' Midterm Election Effort." *ABC News*, April 26, 2010. http://blogs.abcnews.com/politicalpunch/2010/04/obama-launches-dnc-vote-2010-midterm-election-effort.html (accessed July 15, 2010).

Cillizza, Chris. "Obama Announces 'Organizing for America.'" *Washington Post*, The Fix Weblog, January 17, 2009. www.voices.washingtonpost.com/thefix/white-house/obama-announces-organizing-for.html (accessed June 4, 2010).

Clinton, William Jefferson. "Executive Order 12,866: Regulatory Planning and Review." *Code of Federal Regulations*, title 3, p. 638 (1993).

———. "Second Inaugural Address." January 20, 1997, reproduced on Bartleby.com. www.bartleby.com/124/pres65.html (accessed July 18, 2010).

———. "Statement Announcing the President's Signature of the National Missile Defense Act of 1999." In *Pushing the Limits: The Decision of National Missile Defense*. Washington, DC: Council to Reduce Nuclear Dangers, 2000.

CNNPolitics. "Holder Defends Decision to Try Accused 9/11 Terrorists in New York." November 18, 2009. http://articles.cnn.com/2009-11-18/politics/holder.new.york.trial_1_civilian-court-khalid-sheikh-mohammed-suspects?_s=PM:POLITICS.

———. "McCain, Obama Headed to Washington for Bailout Talks." September 28, 2008. www.cnn.com/2008/POLITICS/09/24/campaign.wrap/index.html (accessed June 26, 2010).

Cohen, Andrew. "Maneuvering Room on Signing Statements." *CBS News*, March 3, 2009. www.cbsnews.com/8301-503544_162-4854750-503544.html (accessed March 17, 2010).

Cohen, Richard. "Who Is Barack Obama?" *Washington Post*, July 20, 2010. www.realclearpolitics.com/articles/2010/07/20/barack_obama_introduce_yourself_106374.html (accessed July 20, 2010).

Connolly, Ceci. "How Obama Revived His Health-Care Bill." *Washington Post*, March 23, 2010.

Connolly, Katie. "Busted: The Churchill Flap." *Newsweek*, February 21, 2009. www.newsweek.com/2009/02/20/busted-the-churchill-flap.html (accessed June 26, 2010).

Cooper, Philip. *By Order of the President: The Use and Abuse of Executive Direct Action.* Lawrence: University Press of Kansas, 2002.

Cornfield, Michael. "The Internet and Campaign 2004: A Look Back at the Campaigners, Commentary." *Pew Internet and American Life Project*, 2005. www.pewinter_net.org/~/media/Files/Reports/ 2005/Cornfield_commentary.pdf.pdf (accessed May 28, 2010).

Corrado, Anthony J. "Financing the 2004 Presidential General Election." In *Financing the 2004 Election*, edited by David B. Magleby, Anthony J. Corrado, and Kelly D. Patterson. Washington, DC: Brookings Institution Press, 2006.

———. "Financing the 2008 Presidential General Election." In *Financing the 2008 Election*, edited by David B. Magleby and Anthony J. Corrado. Washington, DC: Brookings Institution Press, forthcoming.

———. "Fund-Raising Strategies in the 2008 Presidential Campaign." In *Campaigns and Elections American Style*, 3rd ed., edited by James A. Thurber and Candice J. Nelson. Boulder, CO: Westview Press, 2010.

Corrado, Anthony J., Michael J. Malbin, Thomas E. Mann, and Norman J. Ornstein. *Reform in an Age of Networked Campaigns*. Washington, DC: Campaign Finance Institute, 2010.

Crabtree, Susan. "Intel Bill Pulled over Controversial Added Interrogation Provision." *Hill*, February 25, 2010. http://thehill.com/homenews/house/83817-gop-cries-foul-over-amendment-to-intel-bill (accessed June 29, 2010).

Croly, Herbert. *The Promise of American Life*. Boston: Northeastern University Press, 1989.

Cronin, Thomas E., ed. *Inventing the American Presidency*. Lawrence: University Press of Kansas, 1989.

Curl, Joseph. "Obama's Census Mark Reveals Race Views." *Washington Times*, April 30, 2010. www.washingtontimes.com/news/2010/apr/30/checked-box-offers-window-into-obamas-views-on-rac/ (accessed July 19, 2010).

Cushman, Barry. *Rethinking the New Deal Court: The Structure of a Constitutional Revolution.* New York: Oxford University Press, 1998.

Davenport, Carol. "2009 Legislative Summary: Climate Change Mitigation." *Congressional Quarterly Weekly Report*, January 4, 2010.

Davenport, Carol, and Avery Palmer. "A Landmark Climate Bill Passes." *Congressional Quarterly Weekly Report*, June 29, 2009.

Delaney, Arthur. "Supreme Court Rolls Back Campaign Finance Restrictions." *Huffington Post*, January 21, 2010. www.huffingtonpost.com/2010/01/21/supreme-court-rolls-back_n_431227.html (accessed July 11, 2010).

Delany, Colin. "Learning from Obama's Online Outreach: How to Find and Build Support on the Internet." March 2, 2009. www.epolitics.com/2009/03/02/learning-from-obamas-online-outreach-how-to-find-and-build-support-on-the-internet/ (accessed June 2, 2010).

DePillis, Lydia. "Disorganized." *The New Republic*, October 29, 2009. www.tnr.com/article/politics/disorganized?page=0,2 (accessed June 4, 2010).

Dionne, E. J., Jr. "Supreme Court Ruling Calls for a Populist Revolt." *Washington Post*, January 25, 2010. www.washingtonpost.com/wp-dyn/content/article/2010/01/24/AR2010012402298.html (accessed June 26, 2010).

Douglass, Frederick. "Oration in Memory of Abraham Lincoln." April 14, 1876. http://teachingamericanhistory.org/library/index.asp?document=39 (accessed June 26, 2010).

———. "The Right to Criticize American Institutions." May 11, 1847. http://teachingamericanhistory.org/library/index.asp?document=1101 (accessed June 26, 2010).

Dowd, Maureen. "Hail the Conquering Professor." *New York Times*, March 23, 2010. www.nytimes.com/2010/03/24/opinion/24dowd.html (accessed March 24, 2010).

Edwards III, George C., and Desmond S. King. *The Polarized Presidency of George W. Bush*. New York: Oxford University Press, 2007.

Edwards, Mickey. *Reclaiming Conservatism: How a Great American Movement Got Lost—And How It Can Find Its Way Back*. New York: Oxford University Press, 2008.

Eilperin, Juliet. "Ozone Rules Weakened at Bush's Behest." *Washington Post*, March 14, 2008. www.washingtonpost.com/wp-dyn/content/article/2008/03/13/AR2008031304175.html (accessed March 22, 2010).

Eisenhower, Dwight D. "I Shall Go To Korea," speech, 1952. http://tucnak.fsv.cuni.cz/~calda/Documents/1950s/Ike_Korea_52.html (accessed June 26, 2010).

Election Law Blog. http://electionlawblog.org (accessed June 26, 2010).

Elliott, Phillip. "Obama Town Hall in Ohio: President Takes Populist Message on the Road." *Huffington Post*, January 22, 2010. www.huffingtonpost.com/2010/01/22/obama-takes-populist-push_n_432749.html (accessed July 11, 2010).

Ely, John Hart. "The Wages of Crying Wolf: A Comment on *Roe v. Wade*." *Yale Law Journal* 82 (1973): 920.

Exley, Zack. "Obama Field Organizers Plot a Miracle." *Huffington Post*, August 27, 2007. www.huffingtonpost.com/zack-exley/obama-field-organizers-pl_b_61918.html (accessed June 3, 2010).

Farrell, Michael B. "Obama Signs Patriot Act Extension without Reform." *Christian Science Monitor*, March 1, 2010. www.csmonitor.com/USA/Politics/2010/0301/Obama-signs-Patriot-Act-extension-without-reforms (accessed March 2, 2010).

Federal Election Commission. *Party Financial Activity Summarized for the 2008 Election Cycle*, May 28, 2009. www.fec.gov/press/press2009/05282009Party/20090528Party.shtml (accessed June 2, 2010).

———. "Presidential Campaign Finance." www.fec.gov/DisclosureSearch/mapApp.do (accessed June 3, 2010).

————. *2008 Presidential Campaign Financial Activity Summarized: Receipts Nearly Double 2004 Total*. Washington, DC: GPO, 2009. www.fec.gov/press/press2009/20090608PresStat.shtml (accessed May 30, 2010).

Ferris, Kevin. "Back Channels: Panther Case Dismissal Needs Explanation." *Philadelphia Enquirer*, July 4, 2010. www.philly.com/inquirer/currents/20100704_Back_Channels__Panther_case_dismissal_needs_explanation.html (accessed July 5, 2010).

Filene, Peter G. "An *Obituary* for 'The Progressive Movement.'" *American Quarterly* 22, no. 1 (Spring 1970): 20–34.

Finn, John. "Enumerating Absolute Power? Who Needs the Rest of the Constitution?" *Hartford Courant*, April 6, 2008. http://articles.courant.com/2008-04-06/news/commentaryfinn 0406.art_1_combatants-presidential-power-constitutional (accessed April 7, 2010).

Finn, Peter. "Justice Task Force Recommends about 50 Guantanamo Detainees Be Held Indefinitely." *Washington Post*, January 22, 2010. www.washingtonpost.com/wp-dyn/content/article/2010/01/21/AR2010012104936.html (accessed January 22, 2010).

————. "Under Panetta, A More Aggressive CIA." *Washington Post*, March 21, 2010.

Finn, Peter, and Joby Warrick. "Under Panetta, a More Aggressive CIA." *Washington Post*, March 21, 2010. www.washingtonpost.com/wp-dyn/content/article/2010/03/20/AR2010032003343.html (accessed June 29, 2010).

Fisher, Louis. *The President and Congress: Power and Policy*. New York: Free Press, 1972.

Fix, The. *Washington Post*. http://voices.washingtonpost.com/thefix (accessed June 26, 2010).

Ford, Gerald M. "Executive Order 11,821: Inflation Impact Statements." 39 *Federal Register* 41501 (November 29, 1974).

Ford, Paul Leicester, ed. *The Works of Thomas Jefferson*. New York: G.P. Putman, 1898.

Fox News. "Congressman Wants Radical Cleric's Citizenship Revoked." April 21, 2010. www.foxnews.com/politics/2010/04/21/congressman-wants-radical-clerics-citizenship-revoked/ (accessed June 26, 2010).

Fox, Susannah. "Privacy Implications of Fast, Mobile Internet Access." *Pew Internet and American Life Project*, February 13, 2008. www.pewinternet.org/Reports/2008/Privacy-Implications-of-Fast-Mobile-Internet-Access.aspx (accessed September 19, 2009).

Frank, Barney, David Obey, and Nita Lowey. "Letter to President Obama." July 7, 2009. www.house.gov/frank/pressreleases/2009/07-21-09-signing-statements-letter-obama.html (accessed March 23, 2010).

"Freedom of Information Act." *Federal Register* 74, no. 12 (January 21, 2009).

Frieden, Terry, and Chris Kokenes. "Accused 9/11 Plotter Khalid Sheikh Mohammed Faces New York Trial." *CNN Justice*, November 13, 2009. www.cnn.com/2009/CRIME/11/13/khalid.sheikh.mohammed/index.html (accessed June 26, 2010).

Friedman, Barry D. *Regulation in the Reagan–Bush Era: The Eruption of Presidential Influence*. Pittsburgh: University of Pittsburgh Press, 1995.

Gerson, Michael. "Political Honeymoon Over for President." *State Journal-Register*, August 8, 2009.

Gerstein, Josh. "Obama: Ignore Signing Statements." *Politico*, March 9, 2009. www.politico.com/news/stories/0309/19795.html (accessed March 24, 2010).

"Getting to Know the Racial Views of Our Past Presidents: What about FDR?" *The Journal of Blacks in Higher Education* 38 (Winter 2002/2003): 44–46.

Ghosh, Bobby. "CIA Chief Panetta Winning Over Doubters at the Agency." *Time*, November 24, 2009.

Gilbert, Steve. "Obama's Courses at U of C Law School." October 2, 2008. http://sweetness-light.com/archive/obamas-courses-at-u-of-c-law-school (accessed June 26, 2010).

Goldsmith, Jack. "The Cheney Fallacy." *The New Republic*, May 18, 2009. www.tnr.com/article/politics/the-cheney-fallacy?id=1e733cac-c273-48e5-9140-80443ed1f5e2&p=1 (accessed June 26, 2010).

Green, John C. "Financing the 2004 Presidential Nomination Campaigns." In *Financing the 2004 Election*, edited by David B. Magleby, Anthony J. Corrado, and Kelly D. Patterson. Washington, DC: Brookings Institution Press, 2006.

Greengard, Samuel. "The First Internet President." *Communications of the ACM* 52, no. 2, (February 2009).

Greenwald, Glenn. "The Case Against Elena Kagan." *Salon*, April 13, 2010. www.salon.com/news/opinion/glenn_greenwald/2010/04/13/kagan/index.html (accessed July 20, 2010).

———. "Confirmed: Obama Authorizes Assassination of U.S. Citizen." *Salon*, April 7, 2010. www.salon.com/news/opinion/glenn_greenwald/2010/04/07/assassinations (accessed April 9, 2010).

———. "New and Worse Secrecy Claims from the Obama Department of Justice." *Salon*, April 6, 2009. www.salon.com/news/opinion/glenn_greenwald/2009/04/06/obama (accessed March 21, 2010).

———. "Obama's Impressive New OLC Chief." *Salon*, January 5, 2009.

———. "The 180-degree Reversal of Obama's State Secrets Position." *Salon*, February 10, 2009. www.salon.com/news/opinion/glenn_greenwald/2009/02/10/obama (accessed March 21, 2010).

Gregg, Gary L., II. "The Symbolic Dimensions of the First Presidency." In *Patriot Sage: George Washington and the American Political Tradition*, edited by Gary L. Gregg II and Matthew Spalding. Wilmington, DE: ISI Books, 1999.

Gunderson, Robert. *The Log Cabin Campaign*. Lexington: University of Kentucky Press, 1957.

Halpern, Stephen. *On the Limits of the Law: The Ironic Legacy of Title VI of the 1964 Civil Rights Act*. Baltimore: Johns Hopkins University Press, 1995.

Hamilton, Alexander. "Federalist No. 70," *The Federalist Papers*, edited by Charles Kesler. New York: Penguin, 2003.

Hamilton, Alexander, James Madison, and John Jay. *The Federalist Papers*, edited by Clinton Rossiter. New York: Mentor, 1999; New York: New American Library, Mentor Books, 2003.

Harris, Chris. "Barack Obama Answers Your Questions About Gay Marriage, Paying For College, More." *MTVNews*, November 1, 2008. www.mtv.com/news/articles/1598407/20081101/story.jhtml (accessed June 26, 2010).

Harris, John F., and Jonathan Martin. "The George W. Bush and Bill Clinton Legacies in the 2008 Elections." *The American Elections of 2008*, edited by Janet M. Box-Steffensmeier and Steven E. Schier. Lanham, MD: Rowman & Littlefield, 2009.

Harris-Lacewell, Melissa V. "African Americans, Religion, and the American Presidency." In *Religion, Race, and the American Presidency*, edited by Gastón Espinosa. Lanham, MD: Rowman & Littlefield, 2008.

Hayden, Michael. "Obama Administration Takes Several Wrong Paths in Dealing with Terrorism." *Washington Post*, January 31, 2010.

———. "Time for CIA to Move Ahead, not Back." *Washington Times*, August 20, 2009.

Healy, Gene, and Timothy Lynch. *Power Surge: The Constitutional Record of George W. Bush*. Washington, DC: Cato Institute, 2006.

Hendler, Clint. "Day One: New FOIA Rules." *Columbia Journalism Review*, January 21, 2009. www.cjr.org/campaign_desk/day_one_new_foia_rules.php (accessed March 31, 2010).

Hendricks, John Allen, and Robert E. Denton, Jr. "Political Campaigns and Communicating with the Electorate in the Twenty-First Century." In *Communicator-in-Chief*, edited by John Allen Hendricks and Robert E. Denton, Jr. Lanham, MD: Rowman & Littlefield, 2010.

Hofstadter, Richard. *Social Darwinism in American Thought*. Boston: Beacon Press, 1992.

Holmes, Oliver Wendell. *The Common Law*. Boston: Brown Little, 1881.

Horrigan, John. "Home Broadband 2008." *Pew Internet and American Life Project*, July 2, 2008. www.pewinternet.org/Reports/2008/Home-Broadband-2008.aspx (accessed September 19, 2009).

———. "Mobile Access to Data and Information." *Pew Internet and American Life Project*, March 5, 2008. www.pewinternet.org/Press-Releases/2008/Mobile-Access-to-Data-and-Information.aspx (accessed September 19, 2009).

———. "Why We Don't Know Enough About Broadband in the U.S." *Pew Internet and American Life Project*, November 14, 2007. www.pewinternet.org/Reports/2007/Why-We-Don't-Know-Enough-About-Broadband-in-the-US.aspx (accessed September 19, 2009).

House Committee on Energy and Commerce. *Presidential Control of Agency Rulemaking: An Analysis of Constitutional Issues that may be Raised by Executive Order 12,291*. 97th Cong., 1st sess., June 15, 1981.

House Committee on Governmental Operations. *Executive Orders and Proclamations: A Study of the Use of Presidential Power*. 85th Cong., 1st sess., 1957, Committee Print.

Institute of Politics, The. *Campaign for President: The Managers Look at 2008*. Lanham, MD: Rowman & Littlefield, 2009.

Jamieson, Kathleen Hall, ed. *Electing the President, 2008: The Insiders' View*. Philadelphia: University of Pennsylvania Press, 2009.

JohnMcCain.com "Celeb." Video, 2008. www.youtube.com/watch?v=oHXYsw_ZDXg&feature=player_embedded (accessed June 26, 2010).

———. "The One." Video, 2008. www.youtube.com/watch?v=mopkn0lPzM8 (accessed June 26, 2010).

Johnson, Carrie. "CIA Videotape Investigation Focuses on Whether False Statements Were Made, Sources Say." *Washington Post*, March 24, 2010.

Johnson, Carrie, and Julie Tate. "CIA Videotape Investigation Appears to Be Nearing a Close," *Washington Post*, March 24, 2010. www.washingtonpost.com/wp-dyn/content/article/2010/03/24/AR2010032402041.html (accessed June 29, 2010).

Johnson, Lyndon Baines. "Remarks at the University of Michigan." Lyndon Baines Johnson Library and Museum, May 22, 1964. www.lbjlib.utexas.edu/johnson/archives.hom/speeches.hom/640522.asp (accessed June 28, 2010).

Johnson, O'Ryan. "Crowley Teaches Racial Profiling Class at Academy." *Boston Herald*, July 23, 2009. www.bostonherald.com/news/regional/view/20090723 crowley_teaches_racial_profiling_class_at_academy/srvc=home&position=0 (accessed June 26, 2010).

Johnston, David. "US Says Rendition to Continue, but with More Oversight." *New York Times*, August 25, 2009. www.nytimes.com/2009/08/25/us/politics/25rendition.html (accessed September 19, 2009).

Kagan, Elena. "Presidential Administration." *Harvard Law Review* 114, no. 8 (2001).

Kantor, Jodi. "Inside Professor Obama's Classroom." *New York Times* Caucus Blog, July 30, 2008. http://thecaucus.blogs.nytimes.com/2008/07/30/inside-professor-obamas-classroom/ (accessed July 3, 2010).

———. "Teaching Law, Testing Ideas, Obama Stood Slightly Apart." *New York Times*, July 30, 2008. www.nytimes.com/2008/07/30/us/politics/30law.html (accessed July 3, 2010).

Katzen, Sally. Testimony before the House Committee on Science and Technology, Subcommittee on Investigation & Oversight, February 13, 2007. http://judiciary.house.gov/hearings/printers/110th/33312.PDF (accessed July 10, 2010).

Keegan, John. *The Mask of Command.* New York: Penguin, 1987.

Keller, Morton. "Fixing the Economy: The New Deal and the New Foundation." Unpublished manuscript.

Kelley, Christopher S. "The Unitary Executive and the Presidential Signing Statement." PhD diss., Miami University, Oxford, OH, 2003.

Kennedy, Caroline. "A President Like My Father." *New York Times*, January 27, 2008. www.nytimes.com/2008/01/27/opinion/27kennedy.html (accessed July 11, 2010).

Kesler, Charles. "The Audacity of Barack Obama." Review of *The Audacity of Hope: Thoughts on Reclaiming the American Dream*, by Barack H. Obama. *Claremont Review of Books* 84 (2008).

Klein, Ezra. "Obama's Gift." *The American Prospect*, January 3, 2008. www.prospect.org/csnc/blogs/ezraklein_archive?month=01&year=2008&base_name=obamas_gift (accessed July 11, 2010).

Knoller, Mark. "White House Not Challenging Rove's Privilege." *CBS News*, February 14, 2009. www.cbsnews.com/8301-503544_162-4803349-503544.html (accessed June 26, 2010).

Knott, Stephen F. *Secret and Sanctioned: Covert Operations and the American Presidency.* New York: Oxford University Press, 1996.

Kornblut, Ann E., and Michael A. Fletcher. "In Obama's Decision-Making, A Wide Range of Influences." *Washington Post*, January 25, 2010.

Kramer, Larry. *The People Themselves: Popular Constitutionalism and Judicial Review.* New York: Oxford University Press, 2004.

Lacono, Tim. *Real GDP Since 1930, Seeking Alpha*, February 4, 2009. http://seekingalpha.com/article/118349-real-gdp-since-1930 (accessed July 18, 2010).

Lamb, Christina. "Democrats in Revolt Over Barack Obama's Troop Surge." *Sunday Times*, November 29, 2009. www.timesonline.co.uk/tol/news/world/us_and_americas/article6936327.ece (accessed June 26, 2010).

Lede, The. http://thelede.blogs.nytimes.com/ (accessed June 26, 2010).

Leiby, Richard. "Obama Delivers the Zingers at Journalists' Dinner." *Washington Post*, May 10, 2009. www.washingtonpost.com/wp-dyn/content/article/2009/05/09/AR2009050902802.html (accessed June 26, 2010).

Leiter's Law School Rankings. www.leiterrankings.com/faculty/2007faculty_impact_areas.shtml (accessed April 2, 2010).

Lemann, Nicholas. "Terrorism Studies: Social Scientists Do Counterinsurgency." *New Yorker*, April 26, 2010.

Levy, David W. *Herbert Croly of the New Republic.* Princeton, NJ: Princeton University Press, 1985.

Lincoln, Abraham. "Cooper Union Address." New York, February 27, 1860. http://showcase.netins.net/web/creative/lincoln/speeches/cooper.htm (accessed June 24, 2010).

———. "The Gettysburg Address." Gettysburg, Pennsylvania, November 19, 1863. http://showcase.netins.net/web/creative/lincoln/speeches/gettysburg.htm (accessed June 24, 2010).

———. "House Divided Speech." Springfield, Illinois, June 16, 1858. http://showcase.netins. net/web/creative/lincoln/speeches/house.htm (accessed June 23, 2010).

Liu, Goodwin. "Rethinking Constitutional Welfare Rights." *Stanford Law Review* 61, no. 2 (2008): 203.

Lowry, Tom. "Obama's Secret Digital Weapon." *Business Week*, June 24, 2008. www.business week.com/magazine/content/08_27/b4091000977488.htm (accessed May 30, 2010).

Loyd, Anthony. "US Drone Strikes in Pakistan Tribal Areas Boost Support for Taliban." *Times Online*, March 10, 2010. www.timesonline.co.uk/tol/news/world/asia/article7055965.ece (accessed June 29, 2010).

Mackay, Jenn Burleson. "Gadgets, Gismos, and the Web 2.0 Election." In *Communicator-in-Chief*, edited by John Allen Hendricks and Robert E. Denton, Jr. Lanham, MD: Rowman & Littlefield, 2010.

Mackey, Robert. "Drone Strikes Are Legal, US Official Says." *New York Times*, March 29, 2010. http://thelede.blogs.nytimes.com/2010/03/29/drone-strikes-are-legal-u-s-official-says/ (accessed June 29, 2010).

Malbin, Michael J., Gregory Fortelny, and Brendan Glavin. "The Need for an Integrated Vision of Parties and Candidates: National Party Finances, 1999–2008." *The State of the Parties*, edited by John C. Green. Lanham, MD: Rowman & Littlefield, forthcoming.

Mann, Thomas E. "Whose Stimulus: President Obama's or the Democratic Congress'?" *The Brookings Institution*, August 18, 2009. www.brookings/opinions/2009/0807_obama_mann. aspx?p=1 (accessed August 18, 2009).

Mansfield, Harvey C. *America's Constitutional Soul*. Baltimore, MD: Johns Hopkins University Press, 1991.

Mayar, Wahidullah. "Obama Calls Situation in Afghanistan 'Urgent.'" *CNNPolitics.com*, July 21, 2008. www.cnn.com/2008/POLITICS/07/20/obama.afghanistan/ (accessed June 26, 2010).

Mazzetti, Mark, and Carl Hulse. "Panetta is Chosen as C.I.A. Chief, in a Surprise Step." *New York Times*, January 5, 2009. www.nytimes.com/2009/01/06/us/politics/06cia.html (accessed June 29, 2010).

Mazzetti, Mark, and Scott Shane. "Interrogation Memos Detail Harsh Tactics by the C.I.A." *New York Times*, April 17, 2009. www.nytimes.com/2009/04/17/us/politics/17detain.html (accessed June 29, 2010).

Mazzetti, Mark, and William Glaberson. "Obama Issues Directive to Shut Down Guantánamo." *New York Times*, January 21, 2009. www.nytimes.com/2009/01/22/us/politics/22gitmo.html?_ r=1&scp=1&sq=Obama%20Issues%20Directive%20to%20Shut%20Down%20Guanta namo,%94%20The%20New%20York%20Times,%20January%2022,%202009&st=cse (accessed June 29, 2010).

McCormack, John. "Assassinating Awlaki." *Weekly Standard*, April 8, 2010. www.weeklystan dard.com/blogs/assassinating-awlaki (accessed June 29, 2010).

McGreal, Chris. "Liz Cheney Accused of McCarthyism over Campaign against Lawyers." *Guardian*, March 11, 2010. www.guardian.co.uk/world/2010/mar/11/liz-cheney-keep-amer ica-safe (accessed June 29, 2010).

McMahon, Kevin J. *Reconsidering Roosevelt on Race: How the Presidency Paved the Road to Brown*. Chicago: University of Chicago Press, 2004.

McPhee, Michelle, and Sara Just. "Obama: Police Acted 'Stupidly' in Gates' Case." July 22, 2009. http://abcnews.go.com/US/story?id=8148986&page=1 (accessed July 19, 2010).

"Media Inquiries: Statement Regarding Barack Obama." www.law.uchicago.edu/media (accessed June 26, 2010).

Melnick, Shep. *Between the Lines: Interpreting Welfare Rights*. Washington, DC: Brookings Institution Press, 1994.

Meyer, Cordula. "Interview with Homeland Security Secretary Janet Napolitano: 'Away from the Politics of Fear.'" *Spiegel Online International*, March 16, 2009. www.spiegel.de/international/world/0,1518,613330,00.html (accessed June 29, 2010).

Milkis, Sidney M. "The Modern Presidency, Social Movements, and the Administrative State: Lyndon Johnson and the Civil Rights Movement." In *Race and American Political Development*, edited by Joseph Lowndes, Julie Novkov, and Dorian T. Warren. New York: Routledge, 2008.

———. *Political Parties and Constitutional Government: Remaking American Democracy*. Baltimore: Johns Hopkins University Press, 1999.

———. "Preface" and "Introduction: Lyndon Johnson, the Great Society, and the 'Twilight' of the Great Society." In *The Great Society and the High Tide of Liberalism*, edited by Sidney M. Milkis and Jerome M. Mileur. Amherst: University of Massachusetts Press, 2005.

Milkis, Sidney A., and Michael Nelson. *The American Presidency: Origins and Development, 1776-2007*, 5th ed. Washington, DC: Congressional Quarterly Press, 2007.

Miller, Joe. "Was Barack Obama Really a Constitutional Law Professor?" March 28, 2008. www.factcheck.org/askfactcheck/was_barack_obama_really_a_constitutional_law.html (accessed June 26, 2010).

Miller, John Chester. *The Wolf by the Ears: Thomas Jefferson and Slavery*. New York: The Free Press, 1977.

Morgan, Dan. "The Big Deal." *Washington Post*, February 1, 2009. www.washington post.com/wp-dyn/content/article/2009/01/30/AR2009013002767.html (accessed June 26, 2010).

Mosk, Matthew. "Obama Rewriting Rules for Raising Campaign Money Online." *Washington Post*, March 28, 2008. www.washingtonpost.com/wp-dyn/content/article/2008/03/27/AR2008032702968.html (accessed May 30, 2010).

Moynihan, Daniel Patrick. *Maximum Feasible Misunderstanding*. New York: Free Press, 1966.

Murray, Shailagh. "A Commission on Enhanced Interrogation? Obama Rebuffs Idea." *Washington Post*, April 23, 2009.

MySpace. www.crunchbase.com/company/myspace (accessed June 2, 2010).

Nagourney, Adam. "Obama Elected President as Racial Barrier Falls." *New York Times*, November 5, 2008. www.nytimes.com/2008/11/05/us/politics/05elect.html (accessed April 5, 2010).

Nather, David. "Congress Suddenly Remembers It Can Cut Off Funds." CQ Balance of Power blog, July 10, 2009. http://blogs.cqpolitics.com/balance_of_power/2009/07/congress-suddenly-remembers-it.html (accessed March 21, 2010).

———. "Obama's Pledge on Signing Statements." *CQ Beyond the Dome* blog, May 20, 2008. http://blogs.cqpolitics.com/beyond/2008/05/obamas-pledge-on-signing-state.html (accessed March 17, 2010).

Nelson, Dean. "Analysis: Obama's Troop Surge Won't Solve Karzai Problem." *Telegraph*, December 5, 2009. www.telegraph.co.uk/news/worldnews/northamerica/usa/barackobama/6703655/Analysis-Obamas-troop-surge-wont-solve-Karzai-problem.html (accessed July 18, 2010).

Nelson, Gabriel. "Obama Overhaul of Regulatory Reviews Now Seen as Unlikely." *New York Times* Greenwire, July 14, 2010. www.nytimes.com/gwire/2010/07/14/14greenwire-obama-overhaul-of-regulatory-reviews-now-seen-45978.html (accessed July 16, 2010).

Newsweek. "Obama Returns Churchill Bust To England: British Press Sees Snub." *Huffington Post*, February 22, 2009. www.huffingtonpost.com/2009/02/22/obama-returns-churchill-b_n_168919.html (accessed July 18, 2010).

Newton-Small, Jay. "Obama's Flag Pin Flip-Flop?" *Time*, May 14, 2008. www.time.com/time/politics/article/0,8599,1779544,00.html (accessed July 11, 2010).

New York Times. "Barack Obama's Feb. 5 Speech." February 5, 2008.

———. "Barack Obama's Inaugural Address." January 20, 2009.

———. "The K.S.M. Files." April 15, 2010.

Nichols, James H., Jr. "Pragmatism and the U.S. Constitution." In *Confronting the Constitution*. Washington, DC: The AEI Press, 1999.

Nixon, Richard M. "Executive Order 11,541: Prescribing the Duties of the Office of Management and Budget and the Domestic Council in the Executive Office of the President." *Code of Federal Regulations*, title 3, p. 939 (1966–1970).

Obama, Barack H. "Address Before a Joint Session of the Congress." February 24, 2009. www.presidency.ucsb.edu/ws/print.php?pid=85753 (accessed August 14, 2009).

———. "Answer Memo." 1997. http://graphics.nytimes.com/packages/pdf/politics/2008OBAMA_LAW/conlaw3.obama.1997.fall.memo.pdf (accessed June 26, 2010).

———. *The Audacity of Hope: Thoughts on Reclaiming the American Dream*. New York: Vintage Books, 2006.

———. "Current Issues in Racism and the Law." 1994. www.nytimes.com/packages/pdf/politics/2008OBAMA_LAW/Obama_CoursePk.pdf (accessed June 26, 2010).

———. "Democratic Convention Speech." Democratic Convention, Boston, MA, July 28, 2004.

———. *Dreams from My Father*. New York: Times Books, 1995; later print edition, New York: Three Rivers Press, 2004.

———. "Executive Order 13,489: Presidential Records." *Federal Register* 74, no. 13 (January 26, 2009): 4669.

———. "Executive Order 13,491: Ensuring Lawful Interrogations." *Federal Register* 74, no. 13 (January 27, 2009): 4891.

———. "Executive Order 13,492: Review and Disposition of Individuals Detained at the Guantanamo Bay Naval Base and Closure of Detention Facilities." *Federal Register* 74, no. 13 (January 27, 2009): 4897.

———. "Executive Order 13,493: Review of Detention Policy Options, Executive Order 13493," *Federal Register* 74, no. 13 (January 27, 2009): 4901.

———. "Executive Order 13,497, "Revocation of Certain Executive Orders Concerning Regulatory Planning and Review." *Federal Register* 74, no. 22 (February 4, 2009): 6113. www.reginfo.gov/public/jsp/Utilities/EO_13497.pdf (accessed April 7, 2010).

———. "Inaugural Address." 2009 Presidential Inaugural. Capitol Building, Washington, DC, January 20, 2009. www.presidency.ucsb.edu/ws/index.php?pid=44 (accessed March 24, 2009).

———. "Keynote Address at Democratic National Convention." July 27, 2004. www.washingtonpost.com/wp-dyn/articles/A19751-2004Jul27.html (accessed July 19, 2010).

———. "Memorandum for the Heads of Executive Departments and Agencies: Regulatory Review." *Federal Register* 74, no. 21 (February 3, 2009): 5977. www.reginfo.gov/public/jsp/EO/fedRegReview/POTUS_Memo_on_Regulatory_Review.pdf (March 21, 2010).

———. "Memorandum of March 9, 2009: Presidential Signing Statements: Memorandum for the Heads of Executive Departments and Agencies." *Federal Register* 74, no. 46 (March 11, 2009): 10669.

———. "Remarks by the President at the Acceptance of the Nobel Peace Prize." *Federal Register* 74, no. 236 (December 10, 2010).

———. "Remarks by the President on the Economy at Carnegie Mellon University." June 2, 2010. www.whitehouse.gov/the-press-office/remarks-president-economy-carnegie-mellon-university (June 26, 2010).

———. "Remarks by the President to a Joint Session of Congress on Health Care." *Federal Register* 74, no. 173 (September 9, 2009).

———. "Remarks by the President to the NAACP Centennial Convention." July 17, 2009. www.whitehouse.gov/the_press_office/Remarks-by-the-President-to-the-NAACP-Centennial-Convention-07/16/2009/ (accessed July 11, 2010).

———. "Remarks by the President at University of Michigan Spring Commencement." May 1, 2010. www.whitehouse.gov/the-press-office/remarks-president-university-michigan-spring-commencement (accessed June 26, 2010).

———. "Remarks of President Barack Obama—As Prepared for Delivery: Signing of Stem Cell Executive Order and Scientific Integrity Presidential Memorandum." March 9, 2009. www.whitehouse.gov/the-press-office/remarks-president-prepared-delivery-signing-stem-cell-executive-order-and-scientifi (accessed June 26, 2010).

———. "Remarks of Senator Barack Obama on the Confirmation of Judge John Roberts." September 22, 2005. www.barackobama.com/2005/09/22/remarks_of_senator_barack_obam_10.php (accessed June 26, 2010).

———. "Remarks of Senator Barack Obama on the Nuclear Option." April 13, 2005. www.barackobama.com/2005/04/13/statement_of_senator_barack_ob.php (accessed June 26, 2010).

———. "Remarks of Senator Barack Obama: Take Back America 2007." June 19, 2007.

———. "Remarks of Senator Barack Obama: The American Promise." August 28, 2008.

———. "Remarks of Senator Obama: A New Beginning." October 2, 2007. www.barackobama.com/2007/10/02/remarks_of_senator_barack_obam_27.php (accessed June 26, 2010).

———. "Remarks of Senator Obama: The War We Need to Win." August 1, 2007. www.barackobama.com/2007/08/01/the_war_we_need_to_win.php (accessed June 26, 2010).

———. "Renewing American Leadership." *Foreign Affairs*, July/August 2007.

———. "Selma Voting Rights March Commemoration." Selma, Alabama, March 4, 2007. www.barackobama.com/2007/03/04/selma_voting_rights_march_comm.php (accessed July 1, 2010).

———. "Senator Obama's Announcement for President." February 10, 2007. www.nytimes.com/2007/02/10/us/politics/11obama-text.html?_r=1&ref=politics&pagewanted=print (accessed July 14, 2010).

———. "Speech on Afghanistan." December 1, 2009. http://abcnews.go.com/Politics/full-transcript-president-obamas-speech-afghanistan-delivered-west/story?id=9220661 (accessed July 19, 2010).

———. "Speech on Race: A More Perfect Union." *New York Times* transcript, March 18, 2008. www.nytimes.com/2008/03/18/us/politics/18text-obama.html?_r=2&pagewanted=r (accessed June 18, 2010).

———. "Statement on Signing the Fraud Enforcement and Recovery Act of 2009." *Federal Register* 74, no. 96 (May 20, 2009).

———. "Statement on Signing the Omnibus Appropriations Act, 2009." *Federal Register* 74, no. 46 (March 11, 2009): 10669.

———. "Statement on Signing the Omnibus Public Land Management Act of 2009." *Federal Register* 74, no. 59 (March 30, 2009).

———."Statement on Signing the Ronald Reagan Centennial Commission Act." *Federal Register* 74, no. 104 (June 2, 2009).

———."Statement on Signing the Supplemental Appropriations Act, 2009." *Federal Register* 74, no. 120 (June 24, 2009).

———. "Take Back America" speech. June 14, 2006. http://obamaspeeches.com/077-Take-Back-America-Obama-Speech.htm (accessed July 19, 2010).

———. "Tort Law—Prenatal Injuries—Supreme Court of Illinois Refuses to Recognize Cause of Action Brought by Fetus Against Its Mother for Unintentional Affliction of Prenatal Injuries." *Harvard Law Review* 103 (1988): 823.

———. "What I See in Lincoln's Eyes." *Time*, June 26, 2005. www.time.com/time/magazine/article/0,9171,1077287,00.html (accessed June 24, 2010).

"Obama Declares He's Running for President." *CNN.com*, May 2, 2007. www.cnn.com/2007/POLITICS/02/10/obama.president/index.html (accessed June 26, 2010).

"Obama Jumps Into 2010 Race with Appeal to Latinos, African-Americans, Women and Youth." *Fox News*, April 26, 2010. www.foxnews.com/politics/2010/ 04/26/obama-jumps-race-appeal-latinos-african-americans-women-youth/ (accessed June 26, 2010).

Office of the Press Secretary. "President Obama Announces Recess Appointments to Key Administration Positions." March 27, 2010. www.whitehouse.gov/the-press-office/president-obama-announces-recess-appointments-key-administration-positions (accessed June 26, 2010).

OMB Watch. "OIRA Nominee Promises Law and Pragmatism Will Guide Decisions." www.ombwatch.org/node/10010 (accessed April 3, 2010).

"Oprah Winfrey Interview with President Barack Obama." *ABC News*, December 14, 2009. http://blogs.abcnews.com/politicalpunch/2009/12/president-obama-grades-self-a-good-solid-bplus.html.

"Outliers Urged to Join Nonproliferation Regime." *Global Security Newswire*, May 7, 2010. http://gsn.nti.org/gsn/nw_20100507_7585.php (accessed June 26, 2010).

Palmer, Anna. "Legislative Affairs Team Gets to Work." *Roll Call*, January 21, 2009. www.rollcall.com/issues/54_75/lobbying/31589-1.html (accessed May 20, 2010).

Parthasarathy, G. "Uncertainty in India-US Ties." *The Pioneer*, April 15, 2010. www.dailypioneer.com/249212/Uncertainty-in-India-US-ties.html (accessed June 26, 2010).

Patrick, Deval, Patricia Madrid, and Judith McHale. "Renewing America's Promise." 2008 *Democratic National Convention*, August 13, 2008. www.presidency.ucsb.edu/papers_pdf/78283.pdf (accessed March 23, 2010).

Percival, Robert B. "Checks Without Balance: Executive Office Oversight of the Environmental Protection Agency." *Law and Contemporary Problems* 54, no. 4 (1991).

Perez, Evan. "Decision on 9/11 Trial Could Undercut Holder." *Wall Street Journal*, March 10, 2010. http://online.wsj.com/article/SB10001424052748704145904575112072380877534.html?mod=WSJ_hpp_MIDDLTopStories (accessed April 3, 2010).

Perkins, Frances. *The Roosevelt I Knew*. New York: Viking Adult, 1946; later edition, Ithaca, NY: Colophon Books, 1964.

Petrilli, Mark. "Russlyn Alli's 'Remedy' Redux." *Flypaper*, March 9, 2010. www.ed excellence.net/flypaper/index.php/2010/03/russlynn-alis-remedy-redux/ (accessed June 26, 2010).

Pew Research Centers. "Obama More Popular Abroad than at Home, Global Image of U.S. Continues to Benefit." *22-Nation Pew Global Attitudes Survey*, June 17, 2010. http://pewresearch.org/pubs/1630/obama-more-popular-abroad-global-american-image-benefit-22-nation-global-survey (accessed June 26, 2010).

Pfiffner, James P. *Power Play: The Bush Presidency and the Constitution.* Washington, DC: Brookings Institution, 2008.

Phillips, Kate. "Senators Take on Czar Wars." *New York Times* Caucus blog, October 7, 2009. http://thecaucus.blogs.nytimes.com/2009/10/07/senators-take-on-the-czar-wars/ (accessed March 17, 2010).

Pickler, Nedra. "Rove, Miers, Will Testify about Prosecutor Firings." *Houston Chronicle*, March 4, 2009. www.chron.com/disp/story.mpl/front/6294041.html (accessed March 17, 2010).

Pierce, Tony. "Gen. Stanley McChrystal Resigns, Obama Nominates Gen. David Petraeus to Lead the War in Afghanistan." *Los Angeles Times* Comments blog, June 23, 2010. http://latimesblogs.latimes.com/comments_blog/2010/06/gen-stanley-mcchrystal-general-david-h-petraeus.html (accessed July 23, 2010).

Pincus, Walter. "House Votes to Revise Intelligence Disclosure Rules for President." *Washington Post*, March 2, 2010. www.washingtonpost.com/wp-dyn/content/article/2010/03/01/AR2010030103310.html (accessed June 29, 2010).

Plouffe, David. *The Audacity to Win.* New York: Viking, 2009.

Political Punch. http://blogs.abcnews.com/politicalpunch/ (accessed June 26, 2010).

Polsby, Nelson W. *Consequences of Party Reform.* New York: Oxford University Press, 1983.

Posner, Richard. *Not a Suicide Pact: The Constitution in a Time of National Emergency.* New York: Oxford University Press, 2006.

Powell, Larry. "Obama and Obama Girl: YouTube, Viral Videos, and the 2008 Presidential Campaign." In *Communicator-in-Chief*, edited by John Allen Hendricks and Robert E. Denton, Jr. Lanham, MD: Rowman & Littlefield, 2010.

"President-Elect Obama Announces Organizing for America." January 17, 2009. www.gwu.edu/~action/2008/chrntran08/orgforam011709pr.html (accessed June 26, 2010).

"President Obama's 'Czars.'" *Politico*, September 4, 2009. http://dyn.politico.com/printstory.cfm?uuid=870D765C-18FE-70B2-A86B4FAE48EF7FBB (accessed April 9, 2010).

Rabkin, Jeremy. *Judicial Compulsions: How Public Law Distorts Public Policy.* New York: Basic Books, 2009.

Rajghatta, Chidanand. "Stay the Course in Afghanistan, PM Manmohan Singh Urges US." *Times of India*, November 24, 2009. http://timesofindia.indiatimes.com/world/us/Stay-the-course-in-Afghanistan-PM-Manmohan-Singh-urges-US/articleshow/5262957.cms (accessed June 26, 2010).

Ramsden, John. *Man of the Century: Winston Churchill and His Legend Since 1945.* New York: Columbia University Press, 2002.

Rasmussen Reports. "Health Care Law." July 26, 2010. www.rasmussenreports.com/public_content/politics/current_events/healthcare/health_care_law (accessed June 26, 2010).

Raum, Tom, and Phillip Elliott. "Obama Town Hall in Ohio: President Takes Populist Message on the Road." *Huffington Post*, January 22, 2010. www.huffingtonpost.com/2010/01/22/obama-takes-populist-push_n_432749.html (accessed June 26, 2010).

Reagan, Ronald W. "Executive Order 12,291: Federal Regulation." *Code of Federal Regulations*, title 3, p. 127 (1981).

———. "Executive Order 12,498: Regulatory Planning Process." *Code of Federal Regulations*, title 3, p. 323 (1985).

———. "Program for Economic Recovery: Address before Join Session of Congress." 17 *Weekly Comp. Pres. Doc.* 130 (February 18, 1981).

Reid, Tim. "Barack Obama's 'Guns and Religion' Blunder Gives Hillary Clinton a Chance." *Times Online*, April 14, 2008. www.timesonline.co.uk/tol/news/world/us_and_americas/us_elections/article3740080.ece (accessed June 26, 2010).

———. "President Obama Orders His First Drone Attacks." *Times Online*, January 23, 2009. www.timesonline.co.uk/tol/news/world/us_and_americas/article5575883.ece (accessed June 29, 2010).

Relyea, Harold C. "Presidential Directives: Background and Overview." *CRS Report for Congress*, April 23, 2007. www.fas.org/irp/crs/98-611.pdf (accessed March 10, 2010).

Remnick, David. *The Bridge: The Life and Rise of Barack Obama*. New York: Alfred A. Knopf, 2010.

Rhee, Foon. "Obama Reaches 2 Million Donors." *Boston Globe*, August 14, 2008. www.boston.com/news/politics/politicalintelligence/2008/08/obama_reaches_2.html (accessed June 2, 2010).

Robinson, Greg. "The Tyrannical History of Military Tribunals for Civilians." *History News Network*, October 5, 2009. http://hnn.us/articles/117429.html (accessed June 29, 2010)

Rodgers, Daniel T. "In Search of Progressivism." *Reviews in American History* 10, no. 4 (1982): 113–32.

Roosevelt, Franklin D. "Acceptance of Nomination for Second Term." June 27, 1936. http://teachingamericanhistory.org/library/index.asp?document=611 (accessed June 26, 2010).

———. "Excerpts from the Press Conference: December 28, 1943." *The American Presidency Project*. www.presidency.ucsb.edu/ws/index. php?pid=16358 (accessed June 26, 2010).

———. "Fourth Inaugural Address." January 20, 1945. http://millercenter.org/scripps/archive/speeches/detail/3337 (accessed July 4, 2010).

———. "Nomination Address." July 2, 1932. http://newdeal.feri.org/speeches/1932b.htm (accessed July 19, 2010).

———. *The Public Papers and Addresses of Franklin D. Roosevelt*, edited by Samuel Rosenman. New York: Random House, 1938.

———. "Second Inaugural Address." January 20, 1937. http://millercenter.org/scripps/archive/speeches/detail/3308 (accessed July 4, 2010).

Roosevelt, Theodore. *An Autobiography*. New York: The Library of America, 2004.

Rosen, Jeffrey. "The Case Against Sotomayor: Indictments of Obama's Frontrunner to Replace Souter." *The New Republic*, May 4, 2009. www.tnr.com/article/politics/the-case-against-sotomayor (accessed June 26, 2010).

Rosenberg, Gerald. *The Hollow Hope: Can Courts Bring About Social Change?* 2nd ed. Chicago: University of Chicago Press, 2008.

Rossiter, Clinton. *The American Presidency*. New York: Harcourt Brace, 1960.

Rozell, Mark. "Washington and the Origins of Presidential Power." In *Patriot Sage: George Washington and the American Political Tradition*, edited by Gary L. Gregg II and Matthew Spalding. Wilmington, DE: ISI Books, 1999.

Rozell, Mark, and Mitchel Sollenberger. "Taking Executive Privilege to Absurd Levels?" *Roll Call*, February 6, 2009. www.rollcall.com/news/32134-1.html (accessed March 19, 2010).

Rozell, Mark J., and Gleaves Whitney, eds. *Testing the Limits: George W. Bush and the Imperial Presidency*. Lanham, MD: Rowman & Littlefield, 2009.

Rucker, Philip, and Dan Eggen. "Protests at Democrats' Health-Care Events Spark Political Tug of War." *Washington Post*, August 6, 2009. www.washingtonpost.com/wp-dyn/content/article/2009/08/05/AR2009080502780.html?sid=ST2009080504000 (accessed June 7, 2010).

Ryan, James E. "Does It Take a Theory? Originalism, Active Liberty and Minimalism." *Stanford Law Review* 58 (2006): 1623.

Salant, Jonathan D. "Obama's Army of E-Mail Backers Give Him Clout to Sway Congress." *Bloomberg.com*, December 1, 2008. www.bloomberg.com/apps/news?pid=20601087&sid=aEVXKOC3s8.k (accessed June 6, 2010).

Sanger, David E., and Peter Baker. "Obama Limits When U.S. Would Use Nuclear Arms." *New York Times*, April 5, 2010. www.nytimes.com/2010/04/06/world/06arms.html (accessed July 18, 2010).

Sargent, James E. "FDR and Lewis Douglas: Budget Balancing and the Early New Deal." *Prologue* 6 (1974): 33–43.

Savage, Charlie. "Barack Obama's Q & A." *Boston Globe*, December 20, 2007. www.boston.com/news/politics/2008/specials/CandidateQA/ObamaQA/ (accessed June 26, 2010).

———. "Holder Backs a Miranda Limit for Terror Suspects." *New York Times*, May 9, 2010. www.nytimes.com/2010/05/10/us/politics/10holder.html (accessed June 29, 2010).

———. "Holder Won't Rule Out N.Y. 9/11 Trial." *New York Times*, April 15, 2010. www.nytimes.com/2010/04/15/us/politics/15holder.html (accessed June 29, 2010).

———. "Obama Looks to Limit Impact of Tactic Bush Used to Sidestep New Laws." *New York Times*, March 9, 2009. www.nytimes.com/2009/03/10/us/politics/10signing.html (accessed March 17, 2010).

———. "Obama's Embrace of Bush Tactic Riles Congress." *New York Times*, August 8, 2009. www.nytimes.com/2009/08/09/us/politics/09signing.html (accessed June 29, 2010).

———. "Obama Team is Divided on Tactics Against Terrorism." *New York Times*, March 28, 2010. www.nytimes.com/2010/03/29/us/politics/29force.html (accessed June 29, 2010).

———. "Obama Upholds Detainee Policy in Afghanistan." *New York Times*, February 21, 2009. www.nytimes.com/2009/02/22/washington/22bagram.html?_r=1&scp=2&sq=bagram&st=cse (accessed July 3, 2010).

———. *Takeover: The Return of the Imperial Presidency and the Subversion of American Democracy.* Boston: Back Bay Books, 2008.

Savage, Charlie, and James Risen. "Federal Judge Finds N.S.A. Wiretaps Were Illegal." *New York Times*, March 31, 2010. www.nytimes.com/2010/04/01/us/01nsa.html (accessed June 29, 2010).

Schandler, Herbert Y. *The Unmaking of a President: Lyndon Johnson and Vietnam.* Princeton, NJ: Princeton University Press, 1977.

Scherer, Michael. "No Testifying for Obama's Social Secretary?" *Time*, December 3, 2009. www.time.com/time/politics/article/0,8599,1945192,00.html (accessed June 26, 2010).

Schmitt, Eric, and Thom Shanker. "General Calls for More U.S. Troops to Avoid Afghan Failure." *New York Times*, September 20, 2009. www.nytimes.com/2009/09/21/world/asia/21afghan.html.

Schwartz, John. "Obama Backs Off Reversal on Secrets." *New York Times*, February 9, 2009. www.nytimes.com/2009/02/10/us/10torture.html?_r=2 (accessed July 3, 2010).

Seelye, Katharine Q. "Obama Wades into a Volatile Race Issue." *New York Times*, July 23, 2009. www.nytimes.com/2009/07/23/us/23race.html (accessed July 7, 2010).

Shane, Scott. "U.S. Approval of Killing of Cleric Causes Unease." *New York Times*, May 13, 2010. www.nytimes.com/2010/05/14/world/14awlaki.html (accessed June 29, 2010).

———. "US Approves Targeted Killing of Muslim Cleric." *New York Times*, April 6, 2010. www.nytimes.com/2010/04/07/world/middleeast/07yemen.html (accessed April 7, 2010).

Shipman, Tim. "Barack Obama Sends Bust of Winston Churchill On Its Way Back to Britain: Barack Obama Has Sent Sir Winston Churchill Packing and Pulse Rates Soaring Among Anxious British Diplomats." *Daily Telegraph*, February 14, 2009. www.telegraph.co.uk/news/worldnews/northamerica/usa/barackobama/4623148/Barack-Obama-sends-bust-of-Winston-Churchill-on-its-way-back-to-Britain.html (accessed July 18, 2010).

Shlaes, Amity. *The Forgotten Man: A New History of the Great Depression.* New York: Harper Collins, 2007.

Shulman, Bruce J. *Lyndon Baines Johnson and American Liberalism.* 2nd ed. Boston: St. Martin's, 2007.

Sifry, Micah. "Section I: Year One of Organizing for America: The Permanent Field Campaign in a Digital Age." January 14, 2010. http://techpresident.com/ofayear1 (accessed June 6, 2010).

Sinkler, George. *The Racial Attitudes of American Presidents: From Abraham Lincoln to Theodore Roosevelt.* New York: Double Day, 1971.

Slevin, Peter. "Obama Makes Empathy a Requirement for Court." *Washington Post*, May 13, 2009.

Smith, Ben, and Alex Isenstadt. "Obama Political Arm Under Fire." *Politico*, January 13, 2010. www.politico.com/news/stories/0110/31428.html (accessed June 7, 2010).

Smith, Ben, and Lisa Lerer. "44 to Reverse 43's Executive Orders." *Politico*, January 13, 2009. www.politico.com/news/stories/0109/17365.html (accessed June 29, 2010).

Smith, Melissa. "Political Campaigns in the Twenty-First Century: Implications of New Media Technology." In *Communicator-in-Chief*, edited by John Allen Hendricks and Robert E. Denton, Jr. Lanham, MD: Rowman & Littlefield, 2010.

SpyTalk. http://blog.washingtonpost.com/spy-talk/ (accessed June 26, 2010).

Stanglin, Doug. "Book Tells of John Edwards' Affair, His Disdain for 'Fat Rednecks.'" *USAToday*, January 27, 2010. http://content.usatoday.com/communities/ondeadline/post/2010/01/book-tells-of-john-edwards-affair-his-disdain-for-fat-rednecks-/1 (accessed June 26, 2010).

Steele, Shelby. *A Bound Man: Why We Are Excited About Obama and Why He Can't Win.* New York: Free Press, 2008.

———. "From Emmitt Till to Skip Gates." *Wall Street Journal*, August 1, 2009. http://online.wsj.com/article/SB10001424052970204619004574322054186035002.html (accessed July 8, 2009).

Stein, Jeff. "Ex-Spies Still Agitated over CIA's Afghan Losses." *Washington Post*, March 22, 2010. http://blog.washingtonpost.com/spy-talk/2010/03/nearly_four_months_after_an.html (accessed June 29, 2010).

Steinzor, Rena. "Eye on OIRA: Sunstein Says Ambitious Efforts to Revamp Regulatory Review Tabled for the Time Being." Center for Progressive Reform blog, March 12, 2010. www.progressivereform.org/CPRBlog.cfm?idBlog=52D5FC2E-F9E4-2834-4EEF1A5EB76DA41B (accessed April 7, 2010).

Stelter, Brian. "The Facebooker Who Friended Obama." *New York Times*, July 7, 2008. www.nytimes.com/2008/07/07/technology/07hughes.html (accessed May, 2010).

Stephanopolos, George. "George's Bottom Line." ABC News, July 22, 2010. http://blogs.abc-news.com/george/2010/07/shirley-sherrod-obama-is-not-someone-who-has-experienced-what-i-have-experienced-through-life.html (accessed July 24, 2010).

Stokey, Edith, and Richard Zeckhauser. *A Primer for Policy Analysis.* New York: Norton, 1978.

Stolberg, Sheryl Gay, and Helene Cooper. "Obama Adds Troops, but Maps Exit Plan." *New York Times*, December 1, 2009. www.nytimes.com/2009/12/02/world/asia/02prexy.html (accessed July 18, 2010).

Stolberg, Sheryl Gay, and Janie Lorber. "White House Blocks Testimony on Party Crashers." *New York Times* Caucus blog, December 2, 2009. http://thecaucus.blogs.nytimes.com/2009/12/02/white-house-revises-rules-for-major-events/ (accessed March 22, 2010).

Stone, Geoffrey R. "Obama's Judges." *Huffington Post*, March 2, 2010. www.huffingtonpost.com/geoffrey-r-stone/obamas-judges_b_483042.html (accessed June 26, 2010).

Sunstein, Cass. "The Minimalist Constitution." In *The Constitution in 2020*, edited by Jack M. Balkin and Reva B. Siegel. New York: Oxford University Press, 2009.

———. "The Visionary Minimalist." *New Republic*, January 30, 2008.

———. "What the 'Unitary Executive' Debate Is and Is Not About." The Faculty Blog, August 6, 2007. http://uchicagolaw.typepad.com/faculty/2007/08/what-the-unitar.html (accessed January 19, 2010).

"Sunstein to Join Harvard Law School Faculty." www.law.harvard.edu/news/2008/02/19_sunstein.php (accessed April 2, 2010).

Sweet, Laurel J., Marie Szaniszlo, Laura Crimaldi, Jessica Van Sack, and Joe Dwinell. "Officer in Henry Gates Flap Tried to Save Reggie Lewis: Denies He's a Racist, Won't Apologize." *Boston Herald*, July 23, 2009. www.bostonherald.com/news/regional/view.bg?&articleid=1186567&format=&page=2&listingType=Loc#articleFull (accessed July 17, 2010).

Sylvia, Ronald D. "Presidential Decision Making and Leadership in the Civil Rights Era." *Presidential Studies Quarterly* 25, no. 3 (Summer 1995): 396–97.

Talbot, David. "The Geeks Behind Obama's Web Strategy." *Boston Globe*, January 8, 2009. www.boston.com/news/politics/2008/articles/2009/01/08/the_geeks_behind_obamas_web_strategy/ (accessed May 28, 2010).

Tapper, Jake. "Dawn Johnsen Withdraws Her Nomination." *ABC News*, Political Punch Blog, April 9, 2010. http://blogs.abcnews.com/politicalpunch/2010/04/dawn-johnsen-withdraws-her-nomination.html (accessed June 29, 2010).

———. "Did Brennan Withdraw His Name from Consideration for CIA Post Before Obama Could Withdraw It For Him?" *ABC News*, Political Punch Blog, November 26, 2008. http://blogs.abcnews.com/politicalpunch/2008/11/did-brennan-wit.html (accessed June 29, 2010).

———. "Obama Administration to Release Detainee Abuse Photos." *ABC News* Political Punch blog, April 24, 2009. http://blogs.abcnews.com/politicalpunch/2009/04/obama-adminis-3.html (accessed March 27, 2010).

———. "Obama Calls for Support of Campaign Finance Reform Bill, Post Citizens-United Ruling." *ABC News* Political Punch Blog, May 1, 2010. http://blogs.abcnews.com/politicalpunch/2010/05/obama-calls-for-support-of-campaign-finance-reform-bill-post-citizens-united-ruling.html (accessed June 29, 2010).

Thach, Charles C., Jr. *The Creation of the Presidency 1775–1789*. Baltimore: Johns Hopkins University Press, 1969.

Thernstrom, Abigail. "The New Black Panther Case: A Conservative Dissent." *National Review*, July 6, 2010. http://article.nationalreview.com/437619/the-new-black-panther-casebr-a-conservative-dissent/abigail-thernstrom (accessed July 15, 2010).

Thomasson, Daniel. "Recess Appointments Another Slap at GOP." *Boston Herald*, April 2, 2010. www.bostonherald.com/news/opinion/op_ed/view.bg?articleid=1244079 (accessed April 4, 2010).

Thrush, Glenn. "Black Caucus Reminds Obama of Pledge Not to 'Forget' Race." *Politico*, December 8, 2009. www.politico.com/blogs/glennthrush/1209/ (accessed June 26, 2010).

Toobin, Jeffrey. "After Stevens: What Will the Supreme Court Be Like Without Its Liberal Leader?" *New Yorker* 86, no. 5 (March 2010): 45–46.

Tribe, Laurence. "The Curvature of Constitutional Space: What Lawyers Can Learn From Modern Physics." *Harvard Law Review* 103 (1989): 1.

Trippi, Joe. *The Revolution Will Not Be Televised.* New York: Regan Books, 2004.

Tulis, Jeffrey K. *The Rhetorical Presidency.* Princeton, NJ: Princeton University Press, 1987.

Tushnet, Mark. *Taking the Constitution Away from the Courts.* Princeton, NJ: Princeton University Press, 2000.

Twohig, Dorothy. "That Species of Property: Washington's Role in the Controversy Over Slavery." *The Papers of George Washington,* 1997. http://gwpapers.virginia.edu/articles/twohig_2.html (accessed June 21, 2010).

U.S. House of Representatives, Committee on Rules. *Statement of Administration Policy: H.R. 2701—Intelligence Authorization Act for Fiscal Year 2010.* 111th Cong., 2nd sess.

Vargas, Jose Antonio. "Obama Raised Half a Billion Online." November 20, 2008. http://voices.washingtonpost.com/thetrail/2008/11/20/obama_raised_half_a_billion_on.html (accessed March 9, 2009).

Verkuil, Paul R. "Jawboning Administrative Agencies: Ex Parte Contacts by the White House." *Columbia Law Review* 80 (1980).

Viser, Matt, Eric Moskowitz, and Martin Finucane. "Obama Stumps for Coakley." *Boston Globe,* January 17, 2010. www.boston.com/news/local/breaking_news/2010/01/a_long_line_wai.html (accessed July 11, 2010).

Waite, Brandon C. "E-mail and Electoral Fortunes: Obama's Campaign Internet Insurgency." In *Communicator-in-Chief,* edited by John Allen Hendricks and Robert E. Denton, Jr. Lanham, MD: Rowman & Littlefield, 2010.

Wallsten, Peter. "Obama's New Partner: Al Sharpton." *Wall Street Journal,* March 17, 2010. http://online.wsj.com/article/SB10001424052748704588404575123404191464126.html (accessed July 7, 2010).

Walsh, Joan. "Barack Obama: The Opacity of Hope." *Salon,* April 5, 2010. www.salon.com/news/opinion/joan_walsh/politics/2010/04/05/david_remnick_the_bridge (accessed April 4, 2010).

Walsh, Kenneth T. "Obama's Years in Chicago Politics Shaped His Presidential Candidacy." *U.S. News & World Report,* April 11, 2008. http://politics.usnews.com/news/campaign-2008/articles/2008/04/11/obamas-years-in-chicago-politics-shaped-his-presidential-candidacy.html (accessed June 26, 2010).

Washington, George. "Message to the House of Representatives, Declining to Submit Diplomatic Instructions and Correspondence." March 30, 1796. http://millercenter.org/scripps/archive/speeches/detail/3461 (accessed July 16, 2010).

Washington, Jesse. "PBS Host Smiley Calls Meeting to Urge Black Agenda." www.wggb.com/Global/story.asp?S=12079353&nav=menu1460_10_27531015 (accessed July 26, 2010)

Weber, Max. *The Theory of Social and Economic Organization.* New York: Oxford University Press, 1947.

Weisman, Jonathan. "Financial-Bill Playbook: Don't Mess Around." *Wall Street Journal,* May 22–23, 2010.

———. "Obama's Fiats Anger Lawmakers." *Wall Street Journal,* June 2, 2009. http://online.wsj.com/article/SB124761651200542351.html (accessed March 21, 2010).

———. "Obama's Symbolic Importance." *Washington Post,* July 30, 2008. http://blog.washingtonpost.com/44/2008/07/obamas-symbolic-importance.html (accessed June 26, 2010).

———. "Signing Statements Reappear in Obama White House." *Wall Street Journal,* March 12, 2009. http://online.wsj.com/article/SB123688875576610955.html (accessed June 29, 2010).

Weiss, Debra Cassens. "McCain Says He Won't Use Signing Statement." *ABA Journal*, February 25, 2008. www.abajournal.com/news/article/mccain_says_he_wont_use_signing_state ments/ (accessed July 14, 2010).

Wells, Tim. "A Conversation with Peter B. Edelman." *Washington Lawyer Magazine*, April 2008. www.dcbar.org/for_lawyers/resources/publications/washington_lawyer/april_2008/ legends.cfm (accessed May 16, 2010).

"What Does 'Viral' Mean?" *e.politics*, January 14, 2009. www.epolitics.com/2009/01/14/what-does-viral-mean/ (accessed June 2, 2010).

White, G. Edward. *The Constitution and the New Deal*. Cambridge, MA: Harvard University Press, 2000.

White House Blog, The. www.whitehouse.gov/blog (accessed June 26, 2010).

Wilson, Scott. "Joint Press Conference with Prime Minister Churchill at Casablanca: January 24, 1943." *The American Presidency Project*. www.presidency.ucsb.edu/ws/index.php?pid= 16408&st=&st1= (accessed June 26, 2010).

———. "Obama Shifts on Abuse Photo." *Washington Post*, May 14, 2009. www.washington post.com/wp-dyn/content/article/2009/05/13/AR2009051301751.html (accessed March 27, 2010).

Wilson, Scott, and Al Kamen. "Global War on Terror is Given New Name." *Washington Post*, March 25, 2009. www.washingtonpost.com/wp-dyn/content/article/2009/03/24/ AR2009032402818.html (accessed June 29, 2010)

WSJDigitalNetwork. "Rahm Emanuel on the Opportunities of Crisis." Video, 2008. www. youtube.com/watch?v=_mzcbXi1Tkk (accessed June 26, 2010).

Wulfhorst, Ellen. "Obama Calls Elitism Attack 'Political Silly Season.'" *Reuters*, April 15, 2008. www.reuters.com/article/idUSN1516902320080415 (accessed June 26, 2010).

Yoo, John. *Crisis and Command: A History of Executive Power from George Washington to George W. Bush*. New York: Kaplan, 2010.

New York Times Bibliography

Alexander, Matthew. "Torture's Loopholes." *New York Times*, January 21, 2010.

Baker, Peter. "In Court Nominees, Is Obama Looking for Empathy by Another Name?" *New York Times*, April 25, 2010.

———. "Obama to Use Current Law to Support Detentions." *New York Times*, September 24, 2009. www.nytimes.com/2009/09/24/us/politics/24detain.html (accessed January 22, 2010).

———. "When 535 Take on Number 1." *New York Times*, October 5, 2008. http://query. nytimes.com/gst/fullpage.html?res=9901E3DB1339F936A35753C1A96E9C8B63 (accessed March 14, 2010).

Dowd, Maureen. "Hail the Conquering Professor." *New York Times*, March 24, 2010.

Johnston, David. "US Says Rendition to Continue, but with More Oversight." *New York Times*, August 25, 2009. www.nytimes.com/2009/08/25/us/politics/25rendition.html (accessed September 19, 2009).

Kantor, Jodi. "Teaching Law, Testing Ideas, Obama Stood Slightly Apart." *New York Times*, July 30, 2008. www.nytimes.com/2008/07/30/us/politics/30law.html (accessed June 26, 2010).

Kennedy, Caroline. "A President Like My Father." *New York Times*, January 27, 2008. www .nytimes.com/2008/01/27/opinion/27kennedy.html?em (accessed June 26, 2010).

Mazetti, Mark. "Interrogation Memos Detail Harsh Tactics by the CIA." *New York Times*, April 17, 2009.

———. "Obama Issues Directive to Shut Down Guantanamo." *New York Times*, January 22, 2009.

———. "Panetta Is Chosen as CIA Chief, in a Surprise Step." *New York Times*, January 6, 2009.

Nagourney, Adam. "Obama Elected President as Racial Barrier Falls." *New York Times*, November 5, 2008. www.nytimes.com/2008/11/05/us/politics/05elect.html (accessed April 5, 2010).

Nelson, Gabriel. "Obama Overhaul of Regulatory Reviews Now Seen as Unlikely." *New York Times* Greenwire, July 14, 2010. www.nytimes.com/gwire/2010/07/14/14greenwire-obama-overhaul-of-regulatory-reviews-now-sesen-45978.html (accessed 16 July 2010).

New York Times "Barack Obama's Feb. 5 Speech," February 5, 2008.

———. "Barack Obama's Inaugural Address," January 20, 2009.

———. "The K.S.M. Files," April 15, 2010.

Phillips, Kate. "Senators Take on Czar Wars." *New York Times* Caucus blog, October 7, 2009. http://thecaucus.blogs.nytimes.com/2009/10/07/senators-take-on-the-czar-wars/ (accessed March 17, 2010).

Sanger, David E., and Peter Baker. "Obama Limits When U.S. Would Use Nuclear Arms." *New York Times*, April 6, 2010.

Savage, Charlie. "Bush-Era Wiretapping Program is Rule Illegal: Judge Rejects 'State Secrets' Argument." *New York Times*, April 1, 2010.

———. "Holder Backs a Miranda Limit for Terror Suspects." *New York Times*, May 10, 2010.

———. "Holder Won't Rule Out N.Y. 9/11 Trial." *New York Times*, April 15, 2010.

———. "Obama Looks to Limit Impact of Tactic Bush Used to Sidestep New Laws." *New York Times*, March 9, 2009. www.nytimes.com/2009/03/10/us/politics/10signing.html (accessed March 17, 2010).

———. "Obama Team is Divided on Tactics Against Terrorism." *New York Times*, March 29, 2010.

———. "Obama Upholds Detainee Policy in Afghanistan." *New York Times*, February 22, 2009.

———. "Obama's Embrace of a Bush Tactic Riles Congress." *New York Times*, August 9, 2009.

Schmitt, Eric, and Thom Shanker. "General Calls for More U.S. Troops to Avoid Afghan Failure." *New York Times*, September 20, 2009. www.nytimes.com/2009/09/21/world/asia/21afghan.html (accessed June 26, 2010).

Schwartz, John. "Obama Backs Off of State Secrets." *New York Times*, February 10, 2009.

Seelye, Katharine Q. "Obama Wades into a Volatile Race Issue." *New York Times*, July 23, 2009. www.nytimes.com/2009/07/23/us/23race.html (accessed July 7, 2010).

"Senate Confirmation Hearings: Eric Holder, Day 1." *New York Times*, January 16, 2009. www.nytimes.com/2009/01/16/us/politics/16text-holder.html?pagewanted=all (accessed April 3, 2010).

Shane, Scott. "U.S. Decision to Approve Killing of Cleric Causes Unease." *New York Times*, May 14, 2010.

———. "U.S. Approves Targeted Killing of American Cleric." *New York Times*, April 7, 2010.

Stelter, Brian. "The Facebooker Who Friended Obama." *New York Times*, July 7, 2008. www.nytimes.com/2008/07/07/technology/07hughes.html (accessed May 25, 2010).

Stolberg, Sheryl Gay, and Helene Cooper. "Obama Adds Troops, but Maps Exit Plan." *New York Times*, December 2, 2009.

Index

~

About the Contributors

David Alvis (PhD, Fordham University) teaches American politics and political theory at Wofford College. His publications include essays on a variety of subjects including multiple articles on Progressivism and American political thought, the films of John Ford, and the origins of the presidency in the Constitutional Convention. He is currently completing a book on political development and the executive removal power. In 2009, he was given the Distinguished Teaching Award from the University of West Florida.

Joseph M. Bessette is Alice Tweed Tuohy Professor of Government and Ethics at Claremont McKenna College, where he teaches courses on American government and politics, political ethics, and crime and public policy. He previously served nine years in public service as Director of Planning, Training, and Management in the Cook County (IL) State's Attorney's Office and as Deputy Director and Acting Director of the Bureau of Justice Statistics in the U.S. Department of Justice. He is author of, among other works, *The Mild Voice of Reason: Deliberative Democracy and American National Government* (1994) and, with John J. Pitney, the new American government textbook *American Government and Politics: Deliberation, Democracy, and Citizenship* (2011). He has also coedited and contributed to two collections of essays on the presidency and the Constitution: *The Presidency in the Constitutional*

308 ~ About the Contributors

Order and *The Constitutional Presidency* (2009). He is currently working on a major new study of the use of the death penalty in the United States.

Andrew E. Busch (PhD, University of Virginia) is Crown Professor of Government and George R. Roberts Fellow at Claremont McKenna College, where he teaches courses on American government and politics. Busch has authored or coauthored eleven books on American politics, including most recently *Epic Journey: The 2008 Elections and American Politics* (2009) and *The Constitution on the Campaign Trail: The Surprising Political Career of America's Founding Document* (2007), along with more than thirty articles and chapters. In 2007, he received a Fulbright fellowship to lecture on American politics at the Diplomatic Academy of Ukraine, and he served as the Ann and Herbert Vaughan Fellow in the James Madison Program in American Ideals and Institutions at Princeton University in the 2009–2010 academic year. He currently serves as Director of the Rose Institute of State and Local Government at CMC.

James W. Ceaser is professor of politics at the University of Virginia, where he has taught since 1976, and senior visiting fellow at the Hoover Institution. He is the author of several books on American politics and political thought, including *Designing a Polity*, *Presidential Selection*, *Liberal Democracy and Political Science*, *Reconstructing America*, and *Nature and History in American Political Development*. Professor Ceaser has also coauthored a series on American national elections for every presidential election since 1992.

Anthony Corrado (PhD, Boston College) is professor of government at Colby College and nonresident senior fellow at the Brookings Institution. He also serves as chair of the board of trustees of the Campaign Finance Institute, a nonpartisan research organization located in Washington, DC. He is the author or coauthor of numerous books and articles on national elections and campaign finance, including *Financing the 2008 Election*, *The New Campaign Finance Sourcebook*, *Campaign Finance Reform: Beyond the Basics*, and *Paying for Presidents*.

Joshua Dunn (PhD, University of Virginia) is associate professor of political science at the University of Colorado–Colorado Springs where he teaches courses on American political institutions, constitutional law, and political theory. His research primarily focuses on constitutional history and judicial policymaking. He is the author of *Complex Justice: The Case of Missouri v. Jenkins* (University of North Carolina Press), which explores the judicial attempt to desegregate the Kansas City, Missouri school system. He coedited, with Martin West, *From Schoolhouse to Courthouse: The Judiciary's Role in American Education.* He also coauthors, with Martha Derthick, a quarterly article on law and education for the journal *Education Next.* Previously he taught at the College of William and Mary and was a fellow in contemporary history, public policy, and American politics at the Miller Center of Public Affairs in Charlottesville, Virginia.

Stephen F. Knott is associate professor of national security affairs at the United States Naval War College. He has served as cochair of the University of Virginia's Presidential Oral History Program and directed the Ronald Reagan Oral History Project. He received his PhD in political science from Boston College and has taught at the United States Air Force Academy and the University of Virginia. He is the author of *Alexander Hamilton and the Persistence of Myth, Secret and Sanctioned: Covert Operations and the American Presidency, At Reagan's Side: Insiders' Recollections from Sacramento to the White House,* and the forthcoming *Bush 43 Reconsidered.*

Marc Landy (PhD, Harvard University) is professor of political science at Boston College. He teaches courses on American political development, the American presidency, and American federalism. His recent articles include "Terror and the Executive" and (with Sidney Milkis) "The Presidency in the Eye of the Storm" in *The Presidency and the Political System,* edited by Mike Nelson. He and Milkis also wrote *Presidential Greatness* (2000) and *American Government: Balancing Liberty and Democracy* (2007). He is an author of the *Environmental Protection Agency From Nixon to Clinton: Asking the Wrong Questions* (1994). He is an editor of *Creating Competitive Markets: The Politics of Regulatory Reform* (2007)._

Melanie M. Marlowe is a doctoral candidate at Claremont Graduate University where she is writing a dissertation on the unitary executive. She is a lecturer at Miami University, where she teaches courses in constitutional law, the presidency, and American politics. She is the author of chapters on executive oversight of regulatory activity, the unitary executive, and the Obama presidency. She teaches summer courses in the masters program for the Ashbrook Center for Public Affairs.

Carol McNamara (PhD, Boston College) is senior lecturer of political theory, politics and literature, and the American presidency in the political science department at Utah State University. The focus of her research is ancient political thought, politics and literature, and the presidency. She has published several articles on Tom Wolfe, Xenophon, and Shakespeare, including most recently: "Science and the Fate of the Human Soul," forthcoming in *Perspectives in Political Science*; "Honor and Eros: Private Goods and Public Neglect in Shakespeare's Troy," forthcoming in *Immortal Longings: Representations of Honor and Love in Shakespeare*; and "Socratic Politics in Xenophon's *Memorabilia*" in *Polis*. She is currently writing *A Political Companion to Tom Wolfe*.

David Nichols is associate professor in the Department of Political Science at Baylor University. He is the author of *The Myth of the Modern Presidency*, coeditor of *Readings in American Government*, and the author of numerous articles on American politics, the American presidency, and politics and literature. He is also senior fellow of the Alexander Hamilton Institute for the Study of Western Civilization.